Iraq
Then and Now

A Guide to the Country and its People

Karen Dabrowska
Geoff Hann

www.bradtguides.com

Bradt Travel Guides Ltd, UK
The Globe Pequot Press Inc, USA

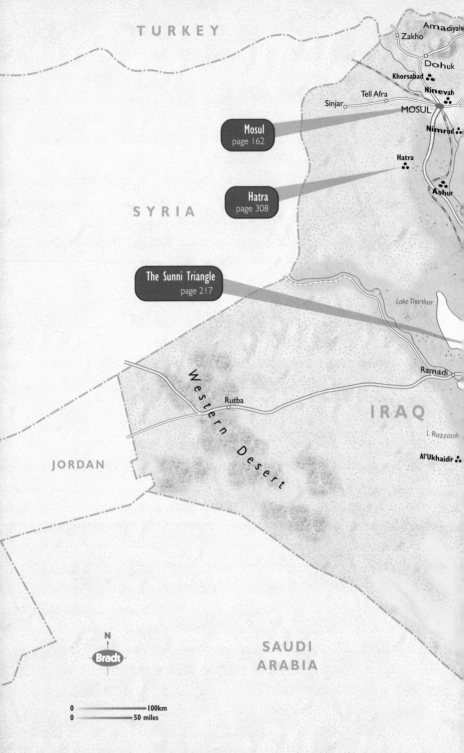

TURKEY

Zakho
Amadiyah

Dohuk

Khorsabad
Ninevah

Tell Afra

Sinjar

MOSUL

Mosul
page 162

Nimrud

SYRIA

Hatra

Hatra
page 308

Ashur

The Sunni Triangle
page 217

Lake Tharthar

Ramadi

Western Desert

Rutba

IRAQ

L Razzazah

JORDAN

Al'Ukhaidir

N

Bradt

SAUDI
ARABIA

0 ————————— 100km
0 ————————— 50 miles

Adapted from Economist Intelligence Unit.

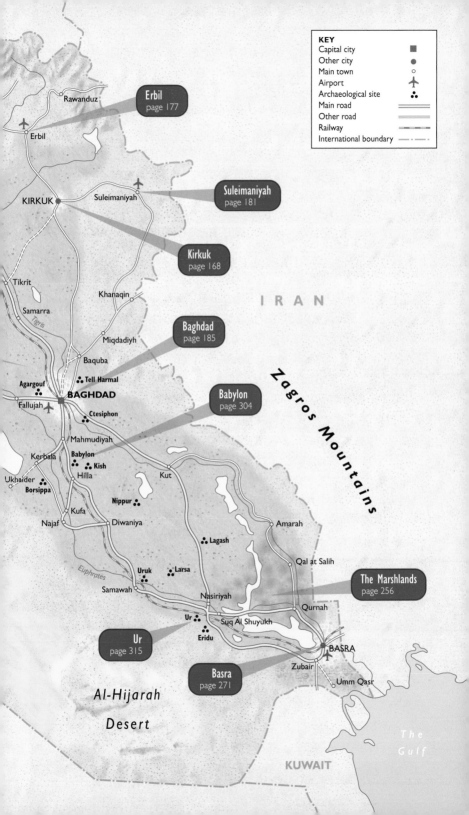

KEY
Capital city
Other city
Main town
Airport
Archaeological site
Main road
Other road
Railway
International boundary

Rawanduz

Erbil
page 177

Erbil

KIRKUK

Suleimaniyah

Suleimaniyah
page 181

Kirkuk
page 168

Tikrit

Khanaqin

I R A N

Samarra

Tigris

Miqdadiyh

Baghdad
page 185

Baquba

Agargouf

Tell Harmal

BAGHDAD

Fallujah

Ctesiphon

Babylon
page 304

Mahmudiyah

Kerbala

Babylon

Kish

Ukhaider

Hilla

Borsippa

Kut

Zagros Mountains

Nippur

Kufa

Najaf

Diwaniya

Lagash

Amarah

Qal at Salih

Uruk

Larsa

The Marshlands
page 256

Samawah

Nasiriyah

Qurnah

Ur

Suq Al Shuyukh

Ur
page 315

Eridu

BASRA

Basra
page 271

Zubair

Umm Qasr

Al-Hijarah

Desert

KUWAIT

Euphrates

The
Gulf

top   The Sinak Bridge spanning the River Tigris, Baghdad (GH) page 200

above Martyrs' Monument, to the Iran–Iraq War, Baghdad (GH) page 344

below Saddam Hussein's Great Arch of Crossed Swords, Baghdad (GH) page 345

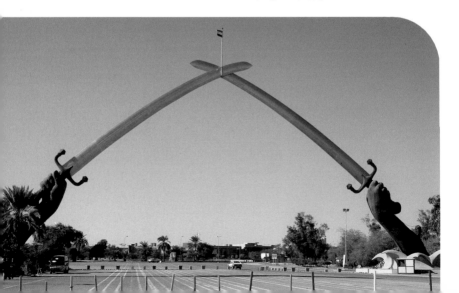

top   Four Shiite Muslim women
walk through the remains
of their Baghdad
apartment building, 2005
(CS) page 274

above   Soldier guards aftermath
of suicide bombing,
Baghdad 2005
(CS) page 117

left   US tank crossing the Tigris
River into Baghdad
(GH)

top   In Kuchteppe, a woman of the Barzani tribe shows pictures of her abducted relatives, 1983 (CK) page 182

above left   Defaced Saddam statue in the former Saddam Art Gallery, Baghdad (CS) page 280

above right   Golden statue of Saddam, Basra (GH) page 272

right   Saddam mural, outside of Diwaniya, 2002 (GH) page 240

above **Toppled statue of Saddam, Kirkuk** (PeerPoint/Alamy) page 85

below **The Monument for Freedom, Baghdad** (GH) page 279

Publisher's Foreword

A lifetime of travel has taught me one thing above all others: that to get the true measure of a country you need to listen to the opinions of the local people. To travel is to realise how much we are dependent on second-hand views and how different the reality is when we talk to the vendor in the market, or our taxi driver or local guide and learn about their every-day concerns.

Bradt guides make a point of setting the tourist information against a background of history and cultural identity, and we have always tried to let the people speak for themselves, rather than impose our own political views. This aim has never been more important than in Iraq, a country on which everyone has an opinion but very few have first-hand experience. Karen Dabrowska and Geoff Hann not only know Iraq intimately, but their love of the country and its people persuaded us to publish their guide to Iraq in 2002. This book helped me form my own opinions about the country; I made the personal decision to join the Hyde Park demonstration in 2003.

Whatever your view on the events that have led to the current situation in Iraq and the publication of this new book, there is no doubting that the Iraq that inspired us to commission the original guide has gone. A new Iraq has emerged, well documented by war correspondents and news commentators, but the focus has, inevitably, been on the war and its effects. *Iraq Then and Now* takes the original background information about the country and its people, and extends it to incorporate the voices of ordinary Iraqis reflecting on the 'then and now' aspect of their lives. Karen and Geoff have tried to represent the various viewpoints; we hope that, if nothing else, this book will offer some new perspectives.

The day will come when all of Iraq is again peaceful and safe for tourism. Then we will publish a new edition of the guidebook as a tribute to its courageous people and the enduring fascination of their country.

Hilary Bradt

AUTHORS

KAREN DABROWSKA Born in Wellington, New Zealand, to Polish parents, Karen Dabrowska worked on a daily paper in New Zealand for six years before emigrating to Britain in 1985, where she completed an MA in International Journalism. She has edited a number of magazines and newsletters dealing with the Arab world, including *New Horizon* and *Al Muhajir* (English section), and has visited most Arab countries. During the 1990s she edited a number of newsletters about Iraq. She is currently Assistant Editor of *Islamic Tourism* magazine. Karen is the author of *Addis Ababa: The First 100 Years* (1987), *Bahrain Briefing – The Struggle for Democracy (December 1994– December 1996)* and *Iraq: the Bradt Travel Guide* (2002).

AUTHOR'S STORY

I received a phone call from a television journalist asking me whether the ongoing violence in Iraq meant a second edition to the Bradt travel guide would be shelved. 'Of course not,' I replied confidently. 'The men with the guns will not win!' But in December 2004, after the assassination of the mayor of Baghdad, Bradt quite rightly decided that publishing a travel guide at this time was unrealistic.

The terrorists may have won a battle, but they did not win the war because early in 2007, in response to the growing interest in the country, it was decided to publish a guide to the country and its people. This guide will bridge the gap until the security situation improves, and a new edition of the traditional travel guide can be published.

Working on the book gave me an insight into the difficulties of life in Iraq after the change. Salem Nasir, a Basra resident, wrote about life in the city. That was easy. But sending his article proved more difficult. He went to an internet café but there was no electricity. When the electricity was on militias were fighting in the street and he could not leave his house. When he finally reached the café and the electricity was on he could not find anyone to type his article. So he scanned it and sent it as an attachment.

Like the tourist guide, the new book introduces the magnificent ancient Iraqi civilisations and provides a historical background to the country. We focus on developments in post-Saddam Iraq, not ignoring the horrors that followed the aftermath of the war, but also highlighting positive developments: the news that the then British Foreign Secretary Margaret Beckett accused the media of ignoring. The boxes interspersed throughout the text describe the hopes, dreams, fears and ambitions of Iraqis from all walks of life.

We believe the Iraqi people will not allow those with the most powerful militias to win the battle for the soul of Iraq. Rather than cursing the darkness we hope this book will be a candle that sheds light on the Iraq of today and looks forward to a future of achievement, development and positive interaction between the peoples of Iraq and their brothers and sisters in the West.

GEOFF HANN Born in High Wycombe and founder/ Director of the Adventure companies Hann Overland and Hinterland Travel, Geoff Hann is an experienced overland traveller and adventurer. Since the mid 1960s he has travelled extensively in the Middle East and Asia taking many groups from London to Kathmandu via Iraq and Afghanistan. More recently he has led groups to India, Bangladesh, Central Asia, Iran and Iraq.

His love of history and taste for exploring little-known routes has led him to travel on almost all roads in and out of Iraq, and during the Iraq–Iran conflict his groups were often the only travellers there. In 2000, after an absence from Iraq due to sanctions and the Gulf War, he re-established his archaeological/ historical tours, which continued until the outbreak of war again. In 2003 he paid a fleeting personal visit as war ended, and then led a rather famous post-war Iraq tour. Then sadly this open window closed. In 2007 he operated two tours of Kurdistan Iraq and now waits for southern Iraq to open again.

AUTHOR'S STORY

After the Second Gulf War, I was determined to revisit Baghdad. My friends were there – how had they coped? What damage had been done? Could we run tours again? What was the future for Iraq? I travelled to Baghdad alone. There were scary moments, once hurriedly leaving a restaurant to bursts of Kalashnikov fire. But the Baghdadis' enthusiasm for freedom after Saddam's constrictive regime was very infectious and apart from looting, there was little damage to the city. So with outrageous enthusiasm I embarked on my post-war tour of Iraq in October 2003, accompanied by people almost as crazy as I was. It was a wonderful experience. There were no restrictions and we totally bemused the military. How could tourists be travelling past their checkpoints as they were hunkered down over their machine guns? The general air of relaxation extended to us mingling with the Pilgrims in Najaf and Kerbala, and being welcomed into the Great Mosque at Kufa. However, this freedom to travel did not last beyond early 2004.

I consoled myself with exploring Kurdistan Iraq, a region difficult to visit under Saddam. In 2007 I arranged two tours. With this book in mind I was delighted to discover the Bavian Gorge with its Assyrian Reliefs (see page 338). But there came a burst of reality when attempting to locate the site of Jarmo, a Neolithic village excavated in 1958, known for its pottery sequence dating back to 6,000BC. Saddam had destroyed the local village and mosque, and we could see little of the site. Returning, we were suddenly stopped and arrested with brutal and fear-inducing efficiency. Our drivers were bound and we were driven at great speed to a police station. Four hours later, following an hilarious interrogation in German between a local interpreter and our German lady client of over 80 years, we were released. Surreal! The Chief of Police offered a guard for another visit, but I politely declined.

A visit to Iraq has always been an adventure.

First published April 2008
Bradt Travel Guides Ltd
23 High Street, Chalfont St Peter, Bucks SL9 9QE, England; www.bradtguides.com
Published in the USA by The Globe Pequot Press Inc, 246 Goose Lane,
PO Box 480, Guilford, Connecticut 06437-0480

British Library Cataloguing in Publication Data
A catalogue record for this book is available from the British Library
ISBN-10: 1 84162 243 5
ISBN-13: 978 1 84162 243 9

Photographs
Angus Beaton (AB), Arjun Clarry (AC), Maysaloun Faraj (MF), Geoff Hann (GH), Chris
Kutschera (CK), Mike Luongo (ML), PeerPoint/Alamy, César G Soriano (CS)
Front cover Abu Dulaf Mosque Samarra (Silvio Fiore/SuperStock); an Iraqi boy rides past a
bullet-ridden mural of Iraqi president Saddam Hussein, near the border of Turkey (Yannis
Behrakis/ Reuters/CORBIS)
Part openers General Information: Baghdad skyline (GH), Iraq Then: Detail from Hatra
(GH), Iraq Now: Minaret, Kerbala (GH)
Back cover Smoke rises over Baghdad, 2006 (CS), young boy poles through date plantations
(AB), Girls in traditional dress, Al-Houtra province (AB)

Photographers have endeavoured always to secure model-release permission for photos in
this guide. On the rare occasions this has not been possible, we have assumed that consent
for publication is implied in the subject consenting to be photographed.

For Bradt: Editorial Project Manager Anna Moores
Edited and designed by D & N Publishing, Hungerford, Berkshire
Cover design James Nunn
Illustrations Carole Vincer
Maps Terence Crump and Steve Munns (colour)
Index Jonathan Derrick

Printed and bound in Malta by Gutenberg Press Ltd

Acknowledgements

KAREN DABROWSKA First and foremost I would like to thank Dr Abdul-Rahim Hassan and John Grigg for their tremendous support and assistance with arranging interviews, reading through the manuscript and offering helpful suggestions. Special thanks must also go to my partner Jabbar Maan Al Khafaji, for his inspiration, patience and encouragement. I appreciate the insightful articles contributed by Raghda Zaid, Fran Hazelton, John Cookson and Julia Duin. For their comments on the text, interviews and insights into life in post-Saddam Iraq my thanks to Dr Mohamed Makiya, Fadhel Ali, Walid Abdul Ameer Alwan, Lamia Al-Gailani Werr, Maysaloun Faraj, Dr Sahib Al-Hakim, Dr Bayan Alaraji, Dr Ayad Allawi, Dr Saeed Shehabi, Dr Ahmed el Dawi, Bayan Sami Abdul Rahman, Yousif Naser, Salam Naser, Ali Kamil, Dr Nabeel Yassin, Hassan Jaber, Dr Salah Al-Shaikhly, Astrid Patsch, Hani Al-Saigh, Riad Al Taher, Abdulkareem Kashid, Ali Kamil, Ehsan Emam, Gbengao Oke, David Lynch, Jahangir Hajipour, Baroness Nicholson of Winterbourne and Teofil Barbu.

GEOFF HANN Firstly I would like to thank the ordinary people of Iraq. They come to my mind when I wish to acknowledge my passion for their country. For so diverse a nation, many of them transcend the divisions of religion, culture and life experiences. Special thanks must go to my guide from Baghdad, (tall) Ahmad, who I really began to understand very slowly, his boss Mr Ahmad and his family, who knew how to fix everything, and my friend in London Mr Saad al Khafaji of IKB, who knows everything that goes on in Iraq. Closer to home my special thanks go to Hilary Bradt, who listened and listened for some years and then made the decision to publish this book, and my wife Janet, who has supported me and for years has shared my passion with ancient Iraq, and Tina and Halina, my sternest critics and organisers. Finally, I would like to thank all my friends who know what it is like to be obsessed with travel and gracefully accept my comings, goings and reminiscences.

This book is dedicated to the memory of Marilyn Paget-Harrison, who passed away on 7 June 2007.

Contents

EXTRACTS

Reprinted with permission, extracts from:
Samir Al-Khalil, *The Monument* (© 1991 Andre Deutsch, London); Leonard
Cottrell, *Land of the Two Rivers* (© 1963 Leonard Cottrell, the Estate of Leonard
Cottrell); © 2007 Vincent L Foulk *The Battle for Fallujah: Occupation, Resistance and
Stalemate in the War in Iraq* (McFarland & Company, Inc., Jefferson); Kenneth
Kattan, *Mine was the Last Generation in Babylon*; Lorenzo Kimball, *The Changing
Pattern of Political Power in Iraq, 1958–1971* (© 1972 Robert Speller, New York);
Tore Kjeilen, extract on Mandeans from *Encyclopaedia of the Orient* (internet
edition); Anton La Guardia, *The Daily Telegraph* reportage on smuggled
antiquities (© 2000 Telegraph Group Limited); Stephen Longrigg, *The Middle
East: A Social Geography* (© 1963 Duckworth, London); Mrs Sue Morris,
quotation from Sir Mortimer Wheeler; Yitzhak Nakash, *The Shi'is of Iraq* (©
1994 Princeton University Press, Princeton); © 2006 Riverbend, *Baghdad
Burning, Volume 2, the Unfolding Story* (Marion Boyars Publishers Ltd); Jeffrey
Robinson, *The Laundrymen* (© 1996 Pennstreet Ltd, Arcade Publishing, New
York); © 2005 Angela M H Schuster and Milbry Polk (eds), introduction by
William R Polk, *Looting of the Iraq Museum, Baghdad* (Harry N Abrams, Inc., New
York); © 2003 John Simpson, *The Wars Against Saddam* (Pan Macmillan,
London); © 2007 Gareth Stansfield, *Iraq* (Polity Press); Freya Stark, *Baghdad
Sketches* (© 1947 John Murray, London); © 2006 Rory Stewart, *Occupational
Hazards: My Time Governing Iraq* (Pan MacMillan, London); © 2007 Charles
Tripp, *A History of Iraq* (Cambridge University Press); Gaston Wiet, *Baghdad:
Metropolis of the Abbasid Caliphate* (© 1971 University of Oklahoma Press); Gavin
Young, *Iraq: Land of Two Rivers* (© 1980 Gavin Young, Gillon Aitken Associates).

Introduction

Iraq, the land between the two rivers, the Tigris and the Euphrates, is a jigsaw puzzle with three main pieces: the mountainous snow-clad north and northeast making up about 20% of the country, the desert representing 59%, and the southern lowland alluvial plain making up the remainder.

The history of Iraq has often been a history of conflict and bloodshed, but during periods of serenity, splendid civilisations have emerged to make numerous indisputable contributions to the history of mankind: it is the land where writing began, where zero was introduced into mathematics, and where the tales of *The Thousand and One Nights* were first told. Iraq was the home of the famous Hanging Gardens of Babylon and the mythical Tower of Babel. Qurnah is reputed to be the site of the biblical Garden of Eden. Splendid mosques and palaces were built by rulers who insisted on nothing but the most magnificent. Through trade, Iraq absorbed the best of what its neighbours had to offer and incorporated the innovations of others into its own unique civilisation.

In the 20th century Arab nationalism was nourished in Iraq – it was the first independent Middle Eastern state and developed a strong Arab identity. Art was encouraged and Baghdad became the venue for many international cultural festivals.

But the 20th century was also the time of the Iran–Iraq War, the Iraqi invasion of Kuwait and the subsequent war. The Iraqi people also suffered from some of the most stringent economic sanctions ever imposed by the United Nations, and from Saddam Hussein's totalitarian regime.

The dream of a better future after the 2003 war, when the US-led coalition toppled Saddam, soon turned into a nightmare. Much of the budget originally allocated by the USA for a massive rebuilding programme has been diverted into maintaining security. Attacks on coalition forces continue on an almost daily basis. Sectarian strife, especially the Shia–Sunni conflict, is also plaguing the country, as thousands of people flee to neighbouring Syria and Jordan, and millions of internally displaced Iraqis face an uncertain future.

But anyone who doubts that the country will emerge from this difficult period and contribute once again to all noble human endeavours does not understand Iraq's resilient nature.

In the words of Gavin Young, author of *Iraq: Land of Two Rivers*:

If the oil should ever run out, the twin rivers will still uncoil like giant pythons from their lairs in High Armenia across the northern plains, will still edge teasingly closer near Baghdad, still sway apart lower down, still combine finally at the site – who knows for sure that it was not? – of the Garden of Eden, and flow commingled through silent date-forests to the Gulf. Whatever happens, the rivers – the life-giving twin rivers for which Abraham, Nebuchadnezzar, Sennacherib, Alexander the Great, Trajan, Harun Al Rashid and a billion other dwellers in Mesopotamia must have raised thanks to their gods – will continue to give life to other generations.

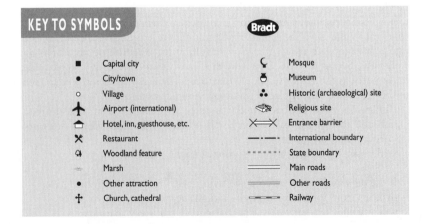

Part One

GENERAL INFORMATION

Size/Area 441,839km²
Population 27,500,000
Location Middle East
Time GMT + 3
Electrical voltage 220V
Bordering countries Iran, Jordan, Kuwait, Saudi Arabia, Syria, Turkey
Flag Three bands, red over white over black, with the words *Allah u akbar* (God is great) written in Arabic on the white stripe
Capital Baghdad
Climate Mild to cool winters; hot, cloudless summers
Main towns Basra, Mosul, Kirkuk
Currency Iraqi dinars (id = 1,000 fils)
Official language Arabic (Kurdish in Iraqi Kurdistan)
Religion 95% Muslim; Christian minorities mainly in villages around Mosul; religious sects: Sabaeans, Yezidis
Ethnic divisions Arabs 75–80%; Kurds 15–20%; Turcoman, Assyrian or other 5%
Type of government Republic
Governorates The country is divided into 18 governorates: Nineveh, Salahuddin, At Ta'mim, Diyala, Baghdad, Anbar, Babil, Kerbala, Najaf, Qadisiyah, Muthanna, Dhi Qar, Wasit, Maysan, Basra, Dohuk, Erbil, and Suleimaniyah
Head of state Jalal Talabani
Ruling party United Iraqi Alliance
Independence 3 October 1932
Economy Capitalist with government subsidies for basic necessities. Main revenue from oil
GDP US$87.9bn
Inflation 64.8%

Overview

HISTORICAL SKETCH

In ancient times, the country now known as Iraq consisted of the kingdoms of Mesopotamia, Assyria, Sumer and Babylonia. The ancient name of Mesopotamia is Greek for 'land between the two rivers'. The name Iraq, meaning 'firmly rooted country', did not emerge until the 7th century in acknowledgement of the country's influence on ancient civilisations. Historians have labelled Mesopotamia as the cradle of civilisation. In 3000BC Sumerian kings, who ruled at the same time as the earliest Egyptian dynasties, developed the first civilisations. Hammurabi (1792–1750BC), a ruler of Babylon, which emerged from a union of the ancient Sumerian and Akkadian kingdoms, developed one of the earliest known codes of law to ensure that 'justice prevailed in the country' and that 'the strong may not oppress the weak'. The hanging gardens of Babylon, a creation of King Nebuchadnezzar (605–562BC), were regarded as the seventh wonder of the ancient world. After Nebuchadnezzar's enlightened rule the area was conquered by a number of different invaders, including the Persians, the Greeks, the Parthians and the Persians again (under the Sassanids). For some centuries (AD60–600) Mesopotamia was often a frontier region being invaded and fought over by the Romans and Byzantines against the Parthian and Sassanian Empires.

In AD637 Mesopotamia was completely subjugated by the Arabs and their new, monotheistic faith: Islam. Between AD750–1258, the era of the Abbasid caliphs (Islamic rulers), Baghdad became the capital and the intellectual centre of the Islamic world, where art, science and philosophy flourished. The writings of Aristotle and Plato were translated in the House of Wisdom and advances in medicine, astronomy and other disciplines laid the foundations for modern Western sciences.

From 1638 until World War I, Iraq was part of the Ottoman Empire governed from Istanbul. After the war, the British mandate followed, and in 1932 Iraq was formally admitted to the League of Nations as an independent state governed by a constitutional monarchy installed by the British. The monarchy was overthrown in 1958 by the nationalist Free Officers in a coup led by Brigadier Abdul Karim Qasim. Qasim was murdered in 1963 during a Baathist-led coup. Nine months later the Baathists were overthrown in a counter-coup, but they succeeded in toppling the government for a second time in 1968. In a country characterised by political instability, where the government has been overthrown 23 times since 1920, the Baath Party became extremely well versed in the art of political survival.

The 1980s were dominated by the Iran–Iraq War, which left an estimated 400,000 dead and 750,000 wounded. Iraq invaded Iran in 1980 in the hope of toppling the fundamentalist Islamic regime and controlling the Shatt Al Arab waterway. Ayatollah Khomeini, the Iranian leader, had tried to incite Iraqi Muslims to rebel against President Saddam Hussein, who was seen as a secular leader by the hardline Shia Iranian regime. The West and some Arab regimes backed Saddam with weapons and intelligence. The war was a total disaster; Iraq was left with demands to repay foreign debts of more than US$75 billion to the countries that helped finance the war, especially Saudi Arabia and Kuwait.

The next military action came with the invasion of Kuwait on 2 August 1990, prompted by Saddam Hussein's unrelenting ambition to turn Iraq into a regional superpower, his anger at Kuwaiti insistence on the repayment of debts, his claim to part of the Rumaila oilfield, and his determination to secure the Kuwaiti islands of Bubiyan and Warbah.

Economic sanctions were imposed as a result of the invasion. Arab and international mediation failed to persuade Iraq to withdraw and the UN authorised the use of force. On 17 January 1991 a five-week bombing campaign, authorised by the United Nations and led by America, began. The bombardment left an estimated 100,000 dead and a further 300,000 wounded. In March 1991, popular uprisings in the north and south of the country, in which disenchanted members of the Iraqi army and civilians took part, were brutally crushed. United Nations Security Council Resolution 688, which 'condemned the repression of the Iraqi civilian population in many parts of the country, including most recently in Kurdish populated areas', was invoked by Britain, France and the USA to establish a safe-haven for the Kurds in the north. In 2003, after 13 years of sanctions, Iraq's alleged non-compliance with Security Council resolutions led to the American-led invasion that toppled Saddam's regime.

Coalition forces are still in the country under a UN mandate to help provide security and to support the government. After the invasion, Iraq was administered by the Coalition Provisional Authority (CPA), which was advised by an Iraqi Governing Council for over a year. Sovereignty was transferred to an Iraqi Interim Government on 28 June 2004. Elections for a 275-member Transitional National Assembly were held on 30 January 2005. The transitional government drafted the country's permanent constitution, which was approved in a referendum on 15 October 2005. The Shias and the Kurds supported the constitution, while most of the Sunnis were against it. A further election under the constitution was held on 15 December 2005 for a 275-member Council of Representatives, Iraq's first constitutional government in nearly half a century.

Even though the institutions of government are in place a shadow state has developed as militias and tribal warlords exert far more authority in the south and centre of the country than the elected government. Iraqi Kurdistan is ruled by the Kurdistan Regional Government in a federal arrangement.

An insurgency against the foreign forces has been underway since the fall of Baghdad on 9 April 2003. It has taken on an increasingly sectarian character and mixed Shia/Sunni neighbourhoods in Baghdad and other cities are becoming a thing of the past. The Kurds are being driven out of Mosul, the Arabs are being driven out of Kirkuk, the Christian minority is persecuted and some analysts believe the country is on the brink of a civil war.

There has been a mass exodus of Iraqis, especially professionals, to neighbouring Jordan and Syria and there are some 2 million internally displaced people within the country.

In his book *Iraq*, Gareth Stansfield concluded:

Quite simply, Iraq as it was cannot be reconstructed as the parts which were used to assemble it in the first place are no more. An attempt can only be made to allow Iraqis themselves to form something new and quite different, whether by purposeful design or civil war, or for the international community to assist in the building of a new state that would look quite different from its predecessor, from scratch.

GEOGRAPHY

Except for the narrow strip of land providing access to the Persian Gulf (the Arabs call it the Arabian Gulf) known as the Shatt Al Arab, Iraq is landlocked, with Iran to the east, Kuwait and Saudi Arabia to the south, Jordan and Syria to the west and Turkey to the north. With an area of 441,839km², it is slightly larger than Sweden.

Iraq's landscape is dominated by two rivers, the Tigris (1,850km long, of which 1,418km are in Iraq) and the Euphrates (2,350km long, of which 1,213km are in Iraq). The two rivers are separated from each other by 400km of open plain when they emerge from Turkey's Taurus Mountains and flow into Iraq. The Tigris flows southwards, the Euphrates to the southeast. Near Baghdad they are separated by a mere 32km. At Qurnah in southern Iraq, reportedly the site of the Garden of Eden, their waters join the Shatt Al Arab.

IRAQ: LOCATION

For centuries the silt of the rivers, deposited in the valleys through which they flow, has ensured the fertility of the soil. The rivers' waters are also essential for irrigation. Floods, most common in March, April and May, have caused serious problems for centuries, as Sumerian legends and the biblical story of the flood tell us. In 1954 Baghdad was devastated by a flood that killed thousands and resulted in an estimated US$50 million worth of damage.

Iraq is made up of the snow-clad mountains of the north and northeast (which account for 20% of the land area); the desert (which accounts for 59%); and the flat lowland alluvial plain in the south, famous for its unique swamps and marshlands. This area was once the home of some 250,000 Marsh Arabs, also known as the Ma'dan, whose unique lifestyle dated back to 3000BC, the time of the Sumerians. Today, the Marsh Arabs are returning to their traditional way of life as Saddam's drainage of the marshes is being reversed.

The Kurds, meanwhile, inhabit the mountainous region, with magnificent snow-clad peaks ranging from 1,000m to more than 3,600m near the Iranian and Turkish borders. On the lower slopes the temperate climate and plentiful rainfall make the growing of fruit, vegetables, grain and tobacco possible. The rest of the country's population is concentrated along the Tigris and Euphrates, whose waters are the lifeblood of the country.

Finally, the desert, where Bedouin live off their herds of camels, goats and sheep, has been described in a geography textbook as 'an area so desolate and uninviting that even a rattlesnake would feel lonely there'.

CLIMATE

Iraq not only has two seasons, hot and cool, but also two climatic areas: the hot Lowlands where crops require irrigation, and the much wetter Northeast where the mountains produce cooler temperatures and precipitation for crop cultivation.

In the Lowlands (mostly southern and central Iraq), there are two seasons, summer and winter. The summer, which lasts from May to October, has high temperatures ranging from 20°C to over 40°C. In Baghdad, temperatures can reach 50°C at their highest, but 40°C+ is more usual. There is usually no rain between June and September. The winter of December to February is mild with temperatures ranging from 2–15°C. Rain occurs between November and April, with an annual mean of 100–180mm.

In the Northeast, the summer lasts from June to September and is usually dry and hot, but with temperatures usually up to 6°C cooler than the Lowlands. Rainfall is mostly in the winter period. The winter here lasts longer and is colder, with mountain temperatures of −4–5°C, but slightly warmer in the uplands or foothills with temperatures ranging up to 12°C. Annual rainfall up to 550mm is typical, but is higher in the actual mountains themselves.

The summer months in Iraq are affected by southern and southeasterly hot and dry winds, which often bring with them destructive dust storms. These occur from April to early June and again from late September to November. However, from mid-June to mid-September the steady wind from the north and northwest called the Shamal brings very dry air, which results in little cloud cover and which in turn causes the land to be intensely heated by the sun; the wind does have a slight cooling effect.

Other extremes to be noted are the range of temperatures that occur in the desert regions, such as the western desert, from below freezing at night to 45°C at the peak of day.

Note that during the summer period the Basra region and the marshes suffer extreme humidity of over 100%.

FLORA AND FAUNA

Finding a date is never a problem in Iraq – there were once over 30 million date trees in the country, with 450 varieties, but only four are commercially exploited. Today there are around 15 million date trees. The trunk of the date palm grows to a height of up to 18m. A female tree bears 200–1,000 dates each season. In date palms of eight years old, the first crop will be 8–10kg per palm; at 13 years, 60–80kg. A cluster of dates weighs up to 12kg, and the annual yield of a single tree may reach 270kg. The tree begins to bear fruit in its eighth year, reaches maturity at 30 years, and begins to decline at about 100 years. Before sanctions were imposed in 1990, Iraq supplied over 80% of the world's dates, but the industry was dealt a serious blow by the Iran–Iraq War (1980–1988) and the draining of the southern marshlands. Many trees and orchards have been destroyed in the battle against the insurgents. USAID has supplied 40,000 date palms for orchards and nurseries.

The landscape determines the vegetation. Oak, pine, walnut, willow, wild vines and buttercups are found in the northern highlands. Reeds dominate the southern marshlands, where saltwort, camel thorn and box thorn are also

RETURN OF THE MONSTER BADGERS

In mid 2007, monster honey badgers, or ratels, appeared in Basra. The rumour mill became active and the British were held responsible for releasing the creatures to frighten the locals.

The honey badger weighs up to 13kg, is one of the world's most fearless creatures and preys on jackals, antelope, foxes, crocodiles and snakes. It is found in sub-Saharan and West Africa, Arabia, the Middle East and India.

Mushtaq Abdul-Mahdi, director of Basra's military hospital, said that older Basrawis called the creature the 'garta' (muncher). Scientists believe the numbers are increasing as the marshlands are being re-flooded (see page 257).

Major David Gell, the British Army spokesman in Basra, denied rumours that his forces had anything to do with the spread of the badgers. (They have also been accused of releasing serpents' eggs into the Shatt Al Arab waterway.) He urged the locals to keep their distance from the badgers. 'If you cornered one and poked it with a stick the smart money would be on the badger', he said.

found. For short periods in the spring the desert blooms provide sheep, goats and camels with spear grass, rock rose, saltbushes and other plants. Orange and lemon trees are grown extensively in the shade of millions of date palms in the centre and south of the country. Wheat and barley are grown in northwest Iraq between the Tigris and Euphrates, and vast areas of rice fields have been planted in the south.

The most fertile region is found on the banks of the Tigris and Euphrates, where a network of irrigation ditches directs water to farmland. About 50% of the land is arable, but only 13% is under cultivation. Agricultural products include wheat, barley, and fruits such as apples, olives, grapes, pears, oranges and pomegranates. The livestock industry is concentrated around sheep, cattle, goats and poultry.

Conservation has not been a priority in Iraq. The oryx, ostrich and wild ass have practically been wiped out. The last lion was killed in 1910. During the 1950s gazelles were hunted from cars, with drastic consequences. Bats, rats of various species, jackals and wildcats are the most common mammals, with wild pig and gazelle found in remoter parts. Reptiles are numerous and include lizards, snakes and tortoises. Otters were once found in the marshes and streams as were fish, mainly from the carp family.

There is a distinct hierarchy among the birds: eagles, vultures, kites and other birds of prey make a meal of smaller birds. Waterbirds include pelicans, geese, ducks and herons. Storks were once a common sight throughout the country. They build their nests on trees, roofs and domes.

The hoopoe is a legendary creature, which sheltered the Prophet Mohammed with its wings when he fell asleep in the desert. In gratitude the bird was offered a gift and the vain creature chose its glorious crown. The sandgrouse, which resembles a pigeon, nests in the desert in temperatures of over 38°C. Water is brought to the young on the breast feathers of their parents, who shelter them with their wings.

Migrating waterfowl wintering in the marshes of southern Iraq have become a favourite target for poachers, who sell them as a cheap alternative to poultry.

The United Nations Environment Programme (UNEP) is helping Iraq clean up the toxic pollution caused by a decade of conflict. UNEP has said it will take many years to clear up the chronic damage to air, water and soil that Iraq has suffered. The Iraqi government has also asked for help in clearing up the depleted uranium left by bombs used in US-led conflicts.

POPULATION

Iraq has a population of 27,500,000, with around 30% engaged in agriculture. The rural-urban drift began in the 1920s after oil was discovered, and increased during the 1970s, at the peak of the oil boom.

Following the 2003 war, sectarian strife and the insurgency have resulted in the displacement of 4.2 million Iraqis. Two million have fled abroad while the remainder are internally displaced persons. A weak central government and the empowerment of local leaders have augmented the traditional authority of tribal sheikhs, which diminished with the development of an oil-based economy and the growth of urban society. Some 75% of the people now live in towns.

The Iraqis have an unquenchable thirst for knowledge and the country is said to have the highest number of PhD holders per capita in the world.

GOVERNMENT

In the elections for a permanent government held on 15 December 2005, political parties submitted lists of candidates and the seats were allocated by proportional representation. The Shia United Iraqi Alliance led by the Supreme Islamic Council and the Dawa Party emerged with 128 seats. The Kurdish list made up of the Kurdish Alliance (with two major parties the Kurdistan Democratic Party and the Patriotic Union of Kurdistan) and other parties such as the Kurdistan Islamic Union and the Islamic Group of Kurdistan received 53 seats, and the third largest bloc was the Iraqi Accord Front of Sunni Arab parties, set up in October 2005, with 44 seats. In theory Iraq is a parliamentary democracy, but the government in Baghdad's Green Zone has limited jurisdiction due to the power of local warlords and militias.

IRAQ GOVERNORATES

Iraq is composed of 18 governorates (*muhafadhat*) (see map overleaf).

Governorate	Population	Governorate	Population
At Ta'mim	949,000	Anbar	1,205,000
Erbil	1,425,000	Babil	1,751,900
Baghdad	7,000,000	Basra	2,600,000
Diyala	1,272,000	Dohuk	510,000
Kerbala	742,000	Maysan	537,735
Muthanna	550,000	Najaf	931,600
Nineveh	2,600,000	Qadisiyah	700,812
Salahuddin	600,896	Suleimaniyah	1,800,000
Dhi Qar	1,454,200	Wasit	643,371

MAJOR TOWNS

Baghdad, with a population of some seven million, is the capital city. It lies in the heart of the Middle East, 692km southwest of Tehran (in Iran) and 805km east of Beirut (in Lebanon). It is an important manufacturing, trade, communications and cultural centre in the Tigris–Euphrates Valley. More than 31% of the country's population is found in Baghdad and the governorate around the capital.

Basra and Mosul are competing for the title of Iraq's second city. Mosul lost some of its inhabitants during the 1960s and Basra became the second-largest city during the mid-70s and early '80s, due to migration of labour to work in construction and development programmes.

Basra (population 1,700,000), characterised by a network of canals, is often called the Venice of the East. It is Iraq's main port, now under the control of Shia militias. **Mosul** (population 1,739,800) is named after 'muslin', the cotton for which it is famous. The country's Christian community is concentrated in this city, which is also home to Arabs, Kurds and Turcomans.

Kirkuk (population 755,700) is Iraq's fourth-largest city. Oil was discovered in the Kirkuk area in 1927. The city is the traditional home of the country's Turcoman minority.

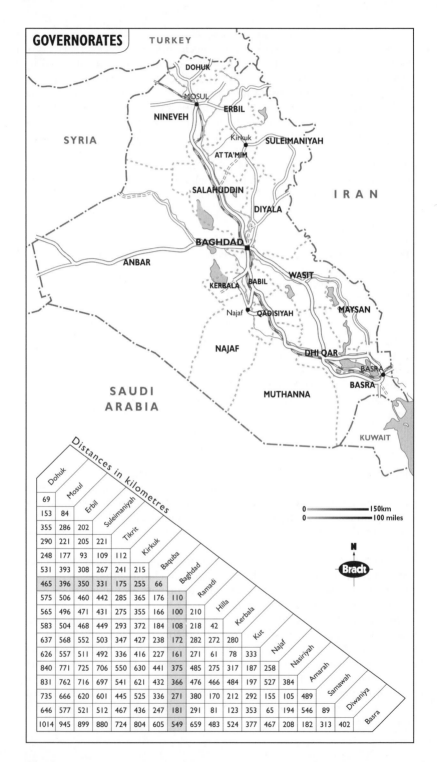

GOVERNORATES

TURKEY

DOHUK

MOSUL

NINEVEH

ERBIL

Kirkuk

SULEIMANIYAH

AT TA'MIM

SYRIA

SALAHUDDIN

DIYALA

IRAN

BAGHDAD

ANBAR

KERBALA

BABIL

WASIT

Najaf

QADISIYAH

MAYSAN

NAJAF

DHI QAR

BASRA

BASRA

SAUDI
ARABIA

MUTHANNA

KUWAIT

Dohuk	Mosul	Erbil	Suleimaniyah	Tikrit	Kirkuk	Baquba	Baghdad	Ramadi	Hilla	Kerbala	Kut	Najaf	Nasiriyah	Amarah	Samawah	Diwaniya	Basra
69																	
153	84																
355	286	202															
290	221	205	221														
248	177	93	109	112													
531	393	308	267	241	215												
465	396	350	331	175	255	66											
575	506	460	442	285	365	176	110										
565	496	471	431	275	355	166	100	210									
583	504	468	449	293	372	184	108	218	42								
637	568	552	503	347	427	238	172	282	272	280							
626	557	511	492	336	416	227	161	271	61	78	333						
840	771	725	706	550	630	441	375	485	275	317	187	258					
831	762	716	697	541	621	432	366	476	466	484	197	527	384				
735	666	620	601	445	525	336	271	380	170	212	292	155	105	489			
646	577	521	512	467	436	247	181	291	81	123	353	65	194	546	89		
1014	945	899	880	724	804	605	549	659	483	524	377	467	208	182	313	402	

Distances in kilometres

0 ⟶ 150km
0 ⟶ 100 miles

N

Bradt

Iraq's economy is dominated by the oil sector, which provides about 95% of foreign exchange earnings. In early 2008, Iraqi crude production was 2.3 million barrels per day, compared with 1.9 million barrels at the start of 2007. According to the US Department of Energy, Iraq contains 112 billion barrels of proven oil reserves, the second largest in the world (behind Saudi Arabia), along with roughly 220 billion barrels of probable and possible resources. Iraq's true potential may be far greater than this, however, as the country is relatively unexplored due to years of war and sanctions.

The Iraq oil law, also referred to as the Iraq hydrocarbon law, will have a major impact on the development of the oil industry. It is a proposed piece of legislation submitted to the Iraqi Council of Representatives in May 2007. The Bush administration hired the consulting firm Bearing Point to help write the law in 2004. The bill was approved by the Iraqi cabinet in February 2007. The Bush administration considers the passage of the law a benchmark for the government of Prime Minister Maliki. It would authorise production share agreements (PSAs) that guarantee a profit for foreign oil companies.

The USA, aided by the International Monetary Fund (IMF), is encouraging the Iraqis to privatise the oil fields. The situation is complicated by regional forces (for example, the Kurdish region) wanting to go ahead to make their own deals with foreign corporations and a growing movement, particularly within the unions, for national control.

Professor Rodney Shakespeare, a barrister, proposed an alternative plan for the development of Iraq's oil industry. He believes that immediately after the 2003 invasion it would have been far better to have announced that the people of Iraq own all its economic assets including the oil fields and that all Iraqi citizens should have a single, non-transferable, life-time share in the ownership of the oil and, in particular, of its income, with the income payable immediately the oil was flowing. If that had been done, it would have given everybody a strong financial interest in the stability and success of their own country.

Oil output has been affected by attacks on oil infrastructure and smuggling. The website Iraq Pipeline Watch recorded 466 attacks on oil infrastructure or employees between 2003 and 2008. According to an article in *The Times* on 1 February 2008, US officials believe that as many as half the industry's most skilled workers fled Iraq or were killed, as the country descended into mayhem. In July 2007 the US Government Accountability Office reported that 100,000 to 300,000 barrels of oil worth US$5–15 million went unaccounted for each day. A US report in 2006 said that insurgents, aided by corrupt officials, were raising US$25–100 million a year from oil smuggling.

The invasion of Kuwait, and subsequent sanctions and damage from military action during the 1991 war, reduced economic activity. Iraq was allowed to export limited amounts of oil in exchange for food, medicine and some spare parts for its infrastructure under the oil-for-food programme during the 13 years of sanctions.

When sanctions were lifted on 24 May 2003, one month after the overthrow of Saddam Hussein, the economic growth of 53% topped the list of the world's fastest growing economies. Under the Coalition Provisional Authority, which ruled the country from 2003–04, a series of orders were issued designed to restructure the state-owned economy along free-market, capitalist lines. Order

39 laid the framework for full privatisation and permitted 100% foreign-ownership of Iraqi assets with the exception of oil.

In December 2006 *Newsweek International* highlighted the findings of a study of Global Insight in London, which showed that:

> Civil war or not, Iraq has an economy and – mother of all surprises – it's doing remarkably well. Real estate is booming. Construction, retail and wholesale trade sectors are healthy, too. The US Chamber of Commerce reports 34,000 registered companies in Iraq, up from 8,000 three years ago. Sales of second hand cars, televisions and mobile phones have all risen sharply. Given all the attention paid to deteriorating security, the startling fact is that Iraq is growing at all.

In a triumph of hope over experience the Iraqi Tourism Board maintains a staff of 2,500 and 14 regional offices throughout the country.

Traditionally Iraq's manufacturing activity has been closely connected to the oil industry: petroleum refining and the manufacture of chemicals and fertilisers. Before 2003, diversification was hindered by limitations on privatisation and the effects of sanctions. Since 2003 security problems have hindered efforts to establish new industries. The most commonly produced goods are footwear, cigarettes, construction materials, processed foods and textiles.

Because of the largely inactive manufacturing sector the range of imports is large and includes food, fuels, medicines and manufactured goods.

The military action of 2003 did little damage to Iraqi agriculture: because of favourable weather conditions in that year, grain production was 22% higher than in 2002. Long-term plans call for investment in agricultural machinery and materials and more prolific crop varieties. The re-flooding of the marshlands, drained under Saddam's regime, is leading to the revival of a traditional rice- and food-producing area.

The main farming area is in the region of the country's two major rivers, the Tigris and Euphrates. Of Iraq's total land area, 77% is not viable for agriculture. Less than 0.4% consists of forest and woodlands situated along the Turkish and Iranian borders. The remaining 22% (about 9.5 million ha) is used for agricultural activities, including seasonal grazing of goats and sheep, tree crops (figs, grapes, olives and dates), field crops such as cereals, pulses, fruit and vegetables, and grains, mostly wheat and barley. The fishing industry is small and centred around freshwater species.

ETHNIC GROUPS AND LANGUAGES

The Iraqi people were once like a necklace, where the thread of nationality united a variety of unique and colourful beads. The Arabs are in the majority, making up at least 75% of the population, while 18% are Kurds and the remaining 7% consists of Assyrians, Turcomans, Armenians and other, smaller minorities

A report by Minority Rights Group International revealed that Iraq's minorities, which consist of some of the oldest communities in the world, are fleeing because of the violence unleashed against them. They tend to be identified with the occupation and are seen as easy targets by kidnappers and death squads. Before 2003 there were 30,000 Mandeans in Iraq. Today there are

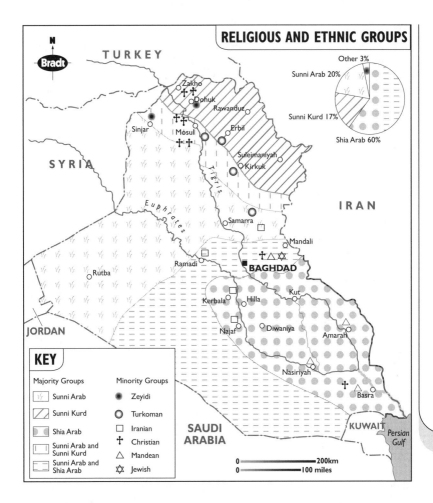

RELIGIOUS AND ETHNIC GROUPS

Other 3%
Sunni Arab 20%
Sunni Kurd 17%
Shia Arab 60%

KEY

Majority Groups
- Sunni Arab
- Sunni Kurd
- Shia Arab
- Sunni Arab and Sunni Kurd
- Sunni Arab and Shia Arab

Minority Groups
- Zeyidi
- Turkoman
- Iranian
- Christian
- Mandean
- Jewish

0 — 200km
0 — 100 miles

fewer then 13,000. The figures for the Turcomans are 800,000 in 2003, now down to 200,000; Jews from a few hundred to 35; Palestinians from 35,000 to 15,000. The Yezidis number 550,000.

Arabic is the official language and English is widely understood, especially in urban areas. Kurdish (the Sorani dialect) is spoken in northern Iraq (generally referred to as Iraqi Kurdistan). The Turcomans converse in Turkish. Farsi is spoken by some tribal elements.

RELIGION: THE SUNNI–SHIA DIVIDE

Islam is the religion of 90% of Iraqis who belong to either the Sunni or Shia sect. Iraq is one of the few Arab countries where the Shia constitute a majority. Estimates of the number of Shias vary from 54–70% (of Arab Muslims). Christians (see pages 40–1) make up nearly 4% of the population. There is a very small Jewish community (see pages 192–3) and esoteric beliefs include those of Yezidis (see pages 170–1) and Mandeans (see pages 262–3).

13

The beliefs of Sunnis and Shias do not differ greatly and theological differences are seldom a source of conflict. Both sects believe in the five pillars of Islam: the profession of faith that there is no God but Allah, to pray five times a day, to fast during the month of Ramadan when the Koran was revealed to the Prophet Mohammed, to give alms to the poor, and to make a pilgrimage to Mecca.

Religious differences include the Shias' veneration of the family of the Prophet (Mohammed and his descendants), and a more centralised and hierarchical clergy. The Shia normally follow the advice of an *ayatollah* on the interpretation of the Koran and Islamic law (*shariah*). In Iraq, Ayatollah Sistani (see page 248) has many followers. The Shias venerate 12 imams, who they see as successors to Prophet Mohammed.

All Muslims believe in the Mahdi who will return to save the earth. There will be a battle between the forces of good and evil followed by a thousand-year reign of peace and the end of the world: hence the occasional apocalyptic rhetoric of the radical Shia cleric Moqtada Al-Sadr. The difference between Shias and Sunnis is that the Shias believe they know the identity of this person. For them he is the son of the 11th Imam al-Askari. For the Sunnis, the identity is not fixed. This is why the Sunnis had a Mahdi in 19th-century Sudan. He believed himself to be the promised one and so did his followers, but his defeat put an end to this belief. In southern Iraq the Soldiers of Heaven cult emerged last year. Its followers believe that their former leader, Dia Abdul-Zahra, who was killed in fighting with the security forces, was the Mahdi. The cult is now led by Ahmed Hassani Yamani, who describes himself as the Mahdi's ambassador.

Major Shia holidays mourn the martyrdom of Imam Ali and Imam Hussein (see pages 233–4). The main Shia holiday is Ashura, marking the martyrdom of Hussein and his followers outside the city of Kerbala in AD680 (see page 233). It is commemorated with a procession to Kerbala, a passion play re-enacting the martyrdom and, in some cases, self-flagellation.

The Sunnis, especially the hard-line clergy in Saudi Arabia, look with disdain upon the veneration of Hussein and Ali and accuse the Shias of a violation of monotheism. Extremist Sunni groups, like Al-Qaeda in Iraq, view the the Shias as *kafirs* (unbelievers), who must be killed.

ORIGINS OF THE DIVIDE The religious divide occurred 1,400 years ago due to a disagreement about who should lead the Muslims after the death of Prophet Mohammed in 632. The Sunnis (followers of the Prophet) believed that any faithful Muslim could become caliph (leader of the faithful) and supported Abu Bakr, an early convert to Islam. The Shias believed that the caliph should come from the Prophet's family. They were called Shiat-Ali (partisans of Ali), after the prophet's cousin and son-in law Ali who they wanted to become caliph. The Shias lost the struggle for leadership of the Muslims (see pages 233–4) and this resulted in their minority status within global Islam. The injustices and discrimination they have suffered since the early days of Islam have resulted in an identification with Hussein, the martyr at the battle of Kerbala.

Although the Shias outnumbered the Sunnis in modern Iraq, the Sunnis maintained their hold on political power and used religious justifications for oppressing the Shia. The Sunni caliphs in Baghdad, mindful of their economic interests, allowed the Shia holy cities to become centres of pilgrimage and even contributed to their development. As long as the Shias did not oppose the ruling elite, they were allowed to run their religious schools unmolested.

THE DIVIDE WIDENS The sectarian divide widened in the 16th century. The Turkish Sunni Ottomans, rulers of the Muslim world, fought with the Shia Safavid dynasty of Persia (see pages 58–60). The Ottomans emerged victorious and consolidated their control of Arab territories. When Iraq came under the British mandate, the power structure was not changed. After World War I, the British left a Sunni monarch to rule Iraq (see pages 68–72).

Before Saddam Hussein assumed power in 1979, Sunni–Shia relations were cordial and tolerant. However, the Islamic Revolution in Iran in 1979 made Saddam fearful that the Iraqi Shias would follow suit; he ordered the murder of a revered Shia cleric, Muhammed Baqr Al-Sadr, and expelled the Feyli (Shia) Kurds to Iran because of their Iranian origin. The Iraqi Shias fought for Iraq during the 1980–88 Iran–Iraq war, but after the war their exclusion from important government and military positions continued.

The Shias and Kurds staged a popular uprising against Saddam at the end of the first Gulf War in 1991. Their revolt was brutally crushed and around 300,000 Shias were killed, many being buried in mass graves. The development of southern Iraq was neglected (see pages 240–1), the marshlands, a traditional place of refuge for anti-regime elements, were drained (see page 257) and a number of Shia clerics were assassinated. Saddam labelled Shia cities 'black' after the uprising. The Wahhabi movement, influenced and financed by the Saudis, was allowed to flourish in Iraq, to undermine the Shias.

But despite the government's machinations, Sunnis and Shias were still friends: they worked and socialised together, new neighbourhoods that sprang up in Baghdad were mixed, tribes and clans included both Sunnis and Shias and intermarriage was common. 'My mother is a Shia and my father a Sunni, so can you tell which half of me is which?' an older woman asked freelance journalist Dahr Jamail. The accompanying smile said it all.

Writing in *The Financial Times* magazine on 30 August 2003, David Gardner pointed out that:

> the Iraq enterprise has set in motion tectonic shifts which are difficult to predict. The US has not just overthrown a rogue regime; it has overturned a Sunni regime in the Arab heartland. By potentially empowering the Shia majority, Bush and the Washington Neo-Conservatives have undermined the nearly millennium-old dominance of Sunni Islam in Iraq and the Arab world.

Two years after Saddam was toppled, the previously cordial ties between the two sects prevented the spread of sectarian violence. The attacks of Al-Qaeda in Iraq against the Shias were not avenged and the Shias sometimes joined the Sunni insurgency against coalition forces. The Sunni supported Moqtada Al-Sadr's stand against the Americans in the summer of 2004 (see pages 254–5) and some of Al-Sadr's Shia Mehdi Army fighters joined the Sunnis in the battle of Fallujah (see pages 220–3). Al-Sadr described himself as a defender of the Arabs and was seen as a hero by the hard-line Sunni Association of Muslim Scholars.

The 2005 elections (see pages 130–2), which were boycotted by the Sunnis, drove a wedge between the two communities. The Shia coalition recruited Shia militiamen into the police force and some of the recruits hid behind their uniforms to settle old scores with the Sunnis. Then came the bombing of Samarra's golden-domed shrine, one of the Shias' holiest shrines, on 22 February 2006, which became a watershed in the simmering Sunni–Shia conflict. The Shias had tolerated previous Sunni attacks, but their patience finally ran out and the sectarian cleansing of Baghdad began, with the Shias ending up in control of 75% of the city (see pages 203–6). Sunni mosques were attacked and reprisals continued in a vicious cycle of violence.

Some Sunni tribes in Anbar Province began co-operating with the Americans in the struggle against Al-Qaeda when the terrorist group began killing Sunnis as well as Shias. The Americans are now paying tribesmen to patrol the province. They are known as 'Awakening Forces' and number 76,000 (see page 225). The Shias fear that the new forces will eventually turn against them. Not all the Sunnis support the Awakening Forces, however, and the Shias (especially the militias of the Supreme Islamic Council and Moqtada Al-Sadr) have fought one another.

WHAT THE FUTURE HOLDS Iraq's many conflicts are a struggle for political domination that is given a religious justification: the Sunnis want to regain the power they have lost after the toppling of Saddam's regime and the Shias want to make sure they hold on to the power they gained through the ballot box and through the power of the gun. In his article in the *Christian Science Monitor*, Dan Murphy points out that:

> while religious differences are real and remain important the
> breakdown over Shia and Sunni in Iraq is about group identity as much
> as it is about disagreements over proper worship. Many Sunnis and
> Shias, who are not particularly devout, are participating in the
> bloodshed, fighting to advance group interests.

Outsiders are reinforcing the sectarian identification that was previously foreign to Iraqis: the Americans set up a governing council based on sectarian and ethnic quotas (see page 125), the Iranians are backing the Shia insurgents and supplying them with weapons, and Al-Qaeda in Iraq is systematically targeting the Shia and their religious sites. Most Iraqis would identify themselves as Muslims or Iraqis without reference to their sectarian identity and questions about sect were once considered rude. An Iraqi diplomat emphasised this when saying:

> The sectarian cleansing in Baghdad and elsewhere is part of a well-
> conceived plan outside Iraq. I strongly believe that if Iraqis could freely
> vote on the issue, they would reject sectarianism outright. Up to 2003
> not a single Iraqi political leader, writer or journalist addressed the
> ethnic issue. This was imported by those who came from outside.

The imposition of a divide by outsiders is demonstrated by the following story. During the first weeks of the occupation, a US military commander showed up in Baquba, the capital of Diyala province, with a mixed Sunni–Shia population. He asked to meet all tribal and religious leaders, who were perplexed when instructed to divide themselves: Shias on one side of the room, Sunnis on the other.

America's Operation Imposing Law, which started on 14 February 2007, may halt the sectarian bloodshed long enough for the two communities to begin the reconciliation process. Economic development, which ensures there is no discrimination between Sunni and Shia neighbourhoods and provision of much needed jobs, could focus the attention of the two communities on resuming normal life rather then perpetuating the cycle of violence.

There is room for optimism. By early 2008, Muqtada Al-Sadr had stood down his militia, but it may well return to fight if attacks against the Shias continue. The politics of sectarianism are being challenged by a new political project agreement called the National Project launched on 17 January 2008 by various Sunni and Shia political groups. MP Usama Al-Najafi of the Iraqi National List of former Prime Minister Ayad Allawi (see page 131) told a press conference in Baghdad:

> The national reconciliation project aims at enhancing the political
> process by building a state of institutions and rule of law, supporting the
> national reconciliation and broadening the base of political participation.

The passing in January 2008 of the Justice and Accountability Law, which allows former members of the Baath Party to return to public life, may aid the reconciliation process. The new alliance could be the first step on the long road to reconciliation. If it fails, a full-blown civil war seems the only alternative. The conflict could move beyond the borders of Iraq, with Iran backing the Iraqi Shias and neighbouring Arab states backing the Sunnis. In Lebanon, Hezbollah supporters chant the name of Muqtada Al-Sadr whose Mehdi Army has killed thousands of Sunnis. In some Arab countries support for the Sunnis in Iraq is tinged with fear of a Shia revival backed by Iran.

Assyrian bull

Part Two

IRAQ THEN

Lion detail, Ishtar Gate

2

The Ancient Kingdoms

Iraq is a jigsaw of deserts, mountains and marshes. And all around lie
centuries of more-or-less remembered histories of vanished civilisations
which pervade the thinking, the attitudes and the lives of the multi-racial
descendants of these civilisations.

K J Whitehead, *Iraq The Irremediable*

CHRONOLOGY

4000–3000BC	The ancient kingdoms of Sumer and Akkad were the first civilisations developed on the banks of the Tigris and Euphrates.
1900BC	Babylon emerged from the union of the Sumerian and Akkadian kingdoms. Hammurabi developed his famous code of law.
1400BC	Rise of Assyria, a kingdom that conquered more than 40 nations. The Assyrians founded the largest empire of their times and built great cities such as Ashur, Nineveh and Nimrud.
606–539BC	Neo-Babylonians. One of the most famous rulers during this period was Nebuchadnezzar, who built a magnificent summer palace and the hanging gardens of Babylon.
539–330BC	Achaemenian Persians. Cyrus the Great, founder of the Achaemenian Dynasty, ascended the Persian throne. He was at first welcomed by the Babylonians, who were the victims of a series of inefficient rulers.
336–323BC	Alexander the Great conquered the Persian Empire, establishing Greek monarchies from Greece to India, marking the beginning of the Hellenistic period. He took Babylon as one of his capitals.
331–129BC	Seleucid Greeks. Seleucus, one of Alexander the Great's generals, ruled Mesopotamia and Persia, which became known as the kingdom of the Seleucids.
130BC–AD226	The Parthian Persians, originally a mixed race of nomads, ruled ancient Iraq from Ctesiphon, and also developed the city of Hatra into a trading centre.

AD227–636	Sassanian Persians. This dynasty challenged Roman control of eastern trade routes. During their rule many of the ancient cities of Mesopotamia were buried beneath the sand of the desert.

EARLY MESOPOTAMIA

Recorded history began at Sumer, a city state in ancient Iraq, but long before the first cities made their appearance in 4000BC Mesopotamia, the land between the two rivers, which we now know as Iraq, was the home of prehistoric man.

Among the world's oldest human remains is a campsite, estimated to be 120,000 years old. It was found in 1949 by Dr Naji Al 'Asil, the Director General of the Iraqi Department of Antiquities. The discovery was made at Barda-Balka, between the northern Iraqi cities of Kirkuk and Suleimaniyah. Four skeletons – one 60,000 years old and the others 45,000 years old – were also discovered in northern Iraq, in Shanidar Cave near the town of Rawanduz.

The great agricultural revolution – when man stopped his wandering existence based on hunting wild beasts and gathering plants and began to domesticate animals and cultivate crops – took place in Mesopotamia around 10,000 years ago. Primitive settlements grew into towns and villages, which eventually evolved into city states along the banks of the Tigris and Euphrates. Writing was developed to record commercial transactions; ceremonies and rituals became part of everyday life. Even the British coronation ceremony has traces of Mesopotamian practices, as do present-day baptism rituals.

As Samuel Noah Kramer points out in the book *Cradle of Civilisation*:

> The Mesopotamians were the first people on earth to live in cities, study the stars, use the arch and wheeled vehicles, write epic poetry and compile a legal code. They also manufactured linen, built sailing ships, laid the foundations of astrology and for 3,000 years engaged in serious scholarship which left its mark on the science, mathematics, medicine, literature, philosophy and religion of subsequent civilisations.

The concept of the tablet of destinies is found in Mesopotamian mythology and in the Jewish tradition, where Moses receives the Torah on two tablets. In the Koran, the Book of Faith mentioned in verse 85 is said to come from heavenly tablets, which were subsequently referred to by Henry IV in Shakespeare's drama: 'O God! That one might read the Book of Fate and see the revolution of the times'. In Uruk (3800–3200BC) cuneiform manuals explained the meaning of dreams. Dream books continued to be used in Byzantine times and in the 20th century had a bearing on Freud's *Interpretation of Dreams*.

Leonard Woolley, who conducted extensive excavations at Ur's royal cemetery during the 1930s, draws attention to the legacy of ancient Iraq when he asks:

> How many of us realise that our superstitious impulse to turn back when a black cat crosses our path stems from the people of Babylon? Do they come to mind when we look at the twelve divisions on our

watch-face, when we buy eggs by the shock (sixty), when we look up at the stars to read our fate in their movement and conjunctions?

The Mesopotamian influence spread through conquest, trade and travelling scholars. The Babylonian cloak was worn from India to Italy, and Mesopotamian goods such as belts and sandals were found in Roman markets. The Bible tells how in the 2nd millennium BC the King of Moab summoned a scholar from Pitru on the Euphrates because of his knowledge of cuneiform texts.

In *The Legacy of Mesopotamia*, which she edited, Stephanie Dalley describes how the Babylonians took foreigners captive in battle and brought them back to Mesopotamia:

Eventually those people might return home, whether for retirement or because they were ransomed, taking with them reports of the marvels they had seen and learnt abroad. Some wonders were practical, such as the pilastered façades of temples, brick vaulting, and other technical skills; others were intellectual, such as the principles on which harps were tuned, or the basis of astronomy.

In the final chapter of the book, Henrietta McCall concludes:

No one concerned with the origins of Western civilisation can afford to disregard its roots in Mesopotamia and the legends handed down to us.

It does not matter that there is so little above ground: no pyramid, no temple, no hypostyle hall, theatre or circus, no forum, no colonnade, only the remains of a few crumbling ziggurats. The visible splendour of proud Babylon and mighty Nineveh may have disappeared from sight, but the dusty mounds that remain are linked with the very start of recorded history. Thus their legacy is unassailable, their renown indelible: legendary, glorious, immortal.

BEFORE SUMER

Ancient Iraq's early farming communities made their appearance between 9000 and 5000BC. Women, anxious to have a fixed abode in which to raise their children, influenced the decision to abandon the nomadic hunter-gatherer lifestyle, as did a decline in edible plants and animals. Jarmo, founded in 6500BC in the foothills of the Zagros Mountains, is one of the oldest known permanent settlements. Its inhabitants lived in mud houses, weaved flax and used tools such as sickles made of obsidian. They buried their dead underneath the floors of their dwellings, a practice that continued in Sumerian times.

People from the Hassuna culture, which dates back to 6000BC, introduced irrigation, were accomplished potters and embarked on trade from the Persian Gulf to the Mediterranean. Some of the world's finest ceramics were produced during the Halaf (north Mesopotamia) period (5000BC) that followed. The villages now had cobbled streets and animals grazed in the surrounding fields. Copper beads replaced clay and stone jewellery.

In south Mesopotamia during the Ubaid period (also c5000BC), the settlements along the Tigris and Euphrates, including Eridu, Ur, Lagash, Nippur and Kish (the forerunners of the Sumerian city states) were built around a shrine. The primitive irrigation system was augmented with small canals and reservoirs, and historians have commented on the division of labour that became evident in society.

The Uruk period (3800–3200BC) was a time of rapid urbanisation. As many as 45,000 people lived in the city of Uruk itself. A collection of temples were dedicated to the goddess Inanna, queen of heaven and earth, and decorated with mosaics and frescoes. The temples became a hive of commercial activity where craftsmen plied their trade. The first pictographs (symbols representing objects) were developed here, as trade could not be conducted without written records, and so writing began. Cylinder seals (devices used for establishing ownership or recording an agreement with your own pictorial marks carved on a small cylinder as a signature) were also an invention of the people of Uruk. The story of the seven sages, part of Mesopotamian mythology dating back to 3000BC, tells of how one of the great gods dispatched seven wise men to the cities to spread knowledge that ranged from music and metallurgy to agriculture and construction.

The Jemdat Nasr period (3200–2900BC) built on the achievements of Uruk. The story of the flood, another Mesopotamian myth that has striking parallels to the biblical story of Noah, is believed to date back to this period. Floods were a common occurrence in Mesopotamian life, but it seems that there was one great flood, which is written about in the *Epic of Gilgamesh* (see page 30). In this epic, Ut-Napishtim, the good, wise man, received a warning from the Gods:

Tear down this house, build a ship!
Aboard the ship take thou the seed of all living things
The ship that thou shalt build
Her dimensions shall be to measure
Equal shall be her width and her length

The importance of the flood is evident from the break in the list of Sumerian kings compiled by the kings' spin doctors (who recorded the exploits of their masters). These chroniclers noted: 'Then came the flood and after the flood kingship again descended from heaven.'

THE SUMERIANS

The seeds of Sumerian culture sown in Iraq's prehistory germinated during the Hassuna, Halaf, Ubaid, Uruk and Jemdat Nasr periods and blossomed in the city states of the 3rd millennium BC, among them Sippar, Kish, Akshak, Larak, Nippur, Adab, Umma, Lagash, Bad-tibira, Uruk, Larsa, Ur and Eridu. The cities began as simple agricultural settlements on the fertile banks of the Tigris and Euphrates. Regular supplies of fish and birds could be relied on if there was a problem with crops. Floods, however, were unpredictable, building materials had to be imported, and the inhabitants of Mesopotamia fought three main battles: the battle against nature, the battle against other cities who wanted to expand their boundaries, and the battle against foreign invaders. After their phenomenal expansion the empires were plagued by internal disputes and were frequently dealt a death blow by their neighbours. Some conquerors assimilated the culture and wisdom of the vanquished, while others were only interested in pillage and destruction.

WORSHIP There was no rational explanation for the forces of nature in the Mesopotamian view of the world, which was run by gods who had to be obeyed and honoured. Fear of the gods, whose decisions could not be understood, resulted in the emergence of an elaborate system of worship centred on the temples, whose requirements controlled the lives of the cities' inhabitants.

By 2500BC much of the land in Sumer was temple-owned and the farmers laboured in the service of the gods. The Sumerians developed a meticulous system of record keeping. The bureaucratic civil service left them in no doubt about what was due to them and what they owed to the temple. Merchants and craftsmen also worked for the temples, the major employer of the time.

The gods, who were treated like human beings, had to receive regular meals and ablutions and were honoured with elaborate rites and rituals. The image of the god was placed in a small room to which only the priests had access. Sometimes they slept next to the statue in the hope that the god would speak to them in a dream.

The hierarchical nature of Mesopotamian society, composed of the aristocracy, the citizens and the slaves, was reflected in the concept of the world of the gods populated by numerous deities of varying status. The common people prayed to their household gods or to the gods who were only honoured with a small chapel in the street. The peasants normally dealt with Ashnan the barley god or Shumuqan the cattle god. But in times of crisis the gods at the top of the spiritual hierarchy – such as the moon god Nanna (who knew the future), Ninurta the warrior-god, the mother earth goddess Ninhursag, and Ishtar, the goddess of love and procreation – could be contacted through the intercession of the priests or with the assistance of the personal god, a special deity to which the individual prayed.

The king had to answer to the supreme deity, hence the magnificent temples built in the service of the gods to secure their favour and protection. Ur, possibly the home of Abraham, was constructed around the mud-brick ziggurat dedicated to the moon god and his wife. The construction of temples and ziggurats was a major preoccupation of the Mesopotamians. Beer was brewed in the temples to make life more pleasant for the workers who laboured on the magnificent structures, and brewing even had a patron goddess, Ishtar. Since excavations of the ancient cities began in the 19th century more than 30 ziggurats have been unearthed. Georges Roux, author of *Ancient Iraq*, likens them to 'prayers of bricks – they extended to the gods a permanent invitation to descend to earth at the same time as they expressed one of man's most remarkable efforts to rise above his miserable condition and to establish closer contacts with divinity'.

But sacrifices and fine buildings to house the deities were not enough; there was also an emphasis on good deeds and actions, which bears a striking resemblance to the dictates of the Bible. Georges Roux says that the favours of the gods went to those who led a good life, who were good parents, good sons, good neighbours, good citizens and who practised virtues as highly esteemed then as they are now: kindness and compassion, righteousness and sincerity, justice, and respect of the law and of the established order. Every day worship your god, says a Babylonian 'Council of Wisdom', but also:

To the feeble show kindness
Do not insult the downtrodden
Do charitable deeds, render service all your days
Do not utter libel, speak what is of good report
Do not say evil things, speak well of people

THE WRITTEN WORD In addition to their religious functions, temples were the focal point of community life and the source of inventions that changed the world, such as the development of writing. Pictographic tablets, said to have made their first appearance in Eanna's temple in Uruk (see page 24) came into everyday use from about 3500BC. The primary motivation was the recording of commercial transactions. If pots were to be exchanged, pictures, which dried in the sun, were drawn in wet mud. The pictures subsequently became impressionistic lines, and the term 'cuneiform', which means wedge-shaped, was coined to describe this form of writing.

As the number of characters became unmanageable, phonetic writing developed: symbols denoting the pronunciation of the word evolved. A new class of scribes were plying their trade by 3000BC and, in addition to commercial transactions, the Sumerians recorded their history and their myths, including the *Epic of Gilgamesh*, the world's oldest literary work (see page 30). A list of kings was also compiled. Before the Seleucid era (from 321BC) there was no calendar and years were referred to according to the rulers, for example the 12th year of Nabuy-na'id, King of Babylon. Around 30,000 inscribed tablets detailing laws, treaties and commercial transactions have been unearthed from Sumerian and Akkadian times, some from great libraries in the cities.

Mastering the art of writing was a serious undertaking. Scribes went to special schools, attached to the temples, where the hours were long, the discipline rigorous and the teaching concentrated largely on rote learning and the memorisation of word lists. There were also private schools in which master scribes taught their skills, passing them on within scribal families, usually from father to son although a few tablets written by female scribes have survived. The first dictionaries were compiled and scholars were eager to pursue their own lines of inquiry and contribute to disciplines such as science and mathematics. Mesopotamian schools could therefore be described as the forerunners of universities.

ROYAL PALACES The second power-house of Mesopotamian city states was the royal palace. A symbiotic relationship developed between the kings and the priests: the temples made certain that taxes were paid to the palace and the kings built fine temples and showed due reverence to the gods, whose protection and favour were continually invoked.

While never neglecting their religious duties the kings also devoted great care and attention to their palaces, which were stocked with the finest imports from far-off lands and displayed with great pride. A palace in the city of Mari in western Mesopotamia, which was destroyed by Hammurabi in the 18th century BC, had 300 rooms and covered nearly 3ha.

But the kings did not just sit in their ivory towers. They held public audiences and took an interest in the affairs of the cities. They were the arbiters in important law suits, dispatched troops to subdue troublesome nomadic tribes who were making incursions into farmland, and discussed commercial alliances with envoys from other courts. The palaces were also places of entertainment, where female slaves, who received musical tuition, played the harp, and poets were among the regular performers.

Like the temples, the palaces were economic institutions in their own right, which sponsored thriving industries and efficient agricultural production. Workers were paid in food and clothing and were eager to avoid the 'private sector', where they were more likely to fall into a vicious cycle of debt from which it was difficult to emerge. (If the worker had borrowed money and seed from lenders or landlords for crops that subsequently failed for any reason, then he and his family were liable to be enslaved.)

SOCIAL STRUCTURE Apart from the palaces and temples, a number of rich and powerful families owned land. From this aristocratic group the king drew his advisors and the temple its senior priests. The farmers ensured a regular food supply and the rest of the population was free to pursue specialised occupations: carpentry, tanning, baking, brewing, pottery, and brick and cloth making. The arts, especially sculpture and painting, developed, and glass was made as early as 2500BC.

The workers toiled away in small, sprawling streets. There was no such thing as town planning, a sewage system or garbage disposal in the cities, which had expanded from small villages along the riverbanks to house up to 100,000 inhabitants. The lower class had to be content with one-storey mud-brick houses. The better-off had a two-storey house with a reception room for guests, a kitchen, bathroom and sometimes servants' quarters, a workshop and storeroom on the ground floor and the family rooms upstairs. During the hot summer months family members often slept on the roof. Household gods were worshipped in a small chapel and deceased family members were buried in a small mausoleum.

Public squares were places of entertainment where professional storytellers told their tales. Amusements included games of chance, wrestling and chariot racing. The bazaars, with stalls overflowing with local and imported items, and taverns and restaurants serving grilled fish and meat, bore a striking resemblance to bazaars throughout the Middle East today. In Sumer, the bricklayers, like their present-day counterparts, worked with standard bricks, drank beer and lived in cities administered by civil servants. The mud houses in the villages of present-day Iraq do not differ much from their Sumerian counterparts: hence the comment from Georges Roux, author of *Ancient Iraq*:

> that there are few countries in the world where the past is more
> strangely alive, where the historian's dead texts are provided with a
> more appropriate illustration.

The merchants traded grain, wool and textiles for essential building materials such as timber, and an extensive trade network with the Near East developed. The main imports included gold, silver, copper and lead, and luxury items such as ivory, pearls and shells. Caravans journeyed to the Mediterranean coast and Iran while boats reached Somaliland and Ethiopia. Information about other cultures was an important commodity and merchants were a vital link in exchanges with foreigners.

It is a tribute to the humanity of ancient Iraq that the lowest class, the slaves, had rights, could take part in business, borrow money and purchase their freedom. Freemen could also sell themselves and their families into slavery to pay off debts. Reforms were introduced against exploitation by the priestly class, who charged exorbitantly for burials and other services.

EARLY SETTLEMENTS The walled cities produced security and stability. Primary allegiance shifted from the family to the group, and unity was fostered by faith in personal gods who protected every settlement and city. The civil service and political institutions could function and develop, and there was time to engage in cultural and leisure pursuits. The Mesopotamians had a passion for organisation and routine, and this characterised all their settlements.

But the growth of cities with fixed boundaries resulted in boundary disputes, a recurrent theme in the history of the Middle East. Each city relied on a section of irrigated land for its survival and the history of Mesopotamia is largely the history of wars and disputes between various city states, each eager to assert its authority over the whole region.

The early settlements were fledgling democracies governed by assemblies appointed by the citizens. But in the face of military threats the citizens felt they needed a leader to ensure their victory in boundary disputes. The term 'big man' (*lugal*) was used to refer to the first leaders, who were only appointed for the duration of a particular conflict. But as the conflicts became more frequent, the leaders became permanent and the institution of kingship developed.

EARLY HISTORY Gilgamesh was one of the legendary early kings of the city of Uruk in around 2600BC, whose fame was assured by the building of the city walls. He emerged victorious in inter-city disputes but his major preoccupation in life was the quest for immortality, the theme of one of man's earliest epics. The prototype of Heracles and Ulysses, the *Epic of Gilgamesh* is the tale of the exploits of Gilgamesh (see page 30). It spread throughout the ancient Near East. The exploits of certain other ancient rulers left such an impression on their subjects that they were deified. Dumuzi, for example, became the fertility god.

With the establishment of the city states, frequent disputes over territory became more commonplace. One documented dispute between two city states occurred in 2700BC, when the people of Umma removed the stele (boundary marker) of their city and marched into the plain of Lagash. In ancient times boundary disputes assumed a religious-metaphysical character as both cities resorted to the assistance of their 'guardian gods'.

The priests, meanwhile, were starting to exploit their status and power, prompting Urukagina, the peace-loving, idealistic reformer and king of Lagash, to introduce a number of anti-corruption measures, so that a high priest was not able to 'come into the garden of a poor mother and take wood therefrom, nor fruit in tax therefrom'. The Mesopotamians also pioneered the concept of freedom of the individual. As many of the inscribed tablets discovered at the various sites tell us, they established laws defining workers' rights under royal patronage, the rights of landlords and their workers, and laws concerning the keeping of slaves. The penalties for breaking these laws are also fully described.

The city states were united in the 24th century BC by Sargon, King of Akkad. His city, known as Agade (which has yet to be discovered), lay to the northwest of the Sumerian kingdoms. Akkadian was adopted as the language of diplomacy and Sargon's empire sprawled into Persia, Syria and along the Mediterranean coast into Lebanon. Sargon proved that a man of humble origins could rise to the highest office. The story of his birth, retold by Leonard Cottrell in *Land of the Two Rivers*, bears a striking resemblance to that of Moses:

Sargon the mighty, King of Akkad am I
My mother was lowly, my father I knew not,
The brother of my father dwelt in the mountains.
My city is Azupiranu, which lieth on the bank of the Euphrates.
My lowly mother conceived me, in secret she brought me forth.
She cast me into the river, which [rose] over me.
The river bore me up, unto Akki, the irrigator, it carried me,
Akki the irrigator reared me up,
Akki the irrigator as his gardener appointed me.
When I was his gardener the goddess Ishtar loved me,
And of fifty-four years I ruled the kingdom.

Sargon does not provide a detailed account of how he rose from the position of cupbearer to be the King of Kish, and hence to establish the first empire in history. During his reign he built the mighty ziggurat at Nippur and brought exotic plants to his kingdom in the hope that they would acclimatise and flourish.

THE EPIC OF GILGAMESH

The story begins in the city of Uruk. Outside the city a distraught wedding guest tells Enkidu that relatives are upset because Gilgamesh has been taking all the brides before the grooms can get to them. At the request of the bridal relatives, the Mother Goddess creates Enkidi to stand up to Gilgamesh. He does this by literally standing outside the door of the bridal chamber. When Gilgamesh swaggers in to exercise his kingly rights Enkidu blocks his way. They fight outside the bridal chamber and become friends.

The next confrontation is with the goddess Ishtar, who falls in love with Gilgamesh, but he spurns her advances and reminds her of the way in which her previous lovers were treated: one was turned into a wolf, another into a spider.

Ishtar responds by sending the bull of heaven to destroy the city of Uruk. With Enkidu's help Gilgamesh slays the bull and throws its right thigh at Ishtar. Such an insult cannot go unpunished and the gods decide Enkidu should die. After losing his friend, Gilgamesh searches for eternal life. He travels to meet Ut-napishtim, whom the gods made immortal after he survived the great flood. Ut-napishtim has some sobering words for Gilgamesh:

Do we build houses for ever?
Does the river for ever raise up and bring on floods?
The dragon-fly leaves its shell
That its face might but glance at the face of the sun.
Since the days of yore there has been no permanence;
The resting and the dead, how alike they are!

Ut-napishtim instructs Gilgamesh to find the plant of life. Gilgamesh dives into the depths of the ocean and picks the plant, which is eaten by a snake when he falls asleep. He then returns to Uruk and embarks on a building programme to ensure his memory lives on.

The message of the epic is that any individual is mortal but the city, meaning the community as well as the buildings, lives on.

After the death of Sargon's son, eastern barbarians known as the Guti destroyed the empire and wiped Agade, Sargon's capital, off the map. Utuhegal, the ruler of Uruk, drove out the invaders only to be deposed by one of his generals, Ur-Nammu, who founded the third dynasty of Ur (2113–2006BC). The kingdoms of Sumer and Ur were united once more. But the unity was more of a partnership in which Ur, with its temple to the moon goddess and 80m ziggurat, was the senior partner. Despite his usurpation of power, Ur Nammu presided over the Sumerian renaissance, a time of increased prosperity during which the arts were given a new lease of life. Ur-Nammu continued the tradition of concern for fairness and justice and inscribed the first law code on cuneiform tablets, three centuries before the creation of Hammurabi's renowned 2.4m stele of black diorite, with its 282 laws. The Sumerian renaissance continued under Ur-Nammu's son, Shulgi.

Ur fell after an attack by the Amorites (Semitic nomads from the deserts of Syria and Arabia) and the Elamites (from an ancient kingdom east of the Tigris).

The attack was a watershed in the history of ancient Iraq: city states were replaced by small kingdoms and kings rented out land. A society in which the temples were the focus of economic activity was replaced by a society of farmers, citizens and traders.

In the book *Cradle of Civilisation*, Samuel Noah Kramer describes how the calamity that had overtaken their land and cities made a deep impression on the poets of Sumer's final days. One of their lamentations may serve as a melancholy epitaph for the people who, more than ten centuries earlier, first crossed the threshold of civilisation, and whose brilliant achievements have enriched most of the great cultures since. It bemoans the day:

That law and order cease to exist...
That cities be destroyed, that houses be destroyed...
That [Sumer's] rivers flow with bitter water...
That the mother cares not for her children...
That kingship be carried off from the land...
That on the banks of the Tigris and Euphrates...
there grow stickily plants

BABYLON AND HAMMURABI

After the Amorite conquest warfare plagued the region as power shifted between rival princes, but in 1780BC Hammurabi, sixth King of Babylon, once again united Mesopotamia. For him unity meant a centralised administration, backed up by the rule of law and an efficient system of justice implemented by magistrates under his control.

Hammurabi was a man of patience and foresight. Before embarking on his empire-building he spent 25 years cementing military and political alliances. His empire, with Babylon as its capital, extended northward from the Persian Gulf through the Tigris and Euphrates river valleys, and westward to the coast of the Mediterranean Sea. Roads were improved to facilitate trade and to enable troops to move quickly and execute their orders. Fifty-five of Hammurabi's official letters to local governors have been discovered. Even ordinary citizens wrote to their ruler. Messengers ensured the efficient flow of correspondence. Even after Babylon's political significance was eclipsed it was respected as an enlightened cultural centre. It was here that the stories of Gilgamesh were brought together in one long epic.

LEGAL PRECEDENT Despite his impressive record as an empire builder, however, Hammurabi is remembered mainly for his famous code of law, which deals with personal property, real estate, trade and business, the family, injuries, labour and rates of pay. A sense of fairness and social justice seems to be the guiding principle, and no-one is excluded from legal protection. Workers are assured of a living wage, but skill is rewarded with higher remuneration. There is no discrimination against women in business dealings: along with their male counterparts they can buy and sell properties and initiate legal proceedings.

Crimes and punishments are set out in detail:

> If the wife of a man has been caught while lying with another man, they shall bind them and throw them into the water. The husband may spare his wife and the king in turn may spare his subject.

Some of the most severe punishments are prescribed for negligent workmanship:

> If a builder constructed a house for a man but did not make his work strong, with the result that the house which he built collapsed and so has caused the death of the owner of the house, that builder shall be put to death.

At the end of the code divine retribution is invoked on whoever alters the just laws. The Babylonians were litigation happy and eager to bring lawsuits, especially in property transactions.

In the 12th century BC the Elamites sequestrated the diorite stele on which the laws are inscribed as war booty and took it to their city of Susa, now in present-day Iran. It was discovered by the French in 1901. The 282 laws outlined in 3,000 lines of cuneiform can be seen today in the Louvre museum in Paris.

EVOLUTION OF RELIGION Despite the magnificence of their empire the Babylonians remained pessimistic. They never forgot that the life-giving rivers could also bring devastation, and that the forces of nature could wipe out their newly found order.

The *Epic of Creation*, a Mesopotamian myth, describes how order was created from a watery chaos when Abzu the sweet waters and Timat the sea created the universe and the gods. Abzu was destroyed by Enki, the god of wisdom, when he conspired against the gods, but Timat continued the conflict and no-one could stop her. Enki's son Marduk made a deal with the gods. He would subdue Timat if he was made head of the gods. They agreed. After Timat was slain Marduk used half of her body to make the sky. Man was made out of the blood of a god who fought alongside Timat.

The Babylonians believed that chaos could return at the beginning of the new year. The struggle in the cosmos, described in the *Epic of Creation*, was not brought to an end. The gods had established order, but they could still be challenged by the forces of chaos, and an elaborate New Year festival was held to elicit the favour of the gods and ensure order prevailed for another year.

After Hammurabi's death in 1750BC his empire was ravaged by the Hittites, a mountain people from Anatolia, who spared Babylon. The next rulers were the Kassites, a mountain people from Persia, who assimilated Babylonian traditions. They signed a frontier agreement with the Assyrian princes, and their rule was characterised by peace and stability, until they were overthrown by the Elamites in 1155BC.

THE ASSYRIANS

Early in the 10th century BC the Assyrians perfected the art of war and conquest and, overthrowing the Elamites, succeeded in establishing their grip on nearly all of the Near East. They came from the state of Assyria in the north, centred around four cities: Ashur, Erbil, Nimrud and Nineveh. At the height of their power Egypt was nothing more than an Assyrian province. The Assyrian Empire stretched for 1,600km, from the Nile Valley in Egypt to the mountains of Armenia.

Their conquests had a religious dimension: the enemies of the king were also the enemies of the god Ashur. Just as Ashur stood at the head of the religious hierarchy, his man on earth, the King of Assyria, had to stand at the head of all other rulers, and battles were seen as crusades.

Conquests went hand in hand with the brutal slaying of the inhabitants of cities that had been subdued. Victory was the Assyrians' *raison d'être*, war was a way of life, and the spreading of terror was their speciality. Shalmaneser III (858–824BC) reigned for 35 years, 31 of which were spent fighting. The vanquished had to pay 'tribute', a form of protection money, to ensure their settlements were left standing.

Military exploits were immortalised in magnificent works of art. The Assyrians are remembered mainly for their reliefs, which depict winged bull-men and lion-men who look down from the gates of palaces. The walls of palaces were decorated with war scenes sculpted in limestone. The sculptures also served as propaganda: remain subservient to the conquerors or perish. Art was no longer a medium for glorifying the gods: it now depicted the exploits of kings and armies.

The army made the Assyrians mighty. As Georges Roux points out in *Ancient Iraq*, the army's success lay:

> in the quality of its troops, the superiority of its weapons and the
> rigidity of its discipline. Originally a conscript army was recruited
> among the peasants of northern Iraq, a mixed race of born warriors who
> combined the boldness of the bedouin with the tenacity of the farmer
> and the toughness of the highlander.

Tiglath-Pileser III set up a permanent army, which consisted of troops from throughout the empire: the horsemen were from Iran, the camel-drivers from Arabia. The use of horse-drawn chariots was fully exploited and ingenious siege weapons for demolishing city walls were developed. The Assyrians never referred to their casualties and the figures for their soldiers were probably inflated; at the battle of Qarqar, for example, Shalmaneser III claims to have commanded 120,000 men.

ADMINISTRATION The exploits on the battlefield were not matched by an enlightened administration of conquered territories, despite the development of a bureaucracy. This oversight was largely responsible for the collapse of the empire. Rule by terror did not inspire loyalty, the vanquished revolted and their revolts were brutally suppressed. Thousands of troublesome subjects were deported to other areas of the vast empire. Areas that came under Assyrian hegemony were regarded as provinces. The conquerors were interested in collecting taxes; they took much, gave little and were despised as cruel masters. The loyalty of governors was sought through a combination of rewards and threats; the threat of punishment if they deviated from the oath of obedience, and rewards in the form of a share in the royal estates and the spoils of war.

The 'Epic of Creation' is described in detail by Leonard Cottrell in *Land of the Two Rivers*:

Every year at the winter solstice the Babylonians gathered to devote eleven days to ensuring the gods' proper attention to their duties during the coming year.

First, for several days they purified themselves by fasting, ceremonial washing and the like. On the fifth day the priests escorted the king to the shrine of the god Marduk; then followed a dramatic incident, which reminds us that all play-acting originated in religious ritual. The king was left alone for a time in the god's shrine. Then the high priest emerged from his sanctuary. He approached the king, took from the monarch his royal robes and crown, forced him to his knees, and then slapped his face and pulled his ears!

On his knees before the god's image the king had now to recite the so-called negative confessions:

We have not sinned, O Lord of the lands,
I have not been negligent regarding thy divinity,
I have not destroyed Babylon.

Then, having made his confession, the king was given absolution and a blessing, after which he could put on his regalia again.

Meanwhile, in the teeming streets of the city, far below the ziggurat in which this drama was enacted, the citizens were acting out their own play. In this they were supposed to be searching for Marduk, who, according to their beliefs, had been held captive in the underworld. Unless he was brought back, the land could not prosper, so mock battles took place between his supporters and those supposed to be detaining him. On the sixth or seventh day he was released by his son and avenger Nebo. On the eighth day the statue of the restored god Marduk was placed in the Chamber of Destinies, together with those of all the other gods who thus presented him with their combined strength in the coming battle against the forces of Chaos. This was in order to determine 'the destinies', that is the fate of society for the coming year. Later, this earthly king, grasping the hand of Marduk's image, was carried along the Sacred Way to the Festival House. Probably another mock battle took place, and then, on the eleventh day, high in the ziggurat, the sacred marriage was celebrated between Marduk and the goddess Ishtar; the deities were represented by the king and a priestess – who may have been of royal blood.

Finally, on the twelfth day all the gods were reassembled in the Chamber of Destinies to ratify their decrees. And so the new year could begin.

As well as having to be on their guard against uprisings in the 'provinces', the Assyrian kings had to curb dissent among their own ruling class. There were disagreements among the nobles regarding the king's successor, who was supposed to have been chosen in consultation with the gods, including the sun god Ashur.

Assyrian kings ruled much like their predecessors: they ensured temples were built and maintained, they received reports from the governors of outlying provinces and they built magnificent palaces. Society was made up of aristocrats, who included the king's advisers and who were often magnificently wealthy individuals with their own courts, and free professional men, including traders, merchants, bankers, physicians and scribes. The craftsmen were organised into guilds, and fathers handed their skills down to sons. The lower class consisted of agricultural labourers, ordinary soldiers and slaves. Prisoners of war were at the bottom of the social hierarchy.

CULTURE AND LEARNING The Assyrians also had an artistic side to their bloodthirsty nature, and valued scholarship and science. The literary and scientific works of the Sumerians, Akkadians and Babylonians were collected in a magnificent library by Ashurbanipal, who issued an instruction in one of his letters:

> Hunt for the valuable tablets which are in your archives and which do not exist in Assyria and send them to me. I have written to the officials and overseers and no-one shall withhold a tablet from you.

Temple libraries, full of baked clay tablets stored by the priests and describing land contracts and laws, were also found in all of Assyria's major towns.

Ivory work was another speciality of the Assyrians. They used it to decorate thrones and it was incorporated in boxes, vases and handles, or inlaid with semi-precious stones. An impressive array of bronze, gold and silver plates, cups and ornaments has also been unearthed. Female slaves wove carpets and Assyrians were also experts in metalwork. The Assyrians made a contribution to mathematics, astrology and medicine, but restricted their studies to the collection of data. Metaphysical doctrines, such as those that attributed sickness to a punishment from the gods for past misdemeanours, hindered the development of scientific theories. Important decisions were seldom taken without consulting diviners who interpreted omens: for example, 'when a star shines forth like a torch from the sunrise and in the sunset fades away, the army of the enemy will attack in force.'

THE ASSYRIAN EMPIRE The Assyrians started to make their presence felt when Babylon was ruled by the Kassites and insisted that Assyria be regarded as an equal by the Kassite Dynasty. The first phase of spectacular conquests began in the 11th century BC when Tiglath-Pileser I's armies reached the Mediterranean and the Assyrians began to receive tributes from Phoenician cities such as Byblos and Sidon. The gods had to be honoured, the main temple of Ashur in the capital Nineveh was restored, and the waters of a tributary of the Tigris were diverted to water the capital's parks.

The brutal hallmarks of Assyrian conquest are summarised in Tiglath-Pileser's account of how he dealt with the Anatolians, who were endangering the region north of Nineveh:

> With their twenty thousand warriors and their five kings I fought and defeated them. Their blood I let flow in the valleys and on the high

A Londoner born and bred, I grew up hearing the sound of ships' fog-horns booming from the Port of London at the end of its 2,000 year history. This gave me a sense of the deep connection between my birthplace and people far, far away. Many a wet Sunday afternoon was filled with a visit to the nearby British Museum, keeping warm and being curious.

One Christmas I found in my pillowcase a book entitled *Man Must Measure*, mainly about ancient Egypt but mentioning Mesopotamia. An illustrated version of *A Thousand and One Arabian Nights* introduced me to Sinbad the Sailor.

Catapulted from a comprehensive school to St Hugh's College, Oxford, to study Politics, Philosophy and Economics, I learned more about oil, and also that 26 million Kurds lived without a homeland promised at the end of World War I. When a Kurdish poet, Rafik Sabeer, showed me a photo of his seven-year-old niece taken before she was hit in a bombing raid on her village by the dictator Saddam Hussein, I was ready to campaign.

I signed up with Liberation, formerly the Movement for Colonial Freedom, headed by (Lord) Fenner Brockway and Stan Newens MP. There I met Iraqis who were setting up the Committee Against Repression and for Democratic Rights in Iraq (CARDRI). In 1979 I became its honorary secretary and enrolled at the School of Oriental and African Studies (SOAS) for a part-time MA in Middle Eastern Studies.

CARDRI campaigned throughout the 1980s and 1990s, chaired by Ann Clwyd MP, to expose the horrors of the Saddam Hussein regime. In 1992 I travelled to the Kurdish Autonomous Region, representing CARDRI as an observer at the first ever free and fair elections in Iraq, under the auspices of the UK Electoral Reform Society.

In 1992–93 I travelled back and forth to Iraqi Kurdistan. I went as a guest to an Iraqi opposition conference. Then I led the first ever package tour to the Kurdish Autonomous Region. The tour, organised by Ishtar Tours, included a visit to the Erbil *qa'ala* or citadel, one of the world's most important unexcavated archaeological sites.

Inspired by my visit to the *qa'ala*, back in London I buried myself in a search for Mesopotamian mythology. In the British Library I discovered academic translations of narrative texts originally written on clay tablets in the two long-dead Mesopotamian languages, Sumerian and Akkadian. I visited the British Museum again and again, buying books. I enrolled in a course on the Myths and Rituals of the Ancient Near East, taught at SOAS by Dr Andrew George.

As I gazed out of the SOAS window I thought how wonderful it would be to have a storytelling group retelling these stories beyond the circle of the academics who knew them. But first I had to study the art of oral storytelling. I found by chance Fiona Collins, a professional storyteller who had been retelling stories of the goddess Inana since 1991. She directed me to the Society for Storytelling (SfS) and a course in

levels of the mountains. I cut off their heads and outside their cities like heaps of grain, I piled them up. I burned their cities, with fire, I demolished them, I cleared them away.

But despite his successes on the battlefield, he failed to establish an efficient administration, the conquered people revolted in 1080BC, and the mighty

Wales, to which I took *Enuma Elish* (the Babylonian creation myth) as my apprentice piece.

Dr Andrew George provided a pre-publication copy of his new translation of *The Epic of Gilgamesh*. From this I prepared a storytelling performance with professional storyteller June Peters.

In 1997 we made our debut at the Kufa Gallery in Bayswater, London. The Kufa Gallery was where Dr Mohammed Makiya and his team kept alight the flame of Iraqi culture throughout the dark years of the Saddam Hussein regime.

As a trio of Mesopotamian storytellers, June Peters, Fiona Collins and I set about developing a wide repertoire of retold stories from the academic translations of Sumerian and Akkadian literature. We performed at many venues, including the Kufa Gallery, Wolfson College Oxford, the Camden Ceilidh storytelling club and the British Museum.

To organise ZIPANG (a Mesopotanian storytelling group) events, and apply for grants to fund them, an educational charity was founded in 2002 called the Enheduanna Society, after the world's first named poet and literary patron. Enheduanna lived in southern Iraq in 2300BC.

In 2004 a series of ZIPANG events was held at the October Gallery in London. Stories retold by the ZIPANG Mesopotamian storytellers were enhanced by Iraqi poetry and music, including the rhythms of Iraq from virtuoso percussionist Farid Zodan and Kurdish folk melodies played on a Celtic harp by Tara Jaff.

Tara Jaff and I had both been speakers at meetings of the Iraqi Women's League 25 years before, in the CARDRI days, and she frequently graced events at the Kufa Gallery with her harp music and singing. Now, in the British Academy, we performed together a retelling of the Sumerian story *Lugalbanda and the Anzud Bird* for the British School of Archaeology in Iraq (BSAI), now the British Institute for the Study of Iraq.

An Arts Council grant funded the ZIPANG project 2006. This included storytelling performances of *Lugalbanda and the Anzud Bird* and *The Epic of Gilgamesh* at the International Festival of Middle Eastern Peace and Spirituality in Edinburgh, the Arabic Community Festival in West London, the Kurdish Cultural Centre in South London, and the Kufa Gallery days before it finally closed. Tara Jaff sang songs in Sumerian and Akkadian, which she put to music from texts provided by Dr Eleanor Robson and Dr Fran Reynolds of Oxford University.

The Enheduanna Society published *Stories from Ancient Iraq* retold by me, with an introduction by Dr Stephanie Dalley. Professor Farouk al-Rawi, an expert on Mesopotamian languages and literature, liked the book: 'Scholars usually describe Mesopotamian literature as a skeleton created by the Sumerians,' he said. 'The Babylonians and Assyrians covered that skeleton with flesh. Fran Hazelton has given it life and dressed it to suit modern readers.'

Fran Hazelton

empire was reduced to a small strip of land on the Tigris stretching for no more than 160km.

The Assyrian Empire rose again 150 years later. The Assyrians once again established their domination over Phoenician cities and returned home with precious stones and metals, wood and exotic animals. One of their rulers, Ashurnasirpal II, had many claims to fame, including the slaying of 1,000 lions.

THE EAGLE PATROL

Tales from the past recounted by Assyrian communities, which have not been verified by historians, describe eagle-assisted flight, which was prompted by the Assyrians' desire for conquest. Before the eagles were put to flight they were kept indoors, blindfolded and without food. They were then attached to strong woven baskets that could accommodate a boy. The baskets were then fastened to the bodies of the eagles, much like a carriage is fastened to a horse (see diagram). The 'pilot' would carry a long cane to which fresh meat was attached with a hook. The starving eagles would take off and fly to get the bait, lifting the basket and the boy into the air, so that he could fly above enemy territory and observe the strength, defensive positions and military installations of the enemy.

Like most Assyrian rulers, Assurnasirpal delighted in both barbarity and beauty. He was fond of describing how he covered a pillar with the skins of his captives. He also built a 2.5ha palace at Nimrud:

> A palace of cedar, cypress, juniper, boxwood, mulberry, pistachio-wood and tamarisk for my royal dwelling and for my lordly pleasure for all time I founded therein. Beasts of the mountains and the seas of white limestone and alabaster I fashioned and set them in the gates.

George Roux, in his book *Ancient Iraq*, describes a magnificent ten-day feast attended by 69,574 guests in Assurnasirpal's new palace.

The conquests continued under Tiglath-Pileser III (745–727BC) and the army grew through the recruitment of foreign mercenaries. War chariots were replaced with cavalry. He tried to reform the administration and curb the disproportionate power of the nobles. The practice of mass deportation began: in total an estimated four-and-a-half million people were deported from their traditional homes and resettled in other parts of the empire. Among them were 30,000 Syrians from Hama who were sent to the Zagros mountains, while 18,000 Arameans from the Tigris area were sent to northern Syria.

THE FALL OF BABYLON Sargon II (722BC), successor to the Assyrian King Shalmaneser V (726BC), had to devote much of his time to quashing revolts. The capital was moved to Sharrukin (present-day Khorsabad) and protected with mud-brick walls more than 23m thick. Sargon's son, Sennacherib, turned Nineveh into a magnificent capital, where 80km of paved canal transported water from the Gomel River – the Tigris was not clean enough! These hydraulic works boosted agriculture. But Sennacherib will be remembered mainly for his savage revenge on Babylon, spared by previous conquerors due to its cultural legacy. The Babylonians had formed an anti-Assyrian alliance with the Elamites and had to be taught a lesson:

> With [the corpses of its inhabitants] I filled the city squares. The city and houses from its foundations to its top, I destroyed, I devastated, I burned with fire.

The Old Testament's Second Book of Kings describes how his forces captured 46 cities in Palestine and besieged Jerusalem, where dissent was also brewing. Sennacherib was killed by a death-blow from a statue of a god: the heavenly beings could not leave the destruction of Babylon unavenged.

Esarhaddon, one of Sennacherib's sons, was a humanitarian ruler who offered food to the famine-stricken people of Elam. He also rebuilt Babylon in 671BC. But the Assyrians were not learning the lessons of history: they never understood how to deal fairly with their subjects and they continued fighting among themselves.

Despite his military and scholarly achievements, Ashurbanipal (668–627BC) laments:

> I cannot do away with the strife in my country and the dissensions in my family; disturbing scandals oppress me always. Illness of mind and flesh bow me down; with cries of woe I bring my days to an end. On the day of the city god, the day of the festival, I am wretched; death is seizing hold upon me and bears me down.

THE END OF THE EMPIRE The Assyrian Empire was dealt a swift death-blow in 612BC when the Babylonian King Nabopolassar joined forces with the Elamites and the Medes (a young and little-known people of the Iranian Plateau from whom the Kurds are said to be descended), and led a combined attack against Nineveh.

The disintegration of the Sumerian city states was lamented, the downfall of Babylon was mourned, but no-one shed a tear at the collapse of the hated Assyrian giant.

BABYLON REVISITED

The Neo-Babylonians ended Assyrian supremacy and resurrected Babylon to its former glory through a dazzling renaissance of Mesopotamia, presided over by Nebuchadnezzar II, crowned on the death of King Nabopolassar in 605BC.

It was essentially a religious revival accompanied by an extensive building program, which focused on the restoration of religious shrines to long-revered Babylonian gods, with an emphasis on religious rituals, especially the New Year festival. The most magnificent was Marduk's temple. Nebuchadnezzar proudly tells us:

2

After the collapse of their massive empire, which lasted for 14 centuries, the Assyrians became ethnic groups of people living at the mercy of their overlords in widely scattered lands in the Middle Eastern region.

They embraced Christianity in the 1st century and today are followers of the ancient church of the East, the Syrian Orthodox Church of Antioch, the Chaldean Catholic Church and various Protestant denominations.

Until the cultural renaissance in the middle of the 19th century, the Assyrians almost lost their ethnic identity when numerous atrocities befell them because of their religious beliefs and origins. Like the Yezidis and Armenians they were the victims of Ottoman massacres. In 1915, the Turks drove them out of the Hakkari mountains where they were living as a semi-independent people under their religious and secular head, Patriarch Mar Shimon, and they joined their brethren in the Urmai and Salams districts of Iran.

The First World War proved disastrous, as their support was enlisted by the allied forces (British and Russian) at dreadful cost. In 1918, just before the war ended, they were forced to retreat from Urmia. More than one-third of the entire Assyrian population perished during the trek to join the British forces in Baghdad. They were settled in camps in Baquba and used to protect the newly installed government of Iraq and British air bases.

Like the Kurds, the Assyrians were promised help by the allies. In Iraq they were offered a special position in the Mosul district, a promise that proved unacceptable to the other interested parties (namely the Turks and Kurds), and that was not kept. In 1933, betrayed by British promises regarding their personal safety, over 600 were massacred in Simeil and 2,000 in the surrounding villages by their Kurdish neighbours and ruling tribal landowners.

Since 1960 hundreds of Assyrian villages have been destroyed by Iraqi forces in the north of the country. Churches and monasteries have been levelled and the Assyrians have been denied the right to practise their religion and preserve their

Silver, gold, costly precious stones, bronze, wood from Magan,
everything that is expensive, glittering abundance, the products of the
mountains, the treasures of the seas, large quantities (of goods),
sumptuous gifts, I brought to my city of Babylon before him [Marduk].

Babylon was also the home of the Tower of Babel, a 90m ziggurat, and 1,179 temples, which once again became the focal point of economic activity. They had their employees, as well as a class of people who laboured for the clergy in return for food and lodgings. When the city was threatened by foreign invaders the people flocked to the temples.

Nebuchadnezzar's architectural boom included the reconstruction of Sumer and Akkad. But the greatest attention was devoted to the rebuilding of Babylon, a city of 100,000 inhabitants that could accommodate a quarter of a million. The city's 16km outer wall was wide enough for two chariots of four horses to ride abreast. Festival Avenue, with a magnificent gate known as Ishtar Gate, led to the royal palace of Nebuchadnezzar. Images of lions, made from glazed tiles and symbolic of the goddess Ishtar, kept a watchful eye on passers-

culture and language. The signing of the 1975 Algiers treaty between Iran and Iraq in 1975, and the attacks on the Kurdish areas in northern Iraq, which are also inhabited by the Assyrians, forced hundreds to flee. During the uprising at the end of the Gulf War in 1991, more than 250,000 Assyrians joined the Kurds, who sought refuge in Turkey, Iran and Syria. Some were eventually resettled in Europe, America, Canada and Australia, while others moved to Baghdad and other large cities in Iraq. One of the largest Assyrian communities abroad is in Chicago where, in 1992, they succeeded in getting a stretch of Western Avenue named after one of their greatest kings, Sargon II (see pages 38–9).

Christianity is a very important part of Assyrian culture, both in Iraq and among the communites in exile, as it has defined the people for nearly two millennia. The major holiday is Easter, followed by Christmas. The fast of the Ninevites is an ancient religious observance still practised by some, during which all animal products are avoided for three days – the length of time Jonah spent in the whale.

As with all Iraqi people, hospitality and visiting are very important among the Assyrians. Music and folk-dancing are part of all festive celebrations.

Since 2003 the Assyrian community has been under siege. In 2003 more than 25 churches were attacked and bombed by terrorists. Priests have been abducted and beheaded, and Christian women have been beheaded for refusing to wear the veil, purportedly by Al-Qaeda terrorists. In October 2006 an Assyrian boy was crucified near Mosul.

According to the United Nations High Commission for Refugees a third of the people who have fled post-Saddam Iraq are Christians. The Catholic Archbishop of Baghdad estimates that half of Iraq's Christians – half a million people – have fled since 2003.

The Christians have received no protection from the 'liberating' forces. They favour the establishment of an autonomous region around the Nineveh Plains, their ancestral homeland in the north of Iraq. Sadly the Islamic/Christian divide, with all its latest prejudice and violence, is alive and strong in the north.

by. The palace's roof gardens, the Hanging Gardens of Babylon, are regarded as the seventh wonder of the ancient world. They were built for the king's wife, Amytas, a Mede, so that she would not miss her mountain home. An elaborate irrigation system watered thousands of trees and shrubs brought from every region of the vast empire.

Jeremiah, an Old Testament prophet, called the city 'a golden cup in the Lord's hand that made all the earth drunken'. The Greek historian Herodotus was equally impressed: 'It surpasses in splendour any city of the known world.'

The transformation of Babylon, however, had to be financed. And while the people did not object to living in a magnificent capital, they did not like paying for it. The temples gave up 20% of their revenues, which were also used to pay for the standing army.

JEWS IN EXILE Nebuchadnezzar was a conqueror as well as a builder. The King of Judea gave up without a fight, but lost about 40,000 subjects who were taken captive. The lament 'by the rivers of Babylon, there we sat down, yea we wept, when we remembered Zion', still sung in churches today, refers to this period of exile. The Jews were greatly influenced by Babylonian culture and ideas, and legends like that of the flood found their way into the Old Testament. In 538BC, when the armies of Cyrus, the great Persian conqueror, invaded Babylon, making it possible for the Jews to return home, many chose to stay. A strong Jewish community developed in Mesopotamia and prospered during subsequent centuries of Arab-Islamic rule. The Jews added to the cosmopolitan nature of society where Phoenicians, Syrians and Egyptians exchanged views, partied together and communicated in Aramaic.

PERSIAN CONQUEST The splendour of Babylon was of no great benefit to the ordinary people who could not make ends meet on their meagre wages. Banking families made a fortune by charging 20–30% interest. As Georges Roux notes in *Ancient Iraq*:

> economic depression contributed to the decline of Mesopotamian civilisation, but the temples kept it alive for almost six hundred years. By a remarkable coincidence, this civilisation was to die, as it was born: under the wings of the gods.

Death came slowly in the form of a slow decline and disintegration. It began with the writing on the wall during Belshazzar's feast in 539BC, when the king's guests were drinking from cups Nebuchadnezzar had removed from the temple in Jerusalem.

The Book of Daniel tells us:

> In the same hour came forth fingers of a man's hand and wrote over against the candlestick upon the plaster of the wall of the king's palace: and the king saw the part of the hand that wrote.

The Prophet Daniel, one of the Jewish exiles, was asked to interpret the message. He replied:

> God hath numbered thy kingdom and finished it. Thou art weighed in the balances, and art found wanting. Thy kingdom is divided, and given to the Medes and Persians.

While the Babylonians were feasting, the armies of Cyrus the Great diverted the waters of the Euphrates into a trench and marched along the dry river bed into the city. For the first time in history the land of the two rivers, the cradle of civilisation, lost its independence and was annexed to a foreign empire. Cyrus proved that empire building could be accomplished with a minimum of destruction. He respected his subjects, and life returned to normal along the banks of the Tigris and Euphrates, until the power-hungry Xerxes levelled a crippling tax on the people of Babylon to finance his military exploits, and tried to replace the Babylonian language with Aramaic. The Persians also monopolised trade with India and the East through the Royal Road from Sardis to Susa, which bypassed Babylon. The people revolted and the empire began to crumble. Magnificent buildings were left to decay, the canals silted up and much of the land reverted to desert.

ALEXANDER THE GREAT From 334BC, Alexander the Great, pupil of Aristotle and army commander from the age of 16, inflicted a series of defeats on the Persians, and conquered their empire and beyond. Crossing the Oxus and the Indus to bring Greek culture to the east, he began the fusion of Greek and Persian society. He wanted Babylon and Alexandria to be his empire's twin capitals. His grandiose ideas of making the Euphrates navigable and constructing canals linking the Red Sea and the Nile, and thus making Babylon a maritime trading centre, all went with him to the grave.

He died, reportedly of malaria, in Babylon in 323BC. But his legacy, the foundation of Greek client kingdoms in the east and the subtle influence of Greek art and sculpture, led to the flowering of Gandhara art, that wonderful fusion of Greek art and artistic influences with the older Buddhist art of India and Central Asia, centred on Taxila, now in Pakistan.

As its masters changed, Mesopotamian civilisation was dying of old age. In the words of Georges Roux:

> Alexander the Great heralded a new age in which the world was bent on extensive commercial intercourse, bursting with curiosity, eager to reappraise most of its religious, moral, scientific and artistic values. There was no room in such a world for a literature which none but a few scholars could read, for an art which drew its inspiration from outdated ideals and models, for a science which evaded rational explanations.

Seleucus, one of Alexander's generals, succeeded him as ruler of Mesopotamia and Persia, then known as the kingdom of the Seleucids, which had its power centre at Seleucia on the Tigris, 32km south of modern Baghdad. Two hundred years later the Seleucids were challenged by new powers to the north, the Parthian Persians, who competed with the Romans for control of the region. During the Parthian period (126BC–AD227) the city of Hatra was constructed 80km south of Mosul, and prospered as a great caravan centre of trade. The buildings and art of the 1st and 2nd centuries BC reflected the culture of the Parthians, with some Roman influence. They accommodated foreign gods, citadels were built on top of old ziggurats and stone replaced mud and brick. Eventually though, the Parthians were pushed aside by a new Persian power, the Sassanian Empire (AD227–636), which revived Zoroastrianism, the major Persian religion.

The history of the region then became the history of a series of wars between Western armies and the Persians. Seton Lloyd, author of *Twin Rivers*, describes a long succession of Western armies marching either down the Euphrates or along the Tigris to attack Babylon, Seleucia, Ctesiphon, or whatever city happened at that moment to be the capital of Iraq. One ancient writer speaks of the springtime as 'when the kings go forth to war'. For the next 500 years one could almost equally well say 'when kings go up against Mesopotamia'.

By the mid-7th century AD the Sassanids and the Romans were exhausted by their struggles and the Sassanian Empire was reduced to a number of small states. The region was ripe for conquest by Arab invaders who had recently converted to Islam, a new monotheistic religion inspired by the teachings of the Prophet Mohammed that were spread by both the book and the sword.

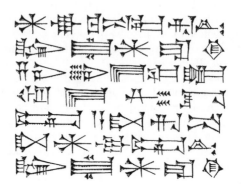

Babylonian inscription

3

Umayyads, Abbasids and Ottomans

The invaders from the desert brought with them no tradition of learning, no heritage of culture, to the lands they conquered. In Syria, in Egypt, in Al Iraq, in Persia they sat as pupils at the feet of the people they subdued. But the seed was sown, and the tree of knowledge, which came into full bloom under the early Abbasids in Baghdad, certainly had its roots in the preceding period of Greek, Syrian and Persian Culture.

Philip K Hitti, *History of the Arabs*

CHRONOLOGY

AD570	Birth of the Prophet Mohammed in Mecca. Emergence of Islam, the third of the monotheistic religions.
632	Death of the Prophet Mohammed in Medina.
661–750	Umayyad caliphs in Damascus. The second caliph (successor to Prophet Mohammed) subjugated Mesopotamia. The time of the greatest expansion of the Muslim Empire. Rebellious Arabs were slaughtered in their thousands at Kufa and a series of brutal governors was installed to keep them in a state of subjugation.
750–1258	The Abbasid caliphs in Baghdad. Baghdad replaced Damascus as the capital of the Muslim Empire. The golden age of wealth and learning (transmission of Greco-Roman philosophy to the Western world). The rulers promoted medicine, chemistry, geometry, mathematics, astronomy and poetry.
1258–1356	Hulagid Il Khan Dynasty. The grandson of Genghis Khan, a great Central Asian conqueror, left behind a trail of horror and destruction.
1356–1410	Jalayrid Dynasty. The Jalayr kingdom was set up by the family of Amir Hussain Jalayr. They were capable rulers and Baghdad once again became an important town.
1410–1509	Turcoman tribes began gaining influence.
1509–33	Safavid Persians. Ismail Shah, founder of the Persian Safavid Dynasty, conquered Iraq.
1534–1918	Ottoman period. Iraq was divided into three provinces (Baghdad, Mosul and Basra) by its Turkish rulers. Ottoman rule was characterised by centuries of neglect

and poverty. Mosul and Basra were important
commercial centres.

THE UMAYYADS

After Prophet Mohammed's death no series of historical events in the
Middle East has ever produced results so immediate, yet so profound
and lasting, as those which followed the unbelievably rapid, unexpected
and complete conquest by the earliest Muslims, under the first
successors (or caliphs) of the prophet, of practically all the territories of
western Asia (except Anatolia) and of north Africa. These conquests
proved final and irreversible, yet were orderly, unmarked by ruin or
massacre, and were preliminary not to a violent but rather to a peaceful
revolution, visible and invisible, in society and policies and men's minds
throughout the region, and far beyond it.

Stephen Longrigg, *The Middle East, Social Geography*

The Muslim conquests were successful largely because the people they sought
to bring under their control resented the oppression and heavy taxation of their
former rulers.

In AD637 the Muslims ended Persian (Sassanid) rule in Iraq at the Battle of
Qadisiya. The gem-laden, panther-skin banner of the enemy was captured. In
Ctesiphon the Muslims discovered remarkable treasures, but resisted the
temptation to attack Persia. The Arab troops, largely nomadic Bedouin, were
stationed at two military garrisons: Basra and Kufa. They soon grew into large
towns, which became the hotbeds of rebellion.

UMAYYAD SOCIETY The Umayyads were responsible for many long-lasting
social changes: they changed the caliphate into an empire, they made Arabic
the language of the state, minted their own coins, and built a number of great
mosques including the Dome of the Rock in Jerusalem, the Umayyad mosque
in Damascus and the great mosque of Qairawan in present-day Tunisia. The
mosques assumed the architectural features of the country: in Syria they were
modelled on a square stone watch-tower, whereas in Iraq the mosque took a
more traditional Arab form until, at a later date, under the Abassids, the spiral
form of minaret originated, inspired by the earlier ziggurats. A regular postal
service, schools, hospitals and charities for the sick were also established, as
was a navy. Basra became an important port for the Islamic Empire, and ships
sailed for Sind in Pakistan, East Africa and China. Stories of Sinbad the sailor
also became popular at around this time.

Umayyad society was divided into four classes: Arabs, who formed the
aristocracy; the neo-Muslims, or converts; the dhimmis (non-Muslims in an
Islamic state, ie: Christians, Jews, Zoroastrians and Berbers); and finally, slaves.

But the Umayyad caliphs never totally abandoned their traditional lifestyle.
The young princes were reared in the desert air and royal courts were held in
tents. Desert castles and palaces were later built on favourite camping grounds.

The first Arab Empire was a politically, culturally and economically self-
contained unit. The world was divided into the House of Islam (Dar Al Islam)

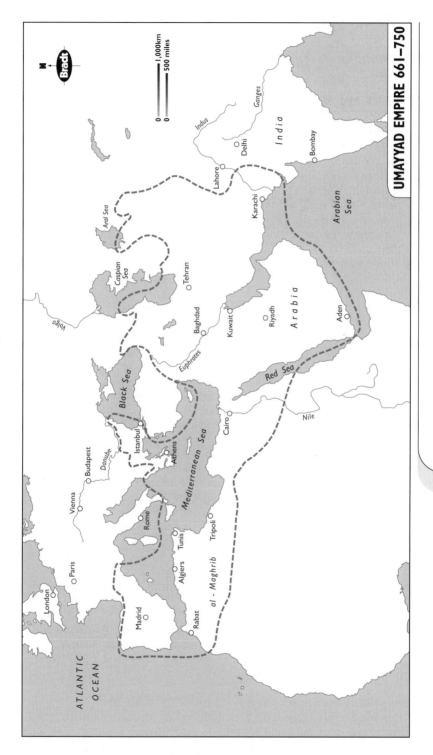

UMAYYAD EMPIRE 661–750

and the House of War (Dar Al Harb). Peace came when the enemies surrendered and converted to Islam. There was little time or need for diplomacy: opponents were quickly subdued and incorporated into the House of Islam.

CONFLICT AND DECLINE But the Iraqis in Basra and Kufa proved to be a continual thorn in the side of the Umayyad rulers. They resented the fact that Umayyad rule meant Syrian rule, they were excluded from government, and they were treated as non-Arab Muslims (*mawali*), who had to pay higher taxes. They also felt the taxes they paid should be spent to develop the areas from which they were collected. Nor did the local people benefit from the land reclamation projects. Their spiritual allegiance was to Ali, the cousin of the Prophet Mohammed, and they were aggrieved by the events at the battle of Kerbala, when Ali's son was killed by the Umayyad ruler Yazid (see page 233).

An attempt was made to rectify the tax status of the Iraqis by Umar bin 'Abd al-Aziz, an Umayyad caliph who ruled from AD717 to AD720. They were taxed as Muslims, who paid only alms (*sadaqa*). But if they sold their land it became the property of the village, on which the full land tax (*kharaj*) paid by non-Muslims was levied.

The governors sent to Iraqi areas ruled by a combination of carrot-and-stick and resettlement. Al-Mughira bin Shu'ba Al-Thaqafi, one of Kufa's first governors, converted to Islam, which annulled all past misdeeds. He adopted a policy of benign oversight as long as his authority was not threatened, and allowed the residents to keep the revenues of some districts.

On his appointment, Ziyad bin Abihi in Basra promised that soldiers' salaries (*ata*) would be paid on time and there would be no arduous, distant military campaigns. In AD671 around 50,000 troops were sent to Khurasan as settlers. This temporary 'cure' proved to be worse than the problem: years later these settlers were responsible for bringing down the caliphate itself.

In AD685 Mukhtar bin Abi Ubayd became a prominent political figure. He claimed descent from the Prophet's early followers, was vehemently opposed to Umayyad rule and made himself master of Kufa. He proclaimed one of Ali's descendants, Ibn Al-Hanafiyya, both caliph and *mahdi*, or divine saviour. The idea proved popular and provided the inspiration for future rebellions. Mukhtar was killed during a siege of the governor's palace in AD687, but his idea of supporting the downtrodden was readily adopted in the propaganda war against the Umayyads.

One of the most brutal governors was Hajjaj bin Yusuf al-Thaqafi, who was in charge of both Basra and Kufa. He leapt onto the pulpit (*mimbar*) in Kufa and made a speech famous in Arabic literature:

> People of Kufa, I see that your heads are ripe for cutting. You are always making mischief but this time you have made too much of it; there must be an end to it. Believe me, an end will be made, and my sword will make it.

Some historians claim the massacre resulted in 100,000 deaths.

Internal conflicts plagued the Umayyad Dynasty, which alienated many of its former supporters and could not provide the leadership expected of Muslim rulers, who became increasing preoccupied with affairs of state. Corruption set in: one of the governors of Iraq was accused of embezzling millions of dirhams.

The Abbasids, descendants of Abbas, the uncle of the Prophet Mohammed, invoked religious legitimacy. They organised themselves into an effective force, which relied heavily on the Persians, and Abu-l-Abbas, the great-great grandson of the prophet's uncle, led a rebellion that toppled the Umayyads in AD750. Abu-l-Abbas called himself the blood-shedder and lived up to his reputation by launching a ruthless extermination campaign against the Umayyads. Arab hegemony over the Islamic Empire was brought to an end, the various conquered populations slowly moved up in the social hierarchy and a new society evolved. The Umayyads appealed to the spirit of Arab nationalism, but the Abbasids could make no such claim, as they appealed to non-Arab Muslims, known as *mawali*, who remained outside the kinship-based society of Arab culture, and were perceived as being of a lower class within the Umayyad Empire. The *mawali* had many grievances, as they were treated as second-class citizens.

THE ABBASIDS – THE RISE OF ISLAM

The Abbasids were convinced that a divinely guided ruler from the family of the prophet would bring the injustices of the Umayyad era to an end. Emphasis was placed on the equality of all Muslims. Persians played an influential role in the political and cultural life of the empire and as the Persians were not Arabs appeals to Arab nationalism could no longer be made. The Abbasids campaigned for the return of power to the family of the Prophet Mohammed and descent from an uncle of the Prophet helped legitimise their religious credentials.

But despite the emphasis on equality and an end to discrimination between Arab and non-Arab Muslims, a ruling elite soon developed and the caliph, surrounded by a vast court, lost touch with his subjects and became an absolute ruler, abandoning the traditional Arab notion of a leader chosen by a council of his peers. The palaces were massive institutions with a complex network of servants and secretaries. The door-keeper (*hajib*) decided who saw the caliph.

The caliph was assisted by a *vizier* (a high-raking adviser). Muslim judges (*qadis*) were appointed by the central government. Ministers and senior military officers were in charge of a wage-earning bureaucracy and an army. Academics were greatly respected. Next in the pecking order came merchants, followed by farmers, herdsmen and slaves, who ceased to be social outcasts. A magnificent cultural renaissance spanned the reigns of the dynasty's first seven rulers (AD750–842), the most famous being the reigns of Mansour (AD754–75), Harun al Rashid (AD786–806) and Mamum (AD813–33).

Kufa was the first capital of the Abbasid Empire, but Caliph Mansour began the construction of a purpose-built capital, Baghdad, which served as a model for many towns and cities, including Cairo. Baghdad soon became the cosmopolitan centre of the medieval world and its richest city, blessed as it was with a plentiful supply of water. The rivers were an important means of communication and there was no malaria. It was a round city with three concentric enclosures, one for the ruler, one for the army and one for the people. Caliph Mansour died a few years after the completion of his capital. He ordered 100 graves to be dug for him to ensure that no-one could find his tomb and desecrate it.

3

Harun al Rashid presided over Baghdad in its heyday, established diplomatic relations with Byzantium and sent the Frankish Emperor Charlemagne an elephant as a present. Prosperity, though, led to ridiculous extravagance. When he was forced to seek shelter in a peasant's hut on the Euphrates the bill for lodgings came to 500 dirhams. The caliph inadvertently gave him a warrant on the treasury for 500,000 and insisted this amount was paid. Zubaida, Harun's wife, only allowed vessels of gold or silver studded with gems at her table; Al-Amin, one of Harun's sons, had boats made in the shapes of animals at a cost of millions of dirhams. But towards the end of his reign the legendary caliph lost interest in affairs of state and allowed the Barmakid family to exercise power in his name.

Social life centred around parties and hunts, chess, intellectual discussions about literature, philosophy, or religion, and poetry and literary symposiums. Outdoor games included polo, fencing, hawking and horse racing. The poet Abu Nuwas provided extensive details about court life.

CULTURAL EXPANSION Harun divided the empire between his three sons, Amin, Mamum and Qasim, but Amin took the office of caliph. He was soon deposed by Mamum, who was supported by the Persians. Amin tried to escape in a boat but was forced to swim back after stones were thrown at the boat. He was captured and executed.

The reign of Caliph Mamum, the middle phase of the Abbasid caliphate, was a time of great cultural expansion. Gaston Wiet, author of *Baghdad: Metropolis of the Abbasid Caliphate*, described how Mamum:

> looked for knowledge where it was evident, and thanks to the breadth
> of his conceptions and the power of his intelligence, he drew it from
> places where it was hidden. He entered into relations with the emperors
> of Byzantium, gave them expensive gifts and asked them to give him
> books of philosophy which they had in their possession. These
> emperors sent him works of Plato, Aristotle, Hippocrates, Galen, Euclid
> and Ptolemy which they had. Mamum then chose the most experienced
> translators and commissioned them to translate these works to the best

POETRY

The Abbasid period was the heyday of a form of Arab poetry that eulogised those with wealth and power and was given the name 'new poetry'. As in Saddam's Iraq, poets who pleased their patrons were handsomely rewarded. Muti'b bin Iyas and Abu Nuwas were the most famous 'new poets' from the Baghdad school. Abu Nuwas advised his patrons to:

Accumulate as many sins thou canst:
The Lord is ready to relax His ire.
When the day comes, forgiveness thou wilt find
Before a mighty King and gracious Sire,
And gnaw thy fingers, all that joy regretting
Which thou didst leave thro' terror of Hell–fire!

FRATERNAL RELIGIOUS ORDERS

Muslim thought was greatly influenced by theologians such as al-Ghazzali, who believed an understanding of life could be gained through ecstatic experience. Individuals who benefited from these experiences, known as *sufis*, attracted followers, and their disciples turned into fraternal orders known as *tariqah*. One of the most famous was the Silsila-i-Qadiriya founded by Sayyid Abdul Qadir al-Jilani (1077–1166) of Baghdad. Another famous order that still has a following today is the Naqshbandiya.

of their ability. After the translating was done as perfectly as possible, the caliph urged his subjects to read the translations and study them. Scholars held high rank and the caliph surrounded himself with learned men, legal experts, traditionalists, rationalist theologians, lexicographers, annalists, metricians and genealogists.

Mamum subscribed to the theology of mu'tazilism, whose central tenet stipulated that the Koran was created and could therefore be altered according to circumstances. It could even be superseded by the judgement of the *imam* (religious leader) – or so the mu'tazilites claimed.

The Abbasid caliphs combined iron-fisted rule with impressive administrative skills and a sharp intellect. Once in power they embraced Sunni Islam

ABBASID EMPIRE 725–1258

BAGHDAD

and disavowed any support for Shia beliefs. This led to numerous conflicts and widespread bloodshed, and the flight of many Shias to the Maghreb. Long periods of stability proved conducive to cultural and intellectual pursuits, the arts were patronised and learning of every sort was encouraged. Classics from many languages were translated into Arabic at the House of Knowledge, erected near the Baghdad observatory. Science and philosophy were studied in the House of Wisdom. The writing of history was prompted by an interest in the life of Prophet Mohammed and the conquests of Islam.

Advanced irrigation systems enabled the introduction of crops such as oranges and sugar. Paper, a Chinese invention, was popularised and assisted academic pursuits. Basra was famous for its glass and soap production, Kufa for its silk, especially silk handkerchiefs.

Abu Bakr Muhammad ibn Zakariya Al-Razi, the chief physician of a hospital in Baghdad, has been acknowledged as one of history's greatest physicians. The philosopher Muhammad Ibn Yarkhan Abu Nasr Al-Farabi wrote about an ideal state and was referred to as 'the second teacher', the first being Aristotle. Muhammad Ibn Musa Al Khwarizmi compiled the first book on algebra and the Arabs were the first people to devote attention to alchemy, the mother of modern chemistry. Ibn Sina became an authority on medicine and philosophy for both the Muslim and European world, and his book on the law of medicine was used as a textbook until the 16th century. Newton was an ardent student of Arab mathematics.

During the reign of the Abbasid caliphs, tales from *The Thousand and One Nights*, including *Sinbad the Sailor*, whose adventures were based on the voyages of Muslim merchants, and *Ali Baba and the Forty Thieves*, were popular. Like the Mesopotamian myths, many of the stories describe the soul's journey through life. The tales were told by Shahrazad, the wife of King Shahryar. Many of the king's wives were killed in vengeance for a previous betrayal by a woman, but Shahrazad stayed alive by keeping him occupied for a thousand and one nights with a series of fascinating tales. They had three children and in the end the king mellowed and was cured from his pain and heartlessness.

TRADE AND COMMERCE It was also a time of intense commercial activity. The ports of the Persian Gulf were connected to Basra and Baghdad through a canal system. Barges transported a wide range of merchandise. Caliph Mansour used to say: 'This is the Tigris – there is no obstacle between us and China. Everything on sea can come to us on it.' Trade was also conducted with Europe and Africa, and even China by the overland route. The commercial sophistication of the caliphate enabled a cheque written on a Baghdad bank to be cashed in Canton. Exports included rugs, tapestries, cotton goods, silk and mosaic tiles with floral designs.

Seton Lloyd, author of *Twin Rivers*, describes the goods that came into the bazaars of Baghdad:

Porcelain, silk and musk from China; spices, minerals and dyes from India and the Malay Archipelago; rubies, lapis lazuli, fabrics and slaves from the lands of the Turks in Central Asia; honey, wax, furs and white slaves from Scandinavia and Russia; ivory, gold-dust and black slaves from eastern Africa. The empire itself supplied rice, grain and linen

The first book on human geography was written during the Abbasid period by Al-Istakhri. It is concerned mainly with Muslim countries. Al-Istakhri constantly revised his work and asked Ibn Hawqal to collect information and make sure that the maps were accurate. Al-Maqdisi, an Arab traveller and geographer, spent 20 years collecting data on most Muslim countries before publishing his famous work, *The Best of Classification for the Knowledge of Regions*.

from Egypt; glass, metal-ware and fruits from Syria; brocade, pearls and weapons from Arabia; and silk, perfumes and vegetables from Persia.

BEGINNING OF THE END However, the seed which grew into a forest of thorns and strangled the Abbasids was sown by Al-Mutasim (AD822–42), who allowed his Turkish bodyguards, numbering some 4,000, to rise to the rank of officers. They slowly wormed their way into positions of control and towards the end of their reign the once feared and revered Abbasid caliphs became nothing more than tools in the hands of strong Turkish generals, the next masters of the Arab world.

As the 20th-century Islamic reformer Rashid Rida, writing in the Islamic magazine *al-Manar* (published between 1898 and 1935), pointed out, the influence of the caliph gradually weakened:

until he became a ghost, decorated by silk and gold, made to say what he does not want or understand, signs what he does not read or know, moves only when his guards or entourage move him. He is enabled to get all the sensual pleasures as long as he obeys. If he refuses, he gets killed and replaced by another ghost. He sees no other way to keep his pleasures and ornaments other than to have no opinion or will.

Fayyaz Mahmud Sayyid, author of *A Short History of Islam*, spoke allegorically about the disintegration of the Abbasid caliphate:

One should visualise a beautiful building with lovely rooms, gorgeous decorations, sparkling gardens, whose foundations are being eaten away by a million rats, white ants and all kinds of vermin, whose walls fall one by one and whose colours and decorations fade gradually, till one day the whole structure crumbles.

The two main problems were finance – maintaining a bloated bureaucracy and large standing army – and the fragmentation of the empire.

Money was raised in three main ways:

- an annual tax on land, or *kharaj*, collected each year
- a farming tax – tax collectors, who were not slow to enrich themselves in the process, collected money from the hapless farmers and paid an agreed sum to the exchequer

- the system of *iqta* – individuals assigned to certain areas supplied the government with troops or money.

Hugh Kennedy, author of *The Prophet and the Age of the Caliphates*, described how revenue-raising became a vicious cycle:

> There was a financial crisis and some ambitious bureaucrat or businessman would then approach the caliph saying that he was in a position to increase the revenue and extract a vast sum from the present *wazir* [chief minister]. The caliph would agree, the hapless wazir would be dismissed and his assistants interrogated, often under torture, and would promise to pay huge fines. The new holder of the office would then discover that the fines were mostly unpaid, since the victims did not have the money, and he was wholly unable to raise the promised sums, whereupon the whole dismal cycle began all over again.

The money was not coming in, the troops were not loyal and the caliph ceased to be in control. The bureaucrats and the ruling class were preoccupied with feathering their own nests. For them the vast empire stretching from the Mediterranean to India ended on the outskirts of Baghdad.

Separate dynasties started breaking away from the central control of the caliphate: Spain in AD756, Morocco in 788, Tunisia in 800 and Egypt in 868. Tribally-based Arab dynasties such as the Hamdanids (929–1003), the Uqailids (996–1096) the Mirdasids (1028–79), the Mazyadids (961–1150) and the Kurdish Marwanids (990–1096) ruled throughout this era.

Before the final curtain fell on the Abbasid Empire, Caliph Muqtadir appointed a Sassanian, Ahmad ibn Buwayh, as commander of commanders. The Buwayhid family members enriched themselves through their new high office but they were not totally without a social conscience and were

OMAR AL-KHAYYAM

The works of Omar Al-Khayyam were translated into English by Edward Fitzgerald in the 18th century. The introduction to the translation published by the Orion Publishing Group describes Khayyam (1048–1131) as a Persian astronomer, mathematician and freethinker. All his life was spent in his native town of Naishapur, where his most celebrated achievement was to direct a commission charged with reforming the calendar, which was done with remarkable accuracy. This brought him celebrity status in the Islamic world, but he was not known for his poetry until several decades after his death, when the now-famous Rubaiyat began to be ascribed to him. His reputation as a poet, more substantial in the West than in Persia itself, was popularised by Fitzgerald's adaptations:

Oh, come with old Khayyam, and leave the wise
To talk; one thing is certain, that life flies;
One thing is certain, and the rest is lies;
The flower that once has blown for ever dies.

responsible for the establishment of a hospital and an academy with a library of 10,000 volumes.

During the 11th century the Seljuk Turks toppled the Buwayhid family. Their reign was peaceful, Baghdad took their fancy and they even toyed with the idea of merging the caliphate with the sultanate. The roads were safer than ever before, attention was paid to the arts, and one of the Seljuk rulers was the patron and protector of Omar Al-Khayyam (see box on previous page).

THE MONGOLS

The years of peace, and the Abbasid Empire itself, were ended by the wanton destruction of the Mongols. Hulagu, a grandson of Genghis Khan, destroyed Diyarbakr, in present-day Turkey, and spent the next two years preparing for the siege of Baghdad with weapons such as fire-arrows, in which naphtha was used. The city surrendered on 10 February 1258 and 800,000 of its inhabitants were slaughtered, along with the caliph and his family. Books from the famous libraries were thrown into the river, the treasures were looted and the palaces and gardens were laid to waste, as described in Fayyaz Mahmud Sayyid's *A Short History of Islam*:

> The city of peace was peaceful no more, nor indeed was it a city any longer: it was a ruin, where corpses lay unburied for weeks and where their stench spread diseases which at last drove Hulagu out of the town. After five hundred years, during which time, despite varying fortunes, the name of Abbas had at least been kept alive, the city of the caliph lay desolate. The longest line of rulers in the world had come to a pitiful end.

THE OTTOMANS

The history of the period between the collapse of the Abbasids, the establishment of the Mongol rule in Persia and Iraq, and the intervening centuries before the Ottomans established their empire, including Iraq, is particularly difficult to describe. This is due to the paucity of the written sources and the nature of the waves of Turcoman tribal invasions, which were the result of the pressures in their homelands in Central Asia by the Mongols. The Turcomans were Turkish tribes and converts to Islam. The use of Turcoman military slaves and military mercenaries in the preceding centuries by the Umayyad, the Abbasid Arab dynasties and the Ghaznavids of Persia and Afghanistan had already introduced Turcoman influences (and often control) in many of the minor dynasties of these areas of the Near East.

By the 10th century AD, one of the invading Turkish tribes, the Seljuk, had established themselves as an important power in Anatolia (modern Turkey) and parts of the Middle East (see the box on the Crusades overleaf). As the Seljuks increased their power, they attracted other Turkish tribes to Anatolia. However, the Seljuks increasingly came into conflict with these nomadic Turkish tribes. As the Seljuk Empire declined, so the power of these Turcoman tribal khanates increased, until the Ottomans, named after Osman I, the founder of the Ottoman Empire, in AD1299, expanded to become the premier power of the region. The Ottomans took Istanbul from the Byzantines in

The period of the Crusades, which started in 1094 and lasted for over two centuries, became a fundamental clash between Medieval Christianity and Islamic forces on the frontiers of their worlds. Jerusalem was always the prize.

The Christians were eager to spread their faith, and rescue Jerusalem, the birthplace of Christianity, which for 400 years had been in the hands of the Muslims, as far back as the Umayyads. For the Muslims the city was, and still is, a very important part of their faith and they could not allow it to fall into the hands of the infidels. The Dome of the Rock in Jerusalem was completed in AD691 to commemorate Mohammed's ascent to heaven as described in the Koran.

By the 12th century the Seljuk Turks were established over much of Anatolia, and at Aleppo and Damascus in Syria. The principalities of Antioch and Edessa and the Kingdom of Jerusalem were won by force of arms by Crusaders and became new Christian-ruled enclaves surrounded by a sea of Muslim faith.

The rise of Saladin, a Kurd from Tikrit, began the end of most of these Christian states. Armoured knights and men at arms were crushed by Saladin at the Battle of Hattin, in Galilee in 1187. Their power was broken, they never really recovered, and in a few weeks Saladin overran much of Palestine. In 1192, the Peace of Ramla, an armistice agreement with King Richard I of England, did no more than consolidate the Muslim victories. Saladin remains an historic hero for the Muslims; his bravery, courteous behaviour and steely faith have always endeared him to them.

However, crusades continued after his death. On the sixth crusade, in 1228, under the Emperor Frederick II, Jerusalem was briefly restored to Christian control, with the exception of Muslim holy places. In 1260 Mamluk Baybers I seized power in Cairo, defeated the Mongol forces entering Syria and proceeded to take most of what remained of Christian Palestine. The last crusade outpost, at Acre, fell in 1291.

AD1453, annexed eastern Anatolia and northern Iraq in AD1514 and were at the gates of Vienna by AD1529. They ruled Iraq as part of their empire for 400 years until 1918.

IRAQ – THE PERIOD FROM THE MONGOLS TO THE OTTOMAN ANNEXATION After the Hulagu Dynasty (1258–1336) came the relative calm of the Jalayrids (1336–1432), a Mongol tribal dynasty that ruled Iraq and Azerbaijan, and made Baghdad their capital. Under this dynasty a flowering of Mongol art took place in Iraq, encompassing poetry, painting and calligraphy, and under the Jalayrid Sultan Ahmed 1382–1409 many architectural projects were undertaken in Baghdad.

However, Tamerlane, a descendent of Genghis Khan, expanded his empire with even more savagery than Hulagu, and ravaged Baghdad. In 1401, when that city revolted against him, he slaughtered its inhabitants and made a pyramid of their skulls. Sultan Ahmed re-established his rule in 1405, when Tamerlane died. He was assisted in this by Kara Yusaf, a chief of the Black Sheep Turcoman from the Kara-Koyunlu principality of Anatolia. Peace did not last

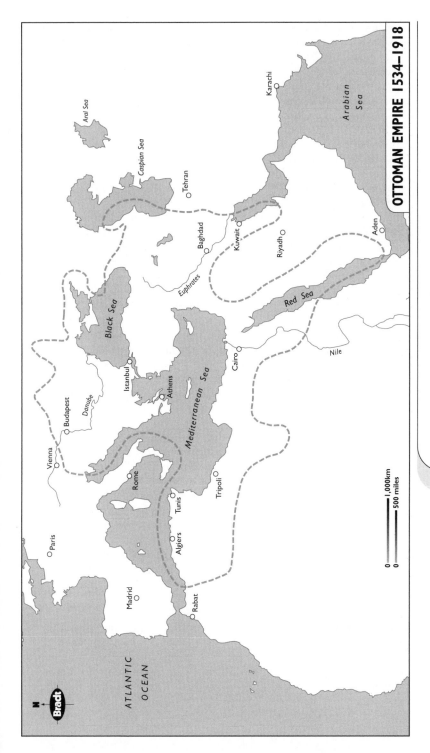

OTTOMAN EMPIRE 1534–1918

Arabian
Sea

Karachi

Aral Sea

Caspian Sea

Tehran

Baghdad

Kuwait

Riyadh

Aden

Euphrates

Red Sea

Black Sea

Istanbul

Athens

Cairo

Nile

Budapest

Danube

Mediterranean Sea

Vienna

Rome

Tripoli

Paris

Tunis

Algiers

Madrid

Rabat

ATLANTIC
OCEAN

0 ___ 1,000km
0 ___ 500 miles

long, however, and in 1409 the two quarrelled and Yusaf killed the Sultan and took Baghdad for himself.

In 1466 the White Sheep Turcoman (another Anatolian tribe from Diyarbakr) under Hassan the Long defeated the Black Sheep Turcoman and took control of the country. But soon Iraq became a battleground between the two main expanding regional powers of the time, the Persians (the Safavids) and the Turks (the Ottomans). It also became a battleground between Sunni and Shia as the Ottomans were Sunni Muslims as were most Turcoman at that time by conversion centuries before. The new Safavid Persian Empire was based in Azerbaijan with Tabriz as its capital. Shah Ismail I was proclaimed as its first Shah or King, and having been tutored at a very early age into the Shia faith enforced this branch of Islam on his mainly Turcoman subjects. In 1508 the White Sheep Turcoman ruling in Iraq were deposed by the Persian Ismail Shah, who then made a pilgrimage to Iraq's Shia shrines and destroyed the tombs of a number of Sunni saints and executed prominent religious Sunni leaders. Although in the minority at this time, Iraqi Shia were able to welcome Persian rule and with the influx of Persian merchants into Baghdad, trade was revived after the years of turmoil.

However, the Ottomans were convinced for both political and religious reasons that the power and influence of the Persians had to be curbed. For example, Eastern Anatolia, although controlled by the Ottomans was populated by Qizilbash (Red Hats) Turcoman, who being Shia were loyal to the Safavids. In 1534 the Ottoman Sultan Suleiman the Magnificent took Baghdad and Iraq was integrated into the Ottoman Empire, which extended over present-day Hungary, Serbia, Albania, Greece, Bulgaria, Romania, the Ukraine, the Crimea, Turkey, Iran, Iraq, Syria, Lebanon, Jordan, Egypt, Libya, Tunisia and Algeria.

Seton Lloyd, author of *Twin Rivers*, notes that:

> Nothing was left undone by the sultan [Suleiman the Magnificent] and his great vizier to encourage the loyalty of their new subjects. Local men of repute were encouraged to visit the court. Official pilgrimages were made by the sultan to the mosque of Shaikh Abdul-Qadir, the tomb of Sheikh Maruf Al-Karkhi and the Shia shrines of Kadhimain. The mosque of Abu Hanifah, which the Persians had demolished and desecrated, was rebuilt and ornamented with a large and stately dome. Canals and dykes were repaired and such encouragement as was possible was given to agriculture and commerce. Finally the sultan returned to Istanbul, leaving Baghdad in the charge of its first Ottoman governor. Iraq acquired the status of a Turkish province, which she was to retain, with one interruption, for four centuries.

PERSIAN CONFLICTS The Persians, however, did not give up easily. They retook Baghdad in 1623 and the repression of the Sunnis began anew under Shah Abbas. Few buildings from the times of the Abbasids were left standing. But the Ottomans, under Sultan Murad IV, once again ousted the invaders in 1638. This time a peace treaty was signed to demarcate the borders between the Persian Safavid Empire and the Ottomans. Sunni shrines were rebuilt, as were bazaars. Gardens were planted and attempts were made to beautify the city.

THE OTTOMAN EMPIRE

The Ottoman Empire began to establish itself in around 1300 and lasted until 1918. At its height, it controlled what is now Turkey, parts of North Africa, southwestern Asia and southeastern Europe. The Ottomans were descendants of Turcoman nomads who entered Anatolia in the 11th century as mercenary soldiers. The term Ottoman comes from Osman, the founder and first sultan of the empire. At the end of the Byzantine Empire in 1453, the Ottomans conquered its capital Constantinople (now Istanbul), which became the capital of the Ottoman Empire. By the mid-1500s the Balkans, present-day Iran, Saudi Arabia and Syria all belonged to the Ottomans. The empire suffered a slow decline during its last 300 years. When World War I began in 1914, the Ottoman Empire held Asia Minor (present-day Turkey), parts of southwestern Asia and part of the Balkans, Syria, Lebanon, Jordan, Palestine, parts of Yemen, Mecca and Medina (in present-day Saudi Arabia) and Iraq. The Ottomans were defeated by the allies (mainly the British and the French) during World War I and their empire came to an end.

The later Ottoman administration, though, was largely corrupt and most of the governors were only concerned with extracting as much revenue as possible for their masters. It was a time of stagnation and poverty. Internal resistance came from the Shias in the towns and the tribes. Between 1620 and 1700, Basra was governed by a local ruler. Tribes such as the Aniza, Shammar, Dhafir, Muntafiq, Cha'ab, Bani Lam, Zubaid and others dominated the countryside, were hostile to the Ottomans and engaged in 'highway' robberies.

In 1730 the Persians had to be repulsed once again when Nadir Shah presented another threat to the Ottomans. The local governors had grown powerful and the sultan could no longer decide who was in charge in the *vilayets*, as the administrative divisions of the Ottoman Empire were known. In their historical work *Iraq*, Stephen Longrigg and Frank Stoakes point out that:

> the sultan-caliph was no longer able to nominate officers of his own choice to the government of these vilayets: he was compelled instead to accept and confirm, often after abortive counter-efforts, the candidates preferred by Baghdad or Mosul themselves. Indeed in the ensuing period, 1747–1831, the pashas of these provinces, while formally correct in their treatment of their sovereign, and willing at times even to remit some token revenue, enjoyed in all but name, effective independence.

The Ottomans employed Christian slaves (Mamluks) from the Caucasus who converted to Islam and were trained in a special school and then assigned military and administrative duties as civil servants in Iraq. Their competent administration led to an economic revival during the 18th and 19th centuries. They cleared the canals, developed industries and permitted the establishment of a British Trade Agency – the Basra office of the East India Company. Between 1747 and 1831 the Mamluk officers became autonomous from the court of the Ottoman Empire and ruled Iraq.

The Shia cities of Najaf and Kerbala were attacked and victimised in 1802 by the Wahhabis, a puritanical sect that became the dominant religious force in Saudi Arabia. The Wahhabis believed they were true Muslims and embarked on a holy war (*jihad*) against all other Islamic tendencies. When the holy city of Kerbala was looted the mosque was stripped of all the treasures and precious offerings that had been left by wealthy Shias throughout the centuries.

Mamluk rule was brought to an end by a fatal combination of disease and flood in 1831. Baghdad was devastated by bubonic plague, with 2,000–3,000 people dying every day. The healthy fled, the administration collapsed and robbers plundered anything worth stealing. The Tigris burst its banks and destroyed hundreds of houses. The population of the city, which had risen to 150,000 during the prosperous rule of Daud Pasha, the last of the Mamluks, was reduced to 50,000.

It was time for the Ottomans to strike. The Mamluks were ordered to convene at an assembly (*diwan*) and were massacred. The ineffective rule of Istanbul returned: between 1831 and 1869 Baghdad had more than ten governors.

SOCIAL REFORM Midhat Pasha, governor of Baghdad between 1869 and 1872, was one of the city's most enlightened rulers, who introduced urgently needed reforms. Emphasis was placed on codes of criminal and commercial law, secular education and local government conducted through provincial assemblies that helped the governor. The Ottomans helped entrench the Sunnis as the dominant, privileged class. But the Western education system from which children of all social classes could take advantage was instrumental in the creation of a new intelligentsia.

The most radical reform, the land reform, remodelled the feudal system into a system of property rights. The tribal sheikhs became landlords, while the tribesmen were turned into share croppers. But the decline of the Ottoman Empire, which had begun three centuries before, was irreversible. The sultans who followed Suleiman were largely incompetent, bribery and corruption were rife and the economy suffered due to inflation. During the 17th century European goods undermined local production. At the same time the Middle East was bypassed as a transit route and the new sea trade routes were controlled by the Europeans. The Sunni religious establishment, convinced of its superiority, was not receptive to new ideas and developments in what it regarded as the infidel West. But the balance of power shifted irreversibly in Europe's favour and the 1877–78 war with Russia and the Treaty of Berlin resulted in the loss of most Ottoman lands in Europe.

EUROPEAN INTERVENTION

As Turkish influence declined, European influence increased. Steam boats started appearing on the Tigris and Euphrates, followed by telegraph lines, a newspaper, military factories, a hospital, schools and administrative councils.

In 1908 the Young Turks, exponents of the Western concept of the nation state, took power in Istanbul and held elections. A parliament, in which members of leading Baghdadi families took part, was reopened. But the policy of 'Turkification' alienated the fledgling Iraqi intelligentsia and prompted the development of the Arab nationalist movement in which the Iraqis, especially the upper and middle classes, were eager to take part. Secret nationalist societies, such as the covenant (*Al Ahd*) made up of Iraqi officers in the Ottoman army, were formed.

According to Longrigg and Stoakes, authors of the historical work *Iraq*, the handling of local nationalism was far from being the only problem for the rulers of Iraq:

> An adequate system of representative government was still to be evolved – or, more broadly, a tolerable relationship was still to be established between government and public. In the field of public enlightenment, everything remained to be done among the backward, ignorant population by education at every level and by every means. National physique was poor, disease endemic and neglected. An almost universal and long-familiar poverty, accepted with hopeless fatalism, afflicted and retarded the public, and precluded all but the lowest standards in nourishment, clothing and manner of life; only immense economic advance on a wide front could improve this, by the comprehensive betterment of agriculture, quantitative and qualitative, the re-establishment of control over the rivers and their scientific exploitation, the intelligent fostering of industry and commerce, the discovery and development of natural resources, and the creation and equipment of modern communications.

At the end of the 19th century conflicts and tensions between various social groups hindered the development of a nation state: there were conflicts between the tribes and the townspeople over the food-growing areas near the rivers, conflicts among the tribes themselves, the Sunnis and the Shias, and the regions. The north had long-standing ties with Syria and Turkey, whereas Baghdad and the holy cities of the south had strong links with Iran. The land reforms led to the development of a market economy and the country became part of the international capitalist system. Social status, traditionally determined by religious knowledge, wealth and noble lineage, became increasingly linked to wealth and land ownership.

After World War I, the Iraqis were hoping to welcome the new dawn of independence. The sun set on the Ottoman Empire and Turkey became a republic. But there was no independence for Iraq. In April 1920 the League of Nations signed a mandate for Britain and France to oversee the lands of the former Ottoman Empire, with Britain responsible for Iraq.

Sumerian head

4

The Emergence of Modern Iraq

The modern history of Iraq is a history of the way in which people who found themselves living in the new Iraqi state were drawn into its orbit.

Charles Tripp

Modern Iraq (ancient Mesopotamia) is a rich country with a splendid cultural heritage. It is also blessed with the world's third-largest oil reserves after Saudi Arabia and two large rivers, the Tigris and the Euphrates. But throughout the 20th century its turbulent political life has prevented it from taking advantage of the gifts of nature and the talents of an educated and creative people. Political instability has dominated 20th-century life. Between 1920 and 1958 senior Iraqi politicians played musical chairs for positions in 24 successive cabinets. The people have been the victims of turmoil, civil strife, bloody coups and counter-coups, and three devastating wars: the Iran–Iraq War (1980–88), the Gulf War, which followed Iraq's invasion of Kuwait in August 1990, and the 2003 war.

Social upheaval and change has characterised 20th-century life in Iraq, which has been greatly influenced by:

- the discovery of oil, which tied the economy to one major source of national income
- the replacement of subsistence cultivation with commercial agriculture
- the decline of nomadism
- urbanisation
- the growth of the middle class, government bureaucracy and the armed forces
- major investment in education, health, housing and other social services
- a weakening of traditional family and tribal links
- the consolidation of the power of the Arab Baath Socialist Party
- a different perception of the role of women, who entered the workforce in large numbers during the 1980–88 Iran–Iraq War
- life under a stringent economic-sanctions regime imposed from 1990 to 2003.

CHRONOLOGY

| 1920 | British mandate established. |
| 1927 | Oil discovered. |

1932	Iraq formally admitted to the League of Nations as an independent state, which became the centre of Arab nationalism and active resistance to Zionism. Constitutional monarchy installed by the British.
1933	King Faisal died. Succeeded by his son Ghazi.
1936	General Bakr Sidqi, a Kurd, overthrew the government in the Arab world's first military coup.
1937	Sidqi assassinated by army officers. Six coups followed.
1939	King Ghazi died in a car accident. Succeeded by his infant son Faisal II.
1941	Government of National Defence headed by the pro-German Rashid Ali Kailani formed. Fighting broke out between British forces and Iraqi army. Kailani escaped to Iran.
1958	'Free Officers' overthrew the monarchy. King Faisal II killed; pro-British politicians eliminated. Brigadier Abdul Karim Qasim became prime minister.
1959	Half a million people demonstrated for communist representation in government.
1963	Prime Minister Qasim was overthrown in a Baathist coup. General Abd al-Salam Aref overthrew first Baathist regime.
1968	Second Baathist coup.
1972	Iraqi Petroleum Company nationalised.
1979	Saddam Hussein became president after ten years of being a key politician. Some 500 top-ranking Baathists were executed.
1980–88	Iran–Iraq War.
2 Aug 1990	Iraq invaded Kuwait.
17 Jan 1991	Gulf War started.

20TH-CENTURY SOCIETY

Iraqi society is a jigsaw puzzle of religious, ethnic, class, family and tribal pieces interlinked through a series of complex relationships. At the beginning of the 20th century there were three main divisions: bedouin camps; villages; towns and cities.

The Bedouin came from four major tribes: the camel- and sheep-breeding Shammar confederation, the sheep-raising Dulaym, and the Muntafiq and Dharfir tribes of the south, once feared because of their raids on pilgrims' caravans. Other important tribes included the Ubaid (found mainly in Tikrit and the surrounding areas up to Kirkuk and Kurdistan's borders), the Jibour (found beside the Tigris River from the outskirts of Baghdad to Mosul), the Azzah (found mainly near the Himreen Mountains, 120–150km north of Baghdad and in Dyala Province) and the Janabis (found in the northern part of Babylon and in the outskirts of Tikrit). The tribes, whose size varied from a few families to hundreds of thousands, traced their origins to a male ancestor. Families who claimed descent from the Prophet Mohammed (*sayyids*) provided the tribes with religious services.

The extended family, made up of three generations, was the basis of tribal organisation. Tribal leaders (*sheikhs*) exercised authority according to their family status and their own abilities. Succession was not always hereditary and tribal leaders could be elected. Decisions tended to be made in the tribal council (*majlis*). Sheikhs traditionally settled family disputes, consented to marriages and divorces, and assumed responsibility for the tribe's welfare – and warfare! As the authority of the central government extended into tribal areas, they also became responsible for tax collection. Business advisers were sometimes appointed to liaise between the tribes and the central government, which put a stop to raiding.

The nomads were gradually absorbed into sedentary life and turned to farming or employment in industry, including the oil industry. Between 1957 and 1965 the bedouin population is said to have decreased by 50%. Today it is estimated at 100,000.

Although most Arabs tend to be sentimental when it comes to their romantic past, there is little aversion to modernisation. Camels are being replaced by Land Rovers and radio and television are turning professional storytelling into a profession of the past.

Helen Metz, author of *Iraq: A Country Study*, has described how as society changed, the lines that separated rural from urban life became increasingly blurred:

> An interesting amalgam developed of the traditional customs of the tribes and the more modern practices of the civil servants sent to rural regions ... the government engineer responsible for the water distribution system, although not a major administrator, in practice became the leading figure in rural areas. He would set forth requirements for the cleaning and maintenance of the canals and the

SOCIAL AND FAMILY LIFE

For men, social life in villages is centred around the coffee houses, described by Helen Metz, author of *Iraq: A Country Study*, as:

> a clearing house for both local and outside news, a political forum, a chamber of commerce, and the place where such family matters as marriage contracts are arranged. Men also gather in the market, while women's social life is centred around home visits.

As in all parts of the Middle East, the family in Iraq is the core around which society revolves. Bahija Lovejoy, author of *The Land and People of Iraq*, has pointed out that:

> In spite of the strong forces from outside that might have destroyed it, this pattern of life, with its roots and traditions, imposes social and economic controls that have persisted through the centuries. A way of life, built around family solidarity, holds true wherever the family lives, whether in a tent or mansion, a mud hut, villa, or house of reeds.

IRAQI FOLK TALES: A SARCASTIC COMMENT ON LIFE'S MISFORTUNES

Throughout Arab history, storytelling was a common profession in the Middle East. Folklore was handed down by word of mouth from generation to generation. The coffee shops and markets were the domain of male storytellers, while women storytellers were welcome in the harems.

E S Stevens, who lived in Iraq at the beginning of the 20th century, was the first writer to collect many of the traditional fairy tales of Mesopotamia. She predicted that folklore would fade into the background when desert tribesmen started listening to concerts and political propaganda broadcasts from Near or Middle Eastern radio stations.

Like their Western counterparts, Iraqi folk tales are full of supernatural beings such as *si'iluwa*, similar to the witch or ogress in Western fairy tales; *ferj aqra'a*, a river demon fond of playing tricks on fishermen and river-dwellers; *dami*, a half-bestial ogress who haunts the outskirts of towns; and *deyu*, a demon who haunts woods and desolate places. Arab storytellers often believe in the supernatural beings whose exploits they describe.

Animal fables, nursery tales and, of course, tales from the Arabian Nights are popular. Some, like the story of the Khalifa Harun Al Rashid (AD786–809), found in Stevens' *Folk-tales of Iraq*, are told in riddles and have a sarcastic, almost bitter flavour:

One day the Khalifa was walking in Baghdad with his minister, and they came to the river, where a fuller stood beating cotton-cloth in the river. It was bitterly cold, and the Khalifa paused by the man and spoke to him.

Said he, 'You have twelve, do you need these three?'

Answered the fuller, 'for the thirty and two they are needed.'

Said the Khalifa, 'And the far?'

Replied the fuller, 'is now near.'

Spake the Khalifa once more, 'If I send you a goose will you pluck it?'

And the fuller made reply, 'Yes, I will pluck its feathers and send it back.'

Then the Khalifa and his minister passed on, and when they had gone a little way the Khalifa turned to his minister, and said, 'Did you understand what I said to the fuller?'

The minister replied, 'O, Khalifa, lord of the age and time, I did not understand.'

tribal sheikh would see to it that the necessary man-power was provided. This service, in the minds of the tribesmen, replaced the old customary obligation of military service that they owed to the sheikh and was not unduly onerous. It could be combined with work on their own grazing lands or agricultural plots, and it benefited the tribe as a whole.

Many Bedouin have been absorbed into village life in Iraq. As in the traditional tribe, the inhabitants of smaller villages, with a population of around 200, are usually related to each other. Village sizes range from 200 to 2,000 inhabitants.

Before the land reforms of the late 1950s, which broke up the large estates, the landless sharecroppers (most commonly found in the villages in southern Iraq) were at the bottom of the village hierarchy. Then came the tenant farmers

Said the Khalifa, 'I will give you a respite of three hours to find out the meaning of what was said and if you cannot read me the riddle, I shall cut off your head.'

The minister saluted the Khalifa and left him. First he went to his house and took a bag of gold, and secondly he went back to the fuller. To him he said, 'O my dear, Allah preserve you and your children and lengthen your life! What was the meaning of what the Khalifa said to you and you to him?'

Answered the fuller, 'Pass on! That is nothing to you!'

Said the minister, 'My brother, my dear, if you will not tell me, the Khalifa will cut off my head! Allah bless you, Allah preserve you! For the sake of Allah the Merciful and the Prophet, on him be peace, tell me the meaning of your conversation.'

Said the fuller, 'If for each riddle, you will give me a hundred pieces of gold, I will speak.'

The minister gave him a hundred pieces of gold.

The fuller said, 'The Khalifa said to me, "You have twelve, do you need these three?" and his meaning was, "There are twelve months in the year, need you work during the three cold months?" and to this I replied, "For the thirty and two they are needed," and I meant my teeth. For if a poor man remains idle three months, his teeth are idle too!'

Then the minister said, 'And now the second dark saying.'

Said the fuller, 'First another hundred pieces of gold!' and the minister counted him out the hundred.

Then said the fuller, '"The far is now near", referred to my sight, which has grown longer with age, as is usual with those getting on in life.'

Said the minister, 'And the third saying?'

Replied the fuller, 'Give me all the gold that remains in the bag and I will tell you.'

The minister handed him the bag, and the fuller said, 'The Khalifa asked if I could pluck a goose, if he were to send me one. By the goose he meant you, and, by Allah, I have plucked you!'

And he held up the gold, and added, 'And now return to the Khalifa!' And the minister departed, shamed.

(usually found in Arab Sunni and Kurdish areas), small landowners, craftsmen and local religious dignitaries. The large landowners (often absentee landlords) were at the top of the village hierarchy. In 1970 the size of land holdings was further limited and middle-level peasants came to dominate the rural hierarchy.

At the beginning of the 20th century Iraq was ruled by the British who, perhaps naively, believed that after 400 years of Turkish rule, the people would embrace a Western version of democracy. The British-installed monarchy was toppled by the Free Officers led by Abdul Karim Qasim in 1958, whose vision of an egalitarian society contrasted sharply with the reality of political intrigue. Qasim was toppled in a coup in 1963. Governments and leaders changed frequently until the Baathist regime seized power in 1968 and held on to it with an iron grip until the Allied invasion in 2003.

As a largely neglected province of the Ottoman Empire, Iraq was catapulted into the 20th century and provided with a modern state structure under British guidance during the 12-year mandate period following World War I (1920–32).

Britain had established a presence in Iraq as early as 1798, when its permanent agent took up residence. The East India Company had an office in Baghdad in 1783. Britain's decision to invade Iraq at the start of World War I was prompted by the Ottoman Empire's alliance with Germany, the need to safeguard British oil production in Persia, and fears for the security of India, which in 1914 was the most important part of the British Empire. The Turks did not give up without a fight. In 1916 the British lost 10,000 men at Kut. Baghdad was occupied a year later. Sensing a British victory the Turks started looting the capital. While the citizens hid in their houses, shops and bazaars were ransacked.

In March 1917 British forces, under the command of General Stanley Maude, captured Baghdad. He read a long proclamation carefully drafted in London, which appealed to the mind and heart and provided an introduction to Britain's ambitions in the country:

> Since the days of Hulagu your city and your lands have been subject to the tyranny of strangers, your palaces have fallen into ruins, your gardens have sunk in desolation and your forefathers and yourselves have groaned in bondage. Your sons have been carried off to wars not of your seeking, your wealth has been stripped from you by unjust men and squandered in distant places.

Maude concluded:

> O people of Baghdad, remember that for 26 generations you have suffered under strange tyrants, who have endeavoured to set one Arab house against another in order that they might profit by your dissensions. This policy is abhorrent to Great Britain and the Allies, for there can neither be peace nor prosperity where there is enmity and misgovernment. Therefore I am commanded to invite you, through your nobles and elders and representatives, to participate in the management of your own civil affairs in collaboration with the political representatives of Great Britain who accompany the British army, so that you may be united with your kinsmen in the north, east, south and west, in realising the aspirations of your race.

The Turks removed all their archives before Baghdad was captured. Eighteen months later the city had electric light and an efficient postal service. A comprehensive street map was also produced.

A British mandate on Iraq was conferred at a meeting of the Allied powers in the Italian town of San Remo in 1920. It was a continuation of the Western division of the Middle East, made possible by the collapse of the Ottoman Empire and following on from the Sykes–Picot Agreement of 1916. This was a secret pact between London and Paris signed by Sir Mark Sykes, a senior British diplomat, and François Georges Picot, a former French consul in Beirut, to divide the Ottoman Empire among Britain, France and Russia after their victory in World War I.

The two most famous British political officers of the mandate period – with a sincere commitment to Arab independence and a remarkable empathy for the Arab people they came into contact with, both kings and commoners – were Col T E Lawrence (1888–1935) and Gertrude Bell (1868–1926).

Lawrence was the architect and inspiration for the organised Arab revolt against the Turks in their search for independence in the Middle East, which he described in his book *The Seven Pillars of Wisdom*. In 1919 he was a member of the British delegation to the Paris Peace Conference of the Council of Four, who were President Woodrow Wilson of the United States, Prime Minister Georges Clemenceau of France, Prime Minister Vittorio Orlandio of Italy and Prime Minister David Lloyd George of Great Britain. He liaised with the Arabs and acted as adviser to the aspiring King Faisal ibn Hussein, but he could not get an agreement to make Jewish immigration into Palestine conditional on the Arabs obtaining their independence.

Lawrence was not satisfied with his achievements. In *Lawrence and the Arabs* Robert Graves points out that:

> He refused to accept his British decoration. He explained personally to King George that the part he had played in the Arab Revolt was dishonourable to himself and to his country and government. He had, by order, fed the Arabs with false hopes and would now be obliged if he might be quietly relieved of the obligation to accept honours for succeeding in his fraud. He said respectfully as a subject, but firmly as an individual, that he intended to fight by straight means or crooked until His Majesty's ministers had conceded to the Arabs a fair settlement of their claims.

A disillusioned man, he effectively resigned from public life and became an ordinary non-ranking airman for most of his remaining life.

Gertrude Bell, meanwhile, was an accomplished archaeologist, political analyst, and in reality one of the principal architects of the modern Iraqi state. In Iraq she is remembered mainly for her efforts to get Prince Faisal of Mecca installed as king, and for her establishment of the Baghdad Museum of Archaeology. In a short biography, Susan Goodman describes the evening of 12 July 1926:

> There was a great public funeral in Baghdad. Thousands of Arabs followed the coffin of Gertrude Bell to the British cemetery on the outskirts of the city. She had died that morning from an overdose of a sleeping potion, just two days before her 58th birthday. She was deeply mourned by the princes and people of Iraq and eulogized by her own king and country.

Her bust and commemorative plaque are carefully stored away – probably somewhere in the museum she established.

In their description of the mandate, Stephen Longrigg and Frank Stoakes, authors of the historical work *Iraq*, pointed out that:

> The temporary administration of the territory retained a character which, while it assured a security, honesty and progressiveness far in advance of anything the three vilayets had seen before, was nevertheless inevitably authoritarian, foreign, Christian, and, largely for these reasons, uncongenial and increasingly unpopular.

REBELLION AND REVOLUTION For its new governors, Iraq proved to be a hornets' nest, with numerous unresolved conflicts: urban dwellers wanted protection against the tribes, and the tribal sheikhs expected the government to confirm their titles to land and give them new land. They also fought among themselves. Merchants demanded legal protection from the courts and the people expected welfare services such as health and education. Canals and roads had to be built and upgraded and agriculture developed. But the British treasury was not a very generous benefactor and attempts were made to keep the administrative costs of the mandate to a minimum.

Nationalist sentiments, originally directed against the Turks, were soon directed towards the British, who at first tried to run the country with the assistance of Indian civil servants. Three anti-colonial secret societies, The League of the Islamic Awakening, The Muslim National League and the Guardians of Independence, were formed.

In 1920 a four-month rebellion, commonly referred to as the Great Iraqi Revolution, which united Sunnis and Shias, tribesmen and urban dwellers, against a common enemy, resulted in 10,000 casualties, cost the British £40 million, and was only quashed when reinforcements arrived from India.

It became obvious that the Iraqis would no longer tolerate a military regime imposed by the British. The time had come to repay Hussein ibn Ali, the Sharif of Mecca, for his assistance during the Arab Revolt of 1916, when he helped the British in their campaigns against the Turks in Transjordan, Palestine and Syria. Sayyid Talib, a prominent political figure in Basra who coined the alarmingly popular slogan 'Iraq for the Iraqis', was invited for tea at the High Commissioner's residence, arrested, and deported to Ceylon (present-day Sri Lanka) on the pretext of the necessity to preserve law and order. Hussein's son, Faisal, was enthroned on 23 August 1921 after a carefully contrived referendum in which he was 'chosen' by around 96% of the Iraqi people.

The fact that Faisal was a British creation is clearly illustrated in a comment made by Gertrude Bell, a political officer in Baghdad: 'We have had a terrific week, but we've got our King crowned' (see page 69).

The king was kept stronger than any one tribe, but could be challenged by a coalition of tribes. This enabled the British to pursue their divide and rule policy and act as arbitrators in local disputes. The king's political legitimacy was derived from that fact that he was a descendant of the Prophet Mohammed, from his role in the Arab revolt against Ottoman occupation in 1916, and his personal and leadership qualities, which could reconcile the various interest groups in Iraqi society.

In 1924 an elected constituent assembly met for the first time. It was a foreign attempt to introduce democracy in which the ordinary people did not participate. The land-owning elites competed with the families in the cities, Ottoman-trained army officers and bureaucrats. As Helen Metz noted in *Iraq: A Country Study*:

> Iraqi politics was more a shifting alliance of important personalities and cliques than a democracy in the Western sense. The absence of broadly based political institutions inhibited the early nationalist movement's ability to make deep inroads into Iraq's diverse social structure. Thus, despite the widely felt resentment at Iraq's mandate status, the burgeoning nationalist movement was largely ineffective.

One of the major contentious issues of the time – the sovereignty of Mosul – was resolved. The Sykes–Picot Agreement placed it under French influence, but under the Long–Berenger Agreement of 1925 France gave up its claim and was instead given a 25% share in the British-controlled Turkish Petroleum Company (TPC), which had concessionary rights in the area. The British believed Mosul was an oil-rich area, but the first major oil strike was in Kirkuk in 1927.

Other issues, especially those of minority rights and independent homelands, are still plaguing Iraq. The Kurds were promised a state at the end of World War I, as spelled out in the Treaty of Sèvres, which was signed by the Sultan in 1920, but this treaty was not recognised by the Nationalist Turks led by Mustafa Kemal, who were seeking to preserve their Turkish homeland. The subsequent Treaty of Lausanne, signed by the new Mustafa Kemal's Government in 1924, made no mention of the promises previously made at Sèvres, and therefore no-one felt bound by them.

The Kurds were, however, given government positions in Kurdish areas and were allowed to preserve their language and culture, a basic right that was denied them in neighbouring states, especially Turkey. But the British had no qualms about bombing rebellious Kurds into submission. Wing Commander Lewis of 30 Squadron recalls how:

> one would get a signal that a certain Kurdish village had to be bombed ... The RAF pilots were ordered to machine-gun any Kurds who looked hostile.

Meanwhile, the Shias continued to resent their exclusion from public life and high-ranking government positions. In the army, Sunni dominance remained, while the Jews were well represented in commerce. When the Baghdad Chamber of Commerce was set up in 1926 there were five Jewish merchants on its 15-member administrative council.

Britain's legacy in Iraq included the establishment of a Basra–Baghdad–Kirkuk railway, a new route that linked Baghdad with Damascus and Beirut; an indigenous Iraqi army in which the Sunnis dominated the higher ranks; the installation of a system of law courts and a modern police force; an overhaul of the Turkish land-revenue system; and the introduction of sterling-based Iraqi currency. Economic assistance was offered through European banks and the setting up of small-scale industries, such as brick-making, cotton-ginning, cigarette–making, soap-making and tanning, was encouraged. Oil exploitation began.

The development of social services was restricted by financial constraints but a number of elementary, primary, secondary and technical schools were set up, along with higher colleges for law, theology, medicine and engineering. Hospitals and clinics were established in all major and many small towns, and agriculture was assisted to a limited extent. Dates were the most important export crop. Flood dykes along the rivers were strengthened and a number of irrigation works were completed in the centre of the country.

In the historical work *Iraq 1900–1950*, Stephen Longrigg notes that:

> the urban life of Iraq, which was taking its modern form and showing its differences of scene and atmosphere from those of the Turkish era, was sadly hampered in its development by poverty. This limited the activities of both the municipalities and of those central government departments whose work was chiefly urban.

The Iraqis were keen to be rid of British influence, but Britain took a step-by-step approach towards independence through four Anglo-Iraqi treaties: 1922, 1926, 1927 and 1930. Iraq was formally admitted to the League of Nations on 3 October 1932; the mandate was over and a new country had joined the international community.

INDEPENDENCE: THE FIRST 26 YEARS

King Faisal died in 1933 and was succeeded by his son Ghazi I, who remained in power until 1939, when he died in a car crash, attributed by Arab conspiracy theorists to Britain's hidden hand. The next king was Ghazi's infant son, Faisal II. Ghazi's first cousin, Amir Abd al Illah, was made regent. With Nuri Said, the most prominent politician during the emergence of post-Ottoman Iraq, he changed the political orientation of the monarchy. He was murdered by a mob in Baghdad when the revolution of July 1958 overthrew the monarchy. The two previous kings were Arab nationalists who opposed the tribal sheikhs, supported by the British. Illah and Said were Pan Arab Iraqi nationalists who relied on the tribal sheikhs to counter the more insular Iraqi urban nationalist movement. Said fought with Sherif Hussein of Mecca, the Arab political and religious leader who began the successful revolt against the Turks in Arabia in 1916 and proclaimed himself king of Arabia.

The Iraqi share of the inherited Ottoman public debt was written off so the country was free of debt. In 1932 payments to Iraq by oil companies reached a million pounds, nearly a quarter of the whole national revenue. By 1952, oil revenues accounted for 60% of the government's income and spending. While politics was an unstable affair characterised by coups and counter-coups, the oil industry, run by the multinationals, grew steadily and efficiently. Light consumer industries were developed by the locals.

However, Edith and E F Penrose, authors of *Iraq: International Relations and National Development*, drew attention to the failure of successive governments to undertake adequate measures to increase productivity on the land, to improve the position of the farmer, and to reform the social and political structure under which in some areas, particularly in the south, landlords were almost a law unto themselves:

This was undoubtedly one of the most serious political issues of the time. It coincided with the expansion of education, which brought numerous students from the countryside to Baghdad, increased political consciousness, and hastened the passing of traditional attitudes, including the attitude of resignation to conditions of deprivation and class oppression.

COUP AND COUNTER-COUP The military entered Iraqi politics in 1933. Disenchanted with their failure to secure a region in which they could set up a nation state, the Assyrians, the largest Christian minority group, living mostly in the north of Iraq, insisted that their patriarch be given some temporal authority. When this was refused some 800 Assyrians headed for the Syrian border. They were denied entry and returned to Iraq, where General Bakr Sidqi, a Kurd, permitted his men to kill about 600 Assyrians in the village of Simeil (see page 40).

Following this incident, the army became embroiled in a series of coups and counter-coups, which began in 1936 when General Sidqi overthrew the government in the Arab world's first military coup. He allied himself with the reform-oriented Ahali group, but it was an alliance doomed to fail due to Sidqi's ruthless crushing of a tribal revolt (which alienated the Shias), his encouragement of the Kurds to join the army (which alienated the nationalist military elements) and his attack on the liberals and socialists (which outraged the Ahali leaders). Sidqi was murdered in 1937 by an army faction that had turned against him. His death was followed by six successive army coups.

The seventh culminated in the setting up of a government of National Defence in 1941, headed by Rashid Ali Kailani, the prominent politician and Iraq nationalist who had been Prime Minister in 1933, 1940 and finally in 1941. Its pro-German stance was motivated by anti-imperialist and anti-British

THE ARAB BAATH SOCIALIST PARTY (ABSP)

The founders of the ABSP came from the al-Maydan area of Damascus, the quarter known for its militant opposition to the French occupation in the 1920s: Michel Aflaq had a Greek Orthodox background, and Salah al-Din al-Bitar traced his descent to a long line of Sunni notables. As Geoff Simons points out in *Iraq: from Sumer to Saddam*, they created the political movement that would come to dominate Syria and Iraq in the modern world:

> One of their first political acts was to create the Syrian Committee, to aid Iraq during the Rashid Ali Kailani episode (see above). The party was officially founded in 1947. The principal inspiration behind Baath philosophy was that of pan-Arabism: the individual Arab states were regarded as 'regions' of the Arab nation, itself a permanent entity in history. The party preached Arab unity, freedom and socialism.
>
> The Iraqi Baath Party was founded in 1951 and by 1954 had attracted some 500 members. Saddam Hussein, then aged 20, joined the Iraqi branch of the ABSP in 1956.

sentiments. Pro-British politicians fled from Iraq. Meanwhile, Kailani tried to modify the terms of the 1941 Anglo-Iraqi Treaty and placed conditions on Britain's request for troop landings in Iraq. The British response was swift and decisive: 2,250 troops landed at Basra and the country was occupied for a second time.

On 30 May 1941 an armistice was signed: Amir Abd al Illah was reimposed as regent and his right-hand man Nuri Said became a dominant figure in Iraqi politics until the revolution of 1958. Kailani and the pro-German generals fled. They were tried *in absentia* and sentenced to death.

WORLD WAR II During World War II Iraq became a base for the military occupation of Iran, Syria and Lebanon. In 1945 it was a founding member of the Arab League. In the same year it joined the United Nations. In 1955 Iraq signed the Baghdad Pact, a mutual defence treaty with Turkey that later included the UK, Pakistan and Iran.

The issue of Palestine was a dominant foreign policy consideration. Some 40% of government revenues were allocated for the army and for Palestinian refugees. Iraq dispatched an expeditionary force to the West Bank in 1948, which withdrew, along with other Arab forces, after considerable Israeli gains throughout the Palestinian territory. Increasing hostility towards the well-to-do Jewish community led to a mass exodus of about 120,000 Iraqi Jews to Israel between 1948 and 1952.

Grievances with the British-installed monarchy and Nuri Said mounted, largely due to foreign policy rather than domestic issues. Iraq's membership of the Baghdad Pact was not widely supported. In 1948 the Portsmouth Treaty, which called for a board of Iraqis and British representatives to decide on defence matters of mutal interest, led to a major uprising, which resulted in the treaty's repudiation.

During one of Nuri Said's stints as Prime Minister in 1954 (in all, he held some 47 cabinet posts during his career), he banned political parties, which he believed were made up largely of opportunists. Newspapers were suspended and a curfew imposed. The period was characterised by rising inflation, poverty among the city dwellers and the salaried middle classes, corruption in government circles and the enrichment of the elite while the Baghdad slums grew. Widespread discontent was contained by repression and a stifling control over the political process.

In the words of Samira Haj, author of *The Making of Iraq 1900–1963*:

The nationalists in the 1930s and the 1940s were largely reformist in nature. After violent repression and the popular revolts of 1948 and 1952 the opposition began to realise that reform was less likely to happen. The potential for reform ended in the 1950s, especially with the rise in the importance of oil in the political economy of the nation. The sharp increase in state revenues from oil made the government less dependent on the domestic economy for its revenues and as a result less responsive to the needs and demands of the opposition situated outside the political process. However, as the government gained more autonomy, it became isolated, factionalised and politically ineffective, thus making the path for its overthrow in 1958 a much easier one.

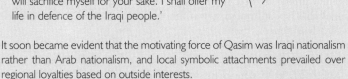

ABDUL KARIM QASIM

Abdul Karim Qasim (1914–63) was a man of the people, a hero of the poor and downtrodden. In *The Changing of Political Power in Iraq, 1958 to 1971*, Dr Lorenzo Kimball described Qasim as a rather quiet, secretive person, born into a lower-middle-class family, who spent practically his entire life in the army:

> He apparently believed he was destined by fate to fulfil a great mission assigned to him by Allah; his dedication finally reached the martyr-complex stage. On August 5, 1958 he declared: 'People, I am the son of the people. I pledge before God that I will sacrifice myself for your sake. I shall offer my life in defence of the Iraqi people.'

It soon became evident that the motivating force of Qasim was Iraqi nationalism rather than Arab nationalism, and local symbolic attachments prevailed over regional loyalties based on outside interests.

Qasim appointed himself Prime Minister and Defence Minister and was known as the sole leader, even though he presided over a civilian-dominated cabinet of 14. In 1969 Qasim hosted a conference for Iran, Iraq, Kuwait, Saudi Arabia and Venezuela to form the Organisation of Petroleum Exporting Countries (OPEC).

An Iraqi lawyer, Jabbar Maan al-Khafaji, now living in exile in London, recalls shaking hands with Qasim when he was leader of a scout group in Abu Ghraib, 30km north of Baghdad, in 1959:

> Qasim was very interested in our activities. Unlike other so-called Iraqi leaders he was not pretentious: he did not live in the Prime Minister's usual residence but in his modest house in the Al Batawein district. He did not amass wealth. He put his salary in his pocket so he could distribute it to the poor. When he was executed he only had a dinar and a quarter on him.

Qasim was executed along with his government members following the coup staged by Baath Party members in 1963.

THE 1958 REVOLUTION AND ITS AFTERMATH

The revolution of 14 July 1958, which toppled the monarchy, was one of the greatest watersheds in modern Iraqi politics. The depth of hatred for the British-installed rulers was illustrated by the killing of King Faisal and his supporters. The body of Nuri Said, the main British protagonist, was run over by buses. Faisal Street in Baghdad became Jamal Abdul Nasser Street.

A request for assistance from the Iraqi military from King Hussein of Jordan, who feared that an anti-Western revolt in Lebanon could spill over into his kingdom, prompted a battalion led by Abdul Karim Qasim (founder of the Free Officers movement, a group dedicated to Iraq Nationalism, with a central committee of 14 members) and Colonel Abdul al-Salam Aref, to move into Baghdad instead of Jordan.

The day after the coup, Qasim issued a public statement in which he proclaimed the liberation of the country from the domination of a corrupt group that was installed by imperialism, announced the formation of an Iraqi republic that would preserve Iraqi unity, and called for brotherly ties with other Arab countries.

Officials of the former monarchistic regime were tried by a special court presided over by Colonel Fadil Abbas Al-Mahdawi. The proceedings were televised live, with Al-Mahdawi often acting as judge and prosecutor, and using his legal position for his own advancement.

In his historical work *The Changing of Political Power in Iraq, 1958 to 1971*, Dr Lorenzo Kimball points out that although many Iraqis were sickened by this travesty of justice and were shocked by the death sentences meted out to once-prominent public figures, it was to Qasim's credit, and also a source of his downfall, that he commuted many of them to prison terms and even rescinded some death sentences.

In March 1959, Iraq announced it was withdrawing from the Baghdad Pact. Two years later Public Law 80 dispossessed the Iraqi Petroleum Company (IPC) of 99.5% of its concession areas. The company could not develop new oil fields: this was left to the newly established Iraq National Oil Company.

SOCIAL CHANGE Unlike the pro-British government, the revolution made dramatic changes to Iraq's social structure: the power of big landed sheikhs and the merchant class was drastically reduced during an extensive land reform programme. The urban centres, Baghdad and Basra especially, grew at a phenomenal rate, with urban dwellers almost tripling between 1958 and 1987. In this period, the population of Baghdad grew by 73%, while Basra's inhabitants increased by 41%. The urban upper class, found mainly in Baghdad, was distinguished from the rest of the population by its political power and wealth. Peasants were drawn to the cities by employment opportunities made possible by an oil-producing country. The construction sector in the cities, and small machine shops, as well as the service industries, made use of their labour. Squatters lived in hastily erected reed and mud huts on the outskirts of the cities.

The middle class also grew during the 1950s and 1960s as education became increasingly accessible to the people and prepared them for civil occupations. The numbers of merchants, shopkeepers, craftsmen, and professional and government officials began to increase steadily.

Qasim believed passionately in bettering the lot of the poor – the urban slum dwellers and the exploited peasants – but not at the expense of the wealthy. A slum reform programme was instituted in Baghdad, political prisoners were released, trade and peasant unions were recognised, rents went down along with food prices, and spending on health, education and housing increased. The Communist Party, once suppressed by Nuri Said and forced to remain underground during the monarchistic era, became an important force in Iraqi politics. Relations with the Soviet Union were re-established and economic co-operation, along with arms sales, began.

INTERNAL CONFLICT In March 1959 army officers from conservative, Sunni backgrounds who objected to Qasim's strong links with the communists attempted to overthrow him. Qasim and his allies mobilised 250,000 supporters in Mosul and a massacre of nationalists and leading Mosul families followed. This was not the only attempt to topple the government. Saddam Hussein, Iraq's future president, took part in an assassination attempt in which Qasim was injured. Abd al-Salam Aref, the man who had been so instrumental in Qasim's coup, also tried to overthrow Qasim after he was relieved of his post as Deputy Prime Minister following disagreements about his pro-Nasser stance.

Despite its attempts at genuine reform, though, Qasim's government was plagued with many problems, both domestic and foreign. For one, the communists were getting too powerful. In Kirkuk one of their rallies resulted in a battle with the Turcomans, and Qasim decided it was time for a crackdown. Iraqi Communist Party (ICP) members were removed from sensitive government positions, union activities were curtailed and communist newspapers were shut down.

The Kurds, who supported the 1958 revolution, soon found themselves at odds with the government, as the new constitution – which clearly stated that they would be equal partners in Iraq's development – was only a paper promise. In 1961 Kurdish *peshmergas* (guerrillas) were involved in extensive fighting with the Iraqi army, who were not as effective as the *peshmerga* in the rugged mountain terrain.

During Qasim's era Iraq lost many of its Arab and foreign 'friends'. It made a claim on Kuwait based on the fact that it was part of Basra during Ottoman times. Those states that recognised Kuwait severed diplomatic relations with Iraq. They included the United States, Japan and Iran.

Qasim left power just as he had gained it – through a military coup. It took place on 8 February 1963. He was executed the next day. The coup was carried out by the Arab Baath Socialist Party (see page 73) with the assistance of the army. One of its main instigators was Abd al-Salam Aref. This time he was successful in toppling Qasim.

In his analysis of the factors that contributed to Qasim's downfall, Kimball identifies the failure to produce a permanent constitution and an electoral system:

> Qasim failed to acquire a political constituency of his own but continually played one party or group off against the other. He quarrelled with and agitated his neighbours, and his foreign policy decisions, especially his claim to Kuwait and Iraq's withdrawal from the Baghdad Pact, put Iraq at odds with a large portion of the world. He seemed endlessly bogged down in a hopeless war to suppress the Kurds and he managed to antagonise a large segment of the Iraqi army. Despite his noble aims, Qasim failed to establish a modern Iraqi state. But his faults and miscalculations are minor misjudgements compared with those of the rulers who followed him and dragged Iraq into the abyss of totalitarianism and futile wars.

BAATH RULE After seizing power the Baathists set up the Revolutionary Command Council as their highest policy-making body. Ahmad Hassan Al Bakr became prime minister and Aref president. But the party was not united and did not have any clear policies. It was dominated by cliques from the same village, town or tribe, and relied on the paramilitary National Guard to counter the lack of support in the regular army.

The Baathists were sharply divided between the hardliners and the pragmatic, more moderate left wing. They too were unable to quell the Kurdish unrest in the north and they only stayed in power for nine months, before being overthrown by military officers in a bloodless coup in November 1963.

Following this coup, Abd al-Salam Aref assumed more effective power, dissolved the National Guard and remained President until 1966. Lorenzo Kimball described how his rule:

> saw the creation of a one-party system dedicated to Arab socialism, an attempt at reconciliation with Egypt, the formulation of an Iraqi Republic with a new constitution, and the development of plans for economic reform which included the nationalisation of insurance companies, banks, the steel, cement and construction industries, and the tobacco industry, tanneries and flour mills.

Abd ar-Rahman Bazzaz, an Iraqi administrator and politician, was appointed the first civilian Prime Minister since the days of the monarchy. He did his best to get the military out of politics, institute the rule of law and implement a five-year economic plan (1965–70).

After the death of Abd al-Salam Aref in a helicopter crash in 1966, his brother, Major General Abd ar Rahman Aref, took his place. The Kurdish insurgency sapped the government's strength and Aref's freedom of movement was limited by the dominance of the officers who put him in power. Bazzaz pacified the Kurds by promising them control over the municipal administration in the north and allowing the use of the Kurdish language. But the army, fearing its power would be curtailed, opposed the rapprochement.

In the opinion of Phebe Marr, a leading authority on Iraq referred to by Helen Metz in *Iraq: A Country Study*, on the eve of the Six-Day War between Israel and various Arab states, which began on 5 June 1967, the Aref government had become little more than a collection of army officers balancing the special interests of various economic, political, ethnic and sectarian groups. The non-intervention of Iraqi troops while Israel was overtaking the Egyptian, Syrian and Jordanian armies and annexing large tracts of Arab territory discredited the Aref regime in the eyes of the masses.

Colonel Abd ar Razzaq an Nayif and Ibrahim Daud, two disenchanted Aref supporters, staged a successful coup but lacked grass-roots support to hold on to power. They were quickly outmanoeuvred by the well organised Baathists, who again took over the government in 1968. The Baathists, though, had learnt from their previous mistakes. This time they were here to stay.

Part Three

IRAQ NOW

5

Saddam's Iraq

Saddam's Iraq is wonderland of terror, a blood-drenched land where the tentacles of the octopus-like security apparatus reach into every nook and cranny, and where no-one is free from the regime's notorious *mukhabarat* [security service].

Ali Karim, political prisoner

The West has created an Iraqi Frankenstein which has turned against them and cannot be controlled.

Hans-Heino Kopietz, Middle East analyst

An estimated three million citizens were killed during the Baath regime's tenure of power after 1968, while approximately four to five million Iraqis (around 15% of the population) were living in exile.

After seizing power the Baathists were determined to establish their credentials as exponents of Arab nationalism. They adopted an uncompromising position on the Palestinian issue. At the beginning of 1969 a public spectacle was made of the hanging of 11 Jews for spying, but this did little to endear the new regime to Arab public opinion. The Egyptian daily *Al-Ahram* commented that hangings in a public square were certainly not a heart-warming sight, nor were they an occasion for organising a festival. When the Egyptian President Anwar Sadat signed the Camp David Accords with Israel in 1978, Saddam Hussein cherished Egypt's isolation in the Arab world and was eager for Iraq to replace Egypt as a leading regional power.

THE KURDS

An attempt was made by the Baathists to fully integrate the Kurds into society and the state of emergency imposed since 1958 in Kurdish areas was lifted. In March 1970 a 15-article peace plan was announced. It stated that the Kurds should participate fully in government, Kurdish officials would be appointed in northern Iraq, and Kurdish would be the official language alongside Arabic. These positive measures were accompanied by the forced relocation of Kurds to other areas, the settlement of Arabs in northern Iraq and the destruction of Kurdish villages along the 1,300km border with Iran. This carrot-and-stick approach did not work and the guerrilla war began again. However, the Kurdish resistance collapsed in 1975 when Iran and Iraq signed an agreement to end their border dispute at an OPEC meeting in Algiers, and Iranian assistance to the Kurdish rebels ceased.

During the 1970s Saddam Hussein worked tirelessly to consolidate his power base. Helen Metz, author of *Iraq: A Country Study*, notes that despite Baath Party attempts to institutionalise its rule, real power remained in the hands of a narrowly based elite united by loose family and tribal ties:

> By 1977 the most powerful men in the Baath Party were all somehow related to the triumvirate of Saddam Hussein, Ahmed Hassan Al Bakr, and General Adnan Khayrallah Talfah, Saddam Hussein's brother-in-law. All were members of the party, its ruling Revolutionary Command Council and the cabinet, and all were members of the Talfah family of Tikrit, headed by Khayrallah Talfah.

Surnames were abolished to disguise the rule of a single clan: ID cards and birth certificates only recorded the child's first name and the name of the father. But Baathist rule did not go unchallenged. In 1973 the Security Chief, Nazim Kazzar, planned a coup against the military faction of the Baath Party. The attempted coup failed, Kazzar was executed and this led to an amendment of the constitution to give the president more power, and to the formation of a National Front consisting of the Baath Party and the Iraqi Communist Party.

Despite their socialist rhetoric, however, the Baathists had many capitalist tendencies. During the mid-1970s the private sector trebled, and by 1980 there were were hundreds of multi-millionaires in Iraq, most with connections to the Baath Party.

Some efforts were made to employ the country's oil revenues for the benefit of the people, especially through investment in the education and health sectors. Legislation was passed giving women equal pay. The number of students in technical fields increased more than 300% between 1976 and 1986 to more than 120,090. In the mid-1980s Iraq also made substantial progress in controlling malaria, trachoma, influenza, measles, whooping cough and tuberculosis. But much of the country's revenue went into the pockets of the ruling elite.

The chapter on 'Funny Money' in Jeffrey Robinson's book *The Laundrymen* illustrates Saddam's financial astuteness:

> In June 1972, Iraq nationalised its petroleum interests. Saddam, who was then Deputy President, convinced the ruling revolutionary council that the commission they'd been paying to Westerners under long-standing agreements should go to the Baath Party. So he took a page out of the life of Calouste Sarkis Gulbenkian.
>
> A Turk of Armenian descent, Gulbenkian was the founding power behind what came to be known as the Iraqi Petroleum Company. For his efforts, he laid claim to a royalty on every drop of its oil. His fee gave birth to his nickname, Mr Five Percent. When he died in Lisbon in 1955, the royalty was passed on to his son Nubar. Some 17 years later, Saddam confiscated Nubar's 5% in the name of the Baath Party. Saddam personally assumed joint custody of the funds, sharing signature authority with Defence Minister Adnan Khayrallah and Petroleum Minister Adnan Hamdani.

According to a document claiming to be a true accounting of those funds, US$51 million was deposited in a major Swiss bank in Geneva in 1972. With interest, the balance in the account climbed to US$92 million the following year and, as the price of oil quadrupled during the Yom Kippur War, to US$327 million in 1974. By the time the Iran–Iraq War broke out – with Saddam now firmly in control of the country – the account held in excess of US$1.69 billion. Overall, Saddam controlled funds worth some US$32 billion.

But the capitalist tendency did not mean a pro-Western foreign policy, and relations with the West, especially America, remained poor. A number of foreigners were expelled for spying. Relations with the Soviet Union were warm, and the Soviets kept the Iraqis supplied with weapons.

On 16 July 1979 Saddam Hussein finally realised his ambition. President Bakr was ousted and he became President of the Republic, Secretary General of the Baath Party Regional Command, Chairman of the Revolutionary Command Council and Commander-in-Chief of the armed forces. Iraq was now Saddam's Iraq, a country ruled with an iron fist and an 'octopus-like' security apparatus that extended its tentacles into every sphere of life.

SADDAM HUSSEIN: A BRUTAL LEGACY LIVES ON

Saddam Hussein, became a brutal dictator and ruled Iraq for 24 years. He was the only man who could prevent repeated coups and keep the country united. The violent policies of confrontation, which managed to subdue his opponents inside Iraq, proved fatal when dealing with foreign powers.

During Saddam's presidency Iraq fought an eight-year war with Iran, invaded Kuwait and was ousted by a multinational coalition. Iraq's defiance of the international community and pursuit of weapons of mass destruction led to the imposition of one of the most stringent sanctions regimes in history, another war in 2003 and American and British occupation. Saddam, a master of the art of survival, escaped American bombs on buildings where he was supposedly staying and was only captured in December 2003. US forces found him hiding in an underground refuge on a farm near Tikrit.

Defiant till the end, he used his trial for the 1982 massacre in Dujail as a political platform, challenging the legitimacy of the court, and claiming that everyone knows Kuwait is part of Iraq and that Bush is the real criminal.

Saddam Hussein was born in 1937 in the poor village of Al-Awja a few weeks after his father passed away. He was taunted for being illegitimate but the bullying stopped when he acquired his first pistol at the age of ten and became a streetwise Tikriti gangster. During his unhappy childhood he had to steal eggs and chickens to feed his family. His stepfather was cruel and beat him with an asphalt-covered stick. He ran away to live with his uncle, Khairallah Tulfa. Eager for knowledge he persuaded his uncle to send him to school, but academic achievements were not his forte. He was rejected by the military academy due to his poor attendance and performance, but after becoming president he forced the academy to change its records and turn him into a star pupil.

In 1955, at the age of 18, Saddam took up residence in Baghdad for further education. He joined the Arab Baath Socialist Party, which was his vehicle for social mobility. He was involved in an unsuccessful assassination attempt against the country's leader, General Abdul Karim Qasim, which prompted him to escape to Egypt where he studied law. Nasser's oratory held him spellbound and he was influenced by enthusiastic talk of Arab unity.

He returned to Iraq in 1963 following the first Baathist coup. In 1969, aged 32, he became the second-in-command of the Baathist regime. The government was headed by a distant relation, General Ahmad Hassan Al-Bakr, but Saddam soon became the power behind the throne. He focused on building up the party's security apparatus and placed his three younger half-brothers, Barzan, Watban and Sabawi, in key security positions.

In 1963 he married his cousin Sajida Talfah and had two sons, Uday and Qusay, and three daughters, Raghad, Rana and Hala. Samira Shabandar became his second wife and gave birth to his youngest son Ali. Uday was a notorious playboy, banished to Switzerland for a time for a murder. Qusay was put in charge of supervising the intelligence and security service. Both sons were killed in Mosul by American troops in July 2003. Saddam took a third wife, dancer Nedhal Al-Hamdani, and had a mistress, Parisoula Lampsos, for three decades.

The '70s were used for bolstering his position within the Baath Party. His notable achievements were an illiteracy eradication programme, building housing for the poor, expanding the education system and developing the petrochemical industry.

The USA assisted him in his endeavours towards self-sufficiency by providing small arms, and an American company supplied the design for his first chemical warfare plant. He imported some of the best brains in the Arab world for Iraq's arms industry. British Foreign Office papers released by The National Archives at the end of December 2007 revealed that defence sales to Iraq in 1976 amounted to an estimated £70 million, and that Iraq paid Britain £500,000 to train Iraqi pilots.

In 1979 Saddam Hussein forced Al-Bakr to resign by threatening him and his family. Those who stood in the way to his acquisition of total power were tried by a revolutionary court 'for plotting against the Arab nation' and sentenced to death. Senior positions in government and the military were filled with members of his tribe. Much of Iraq's new-found oil wealth went into the family's coffers.

Saddam used history to help legitimise his position. He claimed descent from the Prophet Mohammed and had his name engraved on the bricks used in the rebuilding of Babylon. The Iran–Iraq War was known as 'Saddam's Qadisiyah' after the Arabs' early Islamic victory over the Persians. He loved being the boss and was head of 42 government departments. Extravagance was a hallmark of his presidency, with presidential palaces built from Argentine marble costing US$4,000 a square metre. After the 1991 Gulf War he built eight more palaces, one larger than Versailles.

When Ayatollah Khomeini called on Iraqi Muslims to rebel in 1980, Saddam started an eight-year war with Iran, which resulted in more than half-a-million casualties. The West regarded him as a bulwark against Islamic fundamentalism and turned a blind eye to his use of chemical weapons against the Kurds in March 1988, when 5,000 died in the village of Halabja. The war left Iraq with debts of around US$80bn. The oil-rich Gulf states, who no longer felt threatened by Iran, abandoned Iraq, and the West, concerned about Iraq's unconventional weapons programme and its attempts to build an atomic bomb, froze credit.

Unsuccessful negotiations with Kuwait over the issue of oil over-production convinced the ever paranoid Saddam that America and Kuwait were trying to overthrow him. On 2 August 1990 his forces invaded Kuwait and, despite Iraq's disastrous defeat at the hands of a multinational coalition, Saddam insisted that his country emerged victorious in 'the mother of all battles'. The subsequent uprising, in Iraq, of March 1991 was ruthlessly crushed in the south. In the north the Kurds fled to the mountains and the West responded to their plight through the creation of a safe haven, which evolved into a de facto state. The regime's opponents were dealt with with a vengeance: Shia clerics were assassinated, army officers who were suspected of plotting against the regime were executed, and Saddam increased the number of his look-alikes – sometimes they appeared in two places at once.

United Nations' resolutions imposed sanctions requiring Iraq to get rid of its weapons of mass destruction, or WMDs. The country remained under these sanctions for 13 years. Thousands died from malnutrition and Iraq became the Bangladesh of the Middle East. Saddam prospered through the lucrative black market in goods that circumvented the UN's embargo and the Tikritis became increasingly corrupt and despotic. Apparently he enjoyed Western confectionery, especially Quality Street. In 2000 he was listed the 55th richest person in the world by *Forbes* magazine, which put his wealth at US$7bn.

A UN Security Council resolution in November 2002 demanded the return of weapons inspectors to Iraq and acceptance of all previous UN resolutions. When Saddam allowed the inspectors to return the USA and UK raised their demands, accused him of new crimes against humanity and violations of UN resolutions and called for an invasion.

In September 2007 the Spanish newspaper *El Pais* reported that Saddam Hussein had offered to step down and go into exile peacefully just one month before the invasion of Iraq in return for US$1 billion. The offer was revealed in a transcript of talks between US President George W Bush and the then Spanish Prime Minister José María Aznar at the former's Texas ranch. According to the transcript published in *El Pais*, Bush told Aznar in February 2003 that the Iraqi dictator had made the exile offer via the Eygptian government. But Bush made it clear in the meeting that he expected to 'be in Baghdad at the end of March'. 'It's like Chinese water torture,' he said of the UN negotiations. 'We've got to put an end to it.'

Under the pretext of the regime's violation of UN resolutions (no WMDs were ever found in Iraq) American and British soldiers launched a swift military assault on the country. After three weeks the Baathist regime was no more, the army offered only token resistance and a new era began.

In December 2003 Saddam was captured. It took two years to bring him to trial. One of his American guards observed a mellowed tyrant who loved muffins, enjoyed watering plants and took an interest in the guard's family. In one of his last statements, Saddam called on all Iraqis, Arabs and Kurds, to forgive, reconcile and shake hands. On 5 November 2005 he was convicted on charges relating to the deaths of 148 people in Dujail in 1982 and sentenced to death. He was hanged on 30 December 2006, aged 69.

In his newspaper obituary for *The Independent*, David Hirst commented that:

> Like Stalin (who Saddam greatly admired) he had little of the flair or colour of other 20th century despots, little mental brilliance, less charisma, no redeeming passion or messianic fervour: he was only exceptional in the magnitude of his thuggary, the brutality, opportunism and cunning of the otherwise dull, grey apparatchik.

Iraq's first ambassador to the UK after Saddam's overthrow, Dr Salah Al-Shaikhly, observed that the capture of Saddam was a good morale booster:

> But we have to make sure that the demise of Saddam can also mean the demise of Saddamism in Iraq. The singer may have gone but the song will linger for a long time.

On the first anniversary of Saddam's execution black graffiti praising him appeared in his hometown of Al-Awja. The slogans on the town's police, electricity and agricultural buildings read: 'There is no life without the sun and no dignity without Saddam' and 'Paradise for the hero Saddam'. His tomb was covered with flowers.

THE IRAN–IRAQ WAR

Saddam was not content to stamp his imprint on one country: conquest was on his mind and in 1980 oil revenues of US$21.3 billion made him confident he could easily bankroll his political adventures. In the same year, he started the Iran–Iraq War, which permanently altered the course of Iraqi history

For Saddam the time was right for flexing his personal power; he had the money, and he was secretly encouraged by leading American, British, French and Russian politicians and industrialists, who not only saw the political advantages but also the financial benefits in keeping Iran, with its spreading religious influence, to its own side of the Gulf. Saddam knew that the West would not interfere despite the media noise and discussions in their parliaments and assemblies. One of his other strands of motivation came from the old adage 'keep the poor on your side by giving them an enemy.' Large numbers of his foot soldiers were made up of Shias from the south, who readily fought as Iraqis against their Iranian co-religionists.

The war strained Iraqi political and social life and led to severe economic dislocations.

In *Iraq: A Country Study*, Helen Metz said that:

> The outbreak of hostilities in 1980 was, in part, just another phase of the ancient Persian-Arab conflict that had been fuelled by twentieth-century border disputes. Many observers, however, believe that Saddam Hussein's decision to invade Iran was a personal miscalculation based on ambition and a sense of vulnerability. Saddam Hussein, despite having

made significant strides in forging an Iraqi nation-state, feared that Iran's new revolutionary leadership would threaten Iraq's delicate Sunni–Shia balance and would exploit Iraq's geo-strategic vulnerabilities – Iraq's minimal access to the Persian Gulf. In this respect, Saddam Hussein's decision to invade Iran has historical precedent; the ancient rulers of Mesopotamia, fearing internal strife and foreign conquest, also engaged in frequent battles with the peoples of the highlands.

Iraq invaded Iran on 22 September 1980. Prior to the invasion two leading Iraqi Shia personalities, Ayatollah Baqr al-Sadr and his sister Bint al-Huda, were hanged and 97 members of the leading Islamic Dawa Party were executed. Not only were the Ayatollah and his sister hugely respected, but Saddam was taking no chances with the influence of the Islamic Dawa Party in the country, especially in the Shia south, at such a critical time. Ayatollah Khomeini commented that 'the war that the Iraqi Baath wants to ignite is a war against Islam.'

The eight-year war (1980–88) can be divided into several stages: the Iraqi invasion, Iraqi retreats, the war of attrition, the tanker war and the war of the cities.

The Iraqi attacks began with the bombing of Iran's air bases at Mehrabad and Doshen Tappen. At the same time six Iraqi divisions crossed the border into Iran and occupied some 1,000km² of territory, leaving the Iranian army in a state of shock and confusion. But the Iranians refused a settlement offer. In January 1981 Iraqi forces were stopped on the Karun River, largely through 'human wave' assaults in which thousands of recruits in Iran's popular army were killed. The soldiers were convinced that martyrdom in the war guaranteed a place in paradise and some even wore keys to heaven around their necks. The first major Iranian victory was the recapture of Abadan in September 1981.

In March 1982, when it was realised that a quick, guaranteed victory was not a certainty, Iraq indicated it was prepared to negotiate a settlement, but Iran refused. In 1983, three major, unsuccessful human-wave offensives were launched by Iran and the casualties on both sides started rising. An estimated 120,000 Iranians and 60,000 Iraqis lost their lives in the first three years of the war.

Iraq had severed diplomatic relations with the USA following the 1967 Arab-Israeli war, but after 1968 the Iraqi government became interested in acquiring American technology. In her description of American-Iraqi relations, Helen Metz, author of *Iraq: A Country Study*, noted that:

Concern about the 1979 Islamic Revolution in Iran and about the Soviet invasion of Afghanistan prompted Iraq to re-examine seriously the nature of its relationship with the United States. This process led to a gradual warming of relations between the two countries. In 1981 Iraq and the United States engaged in low-level, official talks on matters of mutual interest such as trade and regional security. The following year the United States extended credits to Iraq for the purchase of American agricultural commodities, the first time this had been done since 1967. More significantly, in 1983 the Baathist government hosted a United States special Middle East envoy, the highest-ranking American official to visit Baghdad in more than eighteen years. In 1984, when the United States inaugurated 'Operation Staunch' to halt shipment of arms to Iran

'My story is a complicated one,' Saad Sahib said. 'I was a prisoner of war in Iran for 21 years.'

I had heard stories about captured prisoners in Iran but had never met one. They were captured during the Iran–Iraq war of the 1980s and thousands were held for years in appalling conditions in Iranian jails. Some were recruited into the Shia Iraqi opposition party that was based in Tehran and close to the ayatollahs (The Supreme Islamic Council), but others, particularly the more secular ones, were released only years later and some only when Saddam's regime fell. They lived for years in confinement and then returned to families who thought them dead and to a country dramatically altered by time and by war.

Sahib was an Arab nationalist and he said this had meant he was held longer than most of the other prisoners. He was against Saddam but patriotic to Iraq, and he was in one of the last groups of prisoners to be released, returning to Iraq just one day before the US invasion. He was a poet before he was a soldier, and during his time in jail he continued to write poetry, even though paper and pens were forbidden. It was impossible for him to remember all the poems in his head so he would write on paper he tore out of Iranian cigarette packets. He spent several minutes describing to me an elaborate writing system he and his cellmates had invented. They would dissolve a red antibiotic tablet in water to make a red-coloured liquid, the ink, and they used a disposable syringe to write. Once, they tried to fashion a writing board using empty detergent boxes. They tore strips of cloth from their clothes and sewed them to the board and then covered the cloth in a paste made from detergent and shampoo. They covered the paste with a piece of nylon and would then write on that with a toothbrush, and somehow it left a script that was legible to the prisoners.

I asked what he wrote about. Sahib said his thoughts were mostly about homesickness, about being away from his family, and about his desire for a woman.

by third countries, no similar embargo was attempted against Iraq because Saddam Hussein's government had expressed its desire to negotiate an end to the war. All of these initiatives prepared the ground for Iraq and the United States to establish diplomatic relations in November 1984.

During the eight-year war Iran and Iraq suffered from poor leadership and co-ordination of their forces. Many decisions that should have been taken in the field were referred to the capital. One of the most serious developments was the use of chemical weapons on 40 occasions by Iraq, which was criticised by the then UN Secretary General, Pérez de Cuellar. Both sides were bombing each other's oil tankers. In 1985 population centres and industrial complexes were targeted more frequently. Morale was affected as bodies were returned from the front and funerals in every neighbourhood became a regular occurrence.

When a truce finally came into effect on 20 August 1988 neither country had lost much territory and both countries were still being ruled by the same leaders. Iran consolidated its Islamic revolution and Iraq was now the most powerful state in the region.

I asked him if he could recite one of his prison poems for me. He sat quietly for so long that I thought I had asked too much of him. Then:

> From far, far away, I send longing greetings with
> The wind.
> All my insides are screaming Iraq, Iraq.
> But who carries the papers, who carries the
> Recommendations?
> Our days are strange, our clothes are miserable,
> Mirrors are afraid of our faces,
> I lost my soul and it was scattered from my hand
> In the darkness of the corners.

When Sahib eventually returned home he found his baby sister had grown up and married and his parents were dead. It has been hard for him to adjust to living at home again: when I met him he was unmarried and out of work, surviving on a monthly military pension of just 75,000 dinars – around £30. In jail he and his cellmates had tried to encourage each other by imagining what it would be like on the day they returned, all that they would find again, the tastes, the smells. In the end it had been a great disappointment. He was depressed by the Iraq he had returned to. He sensed that the years of sanctions and the recent war had changed the way people behaved.

'People are so tired. Faith is gone, sincerity is gone. The sincerity between relatives, between husband and wife, it is gone,' he said. 'Selfishness is flooding into our society. I know it is because of the critical circumstances these days, but it is making people greedy. I feel a stranger here.'

Rory McCarthy, author of Nobody Told Us We Are Defeated: Stories from the New Iraq

The cost in terms of human life and resources was phenomenal: 194,931 Iranians and an estimated 160,000–240,000 Iraqis lost their lives. The war cost Iran US$74–91 billion and military imports amounted to US$11.26 billion. Iraq spent US$94–112 billion on the war. Military imports totalled US$102 billion.

Geoff Simons, author of *Iraq: From Sumer to Saddam*, commented on the West's willingness to sell weapons to Iraq:

> The facts are plain enough. The brutal record of Saddam Hussein
> throughout the 1980s was well known: it is still true (however
> unfashionable it is to declare it) that free enterprise business will sup
> with any devil – even a Saddam Hussein – if there is money to be made.

THE INVASION OF KUWAIT

At the end of the Iran–Iraq War Saddam pretended to launch an Iraqi *perestroika* with promises of a new constitution, a multi-party political system and a free press. But just two years after the war with Iran the Iraqi people were once again dragged into another conflict. At the end of July 1990 Iraq and Kuwait held talks that failed: the Iraqis accused the Kuwaitis of not wanting to rectify the harm they had done to Iraq by depressing oil prices in mid-July, which they had achieved by increasing their daily oil production at the behest of the West's industrial nations.

On 2 August 1990 Iraq invaded Kuwait. The response of the international community was swift: on 6 August sanctions were imposed and by 29 November the UN Security Council had adopted Resolution 678, authorising 'all necessary means', including the use of force, to restore international peace and security in the area. A number of diplomatic initiatives to resolve the crisis peacefully failed. On 14 January 1991 the Iraqi parliament decided to go to war rather than withdraw, and two days later the air campaign began. By late February the US-led coalition composed of 28 UN-member states had flown a total of 91,000 air missions over Iraq and Kuwait. On 3 March Iraq accepted ceasefire terms outlined during a meeting of its military commanders and the commander of the multinational force, General Norman Schwarzkopf of the US army. A popular uprising, concentrated largely in the north and south of the country, followed the Gulf War.

DR SAHIB AL-HAKIM: I AM AFRAID THE BAATHISTS COULD COME BACK

Dr Sahib Al-Hakim, 65, has created a custom-made 2007 diary. On the purple cover is a yellow sticker with the sentence: '2007 – the first year without Saddam.'

Reflecting on his 24 years as a human rights activist, Dr Al-Hakim, who set up the Organisation of Human Rights in Iraq in 1982, believes that the trial of Saddam was more important than toppling him. 'Many Iraqi leaders were toppled but none of them were put on trial,' he pointed out. 'It was the first time an Arab, Muslim leader was tried publicly.'

For seven years (1997–2003) Dr Al Hakim organised a weekly picket in London's Trafalgar Square calling for the trial, and over a million people signed the petition. The picket lasted for 333 weeks; Saddam's regime fell on 9 April 2003. 'Three times three is nine – is it a coincidence?' Dr Al-Hakim wonders.

Throughout his 24-year 'career' as a human rights activist Dr Al-Hakim has always used his real name in interviews:

All members of the Al-Hakim family who spoke out against Saddam used their real names, unlike others who call themselves Abu (father of) so and so.

And they paid the ultimate price – 65 members of the Al-Hakim family were executed by Saddam's regime.

It is still unsafe for Dr Al-Hakim to visit Iraq. He has been five times already, but his family is advising him not to return. Saddam's intelligence service wrote a 36-page report about his anti-regime activities and on his first trip to Baghdad two months after the regime fell, he learned that a reward of a quarter of a million dollars had been offered for his capture or assassination:

I will go back but I will adopt a very low profile – no media interviews. I just want to see my city again and my family. I will also have a look at my house from the outside.

Despite the rhetoric of Western leaders who advocated the overthrow of the Iraqi regime and the establishment of a democratic state, however, the multinational force did not intervene to support the Iraqi people in their attempt to overthrow the regime.

Basically the forces were not able to understand or react quickly enough to deal with this political and potentially more long-term solution to Iraqi problems. So much for the superior, sophisticated, intellectual stance of the USA, Britain and Europe in these situations. Many lessons are still waiting to be learnt.

More than two million Kurdish people fled to the mountains after the uprising failed. They were dying at the rate of 450 to 750 a day because of diarrhoea, acute respiratory infections and trauma. This catastrophe prompted the setting up of a 'safe-haven' for the Kurds in northern Iraq. In October 1991, the Iraqi government withdrew all services from Iraqi Kurdistan, and the Iraqi Kurdistan Front (IKF) later held elections for a 105-member Kurdish National Assembly: a de facto Kurdish state had been established and it is now run by the

Dr Al-Hakim's house was confiscated by the Baathists, along with his clinic and the clinic of his wife, Dr Bayan Alaraji.

He commented that the pattern of human rights violations in Iraq has changed:

During Saddam's regime the security forces, intelligence services, and organisations like Baath youth organisations and women's organisations were spying on the Iraqis. Today the Iraqi government is not violating human rights. The culprits are ex-Baathists, Takfiris (extremist Sunnis and Wahabis who class the Shias as unbelievers who must be killed), the Americans and private security firms. The Americans have bombed Diwaniyah, Sadr City, Haditha and Al Washesh. Christians have also been killed by Sunni extremists.

Dr Al-Hakim emphasised that Iraq's most senior Shia scholar, Grand Ayatollah Ali Sistani, has issued a fatwa against the killing of ex-Baathists. Dr Al-Hakim admits there were reprisals against the Sunnis after the destruction of the Al Askari mosque in Samarra in February 2006, 'but this was a reaction to an action.' The deportation of Shias and Sunnis from their traditional places of residence, especially in Baghdad, is one of the most stark violations of human rights.

One of Dr Al-Hakim's worst fears is the return of the Baathists. 'The Baath Party came to power twice and they could come to power again with the help of the Saudis.'

He has over 8,000 documents and photos recording Saddam's scandalous abuse of human rights. His latest publication is a four-volume, 20-year, 3,380-page effort: *The Encyclopedia of Killing and Torture of Religious Shia Leaders and Students of Islamic Schools in the country of mass graves, Iraq, 1968-2003.*

He is currently working on a book about the martyrs who were killed by Saddam's regime. 'Their families are not looked after by the Iraqi government – the new generation will forget them,' Dr Al-Hakim said.

His dream is to house his 8,000 document archive in a museum in Iraq when it is safe to return. But the future 'looks very bad, very gloomy', and he is now scanning the material and publishing it on the internet.

Kurdistan Regional Government. But no similar assistance was offered to the people of the south who were brutally suppressed.

Throughout the Iran–Iraq War the Baathist regime adopted a policy of guns and butter to ensure the civilians did not suffer undue hardships. But the civilians were the main victims of the 1991 Gulf War. This time there were no generous allowances for the parents and relatives of war heroes. The country had been bombed out of the 20th century. Estimates of the numbers of Iraqi soldiers killed in the conflict vary between 30,000 and 100,000. Between 3,000 and 5,000 civilians died in the Allied bombing raids and 105,000 Iraqis died during the subsequent uprising, and from diseases that spread rapidly due to damage to the country's infrastructure.

As reported by the *New York Times* and *Washington Post*, US aircraft alone dropped 88,000 tons of explosives on Iraq, the equivalent of nearly five Hiroshima nuclear blasts. Some 70% of the so-called smart bombs missed their intended targets, falling sometimes on civilian dwellings, schools, churches, mosques or empty fields. But the 30% that blasted on target wiped out Iraq's electricity generating plants and sewage treatment networks. Iraq's infrastructure – its bridges, roads, highways, canals and communication centres – was systematically destroyed.

Felicity Arbuthnot, a journalist who has been to Iraq at least once a year since the imposition of sanctions in 1990, said:

> To reflect on 13 years of visits to Iraq since the Gulf War is to reflect on a decline from the impossible to the apocalyptic. Iraq is a society stripped of assets, infrastructure and human dignity.

WHAT HAPPENED TO SADDAM'S FAMILY?

Raghad Hussein, Saddam's favourite and eldest daughter, is living in a smart suburb of Amman, Jordan. She fled Baghdad at night after the 2003 invasion and was active in organising her father's defence. She was keen to engage Anthony Scrivenor, a former chairman of the Bar Council who said in an article in *The Independent on Sunday* that 'the trial of Saddam Hussein and his colleagues has already degenerated into the realms of a promising theatrical farce.' An Interpol warrant has been issued for her arrest at the instigation of the Iraqi government, who accuse her of 'crimes against life, incitement and terrorism', but the Jordanian government has rejected requests for her extradition. Official conditions of her remaining in Jordan stipulate that she does not engage in political activities. A crew member of the Channel 4 film *Saddam's Tribe* remembers Raghad and her sister Rana spending US$9,000 in 20 minutes at duty-free shops in Qatar.

Ali, Saddam's surviving son, is living with his mother, the dictator's second wife Samira Shahbandar, in Lebanon.

Saddam's sons, Uday and Qusay, were shot by Coalition forces in July 2003. Saddam's half-brother, Barzan, has been executed. His cousin Ali Hussein Al Majid ('Chemical Ali') has been sentenced to death. His execution has been approved by Iraq's presidency.

The Independent, *21 August 2007*

6

Life Under Sanctions

The Identity Card

The name is love
The class is mindless
The school is suffering
The governorate is sadness
The city is sighing
The street is misery
The home number is one thousand sighs

> Poem written by an Iraqi schoolchild who died because
> drugs that could have saved his life arrived too late.

We are in the process of destroying an entire society. It is as simple and
terrifying as that. It is illegal and immoral.

> Dennis Halliday, former UN Assistant Secretary
> General and Humanitarian Co-ordinator in Iraq

CHRONOLOGY

1990

3 Aug	United Nations Security Council passed Resolution 661 imposing international sanctions against Iraq and freezing all foreign assets. The 70% of all foods, agricultural necessities, pharmaceuticals and medical supplies that were imported could no longer be obtained.
2 Sep	Iraq ordered food rationing.

1991

17 Jan	The Gulf War started. For the next 42 days Iraq was subjected to an average of 2,000 bombing raids a day.
13 Feb	Al-Amariyah bomb shelter in Baghdad bombed, killing up to 400 people.
26 Feb	Iraq announced withdrawal from Kuwait. Retreating Iraqi soldiers bombed on the Basra Road.
28 Feb	Ceasefire agreed.

Mar	Popular uprising in 14 out of 18 Iraqi governorates brutally crushed by the army.

1992

27 Aug	No-fly zone declared south of the 32nd parallel and north of the 36th parallel.
24 Sep	*New England Journal of Medicine* stated that an estimated 46,700 Iraqi children under five had died from the combined effects of war and sanctions in the first seven months of 1991.
27 Dec	US shot down Iraqi MIG for flying in the southern no-fly zone.

1993

13–19 Jan	France and Britain bombed anti-aircraft sites in the north and south of Iraq. The Pentagon announced these attacks could continue without further warnings.
26 Jun	Bill Clinton ordered the firing of 23 Tomahawk missiles on downtown Baghdad in retaliation for an Iraqi attempt on the life of George Bush, who was visiting Kuwait.

1994, May	International conference in Malaysia condemned sanctions. Ralph Ekeus of the United Nations Special Commission (UNSCOM) (on Iraq's weapons) stated that Iraq complied with UN resolutions.

1995, Apr	Oil-for-food programme agreed, in principle, allowing Iraq to sell up to two billion dollars' worth of oil in a 180-day period and use the revenue to buy food, medicine and other basic necessities approved by the United Nations.

1996

May	Madeleine Albright was asked whether the death of half a million children was a price worth paying to get rid of Saddam Hussein. She replied: 'It's a hard choice but the price, we think the price is worth it.'
Dec	Oil-for-food programme commenced.

1997, Nov	Iraq demanded a timetable for the end of sanctions and this was denied.

1998

13 Jan	Iraq blocked weapons inspections.
11 Feb	Iraq agreed to inspection of eight presidential sites. Offer rejected by USA and Britain. Crisis escalated.
23 Feb	UN Secretary General Kofi Annan in Baghdad – announced the triumph of diplomacy over sabre-rattling at a press conference with the Iraqi Deputy Prime Minister.

16 Dec	UNSCOM withdrew from Iraq. UK and USA began a four-day bombing campaign stating that Iraq had failed to comply with UNSCOM demands. American and British planes continued to patrol the no-fly zone and to bomb anti-aircraft defences.

1999 US and UK forces flew more than 6,000 sorties and dropped more than 1,800 bombs on Iraq. Around 450 targets were hit. The Pentagon spent more than US$1 billion on its force of 200 airplanes, 19 warships and 22,000 troops in the area.

2000

1 Feb — Hans von Sponeck, the UN Senior Representative in Baghdad responsible for coordinating humanitarian aid, resigned because he believed the sanctions were unfairly harming the civilian population.

Mar — The Iraqi Communist Party reported on the mass execution of prisoners in Makasib and Abu Graib Prisons.

2001

16 Feb — British and US planes bombed the outskirts of Baghdad. The UN was not informed prior to the military action being taken, a fact that was condemned throughout the Middle East.

28 Apr — Saddam Hussein celebrated his 64th birthday. Iraqi exiles estimated the celebrations cost US$8 million.

May — President Saddam's younger son, Qusay, elected to the Baath Party's ruling body, the Regional Command Council, indicating that he is Saddam's likely successor. Huda Saleh Mehji Ammash became the first woman to win a seat on the party executive.

15 May — The Iraqi Health Ministry said 5,696 children under the age of five died of diarrhoea, pneumonia and mal-nutrition-related diseases in April 2001, compared to 347 deaths in the same period in 1989, a year before sanctions were imposed. According to the Iraqi News Agency 1,489,959 people have died as a result of sanctions.

21 May — Iraq rejected 'smart sanctions', a proposed package of restrictions that would see tighter controls on arms, coupled with a relaxation of measures controlling civilian goods.

30 May — The head of the UN oil-for-food programme for Iraq urged the Security Council to put politics aside and focus on improving the humanitarian situation of the Iraqi people.

4 Jul — Two senior Iraqi diplomats requested asylum in the USA.

6 Jul — Iraq accepted a UN resolution extending its oil-for-food programme by another five months.

| 10 Jul | Iraq, for the first time in over a decade, said it was willing to have a dialogue with the UN Human Rights Commission. The moves came after the USA was voted off the 53-member panel in May 2001. |
| 17 Jul | In his speech on the 33rd anniversary of the coup that brought the Baath Party to power, Saddam Hussein urged the Arabs to stand up to Israel. |

INTRODUCTION

Between August 1990 and February 2003 the Iraqi people lived under one of the most stringent sanctions regimes in history. Writing in *The Guardian* in September 1999, James Buchan said:

> Humiliated in war by the West, terrorised by their own government, reduced to paupers, unwelcome anywhere in the world, the Arabs of Iraq are falling to pieces. It is not simply that with their money and savings destroyed and their goods embargoed, their living standards have fallen to the level of at least 30 years ago. In their own eyes, as Iraqis and above all as Arabs, they have been reduced to nothing. I have never seen a people so demoralised. Everybody I met, even the most repellent Baathist thug and extortionist, felt himself a victim.

Corruption was rampant, the crime rate soared and the statistics documenting the fall in living standards and the rise in diseases and infant mortality made horrifying reading.

In July 2001, the official Iraqi News Agency (INA) reported that more than 1.5 million Iraqis, 41% of them children under five, had died from the impact of UN sanctions. Quoting an official report to the United Nations, it said shortages of medicine, vaccines and hospital equipment due to the embargo had, until the end of May, claimed a total of 1,520,417 lives. The deaths included 622,887 children under five. They were caused by diarrhoea, pneumonia and respiratory problems as well as malnutrition, all conditions that were treatable in pre-sanctions Iraq.

The United Nations Food and Agricultural Organisation reported a five-fold increase in child mortality since the imposition of sanctions in 1990. The first surveys conducted by UNICEF since 1991 of child and maternal mortality in Iraq revealed that in heavily populated southern and central parts of the country children under five were dying at more than twice the rate they were ten years before.

The Iraqi opposition, meanwhile, documented the other side of suffering. According to a newsletter produced by the permanent picket of the Iraqi opposition, during the past 30 years Saddam Hussein's regime had killed more than three million citizens, or a million Iraqis every ten years.

The human rights debate took many forms:

> Where are our human rights here in Iraq? We have no electricity, no clean water, no trains, no safe cars, an environment which is being destroyed, and you are bombing us every day. I tell you, we would rather have a real war than this slow death. This is genocide.

The oil-for-food programme, which commenced in December 1996, allowed Iraq to export oil and use part of the money raised to buy basic goods from other countries. Iraq was using its own money to buy these goods: the oil-for-food programme was not humanitarian aid. The nature of the programme was established in an agreement between the UN Secretariat and the government of Iraq from May 1996. This agreement was in turn based upon Security Resolution 986 of 14 April 1995. The UN initially determined that 53% of the oil revenue would be allocated to the humanitarian programme in the areas under the control of the Iraqi government, 30% would go to pay compensation claims arising out of the Gulf War, 13% would go to the UN programme in the Kurdish regions of northern Iraq, and the remainder would be spent on further administrative costs of the UN. The programme was organised in six-month phases. Every six months the Iraqi government presented a proposal of import contracts to be examined and, if judged acceptable, it was approved by the UN Sanctions Committee.

So Nasra al-Sa'adoun, the granddaughter of an Iraqi prime minister who committed suicide rather than surrender to the British, told a journalist from the *New Internationalist* in 1999.

What went into Iraq was determined by the Sanctions Committee. Anything that could be used in the production of chemical, biological or nuclear weapons was banned. That meant no computer equipment, graphite for pencils or chlorine for water. Non-essential items were also prohibited. These included books, magazines, envelopes and paper, coffins, light bulbs, shoes and shoe polish, toys and wheelbarrows. A Briton could be arrested for posting a book or sending medicines to Iraq without permission from the Department of Trade and Industry.

On 7 February 2000 the *Financial Times* stated that 377 oil contracts were on hold in January, while Iraq had received US$300 million out of a possible US$1.5 billion worth of equipment.

In mid-2001 Britain and the USA put forward a 'smart sanctions' programme aimed at easing restrictions on civilian goods and ending smuggling. When these proposals were categorically rejected by the Iraqi government, which demanded a total lifting of sanctions, the oil-for-food programme was extended for another five months.

The Campaign Against Sanctions on Iraq (CASI) emphasised that oil-for-food was never meant to act as an adequate substitute for the independent functioning of the Iraqi economy. Security Council Resolution 986 itself referred to the programme as 'a temporary measure'. The UN Secretary General repeatedly made the same point. In his report of 2 March 2001, he wrote that:

> the programme was never meant to meet all the needs of the Iraqi
> people and cannot be a substitute for normal economic activity in Iraq.

Dr Kamil Mahdi, lecturer in the Economics of the Middle East at the University of Exeter, writing about the sanctions debate in the 24 December 1999 issue of the current affairs magazine *Middle East International*, noted that Iraqis needed to be able to regenerate their economy and resume reconstruction and development:

This means that essential services and the infrastructure have to be given high priority and the import programme has to be geared to raising domestic production. This is impossible under the political and bureaucratic shackles of the Security Council.

The total absence of normal economic activity reduced the majority of Iraqis to a nation of paupers: the damage sanctions inflicted on the regime included collateral damage in a war against society. The average monthly salary of a professional was US$3, compared with US$200 in 1985. It could buy only one of the following: two chickens, one tube of lipstick, four Mars Bars or ten postcards. People sold their possessions to buy food. Those with no possessions to sell sold their bodies, either through prostitution or by providing organs for transplants. A kidney fetched one million Iraqi dinars, or around £320.

Often, when they had nothing left to sell, whole families committed suicide. An academic in his seventies, who had collected books on his travels since he was a child, had three rooms where they were stacked from the floor to the ceiling. They were his friends, his life. One day he walked through the rooms and talked to them saying: 'All my life I've looked after you, I've lavished my money on you and I've loved you and now I have to ask some of you to care for me.' He gathered a few and went to the Friday market where precious, personal collections were sold, bit by bit, and he sat there, week after week, with tears running down his face until not one volume was left.

THE INTELLECTUAL CRISIS

The embargo was not just an economic embargo – it was an intellectual genocide. Addressing the Campaign Against Sanctions on Iraq conference held in Cambridge in 1999, George Joffe, Director of the Centre for North African Studies at Cambridge University, said:

> We are talking about a country where, for the last decade, not a single academic journal has been imported, where there is no means of effective intellectual or social communication with the outside world. In this atmosphere of resentment, isolation and aggravation, extremely violent and antagonistic views towards the West have fermented.

Millions of rich Iraqis fled, either from the regime's repression or for economic reasons. An estimated five million Iraqis, two million of them professionals, are now scattered throughout the Middle East, the Americas and Europe and the exodus is continuing at an alarming rate (see Chapter 14).

Iraq once had the highest percentage of graduates in the Arab world. Under the sanctions regime two or three jobs became the rule rather than the exception for people who could find them. Education and professions were sacrificed on the altar of economic necessity. In the September 1999 issue of *New Internationalist*, correspondent Nikki van der Gaag, who visited Iraq in 1999, pointed out that schooling used to be free and compulsory – parents could be fined if their children did not attend.

But people started turning a blind eye. Children walked the streets, begging, shining shoes, and selling tissues and sticks of incense:

Mohammed cannot attempt to escape the memory of the nightmare that he survived in the shelter at Amariyah, the bombing of a civilian shelter during the Gulf War that killed 400 people. He suffered third-degree burns over 70% of his body and spent many months in hospital. Eventually he returned to his studies but he still has a long road to travel in coming to terms with the annihilation of normality. Journalist and anti-sanctions campaigner Felicity Arbuthnot visited the family in their home. She recalled that as she was about to leave she asked Mohammed:

'What do you feel about those who have done this to your family?' His extraordinarily dignified composure fragmented. Perspiration broke out on his young face, on the backs of his hands and his neck and he said: 'When I am old enough, I will be an officer in the Republican Guard. And if I die, and if I have to wait one thousand years, I will return and get my revenge.'

I apologised for asking him to relive his pain and thanked him for his courtesy for talking to me, we shook hands and I turned to leave. As I reached the gate, he ran after me, touched my shoulder and said, 'Please. I did not mean to attack people like you, people who come to try and understand. I did not mean to hurt you, please wait.' He ran again to the garden, where small amounts of fruit grew, immeasurably precious in a country which imported 70% of herbicides, pesticides, fertiliser and even seeds prior to the embargo, and pushed the fruit into my hands.

When I asked them how old they were they gave an age at least three or four years more than I imagined, and I realised they were now stunted from a childhood with not enough protein. Results of a nutritional survey conducted on 15,000 children under five in April 1997 showed that almost the whole child population was affected. One in every four infants was malnourished.

Obesity used to be the number one problem affecting Iraqi children.

Dr Nadje Al-Ali, a lecturer at the Institute for Arabic and Islamic Studies at the University of Exeter, recalled a conversation with a middle-class woman who left Iraq and now lives in London:

I would feed my children and my husband before eating anything myself. Often I would stay hungry. I would also feed my children before visiting anyone else. Before the sanctions, people were very generous. You would always serve tea and biscuits, if not a meal, when people came to see you. Under sanctions people stopped visiting each other so that they wouldn't embarrass each other.

ILLNESS AND DISEASE

In December 1999, Jason Burke of the *Observer* visited the Saddam Children's Hospital in western Baghdad where the staff were understandably downbeat.

He reported that there was a 100% death rate on the cancer ward. In the West, with plentiful antibiotics and access to chemotherapy, perhaps half of the patients would survive. But in Baghdad even pneumonia was usually fatal. The chronically sick who required long-term drug treatment had a zero survival rate. Before sanctions the survival rate was 95%.

When submitting his resignation to the UN Secretary General in February 2000, Hans von Sponeck, who was responsible for co-ordinating humanitarian aid to Iraq, said that he believed economic sanctions were unfairly harming the civilian population. In 1998, Dennis Halliday left the same job for the same reason, pointing out that sanctions were killing an Iraqi child every six minutes. Both men became active anti-sanctions campaigners.

The devastating poverty was not the only legacy of the Gulf War bequeathed to the Iraqi people. There was also the frightening spread of cancers and deformities. In 1990 the UK's Atomic Energy Authority sent a report to the British government estimating that if 50 tonnes of depleted uranium were left in the Gulf area in the event of a war, then these would lead to an estimated 50,000 extra cancer deaths in a decade. Experts now estimate there may be 900 tonnes remaining. It is not in the public domain as to exactly where this depleted uranium comes from, but the explosives, shells and bombs used by the Allied forces are tipped with this material.

In her article 'Poisoned Legacy' in the September 1999 issue of the *New Internationalist*, Felicity Arbuthnot referred to an Iraqi study of cancers and leukaemias among 1,400 Iraqi soldiers who had been in the heavily bombarded area around Basra. This showed chilling increases: for example, ten cases of lymphomas in 1991 and 106 in 1996. Brain cancer too showed a startling rise: one case in 1991 and 40 in 1996.

THE RULING ELITE

Not everybody suffered from the effects of sanctions: Saddam and his elite, an estimated 500,000 people, lived lives of luxury on goods imported through an entrenched mafia, the new middle class, which controlled the black market. An estimated US$1 billion a year from oil sales outside the oil-for-food programme allowed the import of Swiss chocolates, Italian designer clothes and the latest Mercedes and BMWs. In April 2001 Saddam celebrated his 64th birthday. Iraqi exiles estimated the birthday bash cost US$8 million.

Baron Rea of Eskdale, who was on a sanctions-busting plane to Baghdad in November 2000, commented that as always there are unscrupulous entrepreneurs who have grown rich by exploiting other people's misfortune, and others who profit by trading through the increasingly leaky sanctions regime. In Baghdad's Al Rashid Street it was possible, with dollars, to buy many products found in a Western city such as PCs, and whisky at US$6 a bottle.

Saddam built a magnificent palace on the branch of the Euphrates that ran past the ancient city of Babylon, and construction of the mother of mosques, Saddam's mosque, started in Baghdad. It was designed to hold 45,000 worshippers while appearing to float on water, with eight minarets between 150 and 200 metres high. In one of history's ironies, the cranes on the building site survived the 2003 war and were cited as examples of the reconstruction of Baghdad by foreigners not familiar with the city.

THE FAILURE OF SANCTIONS

Slowly but surely Iraq was breaking out of the stranglehold of sanctions: a number of airlines made regular flights to Baghdad; in 2000 a total of 1,500 firms from 45 countries attended the Baghdad International Trade Fair; and Iraq was invited to the Arab League summit in Cairo for the first time in a decade.

According to an editorial on 7 August 2000 in the *Financial Times*:

The sanctions policy ran out of momentum and the pain it inflicted on Iraq's 22m people eroded support for it in the Arab world and beyond. Among the UN Security Council's five permanent members, only the

THE IRAQI OPPOSITION

After the 1991 Gulf War Saddam's opponents in exile crawled out of the woodwork and attempted to form a united front against the Iraqi dictator. In March 1991, 350 delegates from more than 20 groups, and many independents and personalities, held a conference in Beirut that had three main aims: to unify and organise themselves as a credible alternative to Saddam Hussein's regime; to increase support for the growing resistance of the Iraqi people; and to seek outside sympathy and backing.

There were around 80 anti-Saddam parties in London, Washington, Damascus, Tehran and other Middle Eastern capitals, but only the two main Kurdish parties (the Kurdistan Democratic Party and the Patriotic Union of Kurdistan) and a handful of smaller Kurdish, Turcoman and Assyrian parties, the Iraqi Communist Party, the Islamic Dawa Party and Supreme Council of the Islamic Revolution and the Iraqi National Accord (made up largely of defectors), had a presence inside the country.

America tried (and failed) to unify Saddam's opponents under an umbrella organisation, the Iraqi National Congress (INC), which it financed. Before the regime's troops invaded the safe-haven in 1996 and killed many of its members, the INC tried to encourage rebellious army units to join the ranks of the opposition in northern Iraq and overthrow the regime. The various opposition groups, who published a wide range of newspapers and magazines and held conferences and seminars, could not influence events inside Iraq. In a country once characterised by political instability, where the government had been overthrown 23 times since 1920, the Baath Party has become extremely well-versed in the art of political survival.

In December 2002, before the 2003 war, the largest conference in the Iraqi opposition's history was held in the London Metropole Hotel. Most of the men in the current Iraqi government (first the Governing Council and then the interim government) were present at the conference. They rejected direct rule by America and called for the setting up of an Iraqi government as soon as the regime was toppled.

Today some are still in the beleaguered Green Zone, as their dream of ushering in a democratic Iraq is a dream deferred. A few have been killed while others, disillusioned, their political careers at an end, can be seen shopping in London's fashionable boutiques.

In 2007, the need to blame someone is spread worldwide. The true victims of sanctions were the poor of Iraq. Those with some money could just get by. Medicines and food supplements were available in the late 1990s and early 2000, if you could afford to buy them.

We can blame the USA and Britain, the United Nations, corrupt politicians on all sides of the Iraqi fence, inept bureaucrats controlling the programmes, unfeeling officials 'just doing their job' and smugglers.

Sanctions failed in their stated purpose to control Saddam's ambitions or to produce any real resulting freedom for the Iraqi people.

But in equal if not greater measure, blame should fall on Saddam, his family and his government. For many reasons, it suited Saddam that his people should suffer. A basic supply of medicines and food could have been bought to aid his people. When Saddam was found in his hole in the ground he purportedly had US$700,000 in cash on him. When Uday fled his Baghdad palace many millions of dollars in cash and gold were found bricked up in his secret store. How many aspirins, water treatment tablets or morphine tablets could have been bought with that cash on the world market? Many tonnes.

Blame is where you wish to see it!

US and UK remained staunch backers of the embargo. Though contained, Mr Saddam was firmly in control of Iraq. The exiled opposition, on which the US said it relied to bring about a change of government, was neither credible nor capable of toppling him.

Writing in *Ur*, the journal of the Great Britain–Iraq Society that he founded, George Galloway, MP, said there was not the slightest doubt that Saddam Hussein was stronger than when the sanctions began:

He has become the hero of the Arab streets, the Karachi bazaars, the metropolises from Malaysia through the Moluccas to Moscow and beyond. Quite an achievement for a policy supposedly designed to bring him down!

Only another war could topple Saddam and the Americans and British decided to oust him by force in March 2003. Many arguments were advanced for attacking Iraq. But according to George Packer, author of *The Assassins' Gate: America in Iraq*, it is still not possible to be sure why the USA invaded:

And this remains the most remarkable thing about the Iraq war. It was something that some people wanted to do. Before the invasion, Americans argued not just about whether a war should happen, but for what reasons it should happen – what the real motives of the Bush administration were and should have been. Since the invasion, we have continued to argue, and we will go on arguing for years to come.

7

The 2003 War

Now that conflict has come, the only way to limit its duration is to
apply decisive force... We will accept no outcome but victory.

George W Bush

Therefore, you noble Iraqi people, who are equal to my mother and
father, strike your enemy strongly and accurately, with the force of the
spirit of Jihad.

Saddam Hussein

I'm going to exercise my right of free speech for the first time in my life
– we want you out of here as soon as possible.

Iraqi to US marine interviewed by
BBC correspondents Rageh Omaar and Paul Wood

CHRONOLOGY

2001

11 Sep	Al-Qaeda hijackers plunged aircraft into New York's World Trade Center and the Pentagon.

2002

12 Sep	In his address to the UN General Assembly President Bush said world leaders must confront the 'grave and gathering danger' that Iraq presents or stand aside as the United States acts.
16 Sep	Iraq accepted unconditional return of weapons inspectors.
8 Nov	UN Resolution 1441 passed. 'Serious consequences' threatened if Iraq did not surrender all weapons of mass destruction.
7 Dec	America and Britain said Iraq was 'in material breach' of Resolution 1441 as the dossier it provided about its weapons programmes was incomplete.

2003

9 Jan	The chief UN weapons inspector, Dr Hans Blix briefed the Security Council. The 'smoking gun' had not been found.

28 Jan	In his State of the Union address President Bush said there was a link between Al-Qaeda and Saddam.
16 Mar	The British and Spanish Prime Ministers and President Bush held a summit in the Azores and said 17 March was the final day for negotiations at the Security Council.
17 Mar	President Bush informed Saddam Hussein that if he did not leave the country within 48 hours war would start.
20 Mar	The war started with air strikes on Baghdad.
25 Mar	The port town of Um Qasr was captured by the British.
29 Mar	First suicide bombing.
5 Apr	US army entered Baghdad.
9 Apr	US forces captured Baghdad.
14 Apr	Saddam's home town of Tikrit captured.

WHY WAR?

Three official reasons were given for going to war against Iraq in March 2003: to eliminate Saddam's weapons of mass destruction (WMD); to diminish the threat of international terrorism; and to promote democracy in Iraq and surrounding areas.

Thomas Schoenbaum, in *International Relations: the Path Not Taken – using international law to promote world peace and security*, analysed these reasons and found them wanting:

> The reason given at the time of the invasion was the necessity to eliminate Iraqi weapons of mass destruction (WMD) – Saddam's chemical and biological arms and his suspected nuclear weapons program. However, we now know that US intelligence agencies were – in the words of President Bush's own investigative commission – 'dead wrong' in their pre-war assessments of Iraq's WMD programmes. It has also come out that, before the 2003 war, the Bush administration routinely brushed aside or ignored what turned out to be the correct assessments of the UN arms inspectors and the International Atomic Energy Agency that Saddam's WMD programs had been dismantled.
>
> A second reason for the war that was equally without foundation was that Saddam was connected with Al-Qaeda and Islamist terrorism. But Congressional studies have turned up no evidence of any pre-war connection between Saddam and Al-Qaeda, and paradoxically, the American-led invasion in 2003 opened the way for associates of Osama Bin Laden, such as the cruel and infamous Abu Musab Al Zarqawi, to operate in Iraq. Bin Laden was reportedly surprised by the success of the Iraqi insurgency and offered his support.
>
> Faced with the necessity to justify the 2003 war after the fact, the Bush administration cites Saddam's brutality and tyranny. This is certainly correct, but the question remains whether the United States has a right to invade any country that is ruled by a brutal tyrant. And much of Saddam's brutality – such as his chemical weapons attack on the town of Halabja in 1988, which killed 5,000 Iraqi Kurds – occurred in the 1980s when the US government was secretly helping Saddam.

A final reason advanced for the 2003 Iraq War was the need to introduce democracy into the Middle East – part of President Bush's effort to shake up the undemocratic regimes in the region and to free up the democratic impulses of the Muslim world. Certainly the spread of democracy and freedom is a noble cause, but the question remains whether invasion is the proper or even the most effective method.

The decision to go to war may also have been influenced by America's desire to quash a move by the Organization of the Petroleum Exporting Countries (OPEC) towards using the euro as an oil transaction currency standard.

If America controlled Iraq it would gain de facto control over the Persian Gulf region, where two-thirds of the world's oil resources are located. The Jewish lobby in America also played a role in the decision to pursue the military option. Iraq was not a threat to America but it was certainly a threat to Israel.

In *The Occupation: War and Resistance in Iraq*, Patrick Cockburn explained that almost without thinking, the USA put to the test its claim to be the only superpower in the world:

> It spurned allies inside and outside Iraq: in invading Iraq Tony Blair was Bush's only significant supporter. The first President George Bush led a vast UN-backed Coalition to complete victory in the Gulf War in 1991 largely because he fought a conservative war to return the Middle East to the way it was before Iraq's invasion of Kuwait. It was the status quo with which the world was familiar and restoring it was therefore supported internationally – and in the Middle East. The war launched in 2003 was nothing less than an attempt to alter the balance of power in the world. The US, acting alone, would seize control of a country with vast oil reserves. It would assume quasi-colonial control over a nation which 15 years previously had been the greatest Arab power. Senior American officials openly threatened to change the governments of states neighbouring Iraq. The debate on why the US invaded Iraq has been over-sophisticated. The main motive for going to war was that the White House thought it could win such a conflict very easily.

'LET'S PRETEND' NEGOTIATIONS

Washington began serious war preparations by securing the passage of UN Resolution 1441 on 8 November 2002. Iraq was required to agree to renewed weapons inspections or face 'serious consequences'. The weapons inspections began, but did not produce a 'smoking gun'. Nevertheless, Bush was convinced there was a link between the Iraqi regime and Al-Qaeda, and that Iraq was a sponsor of international terrorism and could even threaten the USA. On 7 December 2002 Iraq's denial (in a massive 12,000-page dossier) that it had any chemical, biological or nuclear-related weapons was the last straw. The USA, UK and Spain presented a draft of a second resolution, which would authorise military action, but France, Russia and Germany said they would not support it.

America's negotiations at the United Nations, the drafting of resolutions and consultations with allies were nothing more than a search for justifications after the decision to attack Iraq had been taken. According to Lieutenant General Michael Moseley, Commander, 9th Air Force and US Central Command Air Forces (November 2001–August 2003), Operation Southern Forces was launched before Bush took his case to the United Nations. It involved dropping 606 precision-guided bombs on 391 targets in an effort to destroy Iraq's air defences, paving the way to use Special Forces early in the war.

One document that could have averted hostilities was written out of history. Milan Rai, author of *Regime Unchanged*, described it as the explosive yet virtually unknown Draft Work Programme of the weapons inspectors, the United Nations Monitoring, Verification and Inspection Commission (UNMOVIC) submitted to the Security Council on 17 March 2003:

> This document should have heralded a new and decisive phase in the inspection process, allowing the UN by solely peaceful means to extract definitive answers to the lingering questions around Iraq's suspected weapons of mass destruction – and to determine whether Iraq had failed the 'final opportunity' to disarm offered in Resolution 1441. The UNMOVIC alternative was not explored. The peaceful route of inspections was shut down on 17 March mere hours after Dr Hans Blix, the head of UNMOVIC, submitted the Draft Programme to the Security Council. At 8pm that night President George Bush announced an ultimatum to Saddam to leave Iraq.

(In late 2004 Chief Weapons Inspector Charles Duelfer stated in his report that there were no weapons of mass destruction, as the programme was never rebuilt after it was brought to an end by inspections, sanctions and bombings during the 1990s.)

THE FIRST AIR STRIKES

The war started as it ended – with an unsuccessful strike targeting Saddam Hussein. Only 1½ hours after the American deadline for Saddam to leave, 2,000lb GPS-guided bombs struck residential quarters in Baghdad where the Pentagon believed the Iraqi leadership was meeting. If Saddam had been killed the war could have ended the day it began. But he appeared on television shortly after.

On the eve of battle, British Lieutenant Colonel Tim Collins told his troops: 'We go to liberate not to conquer… If you are ferocious in battle remember to be magnanimous in victory.' The 'do we fight humanely or do we use decisive force question' dogged Coalition forces throughout the war and in dealing with the insurgency that followed.

Limited air strikes on Baghdad began on 20 March. US and British ground troops entered from the south and 1,000 cruise missiles were fired at targets throughout the country. An entire Iraqi division deserted, leaving the route clear for British forces to capture Iraq's second largest city, Basra.

The presidential palace and the Baath Party headquarters were targeted in the hope that Saddam's inner circle would turn against him and that the army would be too demoralised to fight. Seeing these buildings crumble endeared some of Baghdad's residents to the Coalition, but disaster struck on 26 March when an explosion in Al Shaab, a poor district in northern Baghdad, killed 14 civilians. 'It was an outrage, an obscenity,' wrote *The Independent*'s correspondent Robert Fisk.

> The severed hand on the metal door, the swamp of blood and mud across the road, the human brains inside a garage, the incinerated, skeletal remains of an Iraqi mother and her three small children in their still-smouldering car.

Two days later 55 people died in an air raid on a popular Baghdad market.

After the bombing started, 200,000 people took part in Britain's largest ever wartime protest. There were also massive demonstrations in Europe, America, Asia and the Middle East.

23–28 MARCH – UNEXPECTED RESISTANCE

As thousands of troops swept across the desert the Iraqi resistance seemed non-existent. John Simpson, a BBC reporter and author of *The Wars Against Saddam*, commented that Iraq's armed forces had been reduced to the level of scarecrows. 'They were useful for only one thing, and where Saddam was concerned that was the most important: terrorising the civilians of Iraq.'

Just five days after the war started almost half of Iraq's oil reserves were under the Coalition's control and the port of Um Qasr was secured (see page 275). On 23 March the 3rd US Infantry Division was 240km from Baghdad near the holy city of Najaf. The plan was for the 1st Marine Expeditionary Force to secure the bridges at Nasiriyah and then head towards the capital.

Outside Nasiriyah, the Fedayeen paramilitaries put up a fierce fight. They were a paramilitary, politically reliable force used to eliminate domestic opponents through campaigns of intimidation and assassination, and their fate was intimately linked to Saddam's. There were no ethics in this war – some Fedayeen pretended to surrender, then opened fire on approaching American soldiers.

The Americans had clearly underestimated the Iraqis' will to fight. After 30 helicopters were damaged by anti-aircraft fire, Lieutenant General William S Wallace, the US Army's senior commander, admitted that 'the enemy we are

WHY RESISTANCE?

The Iraqi people viewed the USA with suspicion. It was the United States that failed to support the popular uprising in 1991. There would be no second uprising for fear of the regime's reprisals. America and Britain were responsible for the imposition of 13 years of sanctions, which resulted in untold suffering. How could liberators be bombing the country? While many Americans had the welfare of the Iraqi people at heart, some were trigger-happy.

BBC reporter John Simpson commented that if the Americans had succeeded in killing Saddam on that first morning, 20 March, most Iraqis would have greeted them with gratitude. He said 'None of us should have been surprised that what the Coalition thought was a simple, surgical process was in fact clumsy, unskilful and much resented.'

Saddam's military forces did not put up a fight as the Americans approached Baghdad because many of the senior commanders had been bribed by the CIA to betray Saddam. Eight months after the war, the Films of Record documentary *Secrets of the Iraq War* described a massive Coalition spying operation involving hundreds of exiles. They smuggled satellite phones into Iraq and were at the other end of the lines collecting intelligence from the spies on the ground.

Kassim Ali was one of the Iraqi exiles who assisted the Americans in their secret war. He used the cover of a businessman to smuggle satellite phones into Iraq via Kurdistan. After the fall of the regime Ali returned to the UK, demoralised and crestfallen. He had not been paid for three months by the opposition group that had recruited him to work for the Americans, and he was convinced that the promise of democracy was nothing more than a desert mirage.

Speaking from what he described as 'exile once again' in London, Ali is disgusted that America has given Iraq to the Iranians:

> The present government is taking advice from Iran. The rushed elections were a mistake – they should have left the elections until security was established and the police force and all the ministries were functioning. Alawi [the Iraqi interim prime minister] should have talked to Blair and told him to influence the Americans not to insist on the elections. Time was needed to build the administration. What is the point of two elections in one year? [see pages 130–2, 134]
>
> Now America has to do another occupation. They have got rid of Saddam Hussein and now they have to get rid of the Iranians and all the Shia police who are nothing but Badr and Mehdi militias [the armed wing of the Supreme Islamic Council and the Al Sadr movement]. The Iranians are coming to Iraq with false Iraqi documents. They are in all the cities.

Ali returned to his home in Baghdad, where he lived during 2004–06, and tried to set up a business, but fled again after he felt threatened by Islamist elements because of his secular views. When asked whether he was Sunni or Shia he replied: 'I am an Iraqi – that's enough!' His friends informed him that his house was ransacked by the police, who removed his computer and documents. He is now thinking of buying a flat in Jordan and rebuilding his life. 'I will begin again,' he says. 'I began again when I came to London in 2000, and when I returned to Iraq in 2004.'

fighting is different from the one we had war-gamed against.' Iraq analysts said there were not enough troops in Iraq.

While the Americans concentrated on reaching Baghdad, the British were busy securing Basra (see pages 241–4).

Writing in *The Guardian* on 27 March, Hani Shukrallah, the managing editor of the Cairo-based *Al-Ahram Weekly*, described how the unexpectedly stiff resistance rolled back decades of Arab humiliation. 'We are all Iraqis now,' Shukrallah emphasised. Arab volunteers, mainly Syrians and Algerians, as well as Iraqis resident in Jordan, started arriving in Iraq to fight against the Coalition.

Republican Guard units deployed to stop the Coalition's advance on Baghdad were pounded by B-52 bombers. Before reaching Baghdad the Coalition forces had Sniper Alley, a 3km stretch through the centre of Nasiriyah, to deal with. By the time the marines had left, few houses were left standing on Sniper Alley.

Profound differences between the American and British attitudes soon became apparent. In *War on Saddam*, Patrick Bishop said that many Iraqis are willing to be persuaded that the Americans are in their country as liberators:

> To do that, American soldiers have to not only curb their trigger-happy ways, but also come out from behind their Ray-Bans. Like the British, they should learn to wave at the children and say hello in Arabic to their elders.

Tragically this advice was never heeded. Now, in 2007/8 it is too late.

Fierce resistance was also encountered in Najaf, but the Americans had no desire to get caught up in street fighting. General Tommy Franks ordered the encirclement of the city while the rest of the US 3rd Infantry Division moved on to Kerbala, reaching the Red Zone – the outer ring of Baghdad's defences – on 3 April 2003.

It was here that the Americans had their first encounter with the Republican Guard – the elite of Iraq's fighting force. Up to 1,000 were killed in a slaughter rather than a battle.

By 29 March the Coalition forces were exhausted, and while the air war continued, there was a pause in the ground war. The first suicide bombing at a checkpoint in Najaf signalled a reinterpretation of the Iraqis' perception of the

MARLA RUZICKA, A ONE-WOMAN AID AGENCY

Marla Ruzicka, a one-person aid agency who got US$20 million in compensation for the victims of war in Iraq, became one of the war's casualties herself. At the age of 29 she was killed with her translator on one of Baghdad's most dangerous roads near the airport.

Marla was born in Lakeport California and started her political work at the age of 15 when she was suspended from school for leading a protest against the 1991 Gulf War. During her studies at Long Island University she visited Cuba, Guatemala, southern Africa and the West Bank. In July 2002, Ruzicka began working with USAID and the Senate Appropriations Committee to allocate money to rebuild the homes of families that had suffered losses as a result of military action. After receiving the first report from the Campaign for Innocent Victims in Conflict, an organisation founded by Ruzicka, Senator Patrick Leahy sponsored legislation to provide US$10 million in US aid to innocent Iraqis who had been harmed by the military.

Writing to Human Rights Watch not long before she was killed, Marla said:

> A number is important not only to quantify the cost of the war, but, to me, each number is also a story of someone whose hopes, dreams and potential will never be realised, and who left behind a family.

conflict. As well as a struggle for the survival of the regime it was the patriotic fight against powerful foreign invaders. Iraq announced that 4,000 Arab volunteers were in the country at the same time that the Palestinian Islamic Jihad said it had suicide bombers in Baghdad.

The next major battle was the battle for Basra, which started on 1 April with a 15-hour assault on Iraqi positions. The city was captured the next day and the British began their hearts and minds campaign.

The Kerbala Gap was the final obstacle before the capital. It was on this plain, between Lake Buhayrat and the Euphrates, that Saddam's soldiers were expected to use chemical weapons, but the Republican Guard's Medina Division did not stick around for a fight and only 200 Iraqis engaged in some

THE OTHER WAR: IRAQ VETS BEAR WITNESS

In 2007 *The Nation*, America's oldest journal of progressive political and cultural news, interviewed 50 combat veterans of the Iraq War from around the United States in an effort to investigate the effects of the four-year-old occupation on average Iraqi civilians.

Their stories, recorded and typed into thousands of pages of transcripts, reveal disturbing patterns of behaviour by American troops in Iraq. Dozens of those interviewed witnessed Iraqi civilians, including children, dying from American firepower. Some participated in such killings; others treated or investigated civilian casualties after the fact. Many also heard such stories, in detail, from members of their unit. The soldiers, sailors and marines emphasised that not all troops took part in indiscriminate killings. Many said that these acts were perpetrated by a minority. But they nevertheless described such acts as common and said they often went unreported, and almost always unpunished.

Veterans said the culture of this counter-insurgency war, in which most Iraqi civilians were assumed to be hostile, made it difficult for soldiers to sympathise with their victims, at least until they returned home and had a chance to reflect.

'I guess while I was there, the general attitude was: a dead Iraqi is just another dead Iraqi,' said Specialist Jeff Englehart, 26, of Grand Junction, Colorado. Specialist Englehart served with the Third Brigade, First Infantry Division, in Baquba, about 45km northeast of Baghdad, for a year, beginning in February 2004.

> You know, so what? The soldiers honestly thought we were trying to help the people and they were mad because it was almost like a betrayal [by the people we were trying to help].

Fighting in densely populated urban areas has led to the indiscriminate use of force and the deaths at the hands of occupation troops of thousands of innocents.

'I'll tell you the point where I really turned,' said Specialist Michael Harmon, 24, a medic from Brooklyn. He served a 13-month tour, beginning in April 2003, with the 167th Armor Regiment, Fourth Infantry Division, in Al-Rashidiya, a small town near Baghdad:

> I go out to the scene and [there was] this little, you know, pudgy little two-year-old child with the cute little pudgy legs, and I look and she has a bullet

minor skirmishes. The Coalition gained ground rapidly and raided Saddam's Green Palace 88km north of Baghdad.

'The dagger is clearly pointed at the heart of the regime,' Brigadier General Vince Brooks, the Centcom spokesman said (Centcom is short for US Central Command, which is responsible for US security interests in 25 nations that stretch from the Horn of Africa through the Arabian Gulf region and into Central Asia). The road to Baghdad was lined with the remains of burned-out tanks, abandoned uniforms and gas masks. Hundreds of Iraqi civilians were either heading towards or away from the city. The Americans began to receive the welcome they expected – along Highway 6 hundreds of civilians shouted the few English words they knew, including 'I love you!'

> through her leg... An IED [improvised explosive device] went off, the gun-happy soldiers just started shooting anywhere, and the baby got hit.

Much of the resentment toward Iraqis described to *The Nation* by veterans was confirmed in a report released on 4 May 2007 by the Pentagon. According to a survey conducted by the Office of the Surgeon General of the US Army Medical Command, just 47% of soldiers and 38% of marines agreed that civilians should be treated with dignity and respect. Only 55% of soldiers and 40% of marines said they would report a unit member who had killed or injured 'an innocent noncombatant.'

In June 2003 Staff Sergeant Camilo Mejía's unit was pressed by a furious crowd in Ramadi. Sergeant Mejía, 31, a National Guardsman from Miami, served for six months, beginning in April 2003, with the 1-124 Infantry Battalion, Fifty-Third Infantry Brigade. His squad opened fire on an Iraqi youth holding a grenade, riddling his body with bullets. Sergeant Mejía checked his clip afterwards, and calculated that he had personally fired 11 rounds into the young man.

Raids normally took place between midnight and 05:00 according to Sargeant John Bruhns, 29, of Philadelphia, who estimates that he took part in raids of nearly 1,000 Iraqi homes:

> You go up the stairs. You grab the man of the house. You rip him out of bed in front of his wife. You put him up against the wall. You get the interpreter and you get the man of the home, and you have him at gunpoint, and you'll ask the interpreter to ask him: 'Do you have any weapons?' Normally they'll say 'no', because that's normally the truth.
>
> So what you'll do is you'll take his sofa cushions and you'll dump them. If he has a couch, you'll turn the couch upside down. You'll go into the fridge, if he has a fridge, and you'll throw everything on the floor, and you'll take his drawers and you'll dump them... You'll open up his closet and you'll throw all the clothes on the floor, and basically leave his house looking like a hurricane just hit it.

Specialist Patrick Resta, 29, a National Guardsman from Philadelphia, served in Jalula, where there was a small prison camp at his base. He was with the 252nd Armor, First Infantry Division, for nine months, beginning in March 2004. He recalled his supervisor telling his platoon point-blank, 'The Geneva Conventions don't exist at all in Iraq, and that's in writing if you want to see it.'

The airport was pounded by 2,000lb bombs from the USS *Kitty Hawk*. After Iraqi tanks were pulverised General Brooks announced that Saddam International Airport was now Baghdad International Airport, the gateway to the future of Iraq.

On 8 April an intercepted message indicated that Saddam was in Baghdad's Al-Saa restaurant with his senior leadership. Four satellite-guided bunker-buster bombs flattened the restaurant but Saddam escaped. BBC reporter John Simpson pointed out that:

> Saddam was finished, and his power structure had collapsed. Soon his huge, clumsy statue in Fardous [Paradise] Square would be pulled down by an armoured personnel carrier [see page 202]. But the real image which showed Saddam's fall was the sight of dozens of skinny young men wearing nothing but their underwear, giving up any attempt to resist the implacable force.

There was no last stand in Tikrit, Saddam's home town – just dejected unarmed men making their way back to Baghdad. The only resistance came from small groups of diehard paramilitaries.

The war to topple Saddam and his regime was over when Baghdad fell on 9 April 2003. Coalition casualties stood at 107 American and 31 British, 2,320 Iraqi military casualties and 2,325 Iraqi civilian casualties.

Sir John Keegan, in his introduction to *The Daily Telegraph*'s book *War on Saddam*, concluded that:

> Western civilisation, rooted in the idea that the improvement of the human lot lies in material advancement and the enlargement of individual opportunity, is ill-equipped to engage with a creed that deplores materialism and rejects the concept of individual freedom. The defeat of Saddam has achieved an important respite in the contest between the Western way and its Muslim alternative. But the very completeness of Western victory in Iraq ensures the continuation of the conflict.

8

Post-Saddam Iraq

Of course we are glad Saddam has gone. But things are worse in many ways now. Then, if you stuck your neck out you got clobbered. Now the violence is indiscriminate and everyone is affected.

Sami Al-Mutairy, Iraqi poet

Iraq has moved from tyranny to the fires of hell.

Abul Malik, Shia scholar

CHRONOLOGY

2003

12 Apr	The USA issued 55 playing cards with photos of the most wanted members of Saddam's regime. Saddam was the ace of spades (to date 45 have been captured or killed).
15 Apr	Meeting of 80 opposition personalities from inside and outside Iraq held in Nasiriyah under American auspices in preparation for the establishment of an Iraqi Interim Administration.
2 May	President Bush declared the war was over.
6 May	Paul Bremer appointed new civilian administrator for Iraq. He abolished the Baath Party and the army.
22 May	The UN overwhelmingly approved UNSCR 1483 lifting economic sanctions, and gave its backing to the US-led administration.
Jul	Insurgency intensified.
13 Jul	US appointed, 25-member Governing Council of Iraqis from diverse religious and political backgrounds took office.
22 Jul	Saddam's sons, Uday and Qusay, killed by Coalition forces.
19 Aug	UN Special Representative, Sergio Vieira de Mello, among 20 killed in an attack on the UN's headquarters in Baghdad.
29 Aug	Leading Shia Muslim politician, Ayatollah Mohammed Baqr Al-Hakim, among 80 killed in a bombing in Najaf.
Aug	Saddam's cousin Ali Hassan Al Majid (Chemical Ali) captured.
21 Sep	Iraq allowed foreign investors into all sectors except oil.

27 Oct	Dozens killed in Baghdad bombings, including an attack on Red Cross headquarters.
27 Nov	President Bush made a three-hour trip to Iraq to celebrate Thanksgiving with US troops.
14 Dec	Saddam found in a spider hole near home town of Tikrit.

2004

15 Jan	New bank notes without Saddam's face issued.
1 Feb	At least 101 killed in twin suicide bombings at offices of the two main Kurdish political parties in Erbil.
2 Mar	Around 200 killed in bomb attacks in Baghdad and Kerbala as Shia Muslims celebrated Ashura (see page 14).
8 Mar	Interim constitution signed.
5 Apr	American military occupation of Fallujah began after the murder and mutilation of four American contractors. Over 600 Iraqis died in subsequent fighting.
9 Apr	First anniversary of overthrow of Saddam's regime. Some 40 hostages from 12 nationalities taken. An Italian, Fabrizio Quattrocchi, was executed.
21 Apr	68 people killed in a series of bombings in Basra.
26 Apr	52 former British diplomats sent a letter to Tony Blair urging him to stop backing US Middle East policy. It said that the conduct of the war in Iraq made it clear there was no effective plan for the post-Saddam settlement.
30 Apr	CBS showed photos of American soldiers abusing Iraqi prisoners in the notorious Abu Ghraib prison, where Saddam's regime also tortured detainees.
2 May	Security of Fallujah handed over to the Iraqis.
8 Jun	UN Security Council voted unanimously on Resolution 1546 to transfer sovereignty back to the Iraqi people.
28 Jun	America handed power to an interim Iraqi government.
2 Sep	Iraqi Embassy opened in Britain.
18 Sep	Iraq's national airline resumed international flights 14 years' after war and sanctions forced it to halt operations.
19 Sep	Iraqi prime minister Ayad Allawi visited Britain for talks with Tony Blair.
24 Sep	Iraqi prime minister Ayad Allawi addressed the UN General Assembly and appealed for help to 'defeat the forces of terrorism'.
8 Oct	Ken Bigley, 62, from Liverpool, who was kidnapped on 16 September by the Tawhid and Jihad group, was beheaded. The group had earlier beheaded two Americans, Jack Hensley and Eugene Armstrong, both US citizens. The three men were civil engineers for Gulf Supplies and Commercial Services, a company working on reconstruction projects in Iraq. Over 150 foreigners were kidnapped in Iraq between April 2004 and April 2005.
21 Oct	850 British troops ordered from Basra to help in a massive crackdown on terrorists in the Sunni Triangle.

23 Oct	Bodies of 50 massacred army recruits found close to their training camp in northeast Iraq.
25 Oct	380 tonnes of powerful explosives disappeared from one of the many places in Iraq the USA failed to secure.
5 Nov	The then Iraqi prime minister attended EU summit in Belgium and asked spectator countries to become more involved in reconstruction.
7 Nov	The Iraqi interim government declared a state of emergency for 60 days because of escalating violence.
8 Nov	US and Iraqi national guard forces launched an assault on Fallujah.
16 Nov	Death of hostage Margaret Hassan, Director of Care International in Iraq, shot by her kidnappers.
21 Nov	Creditor nations agreed to slash Iraq's debts by 80%.
21 Dec	Prime Minister Blair made a surprise visit to Baghdad and Basra to support the preparations for elections.

2005

Jan	Increasing attacks by insurgents (90 people killed 3–6 January), estimated to number 200,000 throughout the country, in an attempt to disrupt the elections scheduled for 30 January. Baghdad targeted by suicide bombers.
30 Jan	Iraq held first multi-party elections for 50 years.
20 Feb	Violence directed against the Shias celebrating Ashura left 100 people dead.
22 Feb	Pentagon officials met insurgent leaders for the first time and were pressed to commit themselves to a date for the withdrawal of foreign troops.
27 Feb	Syria handed over Sabawi Ibrahim Al-Hassan Al-Tikriti, Saddam's half brother. Some 44 of the 55 members of the former regime on America's most-wanted list are either in custody or dead.
28 Feb	Massive car bomb in Hilla killed 125.
9 Mar	41 corpses, probably of Iraqi police and national guards who had been shot or decapitated, found in the heartland of Iraq's insurgency near the Syrian border.
21 May	Around a thousand Sunnis assembled in Baghdad and formed an alliance of religious, political and tribal groups to push for a stronger role in the country's Shiite-dominated power structure.
Jun	Massoud Barzani sworn in as regional president of Iraqi Kurdistan.
Jul	Iraq Body Count, a voluntary organisation that records civilian deaths attributable to Coalition and insurgent military action, sectarian violence and criminal violence in Iraq since the US-led invasion, reported that 25,000 civilians had been killed since the invasion.
Aug	Kurds and Shias, but not Sunnis, endorsed a draft constitution.

Oct	Voters approved a new constitution.
15 Dec	Iraqis vote for a permanent government.

2006
20 Jan	The Shia United Iraqi Alliance won the elections but did not gain an absolute majority.
Feb	A bomb attack on the Shia shrine in Samarra unleashed a wave of sectarian violence.
22 Apr	President Jalal Talabani ended four months of political deadlock by asking a Shia compromise candidate, Nouri Al-Maliki, to form a new government.
May/Jun	UN figures revealed that violence was killing 100 civilians per day.
7 Jun	Abu Musab Al-Zarqawi, leader of Al-Qaeda in Iraq, killed.
Nov	Saddam Hussein was sentenced to death for crimes against humanity.
	Iraq and Syria restored diplomatic relations.
Dec	The Iraq Study Group, a bipartisan panel appointed on 15 March 2006 by the United States Congress to assess the situation in Iraq and make policy recommendations, described the situation as grave and deteriorating.
30 Dec	Saddam Hussein hanged.

2007
Jan	President Bush announced the surge during which thousands more US troops were dispatched, mainly to Baghdad and the Sunni Triangle.
	Saddam's half brother Barzan Ibrahim hanged.
	UN reported 34,000 civilians were killed during violence in 2006.
Mar	A former vice-president from the Saddam era, Taha Yassin Ramadan, executed.
May	The leader of Al-Qaeda in Iraq, Abu Ayyub Al-Masri, who had taken over from Abu Musab Al-Zarqawi, was killed in an internal battle between militias.
Jul	President Bush admitted the surge was having only limited political and military success.
Aug	The Iraqi Accord Front, the main Sunni party, withdrew from the cabinet.
26 Aug	Iraqi Shia, Sunni and Kurdish leaders signed a reconciliation deal.
15 Sep	Al-Sadr's radical political movement, which supports the Shias, withdrew from the governing Shia alliance.
26 Sep	Iraqi Senate approved by 75 votes to 23 a non-binding draft resolution envisaging the division of Iraq into three.
13 Oct	Supreme Islamic Council (main Shia party) backed federalism.
21 Oct	Two US marines, including a battalion commander, are to face a court martial in connection with the killing of

	24 Iraqi civilians in Haditha in 2005.
28 Nov	Nearly 6,000 Sunnis entered into a security pact with American forces to fight Al-Qaeda. Tribesmen will man 200 security checkpoints in Anbar Province.
30 Dec	Osama Bin Laden released a new video calling on Iraqis to reject a unity government and warned the Sunnis against joining the Awakening Forces.

2008

12 Jan	Justice and Accountability Law, allowing former Baath Party members to return to public life, passed.
14 Jan	Secretary of State Condoleezza Rice visited Baghdad to press for more progress on political reconciliation.
14 Feb	Legislation setting a budget, providing a limited amnesty for detainees and defining the relationship between Baghdad and local authorities was passed by the Iraqi parliament. The Presidential Council rejected a draft law paving the way for provisional elections.

POVERTY, UNCERTAINTY AND WAR WITHOUT END

On 1 May 2003 President Bush announced the end of the war and 'mission accomplished'. In reality the war was only just beginning. Figures for the number of Iraqis who have died because of the war since the US-led invasion of 2003 vary from more than a million to 89,110. The war is costing America nearly US$2 billion per week. The cost of UK military operations in 2006–07 was approximately £956 million.

A torrent of violence has plagued Iraq, especially the capital. The country has metamorphosed from Saddam's 'wonderland of terror' (see page 84) to a land soaked in blood, where the dream of democracy and a better life has turned into a nightmare. Insurgents are conducting a guerrilla war against Coalition troops and the Iraqi government, army and police; Sunnis are killing Shias; Shias are killing Sunnis; Shia militias are fighting one another; the Kurds are being ethnically cleansed from Mosul; and Arabs are being removed from Kirkuk. Violence has also been unleashed against the Christian and Yezidi minorities, whose very existence is threatened.

A war that was supposed to usher in an era of democracy in Iraq and the region destabilised the Middle East, as America confronted Iran and Syria about their support for the Iraqi resistance. America responded to its failure to bring security to Iraq by sending in even more troops – the so-called 'surge' – in the first six months of 2007. Speaking on 13 October 2007, retired Lieutenant General Ricardo Sanchez branded this strategy a desperate attempt to make up for years of shortcomings, labelled US political leaders as 'incompetent' and 'corrupted' and commented that they would have faced courts martial for dereliction of duty if they had been in the military. Somewhat belatedly, however (February 2008), the surge appears to be showing signs of results in the drop in violence countrywide, but particularly in Baghdad.

Opinion polls conducted by ABC News, *USA Today* and the BBC during the past three years showed that in March 2007, 78% of Iraqis opposed the

8

presence of American troops, compared with 65% in November 2005 and 51% in February 2004.

The human rights organisation Iraq Body Count (IBC) documented 22,586–24,159 violent civilian deaths in 2007, bringing the overall IBC total since the 2003 invasion to 81,639–89,110. The figures reveal that 2007 was the second most violent year since the invasion (exceeded only by 2006): deaths in Baghdad dramatically declined throughout the year; deaths outside Baghdad actually increased until September; deaths caused by the US military significantly increased compared to 2006; and four of the high-violence provinces showed increases in violence compared to 2006.

In commenting on these data, IBC's co-founder and press spokesperson John Sloboda said:

> These figures show beyond any doubt that civil security in Iraq remains in a parlous state. For some 24,000 Iraqi civilians, and their families and friends, 2007 was a year of devastating and irreparable tragedy.

For the Iraqi people every day is a day of bombs, assassinations and killings. Kidnapping is the fastest growing industry. 'We have had two elections and a referendum on the constitution and things have never been so bad,' the Iraqi Vice-President Tariq al-Hashimi admitted.

American policy is characterised by contradictions between noble goals and philosophies of democracy, and the actions of some of its troops inside the country.

The rhetoric became increasingly hollow after the abuse and torture of prisoners in Abu Ghraib prison was revealed in 2004. Thousands of Iraqis are incarcerated in US-run prisons, many arrested on the basis of anonymous tip-offs.

In its 2007 annual report Amnesty International observed that:

> Iraqi security forces committed widespread human rights violations, including killings of civilians and torture and other ill-treatment of detainees, and were suspected of involvement in sectarian killings. Soldiers belonging to the US-led Multinational Force (MNF) also committed human rights violations. The MNF held thousands of people in arbitrary detention without charge or trial. Members of Iraq's most vulnerable groups, including minorities and women, continued to be targeted for abuses. The violence caused many thousands of people to be displaced from their homes, as neighbourhoods in Baghdad and some other centres were increasingly affected by rising sectarianism; hundreds of thousands of Iraqis fled the country and sought refuge abroad. Scores of other people were sentenced to death, after unfair trials. At least 65 women and men, including Saddam Hussain, were executed.

RECONSTRUCTION

Internationally funded reconstruction efforts have been plagued by inadequate security, pervasive corruption, insufficient funding and poor co-ordination among international agencies and local communities. To reconstruct after 20 years of neglect, 12 years of sanctions and three wars is a daunting task. Some local reconstruction has been carried out by the Iraqi people using local resources.

A young boy poles his boat through the
network of irrigation channels among
the date plantations northwest of Qurnah
(AB) page 271

top **Lion of Babylon**
(GH) page 306

above **The Ctesiphon Arch, the largest brick arch in the world**
(GH) page 307

left **Agargouf ziggurat**
(GH) page 303

top left	Relief from the Northwest Palace of Nimrud (GH) page 311
top right	Detail from Hatra city walls (GH) page 308
above left	Mythical beasts of the original Ishtar Gate in the Processional Way protect the ancient city of Babylon (GH) page 305
above right	The Ishtar Gate of Babylon (GH) page 306

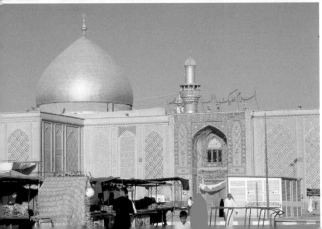

top **Pilgrims and the Shrine of Kadhimain, Baghdad**
(GH) page 238

above **Shrine city of Kerbala**
(GH) page 254

left **Al Askari Mosque in Samarra was destroyed by a bomb in February 2006 but is currently being rebuilt**
(GH) page 238

top left   Minaret detail, Kerbala (GH) page 254

top right   Shrine of Ali, the 4th caliph, the most important shrine in Najaf (GH) page 250

above left   The guard of the mosque, Baha Qu, Hawraman (CK)

above right   Restored 14th-century tomb of Ibn Ali Hasan by the Tigris River in Mosul (GH) page 342

Interior of Al-Mosawi Mosque (The Mosque of Ammer's Sons), in the Al-Fursi area (AB)

Funding of reconstruction began with the creation of the American-administered Iraq Relief and Reconstruction Fund (IRRF) in April 2003. An initial allocation of US$2.5 billion was made for immediate food, medicine and water relief. As of March 2006 the fund had spent US$11.4 billion. The money held by the IRRF has been managed by a series of US agencies, beginning with the Coalition Provisional Authority (CPA).

Charles Tripp in *A History of Iraq* pointed out that three factors undermined economic recovery and reconstruction:

> These were the inadequacy of the CPA in the face of the scale of the economic challenge, the bias, corruption and inefficiencies which beset the allocation of funds, and the rapidly deteriorating security situation which discouraged further investment, or sabotaged the few projects that were up and running. The vast majority of the expanding staff of the CPA, often serving on very short-term contracts, were wholly unfamiliar with Iraqi conditions or Middle Eastern society. They had little contact with Iraqis and were caught up in a system where financial mismanagement was breathtaking.

The CPA worked on the principle that Iraqi reconstruction could best be handled by American private enterprises with links to important figures in the American government. It promulgated laws to assist these enterprises, such as the abolition of customs duties, tax-free repatriation of funds and a flat tax rate of 15%. The Iraqis themselves could only play a small role in this capitalist venture. While most of Saddam's decrees were done away with, the legislation that limited the power of trade unions remained. The Iraqis were dismayed that of the US$1.5 billion worth of contracts awarded from oil revenues, 74% went to American companies.

When the CPA was disbanded on 28 June 2004 the management of re-construction projects was transferred to the Iraq Reconstruction and Management Office (IRMO), a division of the State Department, and the Project and Contracting Office (PCO), a division of the Defense Department.

Funds from the IRRF are disbursed through contracts to private firms. Bechtel of San Francisco received over US$2.4 billion for infrastructure development, a subsidiary of Halliburton of Texas received US$580 million. Another US$1.2 billion was distributed to Iraqi contractors.

In October 2004 Congress created the Office of the Special Inspector General for Iraq Reconstruction (SIGIR), which is charged with oversight of the use and potential misuse of the IRRF. In September and December 2004 and March and December 2005 funds from water resources, sanitation and electricity were shifted to meet security needs.

In October 2005 SIGIR introduced the concept of the 'reconstruction gap' – the difference between the reconstruction planned and that which is delivered. As of February 2006, only 36% of planned water sector projects were completed and only 70% of planned electricity sector projects were completed. This was due to the re-allocation of funds to meet security needs, poor cost estimates and lack of administrative oversight. Without funding for supplies, technicians and fuel there is a danger that the facilities that have been completed may fall into disuse.

At the Madrid Conference on Reconstruction held from 23–24 October 2003 about US$33 billion in grants and loans were pledged. Of this, US$18.4 billion was from the USA, US$812 million from the EU, US$500 million from Kuwait, and offers of loans from the World Bank and the IMF amounted to US$5.5–9.25 billion. Some countries pledged to reduce the debt that Iraq owed them and to provide direct donations in forms such as food and fuel. The funds are managed by the United Nations Development Group and the World Bank. Some 26 donor nations have made pledges of US$1.4 billion as of 30 June 2006. Britain was one of the first donors to fully disburse its Madrid pledge of £544m. It has announced further pledges of £200m, bringing its total commitment to £744m. The rate of disbursement of funds administered by the UN and World Bank has been slow, Iraqi agencies and ministries are often unable to receive or process funds, and many UN agencies have difficulty operating in Iraq due to the security situation.

Reconstruction has only been possible in the areas where the insurgency is weak or the local rulers had curbed violence. Iraqi Kurdistan, for example, witnessed an unprecedented building boom (see pages 158–9, 178–80) and significant foreign investment.

Despite the billions spent and promised for Iraqi reconstruction the Finance Minister, Bayan Jabor, speaking on 21 August 2007, said that Iraq needs at least US$100 billion to rebuild its shattered infrastructure:

> The country is devastated and we are in need of at least US$100–150 billion to restore infrastructure – from sewerage to water to electricity to bridges and basic needs.

Jabor reported that US$4 billion had been spent on infrastructure projects in 2007, more than in all of 2006, when internal violence and the limited capacity of the private sector meant that only about 40% of the US$6 billion allocated in the budget was used.

Speaking to the BBC on 13 October 2007, Radhi Hamza Al-Radhi, a former judge charged with leading the fight against corruption, said that 3,000 cases had been uncovered since 2004, and that US$18 billion was missing. He claimed the Iraqi government frustrated his efforts, and that he and members of his family had been threatened. He is now living in exile in the USA. The Iraqi government has accused Mr Al-Radhi of wrongdoing and has said it will file charges against him.

The failure to rebuild the infrastructure and provide essential services has had a devastating effect on the Iraqi people. On 26 September 2007 a women died of cholera in Baghdad, the first confirmed fatality after an outbreak of the disease in refugee settlements in the north of the country, where at least 2,000 cases were confirmed.

In a report, Oxfam and the NGO Co-ordination Committee in Iraq warned in July 2007 that 70% of Iraq's population did not have adequate water supplies and that only 20% had access to effective sanitation – a figure comparable to sub-Saharan Africa. Nearly 30% of children are malnourished and 15% of Iraqis regularly cannot afford to eat. Nearly a third of the population is in need of immediate emergency aid. The report recognised that armed violence is the greatest threat facing Iraqis but described a population 'increasingly threatened by disease and malnutrition'.

Aid must be provided to two million internally displaced people. Four million Iraqis are registered to receive food aid, but only 60% actually get it, compared with 96% in 2004.

Life during Saddam's time was alright for me. I was still young and didn't know much about life. Saddam offered us good public services and free education. The Iraqi education system was one of the best in the region.

We had something called peace. Many people say that Saddam was a killer. It's true, but if you kept away from him he wouldn't come near you. Saddam had the chance to rule Iraq toward a better future but he didn't. He was interested in himself only, not his people.

In general the situation started to deteriorate after 1991, after I was born. When I started to grow up things in Iraq were already falling apart because of the sanctions. I lived in a time that was better than now, but worse than before the sanctions.

When Saddam's government collapsed most of the Iraqis felt happy because they thought it would be the beginning of a new, better life for them, but they were wrong. At first everything went so well, I could actually travel outside Iraq to see the world for the first time in my life and Iraq became part of the world.

Not long after that things went bad. Horrible things started happening like kidnappings and explosions. Iraqis started to disappear. We couldn't go out walking or even driving. We were afraid of getting killed with no mercy. Those bad people who were allowed to enter our country after the invasion started to control our lives and even told us what to wear and what not to wear. After that we did what most Iraqis did and left.

I really don't know how Saddam prevented these things from happening during his time but we need someone like him to stop the horrible things that are happening in Iraq now.

Iraqis have a voice and no-one wants to hear it. I have a strong desire to save Iraq and bring life to it again, but I am only 16 years old and no-one will listen to me. I hope that our 'leaders' will wake up one day and actually start leading.

Raghda Zaid, a 16-year-old, speaks out

LOOTING, CHAOS AND WISHFUL THINKING

'The Iraqi army has been destroyed. There's no regime command and control in existence right now. This is an ex-regime.' General Franks' elation at Saddam's downfall was short-lived as he went on to describe the maelstrom of violence:

> It began against the symbols of the regime, but degenerated into indiscriminate looting. Like a biblical plague it spread through liberated Iraq. Baghdad was stripped almost bare.

The cost of the looting was estimated at US$12 billion, the revenue budgeted for the country for the first year after the war.

One of the first steps of the occupying powers was to replace Iraqi state television with a new station, which broadcast President Bush's speech of reassurance on 10 April 2003:

Our only enemy is Saddam's brutal regime and that regime is your enemy as well. We will help you build a peaceful and representative government and then our military forces will leave.

The president soon discovered this would not be as easy as envisaged. The people were anxious and uncertain. Their country was free but ruined. Who would put it back together again and in whose image?

In his book *Iraq: People, History, Politics*, Gareth Stansfield noted that:

The alacrity with which the Coalition militarily defeated the Iraqi army was matched by their sluggishness in establishing emergency structures of governance and administration, whether at the local or the national level. Indeed it appears that military planners overestimated the effort needed to defeat Iraq's military and totally underestimated the effort needed to provide some form of civil executive authority in the aftermath period.

The Americans, influenced by opposition parties in exile, believed that Iraqis would embrace democracy once Saddam was toppled. They did not develop a detailed plan for running the country and reacted to developments rather than implementing a strategy.

THE COALITION PROVISIONAL AUTHORITY

The Office of Reconstruction and Humanitarian Assistance (ORHA), led by retired General Jay Garner, who helped set up the Kurdish safe haven in northern Iraq, was charged with rebuilding the state. His efforts were hindered by a 'civil war' in Washington between the State Department and the Pentagon. State Department Arabists were sidelined in the staffing of the ORHA in favour of neo-con supporters. Garner advocated working with existing institutions, a policy at odds with Pentagon thinking, and ORHA was disbanded in mid May 2003, as it was unable to halt Iraq's steady slide into chaos.

ORHA was replaced by the Coalition Provisional Authority (CPA, which the Iraqis concluded stood for Can't Provide Anything) and Garner was replaced by Ambassador L. Paul Bremer III, who had the support of the Pentagon. The Iraqis regarded him as a colonial occupier.

The CPA was the temporary governing body designated by the United Nations as the lawful government of Iraq until the country was politically and socially stable enough to assume its sovereignty.

Bremer started by abolishing the Baath Party and the army – the basis of the Iraqi state. On 15 May 2003 CPA Order No 1 banned anyone serving in the four top levels in the Baath Party from serving in the post-Saddam administration. One hundred thousand people lost their jobs. Order No 2, which followed on 23 May, disbanded the army and 350,000 soldiers were left unemployed. Many joined the insurgency.

The Americans had to start from scratch, establish a new administration and train an army and police force. Their 'new recruits' proved no match for the private militia of the firebrand cleric, Moqtada Al-Sadr (see pages 254–5).

After demolishing two national Iraqi institutions the CPA started working with returning exiles from the opposition. Its approach was top-down, and

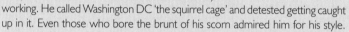

PAUL BREMER: A TOUGH, SHREWD OPERATIVE

Paul Bremer arrived on 12 May 2003 with instructions to assume full governmental control. Bremer seemed made for this task. He was a tough, shrewd operative with strong conservative credentials, who had initially risen through the State Department, but was certainly no diplomatic pansy. In Washington he was considered to be an expert on terrorism.

With his own people he was severe. His attitude was 'You're here for the mission. Get the job done. If you can't cut it, fuck off.' Bremer was not big on compliments. He was smart, flexible and very hardworking. He called Washington DC 'the squirrel cage' and detested getting caught up in it. Even those who bore the brunt of his scorn admired him for his style.

He was the dude exuding power, the anointed one. He would fly around Iraq in the early days, dressed in a business suit and combat boots, responding to the immediate problems he encountered, and snapping out orders to make things right. This was not necessarily the best way to go about running a nation ('I want a law prohibiting potholes') and follow-up turned out to be a problem, but Bremer was confident and decisive.

William Langewiesche, The Atlantic Online

failed to involve the locals in the political process.

In a dramatic policy reversal in mid-April 2004, the US administration decided to reinstate former public sector workers who were members of the Baath Party as long as they had a clean record. It was hoped that by encouraging the former Baathists to get involved in government, the wind would be taken out of the Sunni insurgency. The move was also prompted by serious manpower shortages in the health and education sectors. But the insurgency was growing, and it was clearly a matter of too little, too late.

One hundred days after the American occupation, *The Guardian* journalist Suzanne Goldenberg described Iraq under the US-led occupation as a fearful, lawless and broken place, where murder rates had rocketed, 80% of workers were idle and hospital managers despaired at shortages of basic antibiotics. Police were seen as thugs and thieves, and the American and British forces as distant rulers, more concerned with protecting their troops than providing security. A kilometre away from one of the richest oilfields on earth, the queues at petrol stations stretched for hours.

The statistics were both encouraging and depressing: the USA was spending US$3.9 billion per month on the occupation and US$680m of rebuilding contracts were handed out by the American company Bechtel (US$400m to local companies). Just over one million barrels of oil were being pumped per day, compared with 2.8 million before the war. The International Red Cross spent £60 million on humanitarian aid, yet 1 in 12 children suffered from malnutrition. There were 150 new newspapers, and three plays were performed. Some 15–25 civilians were being shot daily in the capital and 1,000 children were injured by unexploded mines.

The first anniversary of the downfall of the Baathist regime was not a time for celebrations. On 9 April 2004, Firdous Square, where Saddam's statute spectacularly bit the dust a year before, was filled with litter, and barbed wire was on every street leading to it. The Americans declared it a military zone and ordered everyone to stay away. A survey by the BBC and other broadcasters of 2,500 Iraqis revealed that most felt their lives were better a year after the war. The restoration of security was the major priority.

Throughout April the news from Iraq was dominated by the siege of Fallujah (see pages 220–3) and the showdown in Najaf with the radical Shia cleric Moqtada Al-Sadr.

The CPA was advised by the Iraqi Governing Council (see below). On 28 June 2004 sovereignty was formally transferred by the CPA to the Iraqi Interim Government (see pages 127–8) during a ceremony in the Green Zone. Paul Bremer, dressed in his trademark combat boots, left Baghdad on the same day. The staff of the CPA acted as advisers to the Iraqi Interim Government and worked under the auspices of the American Embassy in Baghdad.

The CPA left an unenviable legacy: a chaotic devolution of power to local areas, a variety of insurgent groups, and increasingly powerful militias.

THE IRAQI INTERIM GOVERNMENT – 'MADE-IN-AMERICA'

The Americans had been bankrolling Saddam's opponents in exile, especially the Iraqi National Congress, since 1991. After the war many of these exiles returned home on America's coat tails. Iraq was governed by the Coalition Provisional Authority in conjunction with the Iraqi Governing Council until the transfer of power to an Iraqi interim government on 28 June 2004.

On 16 April 2003 the Americans organised a conference outside the Talil airbase in Nasiriyah for exiled groups, who issued a 13-point framework for a new government. The Shias staged a major demonstration calling for rule by their ayatollahs, not American stooges, and the main Islamic parties boycotted the meeting. The plan was to hold several similar meetings leading to a grand national congress in Baghdad, from which an interim government would emerge – but things did not go according to plan. There were major disagreements between Iraq's main political groups. The Americans decided they could not co-ordinate the diverse ambitions of around 300 national congress delegates, and ended up appointing a 25-member Iraqi Governing Council (IGC) on 13 July 2003.

The Americans tended to see Iraqi politics as a numbers game, which would reflect the composition of society: 13 of the 25 council members were Shia, five Kurdish, five Sunni Arabs, one Turcoman and one Assyrian Christian. Three were women and nine were returnees from exile. Like the CPA, the IGC was headquartered in the Green Zone in Baghdad (see page 203), which bore as much resemblance to the rest of Iraq as a safari park to a real jungle. The area outside the Green Zone (called the Red Zone) was seen as hostile territory, and an unbridgeable gap was created between the rulers and ruled.

Council members were often accused of corruption and filling the ministries with their relatives and friends. The locals treated them with suspicion, and several were assassinated.

THE PROVISIONAL CONSTITUTION

To a backdrop of hostile gunfire, the provisional constitution was signed on an antique desk, which once belonged to King Faisal I, Iraq's first monarch. It stipulated that:

- Islam is the official state religion and one source of legislation.
- Arabic and Kurdish will be the official languages.
- All Iraqis are equal in their rights without any regard to gender, nationality, religion or ethnic origin.
- The Kurdish Regional Government will be recognised as an official regional government within a unified Iraq and will continue to exercise many of the functions it currently exercises.
- The National Assembly will be responsible for drafting the permanent constitution, which will be submitted to a public referendum no later than 15 October 2005.

The Shia tradition is that anyone who co-operated with Saddam is a traitor, let alone someone who co-operates with occupying forces,

warned Dr Hamid Al Bayati, of the Supreme Islamic Council.

As well as being hand-picked by the CPA, the IGC's decisions had to have CPA approval and it was basically an advisory body.

A controversy erupted about whether elections, favoured by the Shias, could be held before the transfer of sovereignty. The UN was called in and the head of the mission, Lakhdar Brahimi, agreed with the USA that it was impractical to hold elections early, but supported the Shia position that they should be held as soon as possible. A compromise was reached: a caretaker government would be chosen to rule after the handover of sovereignty before the first elections were held.

The Iraqi Governing Council's most notable achievement was the signing of a provisional constitution, also known as the Transitional Administrative Law, on 8 March 2004, which set out the framework for how Iraq would be governed after the US-led Coalition ended the occupation and before a new government was chosen.

Getting agreement from the groups in Iraq's diverse political mosaic was not easy. The signing was stalled after five Shia members walked out in protest over a clause that effectively gave the Kurds, about 20% of the population, the power to veto the final constitution. But, in the words of the National Security Adviser Dr Mowaffak Al-Rubaie: 'We started to learn a new trade called compromise.'

RESISTANCE TO THE OCCUPATION AND INSURGENCY

The Iraqi insurgency refers to a variety of groups using armed resistance. It began shortly after the invasion in 2003. At first the insurgents targeted the US-led Coalition forces and the interim government. Attacks on Coalition forces, the Iraqi army and the police force have continued, but the insurgents are now involved in sectarian strife, which some analysts believe is the precursor to a civil war. According to American military estimates, in 2006 the number of insurgents ranged from 8,000 to 20,000. Iraqi intelligence officials believe the figure could be 40,000 fighters with 160,000 supporters. They have brought death to every corner of Iraq.

Civilians have borne the brunt of insurgency attacks. The first official figure for victims of bombings, ambushes and other deadly attacks was 12,000 between January 2005 and June 2006, according to the Iraqi Interior Ministry. Iraq Body Count has documented 73,264–79,869 violent, non-combatant civilian deaths since the beginning of the war (as of 20 September 2007).

Sunni insurgents are made up of ex-Baathists and members of the Iraqi army who were disbanded by the CPA; Sunni nationalists afraid of Shia domination; and foreign Islamic fighters. Al-Qaeda in Iraq has been blamed for the most horrific attacks. When some of the Sunni tribes decided to join the Americans in the fight against Al-Qaeda (see page 104), Osama Bin Laden called on insurgent groups to fulfil their duty to unite so that they become one. In 2006 a statement on the internet from Al-Qaeda said it had joined five other groups, among them the Victorious Sect Army and the Islamic Jihad Brigade, to form the Mujahideen Shura Council. Other Sunni insurgent groups include the Islamic Army in Iraq, the Islamic Resistance Movement, the Islamic Front for Iraqi Resistance, Mohammed's Army, the Islamic State of Iraq and the Army of the Rightly Guided Caliphs. Ansar Al-Islam is a radical Sunni Muslim group with a base in the mountains of Iraqi Kurdistan with suspected ties to Al-Qaeda. The capture and execution of Saddam Hussein had no effect on the insurgency.

Shia political parties have armed wings, which have not been disbanded despite American pressure. The main Shia militias belong to the Supreme Islamic Council (the Badr Brigade) and Moqtada Al-Sadr, who commands the Mehdi Army. Both militias have been accused of targeting Sunnis. The Shias have also formed defence forces to protect local neighbourhoods.

Pentagon data revealed that weekly attacks by the insurgents have been increasing since April 2004, from just under 400 during April–June 2004, to more than 600 a week during August–November 2006. Daily attacks doubled during the first months of 2006, and the number of roadside bombs either discovered or exploded increased from 1,415 in January to 2,625 in July.

Over 500 counter-insurgency operations have been undertaken by the US-led Coalition or the Iraq government. Iraq Body Count reported that in 2006, 536 Iraqi civilians had been killed by Coalition forces in these operations – mainly by Americans.

In addition to the armed forces there are nearly 50,000 armed private security guards working in Iraq. The conduct of private security firms is coming under increasing scrutiny by both the American and Iraqi governments after the American company Blackwater, a well-established private security firm, was involved in an incident on 16 September 2007, which claimed the lives of 11 Iraqis. The Iraqis accuse Blackwater guards, who were protecting an American diplomatic convoy, of firing on innocent civilians, while Blackwater and the State Department claim the convoy came under attack.

THE IRAQI INTERIM GOVERNMENT (IIG)

The American military occupation of Iraq officially ended on 28 June 2004 when Paul Bremer described himself as the 'ex-administrator' at a low-key

I was invited to sit with men on a mattress on the floor, surrounded by weapons – hand grenades, pistols, AK-47 machine guns, RPG-7s and 62-millimetre mortars. These particular fighters were not Baathist remnants. On the contrary, they defined themselves as nationalists and blamed Saddam Hussein for bringing the Americans into Iraq:

> People join us from all walks of life. Those who cannot fight support us financially. We are well trained, as most of us took part in the Iran–Iraq war, but occasionally young recruits ask us for training. We have bases in Basra, Mosul, Baghdad and in five towns in Al-Anbar province: Al Qaem, Haditha, Hit, Fallujah and Al Ramadi. There is plenty of co-ordination going on between these different groups.

I visited a sheikh from the Al-Dulaimi tribe who lived in Samarra. 'Why are the Americans being attacked?' The sheikh asked. He then proceeded to answer his own question:

> It's because they humiliate people – breaking down gates and doors to enter homes and beating and handcuffing husbands. It all leads to bitterness and hatred, and so people resort to violence to take revenge.

I reminded the sheikh of the punishments meted out by the previous regime. 'It's better to be humiliated by an Iraqi than at the hands of strangers and infidels.'

One of the first televised messages addressed to President George Bush from a collective referred to as the Iraqi Resistance in 2003 declared:

> Once again we call upon you, if you are serious about looking after the safety of your soldiers, to leave our country immediately, or we will take revenge for every Iraqi killed or humiliated and every house ransacked. You should know that the Iraqis are now well aware of the big lie you have told them, that you are here to liberate Iraq from dictatorship.

Zaki Chehab, author of Iraq Ablaze: Inside the Insurgency

ceremony that looked more like a coffee morning than a crucial historic moment. UN Security Council Resolution 1546 endorsed the Iraqi Interim Government (IIG).

But just as the downfall of Saddam was not the instant panacea that many hoped would cure the country's problems, the formal end of the occupation did not lead to a reduction of violence. 'The United States does not control the country and handing over sovereignty is like rearranging the Titanic deckchairs,' commented Toby Dodge, author of *Inventing Iraq: The Failure of Nation Building and a History Denied.* More than 110 people were killed and dozens injured in suicide bombings and clashes as Iraq's interim government ended its first month in office amid deepening violence and hostage-taking.

The recommendation of the head of the UN mission Lakhdar Brahimi that the IIG be staffed with technocrats was ignored, and the CPA and Iraq

Reflecting on a lifetime in politics, the first prime minister in post-Saddam Iraq, Dr Ayad Allawi, now 61, recalls his participation in the Baathist coup of 1968:

> I was a medical student. In 1970 I disagreed with Saddam and in 1971 I left Iraq and went to Lebanon. Then I came to London for post-graduate studies. I thought I would not be involved in Iraqi politics. Then I thought I bore responsibility, because I was a partner in the coup and I had to work to undo what Saddam did. So I started working against him. Then I participated in what has happened in Iraq after the downfall of Saddam. Now I feel I have a moral responsibility to bring stability to my country. This is my destiny.

Allawi's priority is fighting for a non-sectarian Iraq:

> Before we had a tyrant and a bunch of people around him, and now we have thousands of militias and corrupt police. Order has disappeared, the country is riddled with warlords and gangs from Mosul to Basra, the Iranians are really running things, and they are getting more and more powerful.

According to Allawi there are three solutions needed to bring Iraq out of its current downward slide: a caretaker government and fresh elections; a change to a non-sectarian government brought about through pressure from the USA, the UK and the international community; and the creation of a new parliament which could vote out the present government.

But he insists that elections must be held under UN supervision and that there have to be fundamental changes to the electoral system:

> We don't want sectarian lists anymore. In the last elections people did not know who they were electing – the names of the candidates were only published a week before. You had a Sunni list, a Shia list, a Kurdish list, a pan-Iraqi list. The candidates were chosen as part of a list rather than for their capabilities and credentials and they were answerable to the leaders of the list and not to the people.

Governing Council decided on the IIG's membership, which could be interpreted as 'payback time' for the exiled opposition. The most influential position of prime minister went to Dr Ayad Allawi, head of the Iraqi National Accord, an exiled opposition party made up largely of ex-Baathists. The President was Ghazi Al-Yawer, a returning Sunni exile from London and a member of one of the leading tribes, the Shammar. The Kurds were given important cabinet posts but failed to get the leading jobs, and made their demands for Kurdish autonomy in future increasingly vocal. The staff of the CPA acted as advisors to the IIG. Sovereignty may have been handed over but Iraq was never truly sovereign, as the Americans were the power behind the throne – in the Green Zone at least.

The whole political process is wrong and the parliament is dysfunctional because it is based on the sectarian divide. The only way to rectify this is to change the election system, hold fresh elections and get a new government. We cannot be a photocopy of the democracy born in Westminster. We have our different circumstances, we have our different culture, we have a different set of problems. I see democracy as a pyramid. The trunk is the rule of law, then come the institutions of state and civil society. And at the end are the elections.

Allawi emphasised it is incumbent on the Americans to come up with a solution:

They brought this government, they are protecting it. They created this problem. They can't make a problem and then not solve it.

He identified three strategic mistakes made by America and its allies: dismantling the state of Iraq, the army, the police and the Baath Party; putting Iraq on the road to sectarianism; and tolerating the intervention of Iraq's neighbours in the country's affairs for too long. 'Ironically America and Iran are at odds with each other, but both of them are supporting the sectarian regime in Iraq.' Allawi is dismayed that members of his party, who are hoping to voice the plight of non-sectarian Iraqis in the USA, have been refused visas for more than a year.

He is convinced Iraq needs a strong man – strong not only in terms of using force, but strong and courageous in talking to enemies and the insurgents. 'You have to be strong in transforming your vision into decisions and implementing these decisions. Without this you will not get a stable Iraq.'

His quest for a stable Iraq is taking him to China, India and France:

I want to engage them in helping Iraq. I will keep on fighting for a non-sectarian Iraq, I will keep on fighting the forces who are trying to wreck Iraq and destroy its fabric, and I will continue to fight forces who are bringing problems to Iraq whether these are regional powers or terrorists. I will keep on fighting to keep Iraq within the Arab and Islamic rank. We do not want to lose our identity and dismember Iraq. This will bring about violence between the three enclaves fighting for territory and economy, it will bring about more sectarian violence, which will spill over into the region and the world. The majority of Iraqis do not think along sectarian lines.

Charles Tripp, author of *A History of Iraq*, commented that despite elections, referenda and all the attributes of representative life, the uneasy question of direct command and indirect influence on the part of the USA persisted, rankling with future Iraqi governments, and at the same time undermining their authority amongst many of their compatriots.

The prime minister, Dr Ayad Allawi, wanted to be seen as a strong man who would not tolerate violence. His detractors pointed to corruption, which they say was rife under his leadership, but Allawi replied that he had ordered an investigation into corruption, and insisted that there would be no media coverage of the investigations until they were completed. 'The head of the Integrity Commission did not flee from Iraq when I was prime minister,' he said (see page 120). Allawi concentrated on trying to crush the insurgents and was gladly assisted by the Americans, as continuing violence derailed reconstruction plans and alerted the American public to the lack of success in creating the so-called new Iraq.

There was a violent confrontation with the Mehdi Army between April and August 2004 (see pages 209–11) and an assault on Fallujah in November 2004 (see pages 220–3), which prompted the Sunni Arab parties to boycott the first elections. Violence increased as the insurgents who fled from the city avenged those they left behind. American military deaths, which reached 1,000 before the assault on Fallujah, continued to rise. Allawi emphasised that before military operations he had made several attempts to resolve the issue through dialogue and had brought several people from Fallujah, including the speaker of the parliament, into the political process.

With a non-arrogant pride he spoke of the achievements of his government: implementing law 91 to dismantle militias (the next government merged them into the security forces and the police) and creating state institutions; reducing Iraq's debt and building up reserves of US$10 billion; stabilising the rate of exchange and spending US$250 million on Sadr City (see pages 209–11); signing economic agreements with Kuwait, Iran, Jordan, Lebanon, Syria, the UAE, Saudi Arabia and Turkey and getting Iraq back into the UN, the Arab League and the international community; and developing relations with Europe and Russia.

THE JANUARY 2005 ELECTIONS

Iraq's first multi-party elections in 50 years were held on 30 January 2005. The pre-election campaign was a low-key affair and many candidates kept their identity secret until the big day. Men with *keffiyah* masks handed out leaflets with a horrific threat: if you want your wife to be a widow, your son an orphan and your house blown up, vote in the elections. The Americans rounded up 2,500 suspected insurgents the day the elections were held, bringing the detainee population to 8,000.

Suicide bombers killed 40 people but did not deter 8.5 million from voting in an impressive 58% turnout. A total of 19,000 candidates contested 275 seats in the National Assembly, 20% of which would be held by women. Political parties submitted lists of candidates and the seats were allocated by proportional representation. Extensive provisions were made for Iraqis abroad to vote, with around 280,000 expats voting in 14 countries. The disdain for the elections among the Sunnis was matched by the enthusiasm of the Shias and the Kurds.

ELECTION RESULTS

The United Iraqi Alliance (a Shia alliance backed by the clergy) 48%
The Kurdistan Alliance 26%
The Iraqi List (headed by the interim prime minister Ayad Allawi) 14%
Others (the Communist Party, the National Rafidian List (Christians), the Iraqi Islamic Party (Sunnis), The Assembly of Independent Democrats (headed by Sunni elder statesman Adnan Pachachi)) 12%

SHIA PARTIES

United Iraqi Alliance – the dominant Shia coalition

Led by two major parties: The Supreme Islamic Council and the Islamic Dawa Party.

Other significant parties: Islamic Virtue Party (Al-Fadhila), a branch of the Sadrist Movement; Iraqi National Congress.

Al-Risaliyun (Upholders of the Message) and National Independent Cadres and Elites represent Moqtada Al-Sadr (see pages 254–5).

KURDISH PARTIES

Kurdistan Alliance

Two major parties: Kurdistan Democratic Party and Patriotic Union of Kurdistan.

Other parties: Kurdistan Islamic Union and Islamic Group of Kurdistan/ Iraq.

SUNNI PARTIES

Iraq Accord Front (Al-Tawafuq)

Major parties: Iraqi Islamic Party, General Council for Iraqi People, Iraqi National Dialogue Council.

Other parties: Iraqi Front for National Dialogue (Al-Hewar) made up of the National Iraqi Front and the National Front for the United Free Iraq.

CENTRIST PARTIES

Iraqi National List

Main parties: Iraqi National Accord Movement, Iraqi Communist Party, Independent Democratic Gathering.

Other parties: National Congress Coalition, People's Union.

MINORITY PARTIES

Iraqi Turcoman Front

Main parties: Turkmen National Party, the Independent Turkmen Movement, the Islamic Movement of Iraqi Turkmen.

Al-Rafidain National List (Two Rivers List) representing the Assyrian, Chaldean and Syriac Christian communities.

Yezidi Movement for Progress and Reform (Al-Ezediah).

Commenting on the elections and the political process, Gareth Stansfield, author of *Iraq: People, History, Politics* said that:

> political life in Iraq moved from being ideologically based under Saddam to being interest and communally based following his removal. The communalisation of Iraqi political life was now codified by the results of the elections. Those who voted did so as Shi'is or Kurds. Those who did not vote did so as Sunnis… Iraqi society is reverting to the communal and is mobilising according to local identities of

ethnicity, sect and tribe. The question is will the pattern ever oscillate back to seeing the ideological superseding the communal once again.

As the political process continued without them and the Shias named Ibrahim Al-Jaafari prime minister, the Sunnis started to regret their boycott. Sunni tribal chiefs issued a list of demands, including participation in the government and drafting the new constitution. 'We made a big mistake when we didn't vote,' admitted Sheikh Hathal Younis from northern Nineveh.

As the violence continued the Americans seemed resigned to the fact that the rebels would not be defeated militarily, and on 22 February Pentagon officials and a number of insurgent leaders held talks for the first time. The insurgents were eager to secure a date for the withdrawal of American troops, while the Americans were hoping to divide the nationalist guerrillas from the fanatical Islamic groups.

Factions suspicious of one another were a hallmark of the first Iraqi government. They entrenched themselves in various ministries, and civil servants from Saddam's era and from the previous administration were purged. The Supreme Islamic Council was given the Interior Ministry and lost no time in giving positions to its own partisans and security forces.

The key figures in the government were referred to as *safawi*, a reference to the Persian Safavid Empire, which occupied Baghdad at certain times. Sunni Arab leaders accused the Interior Ministry of using the Supreme Islamic Council's militia, the Badr Brigade, to murder Sunni religious figures and terrorise Sunni communities. Increasing numbers of murder victims, apparently killed solely due to their religious origin, were being discovered. Sunni insurgent groups were using car and suicide bombs to kill as many Shias as they could.

The government was not able to stop the ever-widening cycle of violence. It did its best to stifle the growing independent trade union movement, especially the General Federation of Iraqi Workers (GFIW), which campaigned against America's privatisation agenda. Throughout 2005 public fears about the withdrawal of the old rationing system and a variety of state subsidies for basic necessities led to demonstrations across the country. The security forces, unaware of how to deal with mass demonstrations, reacted violently.

Shias, Sunnis and Kurds did not manage to reach agreement during the writing of the constitution. Federalism became the major bone of contention. The Sunnis were willing to accept Kurdish autonomy as an inevitability. The Kurds has been running their own affairs since 1991. But they were devastated when some of the Shias also supported federalism, envisaging a break-up of Iraq in which the Sunnis would be left with a region without resources in the centre of the country.

Deadlines for finalising the constitution came and went and in the end the Shias and Kurds passed the draft in the national assembly and the referendum on the constitution followed. The constitution was overwhelmingly rejected by Sunni Arabs and Turcomans, while most of the Kurds and Shias accepted it.

Sadly the new constitution created more problems then it solved. In the words of Gareth Stansfield, author of *Iraq: People, History, Politics*:

THE CONSTITUTION? THEY'VE WRITTEN IT AND THEY'LL RATIFY IT!

'So Umm F., did you have a chance to look at the constitution yet?' I asked.

'Well, Abu F. read me some of it from one the newspapers,' came the disinterested reply. She raised the clippers and furtively snapped away at a couple of branches.

'And what do you think?' I was curious. I had my own ideas about the constitution but I wanted to hear hers.

'I don't care. They've written it and they'll ratify it – what does it matter what I think?' I frowned and tried to hand her the Arabic version.

'But you should read it. Look, I even highlighted the good parts… The yellow is about Islam, and the pink is about federalism and here in green – that's all the stuff I didn't really understand.'

She looked at it suspiciously and then took it from me. I watched as she split the pile of 20 papers in two – she began sweeping the top edge of the wall with one pile, and used the other pile as a dustpan.

'But what will you vote?' I asked.

'You'll actually vote?' she scoffed

'It will be a joke like the elections… They want this constitution and the Americans want it – do you think it will make a difference if you vote against it?'

She put the stained sheets of paper back together and smiled as she handed them back to me. 'In any case, let no-one tell you it wasn't a useful constitution – look how clean the wall is now! I'll vote for it!'

It occurred to me then that not everyone was as fascinated with the constitution as I was, or some of my acquaintances both abroad and inside the country were. People are so preoccupied trying to stay alive and safe, and just get to work and send their children off to school in the morning, that the constitution is a minor thing.

Riverbend, 15 October 2005. Riverbend is the blogging name of a young Iraqi woman posting at riverbendblog.blogspot.com. Extract from Baghdad Burning: Girl Blog from Iraq

Post-Saddam Iraq **THE CONSTITUTION AND THE REFERENDUM**

8

It was something of a mess – promising all things to all groups, yet satisfying no group in particular, disappointing everyone and presenting a series of ambiguities which promised to haunt those who have to interpret its meaning in the future.

FINAL ELECTIONS ON 15 DECEMBER 2005

The results of the December elections were much the same as those held in January. The United Iraqi Alliance received 128 seats and the Kurdish List 53. The Sunnis and Moqtada Al-Sadr were now part of the government for the first time. The third largest share was taken by the Iraqi Accord Front of Sunni Arab parties, set up in October 2005, with 44 seats.

The formation of a government was problematic. The prime minister, Ibrahim Al-Ja'afari, upset the Kurds by visiting Ankara without the Kurdish foreign minister, Hoshyar Zebari. The Sunnis were determined to see another prime minister, as attacks by Shia gangs, associated with the Interior Ministry, increased. The political standoff was finally resolved on 22 April 2006 when the deputy leader of the Dawa Party, Nouri Al-Maliki, was appointed prime minister.

It was now up to Al-Maliki and his government to abandon forever the authoritarian state and usher in the transition to democracy. It was a formidable task as the essential building blocks – political parties, a political culture with democratic ideals and political will – were, if present at all, very weak.

Al-Maliki's government suffered from the same problems as those of his predecessor: ministries were used as power bases from which patronage was exercised, and paramilitary units were established in the name of security. The problems of insecurity, reconstruction, insurgency, unemployment and collapsing public services had to be tackled, but the shadow state made up of local leaders with their own militias was more powerful than the government in the Green Zone.

Charles Tripp, author of *A History of Iraq*, commented that:

> The distribution of portfolios in Al-Maliki's government reflected the power relationships established not simply by the electoral weight of their main figures, but also by the force they could command on the ground in particular localities, the hold they could exercise there, and their capacity to inflict serious damage on any who tried to interfere with the absolute control they enjoyed within their fiefdoms. It appeared to give tacit, even explicit, endorsement of powerful local leaders who would form the new oligarchy of the emerging order.

After the destruction of the Al-Askari Shia Mosque in Samarra in February 2006 (see page 239), some analysts reported that the civil war had started. The violent displacement of Sunnis from Shia areas and vice versa intensified in Baghdad, and the insurgency continued throughout the country. During 2006 and early 2007 around 100 Iraqi civilians a day were being killed.

On 25 June 2006 Al-Maliki put forward a 24-point peace plan aimed at brokering a ceasefire with insurgent groups and involving them in the political process. Ex-Baathists and former military personnel were willing to consider the proposals, but the radical Islamist elements of the insurgency turned a deaf ear.

Political power was rapidly devolving to the localities. An increasing number of provinces, contrary to the instructions of the central government, were turning away refugees from other areas. The Americans began co-operating with tribes in the Sunni Triangle in the battle against Al-Qaeda (see page 225), as the beleagured central governments' efforts were proving ineffectual. This culminated in some 72,000 Iraqis taking part in US-financed Awakening Forces or Concerned Local Citizens Groups. Many of their members were insurgents who had previously fought Coalition forces. Nouri Al-Maliki vehemently opposed American backing for the Awakening Forces, which he fears will become a third military organisation.

On 23 December 2007 the Iraqi Defence Minister Abdul-Qadir Al-Obaidi said in a news conference that these groups would not be allowed any infrastructure like a headquarters building, which could give them longer term legitimacy. The Al-Sadr Movement had accused the American army of opening the doors for Al-Qaeda followers and killers of Shias to reinvent themselves as the Awakening Forces. The Awakening Forces are also rejected by some Sunni groups and their offices have been closed down in Fallujah. 'Those tribal leaders want to control everything everywhere but they are not qualified for leadership. They are just a group of ignorant tribal men', said Ihsan Ahmad, a follower of the Islamic Party in Fallujah. Like the police force and army, the Awakening Forces could be prone to infiltration and exploitation. But the Americans have high hopes for their new allies and General David Petraeus, the senior US Commander in Iraq, would like to see them integrated into the security forces. A national civil service corps is also being considered so they can receive civilian training and become involved in public works projects.

While the Awakening Forces are making their presence felt throughout the country – they are now in 12 out of Iraq's 18 provinces – the survival of Maliki's government is becoming increasingly doubtful. The Moqtada Al-Sadr group withdrew from the governing Shia alliance in September 2007 and the main Sunni alliance withdrew from the cabinet in August. At the beginning of 2008, the cabinet had 17 ministers, with 23 portfolios left unfilled, and despite negotiations Mr Maliki has not been able to find replacements. In mid-January 2008 various Shia and Sunni groups declared a new political project or agreement aimed at confronting the sectarian system and supporting Iraqi national reconciliation.

Relations with Iran and Syria were also problematic. The USA continually accused Iran of arming Shia militias in the south and while the Iraqi government was reaffirming fraternal relations with Iran and anticipating the re-opening of Iranian consulates in Erbil and Basra, the Americans were arresting 'Iranian agents', to the chagrin of the government.

Syria was also suspected of aiding the Sunni insurgency by not paying enough attention to the poorly guarded border, but the Syrians were not inclined to assist the Americans in Iraq due to their policies in Palestine and Lebanon.

An increasing numbers of American soldiers were being killed. With little sign of progress in either curbing the insurgency or rebuilding the country, public support for the Bush administration ebbed away. After the questionable effect of the surge – sending an extra 30,000 troops to the Baghdad area in 2007 (see pages 212–14), both America and Britain focused their energies on taking steps towards the eventual withdrawal of their forces.

In February 2008, the very existence of Iraq as one state is uncertain. The central government is only the government of the Green Zone; the country is breaking up into smaller and smaller regions, localities and parts of cities, where local 'leaders and rulers' are in command, among them the Shia militias that control the south.

In October 2007 Ammar al-Hakim of the Supreme Islamic Council, one of Iraq's main Shia parties, backed federalism, telling his supporters that central government control was tyrannical.

The 2003 war and its aftermath changed Iraq forever. The pottery barnyard rule that if you break it you buy it no longer applies. Despite the best will in the world, America and Britain have not been able to repair the breakages and fragmentations that are a tragic spin-off of their war against the Saddam regime.

Iraq is now ruled by militias, mullahs and warlords, and the views and rights of the ordinary citizens are once again disregarded. The entire society has been transformed, and the language of force and violence is the main political currency. The British and the Americans will leave and the Iraqis will once again have to create new state structures and a political culture. If they broker their own peace agreements and power-sharing deals, a multi-communal, federal state may emerge. But this is a big 'if'.

9

The North (Iraqi Kurdistan)

Nobody should say the Kurds are dead, the Kurds are alive
Our banner shall never be lowered
We are the descendants of the Medes and Key Khasrew
Our homeland is our faith and religion.
We are the heroes of revolution and the colour red
Just look how bloodstained our history is.
The Kurdish people are gallantly standing to attention
Ready to decorate their living crown with blood.
Kurdish youth is ever present and ready
To sacrifice with their lives.

> Kurdish National Anthem, translated by M T Ali

The permanent constitution institutionalised a virtually independent
Kurdistan.

> Peter W Galbraith, author of *The End of Iraq*

After the 2003 war the Kurdistan Regional Government (KRG) continued
ruling the areas in what was known as the safe haven, set up after the 1991 Gulf
War due to concern about reprisals from the central government against the
Kurds who staged a popular uprising. The KRG receives a budget from the
central government in Baghdad.

The northern cities of Mosul and Kirkuk are not under the control of the
KRG. The return of large numbers of Kurds who were expelled from their
homes in Kirkuk has fuelled ethnic tensions with the Turcomans, who regard
the city as their traditional home (see pages 172–3).

The continuation of food aid from the United Nations has hindered the
development of the local economy, especially agriculture. A number of
expatriate Kurds have returned and are encouraging local industries such as
tourism. Expats are also buying real estate, setting up trading concerns and
working in the regional government or as doctors or engineers. The Minister
for Sports and Youth lived in Sweden for more than 20 years and is trying to
introduce many of the ideas he picked up there.

While violence has engulfed most of Iraq following the ousting of Saddam
Hussein, the areas ruled by the KRG have remained relatively trouble-free. The
Kurdish people identify with the regional government and have a stake in
preserving stability and security. Insurgents brought explosives into the region
but were caught, and as such were not able to establish a base.

The Kurds are immensely grateful to the Americans for ousting Saddam Hussein and American soldiers on R&R in Kurdistan are sometimes served free in restaurants and bars. A memorial of gratitude is being built for fallen American soldiers and their relatives will be invited to the unveiling.

A thin, relatively peaceful crescent around the upper rim of the country extending from Dohuk to Erbil and Suleimaniyah has allowed Iraqi Kurdistan to resume its traditional status as an area of refuge from the heat of the plains, both for foreign troops on R&R and for Arab Iraqis. Iraqi Kurdistan has been referred to as 'the other Iraq', an Iraq of peace and stability where the signs of development and construction are everywhere.

KURDISH CULTURE AND SOCIETY

The north of Iraq (Iraqi Kurdistan) is the home of over five million Kurds, the country's largest ethnic group. There are many stories about the origins of the Kurds, whose distinct identity has survived for around 2,000 years.

A widely held belief among historians, and the Kurds themselves, is that they are the descendants of the Medes of central Asia who helped to bring down the powerful Assyrian Empire (see pages 32–9). Some Kurdish Jews believe that Solomon sent genies to collect maidens for his harem. They succeeded the year he died, kept the maidens and lived in the desolate mountains. The Kurds are their children. There are also claims that the Kurds are the descendants of the lost tribes of Israel.

The name Kurdistan refers to the place where the Kurds live. Today this region cuts across the national borders of Turkey, Iran, Iraq and Syria. Large numbers of Kurds are also found in Khanaqin, Diyala and Baghdad.

THE PEOPLE The Kurds embraced Islam during the time of the Arab conquest in the 7th century, motivated in part by a desire to avoid paying taxes imposed on non-Muslims. Some 80% of the Kurds are Sunni Muslims, 15% are Shia Muslims. The remaining 5% are Sufis (members of the Qadiriya and Naqshbandiya brotherhoods); members of Islamic sects such as Ahl al Haqq (People of the Truth); and Yezidis, a cocktail religion that has borrowed from Zoroastrianism, Judaism, Christianity, Islam and other beliefs. The Kurdish Sorani and Kermanji dialects are spoken in Iraqi Kurdistan.

The north of Iraq is also the home of Christians (Assyrians found mainly in Mosul and Dohuk, and Chaldeans concentrated in Shaqlawa and Erbil), Turcomans, Yezidis found in the town of Sinjar on the slopes of the Sinjar mountains and the Shiekhan region, and Armenians.

The history of the Kurds is the history of a proud, rebellious, tribal people who have resisted control by outside forces, and suffered for it throughout the ages. In the words of Teresa Thornhill, author of *Sweet Tea with Cardamon: a Journey Through Iraqi Kurdistan*, 'it is a culture where almost everyone is standing on a mountain of pain and grief.' A popular saying tells us that the Kurds have 'no friends but the mountains' and history suggests this is true.

THE LANDSCAPE In Iraqi Kurdistan the scenery is magnificent, sometimes wooded and watered by turbulent streams, sometimes gaunt and bare, but always dramatic and often awesome.

The bright dazzling colours of tulips, roses, hyacinths, gladioli and daffodils, which appear in spring, are reflected in the costumes of Kurdish women. The men also love flowers and take a special delight in smelling roses. The main crops are wheat and barley grown on the plains of Mosul, Erbil and Kirkuk. Suleimaniyah is a traditional tobacco-producing region. Fruits such as apples, cherries, plums and pomegranates are also grown in Iraqi Kurdistan.

Over 40 different types of fish are found in the rivers and streams. The mountains were once popular hunting grounds for wild boars, bears, hyenas, ibexes and hares. The last lion was reportedly killed in around 1910. Tragically, much of the landscape has been devastated by war and the wanton destruction of the woodlands. Since the 1960s, the Iraqi regime had systematically destroyed the forests that provided a cover for the *peshmergas* (Kurdish guerrilla fighters whose name means 'those who face death').

The use of oak beams in houses in Baghdad and Basra has accelerated deforestation. Animals such as goats, which frequently eat saplings, are also a problem. Attempts at reforestation were made between 1970 and 1974 when the Kurds and the central government were not at loggerheads.

Legendary Arab hospitality is also a Kurdish characteristic and foreigners are often invited to stay with families. During the mass exodus of Kurds to the Turkish and Iranian borders after the failed uprising of 1991 the starving refugees were worried about not having any tea to share with personnel from international aid agencies.

The mountains of northern Iraq, the 'Alps of the Middle East', are traditional areas of retreat from the heat of the plains. They also act as a natural barrier for a society that is eager to preserve its culture. Ethnically the Kurds have no relationship with the Arabs. Many have left Iraqi Kurdistan, often under duress from a government eager to 'Arabise' the area, and settled in towns and cities throughout Iraq and overseas. The Iraqi Kurdish diaspora of around 250,000 people is spread throughout Europe, the Americas and the Middle East.

After the 2003 war, 160,000 Iraqis from outside the mountainous Kurdish north have moved there to flee the growing civil conflict. Refugees International reported that many of the internally displaced are struggling to survive, the victims of inattention, inadequate resources, regional politics (it is easier for Christians to get past the Kurdish border guards than a single Arab man) and bureaucratic obstacles (eg: problems with ration cards to receive food and fuel).

Due to the continuing stability of Iraqi Kurdistan, since 8 January 2007 UK immigration authorities have begun to arrest rejected Iraqi-Kurdish asylum seekers and return them to northern Iraq. But the United Nations High Commissioner for Refugees (UNHCR) has stated that the country cannot deal with the number of displaced persons it already has. Refugees who once had problems with the Kurdistan Democratic Party (KDP), the Patriotic Union of Kurdistan (PUK) or Islamist groups will not be safe, as the KDP and PUK are still in power and the Islamists are exerting their influence. The Kurdistan Regional Government (KRG) responds to frequent protests that take place against poor living conditions and the corruption and incompetence of the authorities with mass arrests.

On 3 July 2007 the US-based NGO Human Rights Watch issued a report detailing torture and abuses in security prisons in the Kurdish area of northern

It was Autumn 1969, in our village Dulbashik near Suleimaniyah. I was outside playing under the nut trees collecting nuts and playing hide-and-seek.

Suddenly out of the clear blue skies two Iraqi fighter planes swooped low across the village, circled round and returned low and loud. The sound was earth shattering. They then opened fire, releasing a spray of large bullets. I found a large rock to hide under. The bombardment lasted around ten minutes but it felt like an eternity. Whilst the shooting was going on, I saw my sister and younger brother nearby and ran to them. When I reached them, I found my younger brother slumped over and my sister with injuries to her hand and leg. I later learnt that my brother had died aged five, and I was only six.

Out of a school class of 20, I was the only one who escaped without injury: the rest were either killed or injured.

In the spring of 1975, in my first year of secondary school, when the peace talks broke down between the Great Barzani and central government, two fighter planes came over our school of 100 children and began to bombard the school. Many children were injured.

In 1978 the Iraqi army occupied all our lands. It was early morning; they came and evacuated the families from the houses, then dynamited all the houses and villages. We all cried as we watched our village being razed to the ground.

There were many such incidents and stories of atrocities as I was growing up. My father lived in fear for my safety and when I was 15 years old he decided to send me abroad to complete my studies. I left Kurdistan in the summer of 1979 and travelled across the mountains to Iran. I spent a year in Tehran and then managed to get a flight to the UK. When I arrived at Heathrow I had no documents and it took two weeks to process my immigration application before I could finally enter the UK formally.

I enrolled on an English language course and then went on to do my A-levels, a degree in civil engineering and finally a masters degree.

In 1996 I wanted to do my bit for my country, which was embroiled in civil war, and I came back as a visiting lecturer to give seminars to the three universities, which

Iraq. It found a consistent pattern of abuse involving detainees being subjected to beatings and stress positions, and allegations of electric shock torture.

When the report was issued a Kurdistan Regional Government spokesperson emphasised:

We have a very high regard for Human Rights Watch for historic reasons. In the early '90s Human Rights Watch was one of the few organisations that did a serious study on the Anfal genocide campaign and even today their report is the most authoritative. The report did acknowledge that the KRG was completely open. We gave them unhindered access to prisons. A lot of Middle East countries do not let them in. We are taking their findings very seriously and some of their recommendations have been implemented. By Middle Eastern standards Iraqi Kurdistan is exemplary, but by the standards we want for ourselves, which is democracy and respect for human rights, we have a lot to learn.

I found to be extremely under-equipped due to Saddam's sanctions. I donated £2,000-worth of civil engineering books to all three universities.

On my return I got a positive welcome from Dohuk University and they proceeded to offer me a position as a civil engineering lecturer. I returned in 2001 with my wife and children and we began to teach at that most sensitive time, with Saddam's troops based only 50km away. At the university we forged many links between UK and Kurdish universities and in the run-up to war we returned to the UK. We were asked by the British Council and the Association of Colleges to brief the UK/Iraq education working group on the situation in the region. Our meeting led to the Rawabit Project, whereby links were made between Iraqi and UK technical colleges.

The happiest day of my life was when I watched the toppling of Saddam on 9 April 2003. It was an event that I thought I would never see, as I always believed that after Saddam the nightmare would continue with his sons, who were worse than him.

In 2004 I made the decision to come back to Kurdistan for good with my family. On my return I immediately set up the Elland Trading Company, and began to import goods supplying to local companies.

My wife resumed her position as an English language lecturer at Dohuk University and with our experience from 2001 we found the education system to be very out-of-date and lacking basic resources, so we contacted a number of publishers to look at providing an English language curriculum. Macmillan did not hesitate and came on a fact-finding visit to Kurdistan. They are now in the process of developing English language textbooks from year-one primary to the final year of secondary school.

This year, following my continued interest in education, I have just opened an English Language college in Dohuk with plans to open a college in November in Erbil. Following the merger of the two political parties in Kurdistan my wife was asked to be Director of Relations for the Kurdistan Regional Government's Ministry of Education.

We now continue to reside in Erbil, Iraqi Kurdistan.

Kamal Kadir

Thousands of Kurdish expats have returned home to set up businesses and take advantage of the increasing opportunities in the region.

RELIGION In Iraqi Kurdistan, religion goes hand in hand with superstition. There is a great awareness of the invisible realm in everyday life and blessings and endearing spontaneous prayers are part of the normal vocabulary. In line with the beliefs of Zoroastrianism, an ancient Persian religion, women are careful when pouring hot liquid into an empty container as a spirit (*jinn*) could be harmed. Angels are seen as God's messengers who can bring rewards or punishments. Amulets for protection against the evil eye are common throughout the area.

Love of nature assumes a spiritual significance: trees and ponds are full of colourful pieces of cloth used as a sign of vigil for a wish. Some 56,000 years ago a Neanderthal man was buried in a flower bed in the area. Today flowers are grown on graves to let the soul rest. They are also a constant feature of Kurdish art and decoration.

SOCIAL STRUCTURE Rural life in Iraqi Kurdistan, a largely traditional society, is centred around land (tribe and village) and blood (family). Traditional village houses are single-storey buildings of mud-brick or stone. The roofs are flat and blend with the terrain. The corrugated iron of 'modernity' has found its way into Iraqi Kurdistan, as has the breeze-block. The villagers gather firewood and tend to their crops and livestock, as they have for centuries.

Behaviour is governed by a strict code of ethics; marriage and family are essential and adultery or free love is not socially acceptable, as a family's reputation depends on the 'honour' of its members. Women guilty of, or even suspected of, adulterous relationships continue to be the victims of so-called 'honour-killings'.

The Kurds place tremendous emphasis on generosity and hospitality. Guests are treated as royalty. Old people are respected far more than in Western society. Loyalty to the tribe and family is essential. Rumour-mongering is frowned upon and bad-mouthing even one's worst enemies is not acceptable.

CULTURE The long Kurdish winters are ideal times for storytelling and many stories describe how to survive in an inhospitable environment. A rich oral culture has been encouraged by the frequent destruction of Kurdish villages and property, which made it unsafe to commit inspiring traditional tales to paper. Some stories detract from the worries of everyday life. There are plenty of satirical tales. Animal stories with a spiritual moral are common. Sometimes

DOMESTIC VIOLENCE AND HONOUR KILLINGS ON THE RISE

Modern technology combined with medieval barbarity when a video showing a 17-year-old Yezidi girl, Doaa Khalil Aswad, stoned to death for falling in love with a Sunni boy in the village of Beshika near Mosul, was posted on the internet in May 2007.

The murder prompted the Organisation of Women's Freedom in Iraq (OWFI) to mount an international campaign to ban honour killings and force the Kurdish and Iraqi legal authorities to bring the perpetrators to justice.

The United Nations' quarterly report on human rights in Iraq states that domestic violence and honour killings are on the rise. In Iraqi Kurdistan there were more than 40 honour killings between January and March 2007. In Erbil rapes quadrupled between 2003 and 2006. Women are being terrorised into wearing the *abaya*, a large black cloak covering the whole body.

A report from Save the Children Iraq revealed that one in eight children die before the age of five and in Baghdad alone there are 300,000 widows. The OWFI said in a statement:

Women of Iraq have gradually let go of most of their 20th-century gains and privileges. The occupation has turned Iraq from a modern country of educated and working women into a divided land of Islamic and ethnic warlords who compete in cancelling women from the social realm. Millions of women's destinies are wasted between the destructive US war machine and different kinds of Islamic rule, which has turned women into helpless black objects of no will or worth.

the animals are portrayed as intelligent beings with their own code of conduct. There are also plenty of legends with a supernatural dimension, and historical epics. Tales of Imam Khidir i Zinde (The Immortal) are among the most common. He is an omnipresent, supernatural being who can be called to come to a person's help after elaborate rituals are performed. But he is the master of disguise and often goes unrecognised.

There is also the story of the avatar Shah Khushin, conceived when his mother was impregnated by the sun's rays, which entered her throat when she yawned during the ritual of bowing before the rising sun. When her family ordered her death for dishonouring their name, the sword was petrified in the air before it struck and the child was born as a speck of light, which turned into a man-child. The birth occurred after only 21 days, the multiplication of the sacred numbers three and seven. Khushin assumed his role as an avatar at the age of 32, one year short of when Christ died on the cross. He disappeared under the waves of the Gamasiyab River aged 61, one year short of when Mohammed died.

Village theatre, a natural progression from storytelling, appeared as a form of entertainment during the Hellenistic period (4th–2nd century BC) when the Greeks established city states in the Zagros Mountains. Some plays have a simple plot and are easy to stage: an old man is played by a miller who powders his beard with flour; a boy with a scarf around his head represents a female character. In two-actor plays the characters abuse each other in a form of slapstick comedy resembling that of Charlie Chaplin. In other plays the lines are all in verse.

Gymnasia were another Greek influence adopted by the Kurds, who were keen on wrestling matches. Games such as backgammon and chess are also popular. So is *ganem ganieh*, a game of chance played with wheat grains.

FESTIVALS The Kurds like to celebrate. Nawruz, or spring rites (similar to Easter), is the main festival, which welcomes spring on 21 March, the Kurdish New Year. It is also the Kurdish national day. The Kurdish calendar begins in AD380, the fall of the last Kurdish kingdom – the Kavusakan Dynasty – with an extra seven years added on.

Spring is a joyous time in contrast to the hardship of winter. It is the most beautiful season, with clear skies, pleasant sunshine and the blossoming of a fascinating range of flowers. Festivities last for more than a week and include breaking pottery for good luck, resolving misunderstandings and giving children presents. A few days before Nawruz bonfires are lit to signify the end of the dark winter season and the beginning of spring, the season of light. Evil spirits are scared off with fire crackers.

According to ancient legend, 21 March is also the day on which the blacksmith Kawa smashed the head of the tyrant Zuhak. Zuhak was suffering from a brain disease and doctors advised him to eat the brains of young people. Kawa offered Zuhak a number of his children but when he wanted to take his last son, Kawa revolted and killed him, emerging as a national hero.

Seasonal festivals, such as the first lambing, are also a feature of rural life. At harvest time the first sheaf reaped is offered to a stranger who passes by.

The comment by the late Mulla Mustafa Barzani, the most renowned Kurdish leader of the 20th century, that 'one who cannot dance is not a Kurd', illustrates the importance of dance in Kurdish culture. Traditional dance is often used by *peshmergas* (freedom fighters), politicians, as well as villagers, to make a political statement when Kurdish culture is suppressed. The dances resemble the Lebanese dabka and consist mainly of handholding group dances round a circle.

Musicians who play for the dancers are often also singers. Kurdish music, which influenced that of Iran and Turkey, tends to be melancholic, a reflection on the trials and tribulations of life. In Iraq, Kurdish music has been influenced by the fast, joyous tempo of Arabic music. Kurdish folk songs, or story songs with heroic, amorous, religious and political themes, are stories told to the accompaniment of music. Travelling Kurdish balladeers once sang about the achievements of epic heroes.

ARTS AND CRAFTS Kurdish art has influences dating back to the Halaf period (6000–5000BC). It is characterised by decorative motifs on painted pottery fired in two-chamber kilns. Some decorative motifs are based on geometric forms found in nature, while others have no connection with natural forms. Flower designs are still used in textiles and decorations.

Rugs and carpets also have a long history. Pile rugs were introduced by the nomads from the cold northern Eurasian steppes. The obelisk of the Assyrian King Shalmaneser III (858–824BC) shows his tribute, which included a pile of rugs. Clay impressions at the site of Jarmo near Suleimaniyah dating back to 8500–7000BC (see page 24) contain the world's oldest records of cloth weaving. Woven products were given as royal presents to the Assyrian court and as Mehrdad Izady, author of *The Kurds: A Concise Handbook*, notes, 'the tradition of fine weaving continued in Kurdistan until at least the end of the medieval period in the 15th century.' The Kurdish economy stagnated after the 15th century due to the decline in international trade and the 'best and handsomest carpets in the world', as described by Marco Polo, became a thing of the past, giving way to more rustic products.

Denise Sweetman, author of *Kurdish Culture: a Cross-Cultural Guide*, describes:

> intricate designs of birds, stars, flowers and leaves which delight the eye and invite a closer look. The colours – crimsons, oranges, golds, blues and greens – distinguish each design from the others. The thick woollen yarn is woven so that the patterns are clear and symmetrical.

Other traditional artefacts include stone- and metal-work, and pottery.

Riotous and gaudy colours, many of them thrown together seemingly haphazardly with absolutely no control or care to match them, is a trademark of Kurdish taste. Mehrdad Izady, notes that unusual dress makes a Kurd stand out in any crowd of conventionally dressed people, in ancient times as now. In days gone by Kurdish men and women wore large amounts of jewellery. Today it is worn mainly by women and is regarded as a source of family wealth and savings, often used to buy land or finance education.

The unique Kurdish colour-madness also runs through Kurdish art, which ranges from a modern abstract to cubist style to the traditional miniature painting style of the East. Artwork varies from socially committed nationalist themes popular with painters Gara Rasul and Rebwar, to the freestyle of still-life scenes, a favourite of Manoor Ahmed.

FOOD The Kurds, as Sweetman observed, are fanatical about fresh food. To share food together is one of the best and most enjoyable ways for people of two cultures to cross boundaries and to establish a friendship.

The land of the Kurds, as the northern part of the Fertile Crescent, offers abundant resources for wonderful cooking. Wheat grows on the sunny plains, as do apricot, peach and plum trees. Apples, walnuts, cherries, almonds and pears offer bounty in baskets. Pomegranates, figs and grapes of all varieties delight any guest who is fortunate enough to visit Kurdistan in late summer. Large flocks of sheep and goats, fattened on the tastiest grass of the mountain pastures, are raised for meat as well as for their milk, which is transformed by skilled Kurdish housewives into creamy cheese, white butter and chilled buttermilk. Grape syrup and honey sweeten bowls of thick yogurt, while wild herbs and mushrooms add their delicate flavours to grilled wild partridge and quail.

Kurdish cuisine, which has been influenced by Turkish and Iranian dishes, is rich and varied. Before urbanisation, a cooked breakfast and dinner were the main meals as people worked in the fields and did not return home for lunch. Today lunch is the main meal, eaten after 14.00 when offices have shut for the day. Meat, lamb or chicken, in the form of kebabs, are nearly always served during the midday and evening meals. If foreign visitors are present an animal may be killed in their honour.

HISTORICAL BACKGROUND

CHRONOLOGY

3000BC	Land of Karda mentioned in Sumerian clay tablet.
612BC	Fall of the Assyrian Empire after wars with the Babylonian King Nabopolassar, and the ancient Kurds, Medes and Elamites.
700–553BC	Median Empire. Kurds assimilated with the Medes, adopted their language and became a Median-speaking nation.
553BC	Median families given high positions in Achaemenid Persian Empire established by Cyrus the Great after his conquest of the Median Empire.
7th century AD	Large-scale conversion of the Kurds to Islam, motivated to some extent by a desire to avoid paying taxes levied on non-Muslims.
1187	Saladin, a Kurdish warrior, took Jerusalem from the Crusaders.
11th century	A number of Kurdish *aghas* (tribal chiefs) achieved total autonomy but most co-existed with the Seljuks.
1514	After a battle at Jalderan between the Safavid Persians and the armies of the Ottoman Empire, most of the Kurds were nominally under the control of the Ottomans but managed to preserve their autonomy.
1878–81	Uprising against the Ottomans led by Sheikh Obeidallah.
1908	First attempts at organising a Kurdish national movement.
1919–30	A period of unbroken struggle against the British carried on under Sheikh Mahmud Berzendji of

	Suleimaniyah. This revolt was accompanied by deportations.
1920	The Treaty of Sèvres envisaged the creation of an independent Kurdistan.
1923	The Treaty of Lausanne (which replaced the Treaty of Sèvres) between the allies and Turkey made no mention of an independent state for the Kurds and the fate of the Mosul region.
1925	The council of the League of Nations adopted the border line between Turkey and Iraq, annexing Mosul to Iraq.
1931	Revolt led by Sheikh Mahmud.
1945	Memorandum from the Kurds to the United Nations Constitutive Assembly outlined national claims. State of Kurdistan Republic established in Mahabad, Iran. Collapsed after a year.
1946	Kurdistan Democratic Party (KDP) formed.
1958	The promulgation of the Provisional Constitution of Iraq. Article 3 stated that 'the Arabs and the Kurds are partners in this fatherland'. Mustafa Barzani, the legendary Kurdish leader (see page 153), returned from exile in the Soviet Union. The KDP legalised.
1960–64	War between the central government and the Kurds. The KDP banned. Barzani negotiated ceasefire with Abd al-Salam Aref.
1961	Fierce battles between the Kurds and the Iraqi army.
1962	Kurdish fighters wiped out an Iraqi battalion in the Zakho region. The Iraqi Petroleum Company's oil pipeline near Kirkuk was sabotaged.
1963	Declaration by the Baath Party's Revolutionary Command Council that it recognised the rights of the Kurdish people. War broke out following the fall of the Baath government.
1966	Iraqi army implemented a policy of total destruction of Kurdish villages. Memorandum on genocide and other atrocities perpetrated against the Kurds submitted to the UN Secretary General and other international bodies.
1970	(11 Mar) Autonomy agreement between the Kurds and the Baathist government.
1971	Unsuccessful Baathist attempt to assassinate Barzani. Another attempt in 1972 also failed.
1974	Kurds rejected watered-down version of autonomy agreement. War with the Baathist government.
1975	Kurdish resistance collapsed and split into three factions after Iran withdrew support following the signing of the Algiers Agreement with Baghdad. Jalal Talabani established the Patriotic Union of Kurdistan (PUK).
1979	Death of Mulla Mustafa Barzani, the leader of the Kurdish national movement. Massoud Barzani, his son, elected president of the KDP.

1987	Iraqi Kurdistan Front formed.
1988–89	Anfal campaign against the Kurds in which 182,000 people perished. Chemical weapons attack on the town of Halabja left an estimated 5,000 people dead.
1990	(2 Aug) Iraq invaded Kuwait, first Gulf War.
1991	(Mar) Kurds rebelled against Saddam Hussein's rule at the end of the first Gulf War and seized control of most of Iraqi Kurdistan. Uprising crushed, thousands of Kurds fled to Iran and Turkey.
1991	(7 Jun) Safe haven handed to the UN by Western allies. Refugees returned.
1992	(May) Kurdish elections in the safe haven. Kurdistan Regional Government (KRG) formed.
1993	A power struggle between the PUK and KDP degenerated into armed clashes.
1994	(May–Aug) Fighting between the PUK and KDP.
1996	(Aug) Iraqi troops entered the safe haven and ejected the PUK from Erbil. USA launched missile attacks on southern Iraq. The Iraqi opposition in the north was crushed and many of its members were executed. A peace agreement, known as the Ankara Accords, brokered by America.
1998	Washington Agreement. The PUK and KDP agreed to share power, reconvene the national assembly and hold new elections. The agreement was not fully implemented and Iraqi Kurdistan was ruled by two parallel administrations.
1999	Attacks by American and British planes on Iraqi forces, challenging their right to patrol the northern and southern no-fly zones.
2000	Elections for local administration held in PUK-controlled regions.
2001	Improvement in relations between the KDP and PUK. Decision for KDP to open offices in PUK-administered areas and vice versa. Iraq called for abolition of the no-fly zone at the Arab League Summit.

2003

Feb	US Secretary of State Colin Powell accused the Iraqi Kurdish Islamist group Ansar al-Islam of playing an important role in linking Al-Qaeda with Saddam's regime. Kurdish leaders rejected proposals to bring Turkish troops into northern Iraq as part of the US military campaign. Widespread anti-Turkish demonstrations in Kurdish towns. The Turks rejected a parliamentary bill allowing US troops to deploy on Turkish soil.
3 Mar	The KDP and PUK created a 'joint higher leadership'. The chairmen were Massoud Barzani and Jalal Talabani.

Mar	Mosul and Kirkuk came under heavy fire as the 2003 war began.
22 Mar	Coalition forces attacked the bases of Ansar al-Islam in Iraqi Kurdistan, leaving dozens of casualties.
27 Mar	Northern front opened up with the landing of hundreds of US paratroopers in Erbil.
9 Apr	Kurdish fighters took control of Mosul and Kirkuk.
Jul	Saddam's sons Uday and Qusay killed in a gun battle in Mosul.

2004

Jan	On a hilltop outside Mosul 2,243 former officers raised their right hands and renounced the Baath Party and all its works.
1 Feb	Some 56 people killed by twin suicide bombings, which hit the KDP and PUK offices packed with guests for the Muslim holiday of Eid al-Adha.
8 Jun	Kurds devastated when UN Resolution 1546 endorsing the transfer of sovereignty to an Iraqi government, did not endorse the interim constitution (agreed to in March 2004), which recognised special Kurdish autonomy in the northern provinces of Dohuk, Suleimaniyah and Erbil.
24 Jun	Forty-four people died and 216 were hurt in a series of car bombings in Mosul.
14 Jul	The governor of the city killed.
Nov	Lawlessness in Mosul after insurgents moved north following the American offensive against Fallujah.

2005

Jan	An alliance of Kurdish parties came second in the national election; 77 Kurdish deputies in the interim parliament.
Apr	PUK leader Jalal Talabani elected interim Iraqi president.
May	Some 50 people killed in a suicide bomb attack on police recruits in Erbil.
Jun	Kurdish parliament in Erbil held its first session. Massoud Barzani became president of the autonomous region.
Dec	Major oil discovery near Zakho.

2006

| 21 Jan | The Kurdistan Regional Government established the first unified cabinet. |
| Sep | The Kurdish flag replaced the Iraqi flag in Iraqi Kurdistan, but the central government protested that only the Iraqi flag should be raised. |

| 13 Jun | Co-ordinated wave of suicide attacks and remote-controlled bombs left 22 people dead and 43 wounded in Kirkuk. |
| Sep | The BBC's *Newsnight* programme claimed that former Israeli commandos secretly trained Kurdish soldiers in counter-terrorism operations. |

2007

6 Mar	Insurgents from the Islamic State in Iraq Movement, of which Al-Qaeda in Iraq is a part, stormed Badoush prison 24km northwest of Mosul and freed 68 prisoners, of whom 57 were non-Iraqis.
2 Apr	A bomb at a Kirkuk police station injured students at a nearby girls' school.
May	American forces transferred responsibility for security in the provinces controlled by the KRG.
1 Jun	Turkey deployed extra troops on the border with Iraqi Kurdistan and announced it could cross any time in pursuit of members of the PKK (the Kurdistan Workers Party, a rebel group that has been waging an armed struggle since 1984 for an independent Kurdish state within Turkey).
4 Jun	Saddam Hussein's cousin, 'Chemical Ali', was sentenced to death for the Anfal campaign of genocide that killed 180,000 Kurds.
7 Jul	Truck bomb in the town of Amirli, south of Kirkuk, killed 105 people and injured 240.
16 Jul	Some 80 people killed in Kirkuk in a co-ordinated attack by a suicide truck bomber in a crowded market and a separate car bomb parked on a busy street.
14 Aug	Truck and car bombs hit two villages of Yezidi Kurds, killing at least 250 people – the deadliest attack since 2003.
	Cholera outbreak in Suleimaniyah and Kirkuk affects internally displaced persons. Over 2,300 cases reported.
20 Aug	Clashes on the northeastern border with Iran between Revolutionary Guards and guerrillas of the Iranian Kurdistan Free Life Party displaced around 1,000 people from their homes.
8 Sep	Turkey announced it is going to build a 470km 'security wall' at the border with Iraqi Kurdistan costing US$2.3 billion.
4 Oct	Kurdistan Regional Government announced four new oil deals.
17 Oct	Turkey's parliament agreed to raids into northern Iraq in pursuit of PKK rebels.
21 Oct	At least 15 Turkish soldiers killed near the Iraq border, in an ambush by Kurdish rebels.

28 Oct	The Kurdish President warned Turkey that an act across the border would be classed as a declaration of war as clashes continued between Turkish troops and Kurdish fighters in Turkey, leaving 20 Kurdish guerrillas dead. He expressed defiance at Turkey's threatened invasion.
17 Dec	Turkish jets bombed PKK targets in Iraq. Incursion by ground forces followed.
22 Dec	More Turkish air raids on PKK targets.

2008

| 9 Feb | Dr Ashti Hawrami, the KRG's Minister of Natural Resources, insisted the KRG would continue to sign production contracts with foreign oil companies despite protests from the central government in Baghdad. |
| 24 Feb | Ten thousand Turkish troops launched a ground offensive against PKK guerrillas. |

INTRODUCTION The Kurds have been living in the Zagros mountains since the beginning of history, when the first written records appeared in the Sumerian city states in 3000BC. The land of Karda is mentioned on a Sumerian clay tablet from the 3rd millennium BC. In the ancient world they were part of the two-way struggle between the people of the plains and the mountain people of the north. The Babylonians referred to the Kurds as valiant or brave (*garda*), the Akkadians used the term Kuti to denote inhabitants of the Zargos and eastern Taurus mountains, while the Persians spoke about the Kurds, a word which was probably derived from the Babylonian word *garda*.

The ancient Kurds waged war with the Assyrian Empire for 700 years. The mountains, the saviours of the Kurdish people from invaders throughout the centuries, were their refuge and prevented their total destruction. In alliance with the Babylonian King Nabopolassar, the Medes and the Elamites, they fought the Assyrian Empire until it crumbled in 612BC.

During the days of the powerful Median Empire (700–553BC) the Kurds coalesced with the Medes and adopted their language. The Median Empire stretched from the southern shore of the Black Sea and Aran province (the modern-day Republic of Azerbaijan) to north and Central Asia and Afghanistan. It included many tributary states, among them that of the Persians, which eventually supplanted and absorbed the Median Empire into the Achaemenid Persian Empire created by Cyrus the Great. During the days of the Achaemenid Empire (553–300BC) the Kurds did not leave their mountain homeland in the Zagros Mountains; they joined the Persians to make a single nation. Cyrus the Great gave Median families the highest positions in his empire.

The Achaemenid Empire was followed by the Parthian (247BC–AD226), an arch-enemy of the Roman Empire in the east. At its height the Parthian Empire covered all of Iran proper, as well as regions of the modern countries of Armenia, Iraq, Georgia, eastern Turkey, eastern Syria, Turkmenistan, Afghanistan, Tajikistan, Pakistan, Kuwait, the Persian Gulf coast of Saudi Arabia, Bahrain, Qatar and the UAE. But the empire was loosely organised and the last king was defeated by one of the empire's vassals of the Sassanid Dynasty.

The Treaty of Sèvres, 10 August 1920, Article 64 states that:

> If within one year from coming into force of the present Treaty the Kurdish peoples within the areas defined in Article 62 shall address themselves to the Council of the League of Nations in such a manner as to show that a majority of the population of these areas desires independence from Turkey, and if the Council then considers that these peoples are capable of such independence and recommends that it should be granted to them, Turkey hereby agrees to execute such a recommendation and to renounce all rights and title over these areas. If and when such renunciation takes place, no objection will be raised by the Principal Allied Powers to the voluntary adhesion to such an independent Kurdish State of the Kurds inhabiting the parts of Kurdistan which has hitherto been included in the Mosul Vilayet.

The Sassanid Dynasty defeated the last Parthian king Artabanus. The Sassanid Empire (AD266–636) witnessed the highest achievement of Persian civilisation and was the largest Iranian empire before the Arab conquest of AD641. Persia influenced Roman civilisation considerably during Sassanid times, and the Romans reserved for the Sassanid Persians alone the status of equals, exemplified in the letters written by the Roman Emperor to the Persian Shahanshah (leader), which were addressed to 'my brother'. The last Sassanid king Yazdegerd III could not stand up to the Arab conquerors and a new era began in Iraqi and Kurdish history.

David McDowall, author of *A Modern History of the Kurds*, notes that with the Arab conquest the Kurds emerged from historical obscurity, rapidly confirming the longevity of their reputation for political dissidence. They first came into contact with the Arab armies who conquered Mesopotamia in AD637.

The pattern of nominal submission to central government, be it Persian, Arab or subsequently Turkic, alongside the assertion of as much local independence as possible, became an enduring theme in Kurdish political life.

One of the most famous Kurds is Saladin, a noble warrior who effectively took the caliphate and commanded the Muslim forces during the Crusades, Christian-Muslim wars that lasted from 1096 to 1453 (see page 56). His forces fought in the territory of present-day Syria, Lebanon and Israel, and Saladin became the ruler of Egypt in 1169 and Syria in 1186. One of his greatest achievements was the taking of Jerusalem from the Christians in 1187, setting limitations on the Crusader kingdoms and principalities. Saladin was born in Tikrit, also the birthplace of Saddam Hussein, and is buried in Damascus.

During the 11th century a number of Kurdish tribal chiefs (aghas) achieved total autonomy, but most co-existed with the Seljuks. In 1514, after a battle at Chaldrian between the Safavid Persians and the armies of the Ottoman Empire, most of the Kurds nominally came under the control of the Ottomans, but managed to preserve their autonomy. Four hundred years later, after the break up of the Ottoman Empire at the end of World War I, the Kurds were promised their own state in the Treaty of Sèvres.

9

This promise was not kept and the traditional Kurdish homeland now cuts across the national boundaries of Turkey, Iran, Iraq and Syria. These countries have many disagreements but they are united in their rejection of the acceptance of an independent Kurdish state, and have reluctantly conceded to some degree of Kurdish autonomy.

THE 20TH CENTURY

After World War I, Britain's attempts to control the region through Sheikh Mahmud Barzinji proved disastrous. He was invited to be the governor, a position he held under the Turks. Barzinji soon came into conflict with Britain as he felt the Kurds should be given greater regional autonomy. He also had differences with the heads of other clans and the long-established Kurdish families settled in Baghdad. In 1931 Sheikh Mahmud revolted, agitating for a united Kurdistan. He was defeated and placed under town arrest in the south of the country. But Kurdish national aspirations could not be arrested.

The establishment of the State of Kurdistan Republic in Mahabad, Iran, in 1945 gave a major impetus to the national aspirations of the Kurdish people. But it collapsed a year later, when Iranian troops marched into Mahabad and ended Kurdish rule in the region.

One of the major nationalist figures to emerge during this time was Mulla Mustafa Barzani, who was appointed commander of the republic's army. After spending 12 years in exile in the Soviet Union, Mulla Mustafa Barzani returned to Iraq when the 1958 coup toppled the monarchy, and formed a friendly alliance with the Prime Minister, Abdul Karim Qasim.

Qasim was the first Iraqi leader to declare that Kurds and Arabs were equal partners. The new Iraqi constitution in fact stated that 'the Kurds and Arabs are partners within this nation and guaranteed their rights within the framework of the Iraqi Republic.' The Kurdish people had great expectations of freedom and democracy, but before long it became apparent that the constitution's fine words could not and would not be translated into actions.

When Qasim could not fulfil the promises he had made to his one-time ally and friend he started arming tribes hostile to Barzani such as the Zibaris, the Baradost, Herki and Surchi. The KDP was banned, the former allies became enemies and the war between the Kurds and the central government continued until Qasim's overthrow in 1963. When the Baathists were firmly in control of the country an 11-point peace agreement was declared on 11 March 1970.

TWO DECADES OF WAR At first the Baathists remained true to the agreement but there was disagreement about three major issues:

1   The demarcation of the Kurdish area
2   The issue of the oil fields and the Kurds' insistence that Kirkuk must be part of the Kurdish autonomous region
3   The Arabisation programme, which began in 1968

Mistrust between the Kurds and the government increased and fighting started again when the government justified increasing its forces in the Kurdish areas on the grounds of an Iranian threat. The Baathists unilaterally declared an

MULLA MUSTAFA BARZANI: LEGENDARY KURDISH HERO

Mulla Mustafa Barzani (1904–79) came from a respected religious family. His name became synonymous with the Kurdish resistance. When he was just two years old he was detained with his mother in Mosul prison following an uprising against Ottoman rule. In 1919 he took part in Sheikh Mahmud's uprising, commanding a force of 300 when he was just 15. His brother, Sheikh Ahmed Barzani, revolted against British rule in 1932. When the State of Kurdistan Republic was founded in Mahabad (Iran) in 1945, Mulla Mustafa Barzani was appointed commander of the republic's army. The Kurdistan Democratic Party of Iran (KDPI) was established in 1945, and in 1946 he founded the Kurdistan Democratic Party – an amalgamation of parties into one party. The KDP was the only Iraqi Kurdish party until the establishment of the PUK in 1976. Barzani remained its president until his death in 1979.

Following the collapse of the Mahabad Republic in 1946, he lived in the Soviet Union until 1958. After the revolution of 14 July (see pages 75–6) he returned to Iraq where he was welcomed by the Kurdish and Iraqi masses. During the 1963 Baathist coup, Barzani welcomed all patriots to the liberated areas. Under his leadership the Kurdish national movement signed the 11 March 1970 agreement with the Iraqi government (see page opposite), on which the government subsequently reneged.

After the collapse of the Kurdish resistance in 1975, when the Shah of Iran withdrew his support, Barzani moved to Iran. His failing health and his distrust of the Shah prompted him to seek medical treatment for lung cancer in the USA, where he remained until his death in 1979. He was buried in Ashnoviya, Iranian Kurdistan. In 1994 thousands of people took part in a mass memorial in the safe haven to commemorate the 15th anniversary of his death. His body was moved to Barzan where he was born.

Autonomy Law on 11 March 1974 and gave the KDP 14 days to agree so they could continue their participation in government. The new law was a watered-down version of the 1970 agreement, which the Kurds rejected mainly because of the Kirkuk issue. The KDP insisted on a proportional distribution of revenues from the Kirkuk oil field. The 14-day period expired and a full scale war began in April 1974.

At first the Kurds, aided by the Iranians, inflicted heavy losses on the Iraqi army, but the Kurdish resistance collapsed overnight after the Algiers Agreement of 1975, between Saddam Hussein and the Shah of Iran, in which Iraq gave up its claim to the Shatt al Arab waterway (the Tigris/Euphrates outlet south of Basra to the Gulf). Iran cut off its assistance to the Kurds and Barzani departed for America, where he died of cancer in 1979.

The war left 7,000 Iraqi soldiers and more than 2,000 Kurdish fighters dead, and displaced 600,000 people. Apart from the KDP, other parties emerged within the Kurdish movement, namely the Patriotic Union of Kurdistan

(PUK) led by Jalal Talabani, and the Kurdistan Socialist Party. In 1987 five main Kurdish nationalist parties set up the Iraqi Kurdistan Front (IKF). Their slogan was real autonomy for the Kurds and democracy for Iraq.

The end of the Iran–Iraq War in 1988 proved disastrous for the Kurds. They were hoping for an Iranian Kurdish victory and the downfall of Saddam Hussein. But when the Kurds expanded the territory they controlled near the Iranian border to an area almost the size of Lebanon, the regime responded with a chemical weapons attack on Halabja and other areas.

On 22 July 1988 Iran accepted the UNSCR 598 ceasefire resolution and Iraq launched a major offensive against the Kurds using 60,000 troops. Thousands fled across the border to Turkey and Iran but the regime continued to use chemical weapons with impunity as the international community did little more than condemn the attacks. On 6 September 1988 an amnesty was offered to the refugees but few returned.

Towards the end of the first Gulf War, the Kurdistan Front was eager to ally itself with the Iraqi opposition committed to the overthrow of Saddam Hussein. During the popular uprising in March 1991 the Kurds controlled nearly all of Iraqi Kurdistan but the Iraqi army brutally sought to re-establish the government's writ over territory controlled by the Kurds, prompting another refugee exodus. Over 1.5 million Kurdish people fled towards the Turkish and Iranian borders to escape from Saddam's forces.

Turkey refused to let the refugees in. The deaths of 1,000 people a day on the Iranian and Turkish frontier prompted the setting up of the safe haven, which was officially handed over by the Western allies to the United Nations on 7 June 1991. The refugee crisis was alleviated and at the beginning of 1992 most refugees returned to Iraqi Kurdistan.

THE SAFE HAVEN Since mid-1991 until recently, the safe haven was administered by the Kurds. Until the 2003 invasion, Coalition war planes regularly policed the no-fly zone to prevent the Iraqi regime from launching air attacks. The safe haven became a de facto autonomous Kurdish entity ruled by the two main Kurdish parties. After the 2003 war the Kurds continued to run their own affairs. Peter Galbraith, author of the *End of Iraq*, highlighted the fact that in the 70 years up to 1991 that Iraq ruled Kurdistan, Baghdad authorities constructed 1,000 schools. The Kurdistan Government built another 2,000 schools between 1992 and 2003, recruiting and training the necessary teachers. When Saddam pulled out of Kurdistan in 1991 there was one university in the region. The Kurdistan government opened two new universities – in Dohuk and Suleimaniyah. All three are of high quality. Medical instruction is in English and Kurdistan's new doctors are qualified by the British Medical Board. Most of the 4,500 villages destroyed by the Iraqi regime since the 1970s and during the Anfal campaign of 1987–89 (see page 182) have been rebuilt by the Kurdistan Regional Government. The area now has more livestock than ever before. Every morning school children sing a Kurdish national song and study from text books printed mostly by the KRG.

A NEW DEMOCRACY The Kurdish elections of May 1992, judged as free and fair by more than 50 observers from 12 countries, were a watershed in Kurdish history, which sent shock waves through the dictatorial regimes of the Arab world. There was an overwhelming eagerness among the young and old to vote. A picture of a man carrying his old mother to the polling station was published by many Western newspapers: the Kurdish democratic experiment was one of the rare 'good news' stories to come out of the Middle East.

The PUK gained 49% and the KDP 51% of the votes, while smaller parties, such as the socialists and the Islamic Union Movement in Kurdistan–Iraq, failed to gain the minimum 7% of the vote required to secure a parliamentary seat. Five seats were allocated for the Christians. Women made up 7% of the parliament, compared with 9% in Britain! A Kurdish Regional Government was formed and the Kurdish Assembly started meeting in Erbil.

CONFLICT, INVASION AND WAR The 50/50 power-sharing deal to prevent autonomy in the governing of the Kurdish region did not work and the ensuing power struggle resulted in armed clashes between the PUK and KDP militias. In 1994 the PUK seized Erbil and the ambitious, idealistic democratic experiment came to an inglorious end. Attempts by both the USA and Britain to bring the two parties to the negotiating table failed and regional powers entered the conflict: Turkey on the side of the KPD and Iran on the side of the PUK.

In 1996, when Iranian forces entered PUK-controlled territory under the pretext of pursuing members of the Kurdish Democratic Party (Iran), the KDP first asked the Americans to intervene. When the plea fell on seemingly deaf ears, Baghdad's help was enlisted: 30,000 Iraqi troops entered the city of Erbil and surrounding areas and assisted the KDP in ousting the PUK from the regional capital. The intervention of the Iraqi army dealt a death blow to the activities of a number of anti-Saddam opposition groups based in Iraqi Kurdistan; after the occupation a large number of Iraqi secret police remained in the area to root out Saddam's opponents. Around 1,500 people were arrested and 2,500 Iraqis and Kurds who were working with the INC (Iraqi National Congress, a coalition of opposition parties and groups) were evacuated to Guam and subsequently re-settled in the USA.

America's attempts to reconcile the two main Kurdish parties culminated in the Ankara Accords of October 1996 and the Washington Agreement of September 1998. Under this agreement Barzani and Talabani agreed to set up a Coalition administration in preparation for new elections.

When hostilities first broke out in 2003 the northern front was almost forgotten. As Ben Rooney pointed out in *The Daily Telegraph*'s publication *War on Saddam*, an unsteady peace had existed in northern Iraq since the 1991 Gulf War and the establishment of the UN safe haven to protect the Kurdish majority. The Kurds were bitter opponents of Saddam, and in them General Franks saw a useful ally. When his plans to open up a second front against Baghdad through Turkey were thwarted by Ankara, he hoped to see the fearsome Kurdish freedom fighters, the *peshmergas*, take on the Iraqis in the north.

On 29 March 2003 American bombing enabled the *peshmergas* to attack the bases of Ansar Al Islam, an extremist group with suspected links to Al-Qaeda. The first major battle on the northern front was fought on 3 April, when the *peshmergas* seized a strategic bridge on the road to Mosul.

Throughout the war the Kurds showed remarkable restraint and did not make a grab for Mosul and Kirkuk. But after the fall of Saddam's regime the

The interests and influence of European and regional powers and the Baghdad government aside, the politics of the safe haven are largely influenced by relations between the leader of the Patriotic Union of Kurdistan (PUK), Jalal Talabani, and the leader of the Kurdistan Democratic Party (KDP), Massoud Barzani.

Jalal Talabani was born in 1933 in the village of Kelkan, in Iraqi Kurdistan near Lake Dokan. In 1946, at the age of 13, he formed a secret Kurdish student association. The following year he became a member of the KDP and in 1951, at the age of 18, he was elected to the KDP's central committee. His political activities prevented him from continuing his law studies, but after the overthrow of the Hashemite monarchy in 1958 he returned to law school and also pursued a career as a journalist and editor of two publications.

The collapse of the Kurdish revolt in March 1975 was a time of crisis for the Kurds in Iraq. Believing it was time to give a new direction to the Kurdish resistance and to Kurdish society, Talabani, along with a group of Kurdish intellectuals and activists, founded the PUK. In 1976, he began organising armed resistance inside Iraq. During the 1980s Talabani, with other Kurdish leaders, led the Kurdish struggle from bases inside Iraq, until the regime's brutal 'Anfal' campaign in 1988, during which 182,000 Kurdish men, women and children were massacred (see page 182).

Talabani worked closely with the USA, UK, Turkey, France and other countries in setting up the safe haven. One of the longest serving figures in Iraqi-Kurdish politics,

Americans could not restrain them any longer. On 10 April they arrived in Kirkuk to a tumultuous welcome as posters of Saddam were torn down and government shops looted. Refugees who had been forced out of the city during the regime's Arabisation programme returned, while the servants of Saddam fled. In Mosul the Iraqi garrison surrendered *en masse*. After the fall of Baghdad the Kurds decided that the POWs should not be considered captives, and the head of the Kurdistan Democratic Party, Massoud Barzani, gave instructions for them to be treated as guests of the Kurdish people. A new chapter in the history of Iraqi Kurdistan had begun.

IRAQI KURDISTAN – THE OTHER IRAQ

Iraqi Kurdistan is referred to by the Kurdistan Development Corporation as 'The Other Iraq' in a major advertising campaign to promote investment and trade in the region. The humming towns are full of well patronised cafés and shops. There are many mobile shops and internet cafes springing up. Liquor is also freely available, sometimes sold by Christians who fled from the troubled south. Neon signs light the streets full of people, including women and girls, who in Baghdad are seldom seen in public. Assad Nejmeddin, an English student at the University of Erbil, said:

he has been a prominent figure in Iraqi opposition activities, and a member of the Governing Council set up by the Coalition Provisional Authority. On 7 April 2005 he became the President of Iraq. On 22 April 2006, he was sworn in for a second term as president, thus becoming the first president elected under the country's new constitution.

Massoud Barzani was born on 16 August 1946 (the day the KDP was founded), in the Kurdish Republic of Mahabad, declared in Iranian Kurdistan. When the republic fell he returned to Iraq with thousands of Barzani clan members who were promptly deported to the southern part of the country. He studied in Baghdad but sacrificed his education at the age of 16 to join the *peshmerga* (freedom fighter) forces. His experiences in the rugged mountains of Kurdistan provided him with the mettle and leadership skills that later propelled him to the helm of the Kurdish movement. He was part of the delegation that signed the autonomy deal with Baghdad in March 1970 (see page 152), and when the government reneged on its pledges he took part in the armed struggle at the side of his father, Mustafa Barzani. He accompanied his father to the USA at the end of the 1970s and after his father's death he returned to Kurdistan and assumed a leading position in the KDP. In 1979 he was elected as its new president, a position that he still holds. He is the author of *Barzani and the Kurdish Liberation Movement*.

Barzani was elected president of the Iraqi Kurdistan region by the Kurdish parliament in June 2005.

I don't know why we're bothering with Baghdad. I and my friends don't even speak Arabic. We have done very well on our own for the past 12 years. Let's continue.

It seems that most Kurds resident in 'the other Iraq' agree with her. Peter Galbraith, author of *The End of Iraq*, noted that:

when the January 2005 elections took place, there were referendum booths just outside, or actually inside, every polling place. Two million Kurds voted in the referendum and 98% chose independence. The outcome put Kurdish and Iraqi leaders on notice that Kurdistan's voters would reject a permanent constitution that required any significant reintegration of the region into Iraq. The permanent constitution institutionalised a virtually independent Kurdistan, the very result Bremer [see page 123] sought to avoid.

(America, which now requires Turkey as an ally, has always been ambivalent towards the creation of an independent Kurdish state.)

The Kurdistan Regional Government (KRG) has two main priorities: to ensure the autonomy of the Kurdish region of northern Iraq and to encourage investment and development.

IRAQI KURDISTAN IN THE PERMANENT CONSTITUTION

The permanent constitution adopted in the October 2005 referendum recognised the Kurdistan region as Iraq's first federal region. It allows Kurdistan to have its own military, called Guards of the Region. Kurdistan law prevails when there is a conflict with federal law. This means that Kurdistan's secular legal system and Western-style constitutional human rights protection will continue to apply as other parts of Iraq evolve towards theocracy.

Kurdistan owns and manages its own land and water. The regional government will have exclusive control over future oil fields and those not yet in commercial production) within the region.

Abridged from Peter W Galbraith's The End of Iraq

At the time of writing in 2008, the Coalition government was led by Prime Minister Nechirvan Barzani. It assumed office on 7 May 2006. The parties in the Coalition are the Kurdistan Democratic Party (KDP), the Patriotic Union of Kurdistan (PUK), the Kurdistan Toilers Party, the Kurdistan Socialist Democratic Party, the Kurdistan Islamic Union, the Kurdistan Communist Party, the Islamic Group and the Turcoman Brotherhood Party. Cabinet members include a Chaldean, an Assyrian, a Yezidi, a Faili and an independent Turcoman.

Following the unification agreement of 21 January 2006, the KRG established the first unified cabinet. Prior to the agreement the governorate of Suleimaniyah was governed by a PUK-led administration, while the governorates of Erbil and Dohuk were governed by a KDP-led administration.

The KRG has an ambitious growth plan. It is trying to follow Dubai's example by attracting foreign investors with job skills and know-how. Ratified in July 2006, the foreign investment law incentives include customs relief, tax holidays and the freedom to repatriate profits.

Warwick Knowles, a Middle East economist at the UK's Dun & Bradstreet Corp, agrees. 'There's a bit of a parallel in the Kurdish region with Dubai. Costs are rising for everything. Infrastructure projects are being built every day.' They include an exclusive new development in Erbil, where some of the houses have as many as 11 bedrooms.

The construction boom is being fed by Turkey. Every day hundreds of trucks cross the border with steel, concrete and other raw materials. Nearly 600 foreign companies are registered in the region, 350 of them Turkish.

Two new international airports have opened in Erbil and Suleimaniyah, with over 80 direct flights scheduled per week to and from Dubai, Jordan, Istanbul, Frankfurt, Stockholm, Amsterdam and other destinations.

Iraqi-Kurdistan produces 50% of the wheat produced in Iraq, 40% of the barley, 98% of the tobacco, 30% of the cotton and 50% of the fruit.

The Kurdistan Development Corporation is keen to draw attention to Kurdistan's rebuilding programme, which started in earnest some 12 years ago. Between 1992 and 1999 around 1,000km of new roads and highways were built in Iraqi-Kurdistan; 600km were repaired and covered with tarmac; and 15 new bridges were constructed. Nearly 132 million dinars (US$110,000) was spent on restoring manufacturing industries by buying essential machinery, equipment and raw materials, especially for textiles, cigarette and canning factories and marble quarries. A total of 26% of the regional budget was spent on construction, repair, re-surfacing and the building of government offices etc.

A campaign of cleaning major cities and towns and building new drainage systems, water supplies, traffic signals, recreational parks etc, has been successfully initiated. Reforestation of burned out villages and areas is also taking place.

But the continuing violence in Baghdad and southern Iraq is taking its toll on the north. Many of Kurdistan's 48 hospitals and 672 primary healthcare centres lack basic medicines and equipment, and the KRG has issued a global plea for medical supplies. It blames violence in other parts of Iraq for the dire shortage. 'With the current situation in the south of Iraq, and particularly Baghdad, it is very hard for us to get the materials, equipment, and pharmaceuticals that we need,' Dr Abdul-Rahman Osman Younis, the region's health minister, said in an appeal issued in June 2007.

The Kurds are very proud of their achievements in the autonomous enclave and tend to talk in superlatives about their 'new democracy', which they believe could be a model for the rest of the country. In the words of Dr Barham Salih: 'We are willing to fight and sacrifice for a democratic Iraq. And we were the ones to suffer the most from the opposite case. If Iraq fails, it will not be our fault.'

But as Kamal Said Qadir pointed out in his article *Iraqi Kurdistan's Downward Spiral* published in *Middle East Quarterly*'s summer 2007 issue, while Kurdish officials and their growing coteries of US consultants praise the region's progress, an increasing culture of corruption, nepotism and abuse of power has both eroded democracy and, increasingly, stability.

There was renewed hope in the wake of Saddam's fall that the bifurcated KRG could fortify its democracy. Such hopes were dashed as the two main Kurdish parties maintained their stranglehold on power. On 30 January 2006 Kurdish authorities held new elections – the two parties ran on the same list so as not to compete – and divided power equitably according to their leaderships' pre-election agreement. Masoud Barzani assumed the presidency of the Kurdistan region, and his nephew Nechervan Barzani became prime minister, overseeing a unified, albeit inactive, parliament. Together they preside over more than 40 ministers, all of whom receive hefty salaries, perks and pensions.

A KRG spokesperson pointed out that:

Kurdistan is part of the Middle East and the Middle East is rife with nepotism and corruption. We have committed ourselves to democracy and part of democracy is to improve on things like transparency and to root out corruption, and we are taking steps towards that. But it takes time. Kurdistan is part of the Middle East and we lived under Saddam Hussein. These are the two big bits of baggage we have to shake off and we are doing our best. ... Now is a critical time for Kurdistan, and it is important for us to have one voice and be united. We actually see it as a strength. The KDP and the PUK are co-operating much more than they used to. We have one unified Kurdistan Regional Government, whereas until 2006 we had two governments.

The Kurdish leaders have also been accused of murder, torture and intimidation to make sure they hold on to power.

Corruption and human rights violations are not the only serious issues the KRG has to deal with. The region remains plagued by the fall-out from Saddam's Arabisation programme and the ever-present threat from Turkey.

The Coalition Provisional Authority (CPA) blocked the return of internally displaced Kurds to Kirkuk and Mosul even though they were forced out of their homes by Saddam's regime. Many have title deeds to their properties. No provision has been made for the return of Arabs brought to the region under the Arabisation programme. A property commission has been set up, but few claims have been made and few disputes have been amicably settled. The administrative boundaries of Kurdistan have to be finalised and the status of Kirkuk and Mosul must be decided.

Guerrillas of the separatist Kurdistan Workers Party (PKK) have long had camps in the Hakurk area, 14km from the Turkish border. On 3 June 2007 Turkish troops shelled the border area but there was no incursion. The leader of the autonomous Kurdish region, Massoud Barzani, said:

We reject any interference in Iraqi affairs and we do not accept any presence of Turkish forces on Iraqi lands. The Turkish army did not enter Iraqi territory yet, but if they did we would consult the Iraqi government and deal with it as an Iraqi issue!

On 17 October 2007, Turkey's parliament gave permission for the government to launch military operations into northern Iraq in pursuit of the PKK. The Iraqi foreign minister called on the rebels to leave the area and thousands of Kurds in Erbil and Dohuk protested against the threat of invasion.

On 18 December, the day US Secretary of State Condoleezza Rice made a visit to Iraq, hundreds of Turkish troops crossed the border into Iraqi Kurdistan and withdrew within 24 hours. The day before, Turkish aircraft had bombed PKK bases. Massoud Barzani refused to meet Rice in protest at the incursion. Turkey gave the USA advance warning of the air strikes but the Iraqi government was not informed. There has been speculation that American military intelligence shared intelligence with Turkey regarding the PKK to curtail its activities.

Turkey's feud with the PKK is linked to issues inside Iraq, among them the tug of war between the Kurds, Arabs and Turcomans over the oil-rich region of Kirkuk. Ankara is also afraid that the independent Kurdish enclave on its border could encourage Turkey's 15 million Kurds to demand autonomy or independence. Increasing insurgency into Turkish territory and acts of terrorism by the Kurdish PKK allied to retaliation by Turkey do not encourage the settlement of the matter. The Ottoman claim to Mosul and Kirkuk as part of the ethnic Turkish state still lingers.

And why not a Kurdish state asks Michael Gunter in *The Kurdish Question and the 2003 Iraqi War*:

What is so sacred about the territorial integrity of a failed state like Iraq? Indeed within the past decade, both the Soviet Union and Yugoslavia broke up into numerous new states. Why do the Arabs so rightfully demand a state for the Palestinians, but so hypocritically deny one for the Kurds? Why do the Turks demand self-determination for the Turkish Cypriots, but so hypocritically deny the same for the Kurds?

Before 2003 Kurdistan was not free of Saddam Hussein, but less in his grasp than previously because of the 1991 no-fly zone and then safe haven.

Since the 1990s we have been able to live autonomously, but there were huge pressures on Kurdistan and the KRG. We suffered a double economic embargo: we had the international embargo on Iraq, but within Iraq Saddam had his own embargo on Kurdistan. The economic pressure was one of the biggest pressures, and it was partly responsible for the civil war that we had between the KDP and PUK. In addition to the civil war we also had attacks from the PKK.

I remember going back in 1992 and 1995 and there was real poverty. That started to ease off in the late 1990s after the UN oil-for-food programme started to kick in. But Kurdistan was not getting its rightful share of the oil-for-food money, as it was administered by Baghdad. We are owed billions of dollars which we are trying to track down. The UN never paid us for projects in Kurdistan [directly]. Some of the money did get through at the end of the 1990s, and at the beginning of 2000 the economic situation did improve, but it was still a very difficult time.

So what has changed since the 1990s is that there is no more economic embargo. That has had a huge impact. Secondly we do not live in fear of Saddam anymore, and fear is very crippling. Even though Saddam Hussein and his regime were kept outside of Kurdistan, you could see his tanks. There was always the danger that the no-fly zone would be discontinued.

The changes that I have seen since 2003 have been dramatic. I go back to Kurdistan every couple of months. Every time I go back I am shocked by the economic development. There are traffic jams because the number of cars on the roads is increasing. Now every family has one car and some families have two or three.

Now that we are free of Saddam and his regime foreign investors are very interested in Kurdistan and they are welcomed. In 2006 we hosted two very high level British trade delegations, and we all know how conservative and cautious the British are. There have also been trade delegations from Austria, Sweden and the USA.

The KRG has representation in a dozen countries, the most high profile being the UK and USA. And the recognition the representations get is also a reflection of the growing interest in Kurdistan as an economic hub for Iraq, and possibly even wider in the Middle East.

Since the liberation we have been able to implement a federal, democratic system more fully. We are under the media spotlight internationally so when we say we believe in democracy we are tested constantly and we are learning from the process.

Bayan Sami Abdul Rahman, High Representative to the UK of the Kurdistan Regional Government

The North (Iraqi Kurdistan)   IRAQI KURDISTAN – THE OTHER IRAQ

These questions, however, do assume the as yet unproven fact that Iraq is a 'failed state'. There have been many false springs for the Kurds, but as this book went to press they were still enjoying their time under an American-warmed sun. But for how long?

TOWNS, CITIES AND SITES

It is not so much the layout of modern cities and towns that is characteristically Kurdish, as their location in the landscape. Like the old settlements depicted in the ancient bas reliefs, their modern counterparts also cling to the hilltops, mountainsides and even cliffs, in sheer defiance of the rationality which would have prescribed the plains nearby.

Mehrdad Izady, *The Kurds: A Concise Handbook*

Mosul and Kirkuk are in northern Iraq but are not under the control of the KRG.

MOSUL This is Iraq's second largest city and was originally built as a citadel or outpost for the Assyrian Empire on a hill called Qlea't, on the right bank of the Tigris opposite the site of ancient Nineveh. The area was inhabited as early as 6000BC. Mosul had many names, including Al-Mosul, meaning the link reaching different destinations between east and west, north and south, or a place of reunion. It was also known as the hunchback (Al-Hadba), the city with two spring seasons, God's city, the city of the prophets, and the green city. The famous cotton fabric 'muslin' derives its name from Mosul, where it was first made. Mosul is also famous for its rich culinary tradition, including kebbet Mosul, a healthy high-fibre food made from the shell of crushed wheat (*burgul*) and stuffed with meat.

History is alive in Mosul: there are plenty of archaeological ruins dating back to Assyrian times. Old Mosul has 38 living quarters called *mahala*, each self-contained with its own market, bath (spa), church, mosque and cemetery. Some quarters even have their own traditions and dialects related to the tribal origins of their inhabitants. Originally all the living quarters were on the west bank of the Tigris within the parameter wall of old Mosul, with nine gates. In 1630 the Ottoman Wali, Bakr Pasha, added four more gates. Visitors and caravans could enter and leave the city only during daylight hours, as all 13 gates were shut at sunset. A deep trench was filled with water for defence and saved the city during the great siege by Nadir Shah (see page 59). The remnants of the city wall and some of the gates can still be seen today.

The city was one of the most ethnically mixed in Iraq: Arabs, Syriac people, Armenians, Kurds, and Turcomans, Jews, Christians, Muslims and Yezidis all called Mosul home. It is the ancient centre of the Christian community, just as the Turcomans have a special attachment to Kirkuk. St Thomas the Apostle lived in Mosul on his way to India. Before the coming of Islam most of the Arab tribes who lived in the area were Christian.

Historical background The city became an important commercial centre from the 6th century BC. In pre-Islamic times the town of Ardashir was named after the Sassanid King Ardashir. It became a Byzantine city after the defeat of the Persians in a battle near Mosul in AD627. But just ten years later it returned to

The Mosque of Nebi Yunis is said to be the burial place of the biblical Prophet Jonah. It is an old Nestorian church converted into a mosque. There is no other church in Mosul for Jonah and the Muslim and Christian pilgrims visit the shrine together to honour the memory of the prophet. An impoverished village surrounds the mosque on the slopes of the mount of ancient Nineveh. Archaeologists attempting to excavate the Assyrian Palace underlying the mosque foundations ran into serious trouble with the clerics and effectively abandoned this work.

The Umayyad Mosque is said to be the oldest mosque in Mosul. It has been built in the vicinity of an ancient church once dedicated to St Paul and 40 martyrs, and subsequently renovated by Marwan (AD744–50). Today, only the minaret of the mosque remains from that era.

The Great Nuriddine Mosque, known as Al-Jami Al-Kabir, built by Nuriddin Zangi in 1172, is famous for its crooked, 52m minaret known as the humped one (Al-Hadba), and its elaborate brickwork.

The Al Imam Muhsin Mosque is a modern mosque situated in the Al-Maidan district of Old Mosul. It was constructed on the ruins of Nour-ul-Din Arsalan school, which was built in AD1210. The only remaining part of the original building is a rectangular room with two flat pulpits made of limestone bricks.

The Mujahidi Mosque, also known as the Al-Khuther Mosque or the Red Mosque, dating back to the 12th century, has a beautiful dome and elaborately wrought *mihrab* (a niche in the wall of a mosque that indicates the direction of Mecca). It stands at the entrance of the Corniche.

The Mosque of the Prophet (Jerjis), an ancient mosque at the prophet's shrine, was renovated and expanded by Tamerlane in 1392 and is now known as the Mosque of Nabi Jerjis. The Mashad (mausoleum or shrine) of Yahya ibn Al Kassen, surmounted by an octagonal pyramid, is one of the many ancient tombs from the Islamic period found in northern Iraq.

Muslim rule during the time of the second Caliph Omar (AD634–44) after one of his commanders, Raba'ibn Akfal Al-Anzi, took control of it without a fight. The Umayyads took a special interest in the development of Mosul and during the reign of the last Umayyad caliph, Marwan II (AD744–50) it became the capital of the province of Jezireh (Mesopotamia).

During the Abbasid era the city was an important trade centre because of its strategic location on the India, Persia and Mediterranean caravan route. The power of its governors increased with Nuriddin Zangi and his son, champions of Muslim opposition to the Crusades. The town was destroyed by the Mongol invasion and rebuilt by Osman I (1280–1324), the first Ottoman Sultan, who divided Iraq into the three provinces (*vilayats*) of Mosul, Baghdad and Basra. The city remained under Ottoman rule for seven centuries until 1918.

After the collapse of the Ottoman Empire, Rashid Rida, the 20th-century Islamic reformer, proposed that it become the neutral seat of the new caliphate, but this proposal, along with attempts to revive the caliphate, came to nothing.

Unlike Basra and Baghdad, Mosul was occupied in peacetime by the British forces after the World War I armistice. Finally the League of Nations decided it should come under Iraqi, rather than Turkish, jurisdiction.

Mosul today Gavin Young, author of *Iraq: Land of Two Rivers*, tells us that:

Mosul improves the closer you get – your first sight of Mosul from the south is a bit disappointing: the buildings are modern and have a utilitarian look. Yet, nearer, you can cheer up. You begin to see better things: the river and the corniche and the old houses that still stand on the water's edge and the parks. Also you see minarets and church spires and domes above the rooftops.

It is a city with a fascinating maze of narrow and wide alleyways (*awjat*), and interesting streets and roads along both banks of the river, which serve as a flood barrier. It is also the place for a panoramic view of the old city – and of an ecological and environmental disaster. Dams upstream in Turkey have turned parts of the mighty Tigris Basin into a giant car park.

Modern Mosul has expanded to both banks of the Tigris and engulfed old Mosul, Nineveh and surrounding areas. There are 67 new modern residential zones. The modern architecture, which uses ornate limestone, is also interesting.

The city has been overtaken by a great burst of modernity. What used to be a discernibly Middle-Ages-type city with many tenements and alleyways has been divided into parts by major roads circling and cutting through it. In 2001 there was much modern building development in progress, and some suburbs had an air of prosperity, with occasional streets of exceptional wealth in evidence.

CHURCHES AND MONASTERIES

The churches of Mosul are fascinating, containing much of the early heritage of 'Eastern Christianity'.

The oldest church still in use today is that of Mar Toma (St Thomas), built on the house occupied by the apostle during his visit to Mosul. The three altars are its most interesting feature. The Church of the Immaculate (Al-Tahira) started life as a monastery in AD300 and became a Chaldean Catholic Church in 1600. It was reconstructed in 1743.

The oldest Chaldean church in Mosul, built in the 13th century, is the Church of Simon Peter (Shamoon Al-Safa). The Church of Mar Soma is alleged to be the oldest Protestant church in the Middle East, established in 1840. The Clock Church (Al-Sa'a) is a Latin church built in 1862. It is named after a clock donated by the wife of Napoleon III, and is known for its fine marble and stained glass.

The Syrian Orthodox Monastery of St Matthew, known locally as Mar Matta or Sheikh Matta (*Mar* means saint in Syriac) is 32km outside Mosul. It was built in the 4th century on Mt Maqlib. In the words of Oswald Parry, author of *Six Months in a Syrian Monastery*, 'it clings like a swallow's nest against a wall'. Parry recalls a glorious view: 'Mosul lay like a small village, in spite of all its domes and minarets on the banks of the Tigris, which curled serpent-like down to the sea.'

On 7 January 2008 – Epiphany Sunday, an important date in the Eastern Christian calendar – bombs exploded outside three churches in Mosul: the Chaldean Church of Saint Paul, the Assyrian Church of the Virgin Mary and the Chaldean Church of Maskanta. There was also an explosion outside a monastery in the centre of Mosul.

Nineveh Street, which runs from east to west through the city, is the main and the longest shopping street in Mosul. Side streets lead to the jewellery market and other shops. Bab Al-Tub Square (Cannongate Square) in the centre of the city is the place for popular cafés, cheap hotels and restaurants. Mosul was known for its ancient cafés. They served as gentlemen's clubs, each frequented on a daily basis by professionals or traders. They were popular meeting places where information was exchanged and contracts sealed. The marketplace near the old bridge that connects the two sides of the city is still an important exchange centre for the agricultural products of the mountains, including watermelons.

As Wayne Bowen, author of *Undoing Saddam: From Occupation to Sovereignty in Northern Iraq*, observed:

> Mosul is the place to shop for Turkish furniture, Chinese electronics, Syrian chocolates, Italian ice cream, English-language books, popular newspapers, flame-broiled chicken, fresh-baked bread, Persian rugs, and fruit from Nineveh's agricultural fields. The prosperity and entrepreneurial spirit of the Iraqis is present everywhere and some of Mosul's quarters resemble southern European street markets. Free markets emerge naturally whenever men and women have the ability to trade with each other without the strong hand of a central state. With the fall of the Baathist regime and the incomplete control over the economy exerted first by the CPA and now the Iraqi government, capitalism is flourishing as much as it can, despite the criminals and terrorists who do their best to disrupt its operation.

Microcosm of Iraq   After the 2003 war Mosul was successful in establishing a democratic administration to run its affairs and held the first election for a local council in post-Saddam Iraq. The Iraqi army based in the city formally surrendered on 12 April 2003. There was an initial period of chaos and looting but the residents of the city agreed that Islamism must exist alongside Arab nationalism and Arabs, Kurds, Muslims and Christians have to live and work together for their own best interests. A 24-member council was elected to run the city.

The council's initial success proved to be a false dawn and the politics of the gun replaced dialogue and discussion. Liberal politicians and academics at the University of Mosul, the largest and most prestigous in northern Iraq, were gunned down. In his book, Wayne Bowen described the killing of the governor of Nineveh province, of which Mosul is the capital.

On today's provisional council the main Kurdish coalition now holds 31 out of 41 seats and all the top executive positions, even though the Kurds only make up 35% of the population.

The city served as the operational base for the US Army's 101st Airborne Division during the occupational phase of Operation Iraqi Freedom. Reconstruction work began and local people were employed in the areas of security, electricity, local governance, drinking water, waste water, trash, roads, bridges and environmental concerns. The US forces have now reduced their bases in the city from four to one – the large airport base. Without Kurdish support the Americans, who the locals see as just another tribe, could not control the city.

The Mosul court was described as the Americans' 'Exhibit A' in a *Washington Post* article on 16 March 2007. When the justice system ground to a halt US advisers brought judges from Baghdad into the city to serve anonymously. In its first three months, Major Crimes Court 15 heard cases against 73 defendants on charges ranging from possession of an illegal identification card to murder. 'Get rid of your Western mind-set,' was the advice from Army Captain Jason De Los Santos, a military lawyer who was intimately involved in the court's formation. 'You have to deal with the "inshallah factor", the fatalistic God willing.'

The American Forces Press Service reported that a total of 194 projects costing US$182 million have begun to pay off. In 2004 alone the Coalition finished 56 projects worth a total of US$61.5 million. They included the rehabilitation, upgrading and building of sewers in many Mosul neighbourhoods, provision of potable water, and installation or improvement of water mains. Another US$15 million is budgeted for water and sewage upgrades. Four electricity projects worth almost US$33 million have been completed and another 17 worth almost US$40 million are moving forward. The Coalition is investing US$25 million in roads, railways, bridges and the airport.

The Arabs, from the powerful Sunni Shammar tribe, traditionally lived on the west bank of the Tigris, while the Kurds and Christians mostly lived on the east bank. Saddam recruited some 250,000 soldiers and 30,000 officers from the city. Many have joined the insurgency. After Saddam's execution some police officers put his picture in their cars. Sunni Arabs, aided by insurgent groups like

Al-Qaeda in Mesopotamia and Ansar Al-Sunna, have driven around 70,000 Kurds out of the city and there are now very few Kurds left in west Mosul. According to the deputy governor Khasro Goran, 40–50 people were being killed in Mosul every week in mid-2006.

The battle for Mosul continues. Goran believes half of the 20,000 police belong to or sympathise with the Sunni resistance, which sees the city as a Sunni town and is trying to get rid of the Kurdish inhabitants.

In his article 'The Shattering of Mosul' in *Counterpunch*, published on 13 April 2007, Patrick Cockburn described Mosul as a city living on its nerves. Bombings and assassinations were not as frequent as in Baghdad, but enough to make life hideously insecure. A professor at Mosul University speaking on condition of anonymity said:

> The condition here is worsening more and more. My office at the college was in havoc by the shrapnel and huge storm of a huge explosion just in the early morning. If I were in my office I should have been torn to pieces.

The professor did not expect life in Mosul to get better and her pessimistic expectations have been fulfilled. For centuries Mosul has been one of the great cosmopolitan cities of the Middle East. Sadly, this is now ending. Kurds are in flight. So too are Christians. Fanatical Jihadi Islamists persecute them as being no different from US soldiers.

Tensions are exacerbated by the Kurdistan Regional Government's attempts to annex large swaths of eastern and northern Nineveh. The constitution gives the KRG the right to the land by the end of 2007 through a popular referendum. The referendum is scheduled and Kurdish political parties are encouraging settlers to move to eastern Nineveh. The problem of relocating Arab settlers who were brought to the area under Saddam's Arabisation programme, and making provision for the return of the half-million displaced Kurds, must also be solved. Deputy governor Mr Goran believes that the poll will result in the Mosul province east of the Tigris, and the districts of Sinjar and Tell Afar to the west of the river, going to the KRG. 'As we get closer to the implementation of article 140, the problems will get worse,' he said.

The Kurds were able to destabilise Iraq for half a century under Saddam Hussein and his predecessors. The Sunni Arabs are certainly strong enough to do the same.

West of Mosul Directly west of Mosul runs a desert road through the Jebel Sinjar. This old desert road runs approximately 185km to the Syrian border, a route once taken by camel trains to the important water and market towns of El Haseka and Raqqa in Syria.

En route lie many important tells, or ancient mounds covering villages, settlements and towns going back to the 3rd and 4th millennium BC. Some 80km along this route is the settlement of Tell Afar, and 20km south is Tell Irmah, with a large artificial hill enclosing the remains of a village grouped around the remains of a ziggurat. The site was occupied until the Assyrian period.

In September 2004 an American attack on Tell Afar, inhabited largely by Turcomans, resulted in 60 civilian deaths. The Americans claimed the area was used for smuggling militants and arms from Syria. A furious Turkish government threatened to stop co-operating in Iraq if the siege was not lifted, while many Turcomans claimed the Kurds managed to get the Americans involved on their side in the continuing conflict between Kurds and Turcomans (see pages 172–3).

Violence in Tell Afar, in between conflict-plagued Mosul and troubled Kirkuk, has been horrifying. In May 2005, clashes between Shias and Sunnis broke out in the town. The following month 8,000 US and Iraqi troops launched an offensive against the insurgents and implemented a reconstruction programme under the 'clear, hold and build' strategy.

Approximately 129km from Mosul is the town of Sinjar, ancient Sinjara, on the slopes of Jebel Sinjar. This town was declared a colony by Marcus Aurelius in approximately AD170 and had a strong Roman garrison. It was captured in AD260 by Shahpur I and captured and recaptured by the Persians and the Romans several times. It was handed back to Shahpur II in AD363 and effectively formed the frontier between the Roman and Persian empires for centuries. It was famed for its prosperity in Abbasid times and in AD1170 Nur ed Din conquered it *en route* to taking Mosul.

The modern town is to the east of ancient Sinjar and contains a Yezidi cemetery and several remains of very old mosques and minarets. The Iraqi/Syrian border is only 57km from the town.

KIRKUK: TO BE OR NOT TO BE KURDISH? The Kirkuk region lies between the Zagros mountains in the northeast and the Lower Zab and Tigris rivers in the west, the Himrin mountain range in the south and the Sirwan (Diyala) River in the southwest. It straddles the strategic trade routes between Turkey, Iran and Iraq.

The discovery of oil during the 1920s turned Kirkuk into Iraq's fourth largest city. There are over 10 billion barrels of proven oil reserves remaining in Kirkuk. It is producing up to a million barrels a day, almost half of Iraqi exports.

Kirkuk dates back to Sumerian times. In 1948 archaeological excavations in the city's Arafa neighbourhood uncovered copper tools and a calf statue. Cuneiform writings found at the foot of Kirkuk citadel indicate that in Babylonian times the city was called Erebga. The Assyrians named it Arrapha, and King Nasirbal II built the citadel between 884 and 858BC as a military defence line. During the Roman era, the city was known as Kergi Sluks and later Kergini. King Sluks was responsible for the construction of a strong rampart with 72 towers around the citadel.

In AD1294 Marco Polo named it Circura. The name Kirkuk first emerged during the time of the Turcoman state of Kara Koyunlu (1375–1468). During Ottoman times Kirkuk was part of the province (*vilayet*) of Mosul. With the development of the petro-chemical industry, the city was given extra importance. Drilling first began at Bawa Gurgur in Kirkuk in 1927 and drilling rigs soon became a constant landmark. Refineries, which provided a good source of employment, were developed in the area and the population increased dramatically.

In addition to oil, the area is rich in natural gas and was referred to in Syriac chronicles as Beth-Garmai – the land of warmth. Natural gas was used for centuries by shepherds and local people for heating and for cooking. Before gas deposits were identified the area was regarded as having supernatural powers. Women used to move the earth with a stick and if flames appeared they believed they would give birth to a boy. Today gas is tapped in commercial quantities.

Kirkuk is a city of stone and alabaster buildings. One of the city's governors decided to paint the buildings of the 1930s and 1940s white. The oldest monument still intact is the citadel. Near the castle is a shrine to the Prophet Daniel, Governor of Babylon when the area was ruled by Nebuchadnezzar.

Efforts have been made to restore the citadel, a number of old houses (such as the one belonging to a merchant named Ali Agha) and the bazaar, which has more than 300 stalls. Kirkuk is a market for the region's produce, including cereals, olives, fruits and cotton. It has a small textiles industry. There is also a Turcoman khan, similar to a medieval inn, and Takia, an old-style Kurdish guesthouse.

As in Mosul, the cosmopolitan nature of Kirkuk is under threat. In the cafés the locals drink tea and flick dice. When they speak, their sentences are mixed with Arabic, Turkish and Kurdish words but sectarian tensions, fuelled by uncertainty and fear of the future, are rising.

After the fall of Baghdad on 10 April 2003, Kurdish *peshmergas* from the Patriotic Union of Kurdistan (PUK) took control of Kirkuk virtually unchallenged. The Turkish Foreign Minister announced that Turkey would do 'whatever is necessary to protect its interests'. His statements were prompted by fears of Kurdish demands for independence. Aware of the sensitivities in the city, PUK leader Jalal Talabani ordered his fighters to leave.

But the Kurds are adamant that Kirkuk, which Talabani described as 'The Kurdish Jerusalem', will be the capital of the autonomous region under the control of the Kurdistan Regional Government. The constitution mandates a referendum on the status of the city by December 2007 and the Kurds are sure they will win. They want Kirkuk, and not just for the oil. They say it's their capital. The Turcomans (see pages 172–3) feel the same way. On 26 December 2007, the autonomous parliament of Iraqi Kurdistan approved a United Nations plan to delay by six months a public vote on Kirkuk's future.

The Sinjar highlands on the Iraqi-Syrian border and in the region northwest of Mosul are the home of the Yezidis, who make up less than 5% of the Kurdish population. They are an esoteric sect whose beliefs are drawn from paganism, Zoroastrianism, Christianity and Islam.

The chief divine figure is Malak Taus, the peacock angel, who rules the universe with six other angels, all subordinate to the supreme god, who has no direct interest in the universe since he created it. The Kurdish word for Yezidis is *Ezdisd*, meaning 'those who are close to God'.

The Yezidis believe that when the devil repented of the sin of pride he was pardoned and reinstated to his previous position as chief of the angels. This has earned them the undeserved reputation of devil worshippers. A number of religious taboos forbid the wearing of blue and eating lettuce and olives. The New Year is in April, the holy day is Wednesday. Yezidis may have up to seven wives. They cannot marry outside their religion as they fear they will lose their identity, but this policy may be revised, as their numbers are decreasing.

The society is well organised, with a chief sheikh as the supreme religious figurehead and an emir as the secular head. The main religious text is the 'black book' (Mes'haf i Resh). Sheikh Adi was the author of a 500-word scripture known as revelation (*khlwa*). Lam is the most important celebration, which consists of a seven-day feast. Worshippers are shown the bird icon, called Anzal, of Malak Taus (the ancient one).

During the days of the Ottoman Empire the Yezidis were persecuted and at least 20 major massacres occurred between 1640 and 1910 when they refused to convert

The Kurds are now determined to reverse Saddam's Arabisation of the city. Between the 1970s and 2003 the Baathist regime expelled more than 200,000 Kurds from Kirkuk and the surrounding areas. Other non-Arabs, including Turcomans, were also expelled.

The Kurdish claims to the city date back to the late 19th century when they made up three-quarters of the population of Al-Tamim province around Kirkuk. Under British occupation the population was 61% Kurd, 28% Turcoman and 8% Arab. According to the 1957 census 48.3% of the residents were Kurds, 28.2% Arab and 21.4% Turcoman.

Arab control of Kirkuk's oil fields was always a priority for the central government. From the 1970s Saddam's Baath Party embarked on a major relocation programme transferring tens of thousands of families from Kirkuk, Sinjar, Khaniqin and other areas to purpose-built resettlement camps. The relocations intensified after the failed 1991 uprising.

At the time of writing Arabisation seems to have been replaced by Kurdification. According to Arab and Turcoman politicians, around 350,000 Kurds have returned to the area since 2003. On 1 January 2006 the *International Herald Tribune* described clusters of grey concrete houses that dot the barren plains surrounding Kirkuk, their purpose as blunt as their design. According to US commanders at least 30 assassination-style killings occurred in the Kirkuk area at the end of 2005, making it one of the deadliest mid-sized cities in Iraq.

to orthodox Islam. Attempts have also been made to replace their Kurdish identity with that of the Arabs or to describe them as an independent ethnic group. They have also been incorrectly linked to the Umayyad caliph Yazid ibn Muawiyya and called Umayyad Arabs by both the Syrian and Iraqi governments.

The burial place of Sheikh Adi has the magical atmosphere of a Yezidi shrine. He is said to have been a reincarnation of Malak Taus. The tomb, with its black stone snake and sacred signs, is in the valley of Lalish. The temple has cave formations dating back to 512BC. All Yezidis are required to visit the temple once in their lifetime. They pray five times a day. The village of Ain Sifini, home of the Yezidi leader worldwide, is close by.

The Yezidis (ethnic Kurds) were doubly persecuted by Saddam's regime, which resented their attempts to preserve their ethnic identity and also saw them as heathens. Some escaped to European and other countries but most remained in Iraq. During the Arabisation programme they were forced out of their villages, denied national identity cards, and prevented from holding government jobs and from visiting Lalish temple.

After the establishment of the Kurdistan Regional Government, the 50,000 Yezidis began to enjoy freedoms they never had, got government jobs and flocked to Lalish temple.

They have also been the perpetrators and victims of sectarian hatred. On 22 April 2007, 23 Yezidis were forced off a bus travelling from a textile factory in Mosul, where they were lined up against a wall and shot. It was a revenge killing for the stoning of a woman who converted to Islam after falling in love with a Sunni Arab. The cycle of revenge was followed with a car bombing in the town of Teliskof in Mosul. Ten Yezidis and Kurds were killed and more than 200 people injured.

A KRG spokesperson pointed out that:

Kurdish people were forced out of their homes at gunpoint and Shia Arabs were brought in. In 2003, when Iraq was liberated, a lot of those Arabs left Kirkuk, but Bremer [Coalition Provisional Authority Administrator from 2003 to 2004] said the issue should be settled and that slowed everything down. Those Arabs came back. They thought 'I am in line for a windfall.' Why should I leave Kirkuk? I will stay until they pay me. So the issue has dragged on and on. We have always said allowing the issue of Kirkuk to drag on will not solve it and we were right. Today Kirkuk is very, very violent. There is no forcing out of Arab families. The constitution sets out a mechanism for normalisation which means allowing the people who can prove they have a claim they lived in Kirkuk to return to their homes and allowing the Arab families to return to where they came from. They will be given help in rebuilding their homes.

Some of the Kurdish people forced out of their homes by Saddam's regime were living in ghettos in other parts of Kurdistan, and now that they had the chance to go back to what was rightly theirs, they have of course gone back. Arab families have taken the compensation and left voluntarily. The KRG has chosen a transparent means of reversing injustices.

Throughout the modern history of Iraq, life has been cruel to its third largest ethnic and cultural minority, the Turcomans, numbering some two-and-a-half million (less than 2% of the population).

Turcomans began to settle in Mesopotamia in the 11th century at the time of the Abbasid Caliph Mutassin. A number of Turcoman states were founded in Iraq following the collapse of the Abbasid state in 1258, including Akkoyunlus, Karakoyunlus, Ilhanis and Celayirlis. The Ottomans encouraged the Turcomans to settle at the entrances of valleys that provided access to Kurdish areas and repel raids.

Following the collapse of the Ottoman Empire in 1918, the British – having occupied Iraq in accordance with the Armistice of Moudros – pursued a policy of attempting to assimilate the Turcomans into Arab and Kurdish society. When Iraq became independent in 1932, the lot of its Turcoman minority did not improve. They were subjected to savage massacres between 1924 and 1959. When the Baath Party came to power in 1968 it promulgated a seven-point Declaration of Cultural Rights for all minorities, but the provisions of the declaration were more honoured in the breach than in the observance.

Today, Iraq's Turcoman minority is found mainly in the northeast, along the border between the Kurdish and Arab regions under KRG control, and in the city of Kirkuk, its historical and cultural base. But in the 1970s the Iraqi government embarked on a policy of dispersing Turcoman (and Kurdish) families from the oil-rich city and replacing them with Arab families (Arabisation).

For the Turcomans, Kurdification continued where Arabisation left off. The *Washington Post* and Reuters reported that in the days following Saddam's fall, Kurdish militiamen sacked the Turcoman towns of Altin Kopru, Kirkuk, Daqua, Tuzkhurmatu and Mandali. US forces did little to prevent the pogroms and looting. The *peshmerga* plundered abandoned government offices in Kirkuk. They burned land deeds and birth registries so as to remove evidence countering their claim that Kirkuk is a Kurdish city.

'The Kurds are building houses on land they don't own,' according to Sangul Chapuk, a Turcoman politician who served on the American-appointed Governing Council.

The Turcomans are now aligning themselves with the Arab settlers against the Kurds. They are also strengthening their links with Turkey. In Autumn 2003 a delegation from the Al-Obeid tribe visited Ankara to create an Arab-Turcoman body.

Writing in *The Kurdish Question and the 2003 Iraq War*, Mohammed Ahmed described the damage to a Shia Turcoman shrine in the town of Tuz Khormatu,

The Kurds now control the key government posts: the provincial governor, provincial council chairman and chief of provincial police are all Kurds. They are insisting that Kurdish is the language of government even though many of the city's residents do not speak it. The Kurds have also been accused of coercing Arabs into selling their properties at knock-down prices, but they deny the accusations.

On 15 June 2005 a confidential State Department cable obtained by the *Washington Post* and addressed to the White House, Pentagon and US Embassy in Baghdad said 'extra-judicial detentions' were part of a 'concerted and widespread initiative' by Kurdish political parties 'to exercise authority in Kirkuk in an increasingly provocative manner'.

which led to clashes between Kurds and Turcomans. He pointed out that Sunni Turcoman nationalists, the Turcoman Front, may have been responsible for the incident in order to create a pretext for the Turkish army to occupy Iraqi Kurdistan. Turkey is using the pretext of support for the Turcomans to intervene in Iraqi Kurdistan, as it is fearful that the successful experiment in autonomy may provide inspiration to Turkish Kurds, who are described as 'Mountain Turks'. Attempts to stifle Kurdish ambitions included attempting to supply weapons to their Turcoman allies in Iraqi Kurdistan and reportedly plotting to assassinate the newly-appointed Kurdish governor of Kirkuk. Moderate Turcoman parties are aligning themselves with the radical Iraqi Turcoman Front, in opposition to the increased Kurdish political power in Kirkuk.

According to a KRG spokesperson, Turcomans in Kirkuk very broadly fall into two groups:

> One group is led by the ITF, the Iraqi Turcoman Front, which is very openly supported and funded by Ankara, so they are basically the mouthpiece of Ankara. They make many claims on Kirkuk and against the Kurds, and make charges of ethnic cleansing. But they are in the minority and they are wrong.
>
> The majority of Turcomans have no problem living in peace with the Kurds and the Arabs. There are Arabs who have been in Kirkuk historically and we are not saying Kirkuk should be entirely Kurdish. We are saying that the people who replaced Kurdish families and took their homes should go back. Kirkuk is a mixed city and there are Arab families who have lived there for centuries, and they have every right to remain, and so do the Turcomans and the Assyrians.
>
> Some of the Turcoman groups resent the statements made by Ankara. When Saddam Hussein was persecuting people in Iraq, Ankara very rarely raised its voice about the treatment of Turcomans, so why is it so concerned now? They never said anything, but now suddenly they are concerned about their countrymen.

Writing in the *Middle East Quarterly* in the winter of 2007, Yucel Guclu, the first counsellor at the Turkish Embassy in Washington, emphasised that it is incumbent upon both the international community and the new Iraqi government to protect the rights of the Turcomans, now threatened both by Kurdish expansionism and the intolerance of some central government factions.

Tensions escalated in February 2007 after the Baghdad government's Iraqi Higher Committee for the Normalisation of Kirkuk offered Kirkuk's non-Kurdish residents financial compensation and a plot of land elsewhere in the country. Shia militias have vowed to fight any attempt to shift control over Kirkuk to the KRG. They used the bombing of the Al-Askari shrine (see page 239) as a pretext to expand their presence in Kirkuk, ostensibly to protect the mosques. The Kurds responded by increasing guards at government buildings to around 15,000.

Prime Minister Nouri Al-Maliki has refused to set a date, and the normalisation process whereby the Kurds return and the Arabs leave is in shambles. The Property Claims Commission has not been empowered by central government, so thousands of Kurds who have returned now live in squatter camps.

Even though it is the jewel in the Turcoman and Kurdish crown, Kirkuk is now a dismal place, the main street resembling an Afghan shanty town. In the Arab districts of the city garbage mixes with sewer sludge, and sheep carcasses that have seen better days hang from shop fronts.

In his article *Where Kurdistan Meets The Red Zone* (published on the blog www.windsofchange.net), Michael Totten observes that:

> Kirkuk's cars are old and beat up. Its buildings are shabby. The streets are utterly bereft of beauty and grace. Residents live behind walls. There are no trees to walk underneath, no social places to hang out in, no sights worth sighing at and nothing to take pictures of. It induces agoraphobia and a powerful urge to get inside and hunker down somewhere safe. With all its resources, if properly managed, it should be as prosperous as Kuwait and Dubai. Instead it is a sprawling catastrophe of a place ground down by decades of fascism and war.

IRAQI KURDISTAN: REGIONS UNDER THE CONTROL OF THE KRG

There are three governorates in the autonomous region of Iraqi Kurdistan: Dohuk, Erbil and Suleimaniyah. Until 2006 Dohuk and Erbil were under the control of the Kurdistan Democratic Party and Suleimaniyah was under the control of the Patriotic Union of Kurdistan. A unified administration has now been established.

DOHUK Dohuk governorate joins three parts of Kurdistan: Syrian, Turkish and Iraqi. It is a region of caves, hundreds of archaeological sites, ancient tombs, castles, woodlands and rivers. It is also the garden of Iraq, rich in fruit and vegetables and arable crops: wheat, barley, lentils, chickpeas, rice, tomatoes, onions, garlic, tobacco, peas, beans, grapes, peaches, sumach (small trees with red, hairy fruits), apricots, quinces, walnuts, figs, apples and nuts all grow in abundance.

An oil pipeline from Kirkuk to Turkey passes through the governorate, which suffered severely from the Anfal campaign and the regime's Arabisation programme. But since the establishment of the safe haven, the reconstruction of villages has started, and many of the region's residents who were expelled have returned.

Dohuk city, whose name means small village, lies in a wide valley with the White Mountain to the north, the great Dakhan (Shinodokha) Mountain to the south and Mamseen Mountain to the east. The Sumeal agricultural plain is to the east. Two rivers meet in the southwest of the city and water the fruit farms on their banks. The region is famous for its grapes.

Dohuk is peaceful and thriving. The residents' only concern is the Turkish army on the border, and threats of invasion in pursuit of PKK rebels (see page 160). The small industries, such as the canning factory, which stopped operating as Saddam's regime restricted industry in the Kurdish areas, are back. In his online blog (*www.michaelyon-online.com*), Michael Yon commented that:

> this Iraqi city appears to be doing at least as well as – and perhaps remarkably better than – many comparably-sized towns in Italy. It may

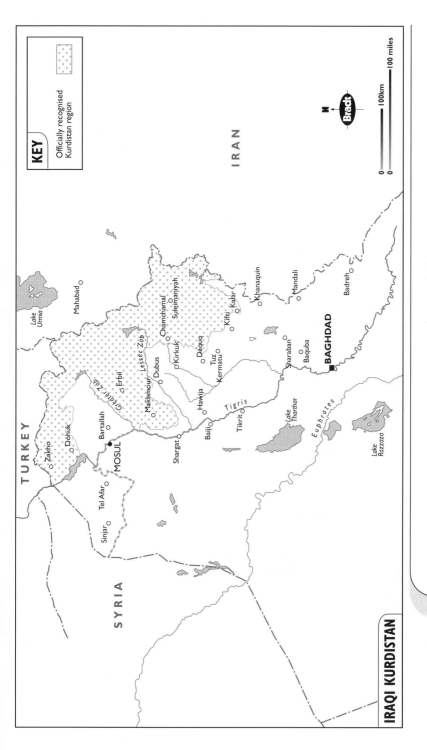

IRAQI KURDISTAN

KEY

Officially recognised
Kurdistan region

TURKEY

SYRIA

IRAN

Lake
Urmia

Mahabad

Zakho

Dohuk

Tel Afar

Sinjar

Bartallah

MOSUL

Greater Zab

Lesser Zab

Erbil

Makhmour

Dubus

Chamchamal

Suleimaniyah

Kirkuk

Daquq

Tuz
Kermatu

Kifri

Kalar

Khanaquin

Mandali

Badreh

Hawija

Shargat

Baiji

Tikrit

Tigris

Sharaban

Baquba

BAGHDAD

Lake
Tharthar

Euphrates

Lake
Razzaza

N

100km
100 miles

0
0

Bradt

be hard to believe, but about 20 % of the cars are either a Mercedes or a BMW. A visit to this place affords more than a break from the rugged routine of war; it also provides a postcard of a possible future for all of Iraq. There are shoeshine boys, flower shops and computer stores. The computer stores in little Dohuk are much better stocked than those in Milan. I walked into a store called Zanest Computer & Electronics, at 14th Anthar Street, and there I sat with Mr Abdul Shukry, and asked him about business. Mr. Shukry said business was good, and that the US Army had come a few days earlier and purchased sixty computers, and gave them all to Dohuk University.

The city's strategic importance dates back to Assyrian times when the roads passing through it connected the empire with other ancient kingdoms. It was part of the Badinan Emirate, a Kurdish principality like the principalities of Baban and Soran, which contracted or expanded as the powers ruling the area (the Ottoman Empire or Persia) became stronger or weaker. Villagers and farmers who migrated to the city of Dohuk over the years settled mainly in the southern, western and eastern suburbs. The Post and Communications Office now stands on the site of Dohuk Castle, a place of court intrigues. Only the castle wall, overlooking the river, remains.

At the entrance to the city when travelling from Mosul or Zakho is Malta, a family-oriented area with swimming pools, cafés, restaurants and bakeries. A small cemetery on the hill pre-dates the city. The zoo is on the road out of Malta.

The tourist hotels are excellent and used by foreigners, especially American soldiers, who come here for R&R. They are given a liberators' welcome. Throughout the autonomous Kurdish region soldiers are sometimes given free meals and souvenirs in appreciation for ousting Saddam. Mazi supermarket is the place for anything and everything. The town centre has a large, indoor market. Behind the supermarket is an amusement park called Dream City, with rides and games for children, and the five-star Dasinia restaurant. (Dohuk was known as Dasinia at the time of the Assyrians). Nearby is Dohuk University, established in 1992. The building was once an army barracks for Saddam's soldiers. The American Development Center is offering advanced English training and exchange programmes through the University of Dohuk as well as other universities in the Kurdistan region. The owner of a well-established souvenir shop with traditional artefacts is happy to expound on the history of the area, as are many of the locals, lacing their narratives with family history, personal experiences, myths, facts and dreams.

Chewar Stoon Cave, an ancient temple with the symbols of five gods (including Ishtar) carved on the rock, is found to the east of the city in the narrow Geli Dohuk passage. Malathaya (Malta) Hill on the Dohuk–Mosul road, where Assyrian earthenware was discovered, is believed to be the site of an important Assyrian castle. In Halamata Cave at the foot of Shindokhan Mountain, four carved images depict a procession of six gods (Ashur, Anilil, Seen, Sun, Ishtar and Adid) riding on sacred animals with the king in front. St Thomas the Apostle (Doubting Thomas) is said to have passed through the Dohuk area *en route* to India.

The town of Simeil on the road to Zakho was the site of the 1933 massacre of Assyrians (see page 40). Zakho is the most northerly location in Iraq. The stone bridge across the Khabour River, dividing the city in two and dating back to Abbasid times, is still in use. Khabour is the border crossing point for trucks that make their way daily from Turkey to northern Iraq and vice versa. Many of the townspeople are engaged in trade. The traditional clothing industry, which specialised in fine woollen clothes including shawls, is a shadow of its former self because the men have adopted other fabrics.

Zakho Castle, built from large pebbles and coated with gypsum from the days of the Badinan Emirate, is in the centre of the city. Qubad Pasha's hexagonal-shaped castle is in Zakho cemetery. The ruins of Kesta, an ancient Assyrian city where Assyrian, Greek and Islamic coins and statues were found, is in the centre of Dohuk governorate.

The town of Ibraheem Khalil is the last stop before the Turkish border. It has been named after the Prophet Ibraheem Khalil and is a tourist and recreation area for the people of Zakho.

Amadiya   In the north of Dohuk governorate is Amadiya, another town that dates back to Assyrian times. It is surrounded by many natural beauty spots, waterfalls, orchards and vegetable-growing areas. The town's huge western marble gate has four carvings of smaller-than-life-size people, perhaps Parthian kings who fought the Romans in AD226. It is possible to climb the steps inside the Amadiya Mosque minaret built by Sultan Hussein Wali in the 14th century. Little remains of the Cemetery of Amadiya princes in the east of the town except two marble domes. On Hussein Wali's coffin there is a carved quotation from the Koran: 'everything is fatal except His face'. An ancient religious school that flourished during the reign of the Badinan princes (1376–1843) and remained open to students until the 1920s is near Amadiya River, also the site of an underground store, Inge Castle and Issa Dala Bridge. Dergani village nearby is famous for its vessel pottery.

In the 6th century BC King Sennacherib constructed a canal to bring water from the Gomil River to Nineveh. A stone statue with carvings of winged oxen remains. Charwana Viaduct is one of 18 canals in Sennacherib's canal construction project in which two million stones were used. An archaeological team from Chicago University visited the area in the 1930s and discovered Sennacherib's chamber, and details about the construction of the viaduct.

Gondik Cave, in the Akri region, has stone carvings both inside and outside the cave dating back to 3000BC. They represent a hunter killing a mountain goat and scenes from a feast. The ruins of Akri Castle, on top of a mountain overlooking the town, include the remains of monasteries. Showsh Castle, higher than Akri Castle, lies to the northwest of Akri town. The great mosque built by Sultan Hussein Wali has a collection of ancient texts.

ERBIL (HEWLER)   Erbil (known in Kurdish as Hewler, seat of the Gods), today the home of a million people, is believed to be one of the world's oldest continuously inhabited cities. Neanderthal man left his imprints in the area, as did the Assyrians, the Romans and Alexander the Great.

Erbil is first mentioned in the 23rd century BC. It has been referred to in Sumerian writings as Orbelum or Urbilum, where the Assyrian goddess Ishtar was worshipped.

After the downfall of the Assyrian Kingdom in 612BC the city fell, consecutively, under the control of the Medes (possibly the ancestors of the Kurds), the Persians, and the Greeks under Alexander the Great (who defeated the Persian King Darius III in the Battle of Gaugamela in 331BC), fought 100km west of the city. The Parthians ruled from 126BC to AD226.

During the Parthian era Erbil was the centre of the Hidyab region, where an important kingdom was established. It was invaded by both the Armenians and the Romans and was an important Christian centre in the early centuries after Christ's death. In the Sassanian era (AD226–642) it was an administrative centre.

The Muslims arrived in AD642 and established the Atakakian principality. In Abbasid times (1128–1232) the city was an Islamic social and cultural meeting place, and leading Muslim scientists and men of letters made it their home. The Mongol occupation, which destroyed the Abbasid Empire, lasted from 1258 until 1410.

The city was ruled by the Turcomans between 1410 and 1508 and the Persian Safavids between 1508 and 1514. They were ousted by the Ottomans who remained until 1918 when the British army entered. The governorate of Erbil was established in 1918. Throughout its history Erbil has been a major trading centre on the route between Baghdad and Mosul.

Since the 1970s, the city has been the home of the Kurdish parliament. The first parliament of the Kurdish Autonomous Region was set up by Saddam and housed in an impressive building. It was totally under the thumb of the central government. After the uprising at the end of the 1991 Gulf War, the Kurds held elections and set up a parliament, which functioned until 1996, when fighting broke out between the Kurdistan Democratic Party (KDP) and the Patriotic Union of Kurdistan (PUK). The PUK set up an alternative government in Suleimaniyah. The parliament reconvened again in Erbil after a peace agreement was signed in 1997. The Kurdistan Regional Government was officially recognised in the 2005 constitution and the KDP and PUK set up a unitary government in May 2006.

Since the overthrow of Saddam there has been little violence in Erbil. The most horrific attack was a parallel bombing against Eid celebrations arranged by the PUK and KDP, which killed 109 people on 1 February 2004. There was another bombing on 10 May 2007 when a truck bomb killed 12 people and wounded 53. On 11 January 2007 US forces arrested six people from the Iranian consulate in Erbil on suspicion of being 'closely tied to activities targeting Iraqi and Coalition forces'.

The city is modernising and developing as a regional capital. In fact it is the fastest growing city in Iraq. A new terminal is under construction at the international airport opened in 2004, and the first phase of the 1 million m^2 Nishtiman complex, with 8,000 shops and 4,000 offices, has been completed. It is the brainchild of Nizar Hana, an Iraqi Christian from Kirkuk who ran a trading company in Baghdad until 1993, when 43 private traders were executed on dubious charges. He and his brothers fled the country, set up businesses in Turkey, Paris and Greece, and returned to Kurdistan to make their first investments, waiting for a conducive business environment in the rest of Iraq. Hana described his complex as 'the biggest single development in the Middle East'.

Ein Kawa, a Christian suburb of the city, is the place for restaurants, entertainment and an amusement park. Among the recent additions is a new

DEVELOPMENT FEELS LIKE A SHELL, A HOLLOW RIND

Azad Mala [a pseudonym] is a Kurdish teacher from northern Iraq. He says that while the region has been spared much of the violence of the capital, the local government is failing to tackle corruption and inefficiency.

Throughout Kurdistan, whenever you leave your home in the morning, the first thing you see is usually a construction project – an overpass, an underpass, a hotel, a mall.

The next thing you see is traffic, as now pretty much everyone has a car. The city is full of people coming here to find work, from the rest of Iraq, from Turkey, from the Philippines, Bangladesh or Ethiopia.

The development here feels like a shell, a hollow rind.

The government is building lots of impressive new buildings, but does not seem to care much about having an effective workforce.

I teach at a university, and things aren't encouraging any more. A few of my students are very good. But most don't seem to care. They can't even be bothered to conceal their cheating.

The first thing I do when I go home is ask my wife if there is electricity. If not, I have to go outside and start the generator. This month we started to get 10 hours of power a day, but prior to that it was three – less than Baghdad, even.

In 1996, I made US$80 a month working for an international organisation, and I could live on it – my rent was US$30 a month. Now I make US$1,200 and it is still not enough. I pay US$700 on rent. Add in the cost of fuel, food, and other expenses and I have nothing left over at the end of the month.

At the end of the day I watch Iraqi satellite news – mostly car bombs and killings. We don't have this violence here in Kurdistan. But in some ways, it seems Baghdad is better than the north. In Baghdad, you hear, they send ministers to prison for corruption.

The government will play this card with us whenever we question their policies. 'Do you want to be like Baghdad?' We still hear the same implied but very clear message from our government: 'You should leave us to be corrupt, to defraud the country, because we give you stability.'

This government sometimes says that this country will be like Dubai. By this they mean that it will be prosperous, thanks to its new-found oil wealth. Kurds never used to have housemaids or servants. It's not really part of our society. But now some of the party elites employ servants from Africa or East Asia, just like elites in the Gulf.

I think this country may well one day be like Dubai, where the 'sheikhs' control everything, the foreigners are given all the challenging work, and the rest of the population is paid to stay out of sight.

The Financial Times, *20 June 2007*

The North (Iraqi Kurdistan)   **IRAQI KURDISTAN: REGIONS UNDER THE CONTROL OF THE KRG**

mosque: a replica of the blue mosque in Istanbul. The Spider Computer Game Centre, near Raperin and Brayeti streets, is popular with children.

The Kurdistan Company For Real Estate is planning a US$120 million mall with a hotel, offices, market, shopping centre, apartments and a recreational area. The Park Kempinski Hotel is one of the first major foreign investment projects in the region. Byblos Bank, Lebanon's third largest lender, has opened a branch in Erbil in the hope of heralding a new financial era in a region where banking services are underdeveloped and people buy houses with piles of cash.

Attempts are also being made to promote Erbil as a major tourist attraction and Kurdish cultural centre. The ancient citadel, recognised as an historic site by UNESCO, is being renovated and, for the first time in its history, is uninhabited. The government compensated refugees who had to leave. The citadel houses a museum of Kurdish tribal textiles, mainly rugs. Lolan Mustefa opened the museum to house his magnificent collection and is hoping for a weaving renaissance by bringing back old looms.

Three large houses from the 19th century have been turned into museums, with displays from the Sumerian to the Abbasid period, handicrafts and an art gallery.

But not everyone is keen to preserve Kurdish heritage, which is threatened by the new wave of modernisation. The amazing covered market selling everything from fabrics and jewellery to cheese made from sheep's milk was described as 'full of rubbish' by Nizar Hana, who is convinced stall-holders should move into his giant mall.

The town of **Shaqlawa** is 90 minutes' drive east of Erbil. Built on a mountainside, with its luscious springs and trees, it is scenic but under-developed. The city is not well kept but people are buying land, so change is in the air. The Iraqi Communist Party has a massive building in the town.

SULEIMANIYAH Koi Sanjac, on the road between Erbil and Suleimaniyah, was one of the most significant trade centres in Abbasid and Ottoman times. It has a building known as the Great Khan, once a bazaar, where the owner rents storerooms.

Dokan Lake, 71km from Suleimaniyah, and Darbandikan Lake are very popular for swimming, water skiing, picnicking and fishing. Dokan was once a sleepy town of 5,000 inhabitants. After the fall of Saddam business started booming: cabins for tourists were constructed and visitors are keen to feast on marinated apricots, the local speciality. The tourist village is owned by the PUK and the local militias get some of the profits.

The Dokan Dam is an important source of electricity for the area. Other mountain resorts include Sarchinar (5km from Suleimaniyah), a place of beautiful forests and a pond formed by several springs. Darbandikan Lake (65km from Suleimaniyah) is the meeting point of two rivers, the Tanjarow and Sirwan, with boating and tourist facilities.

An hour's drive from Suleimaniyah after Darbandikan Lake and dam is the town of Karlar, with an ancient castle. In April 2004, there was an influx of 2,000 Iraqi Kurds into Kalar. They had fled from their homes in Fallujah after being threatened by Arab insurgents for supporting the Coalition and refusing to fight against the US military.

Penjwin, 35km east of Suleimaniyah, is a popular picnic area. A famous Kurdish personality, the writer, politician and philosopher Tawfiq Wahbi, is buried there.

The sunset at Asmar and the view of Suleimaniyah is breathtaking. A new hotel, the Asmar, has recently opened and there are a number of small shops and restaurants, among them the Azmir Palace. New restaurants are also opening up on the road winding down from Asmar.

When Saddam was in power the area was the scene of heavy fighting between Iraqi forces and *peshmergas*. The remains of ditches where tanks used against the Kurds were stationed are still visible.

Hamran, east of Suleimaniyah on the Iranian border, is an area of quaint mountain villages and walnuts. The town is famous for its handmade shoes.

Suleimaniyah city was founded in 1784 by Suleiman Pasha, the King of Baban, who ruled the Emirate of Baban. At that time the area was divided into small emirate-like states, each with its own ruler. One day the king went hunting on Asmar Mountain and on the plain below saw a woman called Malaka Khan. After falling in love with her he started building the foundations of Suleimaniyah, a large, elegant city with wide tree-lined streets smelling of wood smoke, and large villas, the homes of well-to-do Kurds. The riverside walk is a pleasant way to spend an afternoon. The market is the place for rugs at bargain prices and interesting souvenirs such as stuffed partridges and jackals. Baby hawks (live) are also available, along with bowls and pots made of wood.

The 21st century also makes its presence felt in the form of three large supermarkets, the most popular being Altun.

Great attention is paid to the promotion of Kurdish culture. The university has a Kurdish language faculty and Kurdish poetry festivals are held here amid much fanfare.

The University's Cultural Centre is accommodated in one of Suleimaniyah's oldest houses. It has a collection of traditional Kurdish artworks and a folklore centre. Serchnsar, a suburb with coffee shops and restaurants, is being developed into a tourist city. The area has the appearance of a local Coney Island, with Christmas lights illuminating the restaurants, but something has to be done about the smell of sewage from the river below.

Like Erbil, Suleimaniyah is a metropolis of Iraqi Kurdistan. Once the centre of Kurdish nationalism – Sheikh Barzainji (see page 152) organised his first rebellion against the British from the city – it is growing and developing rapidly, seldom scarred by suicide bombers. The international airport opened in July 2006 and, due to its prosperity and natural beauty, local Iraqis and Middle Easterners are coming to the city as tourists. A 400-bed hospital, two highways, universities and new houses are also planned by the regional government. Faruk Rasool, a communist turned chief executive, was able to donate US$1 million to help establish an American University in Suleimaniyah. He made his money from Kurdistan's first cell-phone company and has deals for cement factories, a steel plant and a 28-storey, five-star hotel, and predicts that Suleimaniyah will be one of the most developed cities in the Middle East.

Despite the rapid development, the city's administration is not always what it could be. 'Many people have become rich while thousands of families are suffering from lack of water, electricity and housing,' complained Halmat Shareef, a musician. The local rubbish dump, in an industrial area 11km southwest of the city, has become a source of income for some families.

Rising house prices have put a home out of the range of many young couples. Shwan Mahmood of the Pasand real estate firm, said house prices have increased rapidly as private companies, government agencies and NGOs are now operating from residential properties rather than renting limited office space. The population is rising by 3% annually as refugees from other parts of Iraq settle in the city. Local farmers are leaving their land in pursuit of higher-

Relatively close to the Iranian border, just over an hour's drive from Suleimaniyah, is the town of Halabja. It was brought from obscurity by the horrific poisonous gas attack on its inhabitants during the Anfal, the anti-Kurdish campaign led by Saddam's regime between 1986 and 1987 while fighting the Iran–Iraq War. (There were 180,000 victims of the Anfal, during which civilians were killed by chemical and conventional bombardments and thousands of villages destroyed.)

At Halabja, over 5,000 inhabitants, mostly women, children and old men, were killed in about 20 minutes on 16 March 1988. This brutal and inhuman retaliation to the possession of the town by the Iranians and Kurdish *peshmerga* was perpetrated by Saddam's cousin, Ali Hassan Al-Majid (Chemical Ali). Unbeknown to the Iraqi command was the presence of an Iranian news team who filmed the attack and subsequent grotesque deaths. Images of children's corpses shocked the world. This one attack played a significant role in changing the attitudes of many, particularly those from Europe, who had initially supported the Iran–Iraq War as begun by Saddam's regime.

The dead were gathered by the *peshmerga* and Iranians and hurriedly buried in five large pits scattered around the outskirts of the town. The long-term effects of the poisonous gas were not known then and few of the bodies were identified individually. Today, the pits are marked and simply enclosed.

The town cemetery, whose gate has a sign 'Baathists should not enter here' in English, has an area set aside for the headstones marked with each family's name, their only record.

Halabja was effectively abandoned for some time and a 'new Halabja' was built a few kilometres away, although this is now in decline. In September 2007 the original Halabja has recovered and has a busy air with many reconstructed buildings. Families take their children to play in the wooded areas near some of the death pits and life goes on.

But the turbulence that seems inherent in Kurdistan Iraq has not finished in Halabja. A somewhat grandiose monument set in gardens funded by the regional government and others was attacked by the local people on 3 March 2006. Some say the mob was stirred by various political agents, angered at government funds going to the monument instead of the town and its people, desperate for many facilities.

The interior of the monument was burnt, its wall paintings and sheets of inscribed victims' names on the walls partially damaged. The monument now stands forlorn but guarded and, apart from the gardens, awaiting funds for restoration and the will to do so. On an adjacent site is an information office run by the director, Sarkhel Gafar, whose family were among the victims of the atrocity.

paid jobs, especially in the police force. Suleimaniyah has strong economic ties with Iran.

Corruption is another problem. At the end of 2005 *Chawder*, a PUK newspaper, published a long report, which revealed that there were no personnel files for 80 high-ranking government employees.

Kurdistan's local Islamic parties (the United Islamic Party and the Islamic Movement) have threatened Marywan Halabjaye, author of *Sex, Sharia and*

Women in the History of Islam. Al-Qaeda in Iraq has threatened to kill Muslims who convert to Christianity or Zoroastrianism.

The city and the neighbouring town of Halabja are no strangers to the atrocities of the Iraqi regime. The Palace of Hamid Beg, the last Baban Prince, was destroyed during the 1958 revolution, which overthrew the monarchy (see pages 75–6). The former communications centre of the Iraqi army has been turned into a cultural centre that includes a kindergarten and swimming pools. The headquarters of the intelligence service (*mukhabarat*) and the graves near it have been preserved as a reminder of the inhuman acts perpetrated here.

Lady Adila's palace at Halabja, the last relic of traditional princely architecture, was destroyed during the Anfal campaign of 1986 and 1987.

MOUNTAIN REGIONS AND RESORTS The mountains of Iraqi Kurdistan form a natural barrier between Turkey and Iran. Halgurd is the highest peak in the Hasarost Mountains, 3607m above sea level. Lesley Thornton, who joined the first group tour to Iraqi Kurdistan since the establishment of the safe haven, commented on the wonders of nature: jagged molars of mountains, pale striated pyramids of hills, meadows packed with May flowers – small poppies, purple and yellow vetch, blue flax, huge wild hollyhocks in maroon and white – more in a square metre than in hectares of a British field.

Mountain villages are fascinating places. They may only be a few kilometres apart but every settlement has its own unique character and a well-developed sense of community. The single-storey houses are made of mud-brick or stone.

Model villages, built by the Iraqi government for the former inhabitants close to the Turkish and Iranian borders and scattered on the plains from Dohuk to Suleimaniyah, have been demolished.

Popular mountain resorts include **Salahuddin** on Mount Pirman overlooking the plain (19km from Erbil); **Shaqlawa** on the slope of Mount Safin (about half an hour's drive from Salahuddin); and **Gali Ali Beg** (50km from Shaqlawa), where a waterfall tumbles 800m above sea level. This waterfall has been immortalised on the Iraqi dinar. It forms a small pond where, on the hottest days, veiled Arab women can be seen jumping into the water. The spot is a favourite with Baghdadis who often outnumber the Kurds. It is an area of quaint local cafés and hundreds of yellow chairs from which to enjoy the view.

Beyond the waterfall is the town of Diana where the road divides. One leads to the spectacular waterfall (Beikhal), which can be seen 10km out of **Rawanduz**, an area of outstanding natural beauty. A US$20-million hotel with a golf course, swimming pool and tennis courts opened recently near Beikhal.

The other road goes to the Joodian waterfall. This is an amazing construction where very cold water from the spring atop the hill pours down several staircases. Iraqis camp on the terraces around the falls and run up and down the stairs to cool off.

On the way back from Gali Ali Beg, car engines cool off courtesy of an amazing set of hoses by the side of the road – an informal engine-cooling system.

Zawita (90km from Mosul in Dohuk governorate) is in the heart of a romantic pine and elm forest. King Faisal II built a rest-house in the area, which

I met Mivan Majid in a mountain park above the city of Suleimaniyah. To the north and east the jagged ridges of the Zagros Mountains, marking Iraqi Kurdistan's border with Iran, were receding into dusk. To the south, the immense Mesopotamian plain was a sunset-gilded carpet stretching toward Baghdad and the Persian Gulf. I involuntarily flinched when a tall, gangly teenager in faded blue jeans tapped me on the arm.

'Hey,' she said, 'are you guys American?'

That can be an uncomfortable question in the Middle East today, but her casual manner put me immediately at ease. She had remarkable poise and proceeded to grill me in near-perfect California slang, which she'd picked up from an expatriate girlfriend.

When I learned her age, it struck me that Mivan Majid was the Kurdish dream personified. She had never known a day under the rule of Baghdad. Suleimaniyah, her hometown and the capital of Iraqi Kurdistan's eastern sector, has been under unbroken Kurdish control since 1992, the very year of her birth. She wanted to be an engineer, Mivan told me, 'because they build such cool things: houses, roads, shopping centres. It's like, when you're an engineer you don't get hung up on our terrible history. You look ahead.'

Frank Viviano, National Geographic, *January 2006*

is a popular recreational spot for the people of Dohuk. **Swaratouka** (114km from Mosul) has specially built tourist houses.

One of Saddam's former palaces is in **Sarsang**, 120km from Mosul. The famous Ashawa waterfall and the Christian village of Aneshkey, with its large cave, are nearby. The cave has been converted into a restaurant café with beautiful views and an indoor fountain. It was once used as a base and makeshift hospital for *peshmergas*.

Haj Omran on the Iranian border boasts spectacular scenery. In the future it has potential for winter sports, as does much of Iraqi Kurdistan. It is also a haven for the illicit transfer of goods between the two countries.

The plain of **Harir Batass**, accessible by road from Shaqlawa, is the place for ancient tells (artificial mounds formed by the accumulated remains of ancient settlements) that date back to different ages in the country's history.

10

Baghdad and the Sunni Triangle

The story of the City of Peace is largely the story of continuous war.
Where there is not war, there is pestilence, famine and civil disturbance.
Such is the paradox which cynical history has written across the high
aims implied in the name bestowed upon the city by her founder.
                    Richard Coke, *Baghdad: The City of Peace* (1927)

Buildings that were once thriving now look decrepit and dilapidated.
An internet café is now an empty shell of concrete. Some restaurants
have been hit four or five times in car-bomb attacks. Wires and cables
are strewn like drunken, haphazard spider webs from building to
building and street to street. I saw the hotel room where I lived for six
weeks in 2004. Not because the desk manager let me in – the place is
now shuttered and boarded up – but because the windows are blown
out. Banks, mosques, and hospitals, in addition to whole
neighbourhoods and private houses, are barricaded.
                    Daniel Pepper, *Time*, 7 January 2008

In Iraq all major roads lead to the capital, Baghdad, a city that has risen like a
phoenix from the ashes many times after being devastated by floods, fires and
brutal conquerors. Despite its ever-changing fortunes, the city seldom lost its
importance as a commercial, communications and cultural centre. It is located
in the heart of the Middle East, in the historic Tigris–Euphrates valley, 692km
southwest of Tehran (Iran) and 950km east of Beirut (Lebanon).

Baghdad began as a series of pre-Islamic settlements. In the 8th century it
was transformed into the capital of the Muslim world and remained a cultural
metropolis for centuries. In 1258, after its destruction by Mongol invaders, the
Persians and Ottomans (Turks) vied for control of the city, which was
incorporated into the Ottoman Empire in 1638 as the vilayet of Baghdad, an
important provincial centre. In 1932 it became the capital of modern Iraq.

HISTORICAL BACKGROUND

CHRONOLOGY

AD762	Abu Ja'far Al-Mansour, the second Abbasid Caliph, built the circular city of Baghdad.
768	Construction of Risafah (East Baghdad).
775	Harun al Rashid, the fifth Abbasid Caliph, came to the throne.

836	Mutasim, the eighth Abbasid Caliph (son of Harun), relocated the capital to Samarra.
882	Baghdad became the capital once again.
1048	Buyids (a Persian dynasty) in power.
1055	Tughrul Bey, a Turkish prince, captured Baghdad.
1063	Alparslan, Tughrul's son, succeeded his father.
1065	Nizam ul Mulk, Alparslan's famous vizier, built Nidhamiyah College in Baghdad.
1094	Malakshah, Alparslan's son, succeeded his father. End of the Seljuks.
1118	Mustarshid, the 29th Abbasid Caliph, regained power before being assassinated.
1187	Reign of Nassir, the 34th Caliph. During this time Saladin recaptured Jerusalem.
1235	Mustansir built Mustansiriyah College. Mongol invasion began.
1242	Death of Mustansir.
1258	Hulagu, Genghis Khan's son, captured and completely destroyed Baghdad.
1340	Reign of Hasan Al Jalairi, a Tartar king.
1362	Mirjan, a slave of Greek origin, became the governor of Baghdad. He built Mirjan Mosque, Khan Mirjan and many schools.
1377	Tamerlane, Hulagu's grandson, sacked Baghdad.
1419	Reign of Turcoman Black Sheep Dynasty.
1473	Reign of Turcoman White Sheep Dynasty.
1504	Safavids (Persians) captured Baghdad.
1543	Suleiman the Magnificent (Ottoman Sultan) captured Baghdad.
1632	Safavids recaptured Baghdad.
1638	Murad IV, Ottoman Sultan, captured Baghdad.
1817	Daud Pasha became the governor of Baghdad.
1830	Year of calamity: the bubonic plague devastated Baghdad.
1868	Midhat Pasha, an enlightened governor, came to Baghdad. He built the Serai, a magical palace, and a number of factories, introduced the printing press and published a weekly paper.
1917	The British army captured Baghdad.
1932	Baghdad started to expand; attention paid to the infrastructure, traditional districts disbanded.
1950s	Rural urban drift, shanty towns grew up on the outskirts of Baghdad.
1970s	Four-fold increase in oil price led to a construction boom. Some districts of Baghdad bombed as Iran and Iraq launched a 'war of the cities' during the 1980–88 Iran–Iraq War.
1991	Baghdad bombed during first Gulf War.
1990s	Rebuilding after Gulf War. Saddam started construction of the world's largest mosque. Iraq under sanctions.

2003

20 Mar	The war to change the Iraqi regime began. Baghdad was heavily pounded by cruise missiles on 21 March.
9 Apr	Baghdad captured by American forces. Saddam's statue toppled in Fardous Square. Widespread looting.
13 Apr	Saddam's home town of Tikrit captured.
27 Apr	US soldiers arrested self-proclaimed mayor of Baghdad and accused him of trying to sabotage Coalition efforts to restore basic services.
3 May	Schools re-opened.
30 May	New statue of an Iraqi family holding a crescent moon and a sun replaced Saddam's in Ferdous Square
Aug	Deadly bomb attacks on Jordanian embassy and UN HQ. The UN withdrew personnel from Baghdad.

2004

15 Sep	Suicide bomber killed 47 police volunteers.
8 Nov	Major assault on Fallujah to root out insurgents. 70% of the town was destroyed.
27 Dec	13 people killed in a car bomb outside the offices of the Supreme Islamic Council.

2005

28 Feb	At least 114 people killed by a massive car bomb in Hilla, south of Baghdad – the worst single such incident since the US-led invasion.
Aug	More than 1,000 people killed during a stampede at a Shia ceremony in Baghdad.

2006

7 Apr	85 killed in triple suicide bombing at a Shia mosque in Baghdad.
23 Nov	More than 200 died in car bombings in the mostly Shia area of Sadr City in Baghdad. An indefinite curfew is imposed after what is considered the worst attack on the capital since the US-led invasion of 2003.

2007

10 Jan	President Bush announced a new security plan for Baghdad involving an extra 30,000 troops.
3 Feb	130 killed in lorry bomb in a Baghdad market in a mainly Shia area.
Mar	90 killed in a double suicide bombing in Hilla. Insurgents detonated three trucks with toxic chlorine gas in Fallujah and Ramadi, injuring thousands.
29 May	Five Britons kidnapped in Baghdad.
12 Apr	A bomb blast rocked parliament, killing an MP.
18 Apr	Bombings in Baghdad killed nearly 200 people in the worst day of violence since a US-led security drive

	began in the capital in February.
Jun	A record 168,000 US troops are in Iraq after 30,000 arrived between February and June.
8 Aug	US aircraft and soldiers raided Sadr City, killing 32 and capturing 12 militiamen.
3 Sep	President Bush paid a surprise visit to Anbar province and met Sunni tribal leaders who started co-operating with American forces in the fight against Al-Qaeda.
10 Sep	The top US military commander in Iraq, General David Petraeus, said the objectives of the troop surge 'are largely being met'. Many American politicians and Iraq analysts disagreed.
26 Sep	A woman died of cholera in Baghdad. Iraq's health ministry said it was the capital's first confirmed fatality in the country's recent outbreak.
6 Oct	25 suspected insurgents killed by the US military near Baquba. The target of the operation was a militia commander linked to the Quds Force of Iran's revolutionary guards.
21 Oct	America claimed 49 criminals were killed in three raids on Sadr City, while Sadr's officials claimed women, children and the elderly had been killed.

2008

11 Jan	US bombers dropped over 18 tonnes of explosives on Arab Jabour, a Sunni district on the southern outskirts of Baghdad, flattening what the military described as safe havens for Al-Qaeda in Iraq.
24 Feb	A suicide bomber killed at least 40 people and injured 60 Shia pilgrims on the way to Kerbala to commemorate Ashoura.
1 Mar	Statistics quoted that the surge has worked! Certainly the daily menu of deaths was much diminished throughout Iraq in the last few months.

INTRODUCTION The banks of the Tigris, where the land was fertile and the river constituted an important trade route, were a popular site for settlements long before AD770 when the Abbasid Caliph Abu Ja'far Al-Mansour created the round 'wagon-wheel' city, the setting of the tales of *The Thousand and One Nights*.

Throughout the centuries, settlements with names similar to Baghdad were located on the site of the present-day Iraqi capital. A legal document dating back to 1800BC, the time of Hammurabi, mentions a city called Bagdadu. Archae-ologists have recovered boundary stones from a city known as Pilari in the district of Bagdadi during the reign of the Assyrian King Nazimaruttas (1341–1316BC). A boundary stone from the reign of the Babylonian King Marduk-Apaliddin (1208–1195BC) mentions Baghdad, which was said to be an Armenian settlement in the 8th century BC. Baghdad has had more than 20 names, including City of Peace (Madinat Al-Salam), House of Peace (Dar Al-Salam), Dome of Islam (Qubbat Al-Islam) and Mother of Iraq (Umm Al-Iraq).

Like the Mesopotamian myths, many of the stories from *The Thousand and One Nights* describe the soul's journey through life. The tales, thought to date from the 10th century AD, were narrated by a character called Shahrazad, the wife of a fictional Sassanid king, Shahryar. His other wives were killed, as he sought vengeance for a previous betrayal by a woman. But Shahrazad stayed alive by keeping him occupied for a thousand and one nights with a series of fascinating tales.

The tales, which include *Sinbad the Sailor*, *Ali Baba and the Forty Thieves* and *Aladdin and the Magic Lamp*, became popular in 9th-century Baghdad, the capital of the Abbasid Empire, when they were translated from Indian languages and Persian into Arabic. Their subsequent translation into French and other European languages guaranteed their universal popularity.

During the 19th century, Richard Burton's complete translation of *The Thousand and One Nights* was banned in Britain, as the erotic content of many of the stories offended prudish Victorian society.

During the reign of the Abbasid Caliphs (AD750–1258) Baghdad became the capital of the Muslim Empire (see pages 49–50). The Abbasids who overthrew the Damascus-based Umayyad Dynasty naturally wanted the centre of their empire to be close to their power base. Persian civil servants played an important part in the running of the caliphate. A permanent civil service was created, headed by a Minister of State, known as the *wazir*. Even though the Abbasids emphasised the equality of all the Muslim subjects of the empire, the caliph tended to be a remote, unapproachable figure.

THE FOUNDER OF BAGHDAD In *The Monument*, Samir Al-Khalil describes the building of Baghdad.

The city's founder, the Abbasid Caliph Abu Ja'far Al-Mansour, fancied himself an architect. He imagined the new seat of government as an elaborately walled fortress perfectly circular in shape. A splendiferous royal palace, to which was attached a great mosque, was placed in the exact geometrical centre. The rest of the city radiated outwards like the segments of an orange. Given the singular geometry of this vision, the only critical decision concerned the dimensions of the circumference. It seems the caliph did not trust drawings. Nonetheless, he had to judge the rightness of his decision correctly before construction could begin. So he had his labourers dig a shallow trench into the soil following the outline of the intended circle. Into this a mixture of oil and cotton seeds was placed and set ablaze. The caliph watched the magnificent spectacle from a spot overlooking the great River Tigris, which had seen so many civilisations born of its fertility come and go, pronounced himself satisfied, and ordered construction of the massive outer ring's walls to begin.

The *Encyclopedia of Islam* points out that the site was chosen for military, economic and climatic reasons. The plain was fertile and could be cultivated. It was a meeting place of caravan routes, and monthly fairs were held there,

Baghdad and the Sunni Triangle **HISTORICAL BACKGROUND**

10

ensuring provisions would be plentiful for the army and the residents. It was in the middle of Mesopotamia and enjoyed a temperate and healthy climate, without malarial mosquitoes.

On advice from the geographer Mukaddisi, the notables of Baghdad gave the caliph the following advice, referred to by Richard Coke, author of *Baghdad: The City of Peace*:

> We are of the opinion that thou shouldest found thy city here: thereby shalt thou live among palms and near water, so that if one district fail thee in its crops or be late in its harvest, in another will the remedy be found. Also the city being on the Surat canal, provisions will be brought thither by the boats of the Euphrates, and by the caravans through the plains, even from Egypt and Syria. Hither, up from the sea, will come wares of China, while down the Tigris from Mosul will be brought goods from the Byzantine lands. Thus shall thy city be safe standing between all these streams, and thine enemy shall not reach thee, except it be by a boat or by a bridge, and across the Tigris or Euphrates.

BUILDING BAGHDAD Caliph Mansour referred to his settlement on the west bank of the Tigris as City of Peace (Madinat Al-Salam), despite its fortress-like appearance, which gave it the air of a city ready for war. The design was in fact based on a circular Roman military camp with four gates equidistant from each other: Al-Basra (south), Al-Kufa (north), Damascus (west) and Khorasan (east) led to four main roads that linked the city centre with the regions outside. It was surrounded by a deep ditch followed by the first wall. A space of 57m was left empty for defence purposes. Then came another brick wall with 28 great towers and a space of 170m where the caliph's loyal subjects built their houses.

Another wall separated the caliph's palace, with its famous green dome, and the mosque. The mosque's area was a quarter of that of the palace, but it was gradually expanded because of the increasing number of worshippers. The ceiling of the mosque was decorated with golden crescents and its walls were inlaid with green mosaics surrounded by teak wood.

It is said that Caliph Mansour employed 100,000 workers and craftsmen to turn his dream city into reality. The cost remains unknown as the caliph did not have to account to anyone for his spending. Materials were brought from neighbouring towns. Wasit lost its five famous wrought-iron gates and both Damascus and Kufa had to supply a gate. The bricks from the ruins of Babylon and Ctesiphon were also used.

The city was finally completed in AD766. It only covered 85ha. Mansour was obsessed with security and the city had its own prison: Matbak prison. He ordered 100 graves to be dug for him to escape desecration at the hands of his enemies. The real place of his burial was such a well-kept secret that today no-one is sure where he is buried.

Mansour's city was a city for the government and the court and not for the people. Commercial activities were severely restricted, prompting a merchants' town called Karkh to grow up outside Kufa Gate. The canals were the focal point for trade, where coppersmiths, reed-weavers and sellers of cooked meats congregated. New suburbs were built and Mansour's round city soon became the nucleus of a larger town.

Mansour also built an army camp on the east side of the Tigris named Rusafa. In AD768 a new mosque and palace were constructed in Rusafa, near a great cemetery where many of the caliphs were buried. Today part of central Baghdad has retained this name.

Richard Coke, author of *Baghdad: The City of Peace*, describes Mansour as an exemplary individual in his private life and notes that nothing of an unseemly nature was ever permitted at his court:

> His reign was almost continually interrupted by rebellions, religious disturbances and wars with foreign foes. In spite of all, he not only founded a new capital, but placed the imperial administration on a firmer footing than it had known for a generation. To him more than to any other single man was due the stability which permitted the material glories of the reign of Harun and the intellectual and literary activity of Mamum. To the excellence of his work as a builder witness is given by the fact that his descendants continued to occupy the caliphate throne, in the capital city which he had created, for five hundred years. The founder of Baghdad may justly claim a place as one of the great organising monarchs of the world.

GROWTH AND PROSPERITY The 8th and 9th centuries were Baghdad's golden years. Gavin Young, author of *Iraq: Land of Two Rivers*, described how:

> Baghdad became the richest city of the world. Its wharves were lined with ships – from China bringing porcelain; from Malaya and India with spices and dyes; from Turkestan with lapis lazuli (used as a gem) and slaves; from East Africa with ivory and gold dust; and from Arabia with pearls and weapons.

A fledgling banking system fostered the growth of trade. There was self-regulation of fraud by merchants and traders who formed a specific guild to root out corrupt practices.

As well as a focal point of trade, Abbasid Baghdad was a preserver and translator of past knowledge. The foundation of the city corresponded with the introduction of paper from China, which encouraged literary endeavours – especially as paper was manufactured in Baghdad.

The city became a leading centre of learning from which Greco-Roman wisdom was passed on. The writings of Aristotle and Plato were translated in the House of Wisdom and advances in medicine, astronomy and other disciplines laid the foundations for modern Western sciences. In 1235 Caliph Mustansir built Mustansiriya University on the banks of the Tigris. It was also the time of the poet Abu Nuwas, a famous literary figure whose works are often quoted today. Educational institutions similar to the ones developed in Baghdad were also introduced in the other cities of the Abbasid Caliphate, which extended from the Mediterranean to India.

ADMINISTRATION During Abbasid times social and welfare services, financed by the paying of *zakat* (an offering for the poor and needy similar to the Christian tithe), were developed, along with free hospitals where only

The Jews were an ancient, respected community in Mesopotamia. Even when Cyrus allowed them to return to Palestine in the 6th century BC (see page 42), many chose to remain in Babylon (present-day Iraq), where the famous Babylon Talmud was produced.

During the time of the Abbasid Caliphate and the subsequent years of Ottoman rule, Jews played an important economic role in Iraqi society. Abbas Shibblak, author of *The Lure of Zion: the Case of Iraqi Jews*, notes that:

> They worked in commerce, crafts and credit and money exchanges, while the enlightened middle strata secured a significant share of public office ... the Iraqi Jews continuously maintained their communal identity and were among the wealthiest and most fully integrated of all Jewish communities in Arab countries.

Among the Ottomans, they lived as protected minorities (*dhimmis*) who were given freedom to worship, conduct business and own property. Towards the end of the 19th century many Baghdadi Jews moved to other towns, especially Basra, a thriving port after the Suez Canal was opened.

Kenneth Kattan, author of *Mine was the Last Generation in Babylon*, described Souk Hinnouni (Hannoon market), in the heart of the Jewish neighbourhood in Baghdad:

> It was the main food market for more than 60,000 people and it was situated inside the residential area. All the vendors and customers were Jews. There was even a synagogue situated in its middle. It consisted of multiple intersecting alleys, each not more than three metres in width. They were unpaved, and they became muddy during the rainy days, autumn and winter.

These conditions improved after World War I. During the 1930s, relations between Jews and Muslims began to deteriorate due to Jewish agitation for a Zionist state in the Middle East. Iraq, the first Arab state to gain independence and be admitted to the League of Nations, saw itself as the centre of pan-Arabism and Arab resistance to Zionism. The Germans established an influential embassy in Baghdad and began disseminating anti-Semitic ideas.

In 1934 the Arabisation programme led to the dismissal of Jews from administrative positions under the pretext of reorganisation, so their places could be filled by a rising generation of educated Arabs. The year of 1941 was the year of the Farhud, a word denoting the breakdown of law and order. Jewish properties were

doctors with a diploma could practise. Zakat is one of the five duties (pillars) of Islam and the welfare system was centred around the mosques that financed the services through the social funds (*waqf*) to which believers contributed a percentage of their income. The care of the sick was also financed by the caliphs. Most of the leading physicians were Christians and relations between the Christian and Muslim communities were extremely cordial. At holiday time monasteries were the venues for singing, dancing and feasting.

looted and burned, and Jews were beaten up and killed in Baghdad, Mosul, Kirkuk, Erbil, Basra, Amarah and Fallujah. Official figures put the dead at 187, but Jewish sources claim at least 400 people lost their lives. Not all Iraqis condoned the indiscriminate violence and rape: many Jews were sheltered by Muslim families and Salih Bashayan, a prominent Muslim figure, assigned his men to guard Jewish properties.

But despite these humanitarian gestures the tradition of hundreds of years of co-existence between the Jews and Muslims had come to an end, prompting a mass migration of Iraqi Jews to Palestine or the USA in the 1950s, after the Suez War of 1956 and the Arab-Israeli War of 1967.

In the words of Daphine Tsimhoni, one of the contributors to the book *Nationalism, Minorities and Diasporas: identities and rights in the Middle East*:

> the Jews left carrying with them their attachment to Iraq, its culture and its literature ... They continued to cherish their memories of the unique Jewish-Muslim relationship in Iraq, carrying their Iraqi Jewish identity with them.

The Arabs' disastrous defeat during the 1967 war with Israel led to mass executions of Jews as spies, who were hanged in public in Baghdad.

After the 2003 war American forces found hundreds of documents relating to Baghdad's ancient Jewish community in the basement of a building that once housed Saddam's secret police.

According to the Jewish Agency's emissary to Iraq, Jeff Kaye, there are now 34 Jews in Baghdad. Half of them are over 70 and most of the others are in their 30s. There are no Jewish children acknowledged by anyone, although it would be surprising if they did not exist, but all prefer concealment. The last Jewish wedding was held in 1978. The 2,600-year-old community's last remaining synagogue is in the city centre neighborhood of Bataween. 'It is surrounded by a high wall – you wouldn't know there's a synagogue there until you entered the forecourt,' Kaye told the *Jewish Chronicle* in June 2003. 'The building is well preserved, contains some beautiful ancient artifacts and is large enough for 300 worshippers.' In July 2003 the Jewish Agency flew six elderly Iraqi Jews to Israel.

Some Iraqi Jews, among them Naim Dangoor, whose grandfather was Iraq's chief rabbi, were hoping to return and seek compensation for their lost property. But the rise of radical Islam in the country makes this increasingly unlikely.

The respect for their heritage connections to Baghdad and Iraq is still alive amongst the Jewish communities who fled to Europe or settled in Israel. The Sassoon and the Saatchi families in the UK are prime examples.

Order was maintained by the police force, the legal system, and an army made up of 125,000 regular troops in addition to irregulars known as *harbiyah*. Spies were sent to all major foreign capitals, especially Constantinople. The Board for the Inspection of Grievances eased the caliphs' judicial responsibilities. Judges (*qadis*) presided over both civil disputes and matters pertaining to religious law. The Islamic ideal that every Muslim should be able to complain about injustice brought the Office of the Censor of Morals (*muhtasib*) into being. He dealt with matters ranging from the provision of water supply and the control of weights and measures, to inspection of dolls to make sure they did not contravene the religious ban on idols. He even found husbands for widows.

THE DECLINE OF BAGHDAD Caliph Mansour was succeeded by his son Mahdi. Aware of the harshness of his father's reign, Mahdi's generosity seemed boundless, especially on pilgrimages to Mecca and Jerusalem, during which he distributed millions of dirhams. The next caliph was Harun Al Rashid (the orthodox). As the caliph of *The Thousand and One Nights*, he entered almost every home and his name is as familiar to the world at large as that of Baghdad itself.

Harun left many of the administrative duties to Jaffar the Barmecide, who built a new palace on the east bank of the river that was the scene of wild drinking parties. Some of the more important government offices were moved across the river and East Baghdad, close to Barmecide's residence, became an administrative centre, a role that it maintained until the beginning of the 20th century.

But Jaffar's luck ran out when, in a fit of anger, Harun threw him into prison and had him executed. This left the caliph with immense administrative responsibilities, which he found difficult to bear in his old age. Another serious political mistake was the division of the empire between his three sons: Mamum, Amin and Mutasim. The conflict between the brothers played itself out in the struggle between the Arabs and the Persians in the empire who supported one brother against another.

When Harun died in AD809, Amin was firmly ensconced in Baghdad with his father's treasure. He took up residence in Mansour's old Golden Gate Palace. This prompted Mamum, supported by the Persians, to launch an attack on the city. The tide had turned and the slow decline of Baghdad began with an attack on its western suburbs. The siege lasted for almost a year. In the end Amin tried to escape in a small boat, which overturned when it was pelted with stones. He was taken prisoner after he managed to swim ashore, and was promptly put to death.

RE-BIRTH AND CONFLICT The life of the city was now focused on three districts on the east bank of the river. During the reign of Mamum, Baghdad was a city of intellectual brilliance. In the House of Wisdom an army of translators worked around the clock to make sure all significant foreign works were

HARUN AL RASHID AD766–809

Harun became the fifth caliph of the Abbasid Dynasty in AD786. During his rule the Abbasid Caliphate reached the height of its power and his court was famous for its splendour. Harun's empire extended from the Mediterranean to India. He was a great patron of the arts and a single sonnet could earn a poet 5,000 gold pieces, a robe of honour, ten Greek slave girls and a horse from the royal stables. Harun was responsible for the rebuilding of the mosque of Mansur. In AD802 Mosa Al-Kadhim was buried in the cemetery outside the Straw Gate suburb of West Baghdad. He was poisoned on the orders of Harun Al Rashid after spending 19 years in Al-Sindi ibn Shahek prison. Thirty years later his grandson was buried in the same place and the area was named Kadhimain (the two Kadhims).

available in Arabic. Poets shed the restrictions of rigid classical forms, and prose writing in Arabic began. Religious debates centred around the mustazilates, who advocated free will and reason, and the sufis, oriented towards pure mysticism. Both schools of thought had a profound influence on the Islamic faith.

Mamum was also a religious scholar and the second of the only two caliphs in Islamic history who knew the entire Koran by heart. Richard Coke, author of *Baghdad: The City of Peace*, notes that under his regime one day a week was always set aside at court for literary, scientific or philosophical discussion. One day at the opening of a session for religious debate the caliph said:

> Advance thine arguments and answer without fear, for there is none here that will not speak thee well. Let everyone speak who has the wisdom to demonstrate the strength of his religion.

There are many records of court debates on religious subjects between Muslims and men of other faiths.

Mamun's successor Mutasim, the third son of Harun, surrounded himself with Turkish bodyguards who resembled a Praetorian guard. They became a law unto themselves and abused the citizens of the city. Between AD836 and 892 the capital of the Abbasid Empire was transferred to Samarra, 111km north of Baghdad, the city where Mutasim decided to isolate potential rebels who could threaten his authority. But Baghdad maintained its importance as a leading trading and cultural centre.

The Turks were now the masters, whose allegiance to Samarra amounted to little more than the payment of taxes. Musta'in, a grandson of Mutasim, could not tolerate this situation any longer and decided to enlist the support of the Arabs to rid the empire of the usurpers.

The confrontation took place in Baghdad, which suffered its second siege. Coke describes the decline of the city:

> Just as the first siege had marked the end of West Baghdad as the administrative and social heart of the metropolis, so this second siege marked the beginning of the decline of the original East Baghdad. The three quarters of Rusafah, Shammisiyah and Mukharrim only recovered in part from the effects of the hammering which they received at the hands of the Turkish troops. The new wall erected by Musta'in, as well as the older palaces, bazaars and houses, fell into gradual ruin; the next development was the growth of a new city based on the Jafari palace in a smaller and more southerly East Baghdad, destined to form the principal part of the city in modern times.

Musta'in and his men were defeated but the people of Baghdad became increasingly rebellious and unwilling to submit to Turkish domination. During the last 350 years of the Abbasid Caliphate Baghdad remained the capital. In AD892 Mutadid, one of the greatest of the Abbasid caliphs, overhauled the local government of the city, did his best to root out corruption, enlarged and renovated the Jafari palace where he took up residence, and built a new palace known as the Castle of Paradise, with an artificial lake.

MONGOL RULE The final years of Abbasid rule were characterised by internal strife and struggles between various religious sects, which resulted in frequent bloodshed. In 1256 much of the city was destroyed by floods and two years later the Mongols invaded, leaving between 800,000 and two million people dead.

Genghis Khan, the famous Mongol leader, united a number of ferocious tribes and turned them into a formidable war machine that devastated western Asia and threatened Europe. The caliphs underestimated the strength of the barbarians and at first successfully repulsed their raids and drove them out of Iraq.

Hulagu, Genghis Khan's son, followed his father's edict 'to treat those who submitted to his arms kindly, but to exterminate those who resisted; to conquer the lands from the banks of the Oxus River to the borders of Egypt and to compel the caliph of Baghdad to be submissive.' He began by sending the caliph a letter complaining that he had not received assistance in his campaign against the Assassins (an esoteric Muslim sect), and reminded him of the Mongol's previous conquests.

The caliph was not intimidated and replied:

O young man, just commencing your life, who, drunk with the prosperity and good fortune of ten days, deem yourself superior to the whole world, and think your orders equivalent to those of destiny: why do you address me with a demand which you cannot secure

War was inevitable. The people, sensing the imminent disaster, paid boatmen exorbitant prices to transport them to what they saw as the safety of the city walls.

But only the Christians were spared at the request of Hulagu's Christian wife. After a week of merciless slaughter the people of Baghdad sent a delegation to Hulagu begging him to stop the bloodshed. He agreed, but by this time all the city's major buildings had been either damaged or destroyed and the city's treasures were looted. Famine and disease followed the Mongol onslaught and Cairo replaced Baghdad as the cultural centre of the Muslim world.

The Mongols appointed a governor of Iraq and divided the country into two provinces, Iraq Arabi with its capital in Baghdad, and Iraq Ajemi with its capital in Isfahan. A new province of Dyarbekr was created in northern Mesopotamia, with Mosul as its administrative centre.

One of the most successful Mongol rulers was Orud Kia. In 1284, under the influence of Jewish doctor Said ud-Dawlah, the taxation system was reformed and the power of the military curbed. In 1302, Ghazan was the greatest Mongol ruler: he introduced a new standard of weights and measures, redeveloped lands devastated during earlier invasions, set up an efficient postal service, and built mosques and public baths in poor areas and ensured their upkeep.

After a revolution in central Asia in 1400, Tamerlane emerged as the head of the Mongol Empire. He was a master opportunist who used Islam to justify whatever act of megalomania he wished to pursue. In 1401 he unleashed his wrath on Baghdad, where the Jalayrids had created a new kingdom, ordering only the preservation of mosques and hospitals. The destruction of all other buildings and the killing of citizens 'from eight to eighty' was decreed. His

90,000 men were instructed to bring at least one human skull each to camp. Those who failed would pay with their lives.

Coke described the fate of the city:

> The old civilisation which had survived the first Mongol deluge was effectively wiped out. For the second time in a century and a half the City of Peace had to suffer the virtual annihilation of her population. Such hopes of progress and restoration as might have been entertained in the interval were now dashed to the ground. Before the coming of Timur, Baghdad had sufficiently recovered her old position to be regarded as a rival, if an inferior one, of the great Tabriz. Henceforward, any aspiration of so lofty a kind becomes merely ridiculous. The city, with the country around it, can now do no more than mourn its great past and adjust its point of view to a future which seems to become only narrower and narrower, even more confined and less attractive.

The first Mongol capture of the city left it with a ruling foreign dynasty. The second capture was more like a raid and the invaders did not establish themselves as a ruling power. Turkish tribes then displaced the Mongols as rulers of Baghdad: the Black Sheep (1419) and White Sheep (1473) Turcomans took turns at misruling, rather than ruling, the city and the country. The nomadic Arab tribes turned large areas into pasture lands for their flocks and were more occupied with their internal disputes than the establishment of a centralised administration. The destruction of the irrigation system led to the further marginalisation of the city, which was no more than a bargaining chip between rival Turcoman tribesmen, a town of half-ruined bazaars through which foreign travellers passed unimpressed.

THE OTTOMAN ERA During the 15th and 16th centuries the Ottomans and the Safavid Persians competed for control of Baghdad. In 1508, Shah Ismail of Persia occupied the city, destroyed the tombs of Sunni saints, constructed a large hostel for Persian pilgrims at Kadhimain, and appointed Ibrahim Khan as the first Persian governor of Baghdad. The city was once again developed as a commercial centre.

But the Turks could not accept Persian domination. Thirty years later the Ottoman Sultan Suleiman the Magnificent took Baghdad from Persia, but his rule was detested by the Sunnis and the non-Muslim population. In 1621 the Persians again took Baghdad but lost it 17 years later to the Ottoman Turks. The popular song 'between the Persians and the Rum (barbarians) what woe befell us' summed up the city's unenviable fate as a political football passed from one conqueror to another. From 1638 until World War I, Baghdad was part of the Ottoman Empire, governed from Istanbul.

THE YEARS OF CONFLICT When they retook the city the Turks were eager to ensure the loyalty of the citizens, so local dignitaries were encouraged to visit the Turkish court, Sunni mosques were rebuilt and agriculture was encouraged.

Baghdad became the regional capital of a Turkish province. The finances and the government of the city were in Turkish hands. They continued to repair mosques and built rest-houses, bazaars and coffee houses, as well as a ditch around Karkh to deter Bedouin attacks. Mahmudiyah, a village on the Baghdad–Hillah road *en route* to Babylon, was built as a retreat for Mahmud, a Pasha of Baghdad at the beginning of the 15th century.

Some of the Turkish governors were strong, resourceful and forward-looking, while others were weak and incompetent. Yusef Pasha was in the latter category and the city fell into the hands of Bakr, an officer who asked the sultan to legalise his rule. The request was refused and Bakr enlisted the aid of the Shah of Persia, Abbas, to defeat the Turkish troops sent to oust him. But he did not allow the Persians to take over the city on behalf of the Shah. During the siege that followed famine set in and many of the city's hapless citizens deserted at night to the Persians. In the end Bakr's son Muahhad smuggled Persian troops into the city, the gates were opened and the keys handed to the Shah. Bakr was executed, many Sunnis were sold into slavery and the city was left in a state of disrepair. The Turks, led by Sultan Murad, made several attempts to re-take the city and finally succeeded in 1638 with the assistance of the Abu Rishah tribes on the Euphrates, who sent 10,000 camel loads of provisions. The importance Sultan Murad attached to the city was described by his chief falconer in a letter to Mustafa Bey of Egypt, quoted here by Richard Coke:

> The grand seignior caused the pavilions of all the surgeons of the army to be pitched near his own, ordering all the wounded men to be brought thither and he himself comforted them with good words. The pay of those who died was given to their children or their nearest relations.

The sultan left the city at the head of his victorious army by the Talisman Gate, which was bricked up and remained so until 1917, when the Turks destroyed it in the midst of the British takeover.

TURKISH DOMINANCE The sultan's governors were a weird and wonderful collection of interesting characters. There was Hosein Pasha (nicknamed 'The Mad') who wandered round Baghdad at night in disguise to find out what was happening in the city; Ibrahim Pasha, who was vain and pleasure-loving; and Murtadha Pasha, who terrorised high officials, but who was incredibly generous to the poor – he even allowed a Bedouin with a grievance to talk to him in his private apartments.

During the reign of Salhadar Hosein Pasha in 1671, a new bazaar and a new mosque were built and the mosque of Abdul Wadir Gilani was decorated.

A new era began in 1704 when Hassan Pasha exported the tradition of employing Circassian slaves, who were organised in a strict hierarchy of civil servants, to Baghdad. These Mamluks (white slaves) ruled the city wisely during the next 130 years and held the threat of invasion by the Persians and Arab tribes at bay. Baghdad prospered under Hassan's son Ahmed, who brought peace and order to the city and added the provinces of Mardin, Mosul, Kirkuk and Basra to his domain.

As the Mamluk court expanded, prospered and became increasingly extravagant, the people got poorer and a crippling taxation regime did little to endear the people to the Mamluks. The Persian threat never completely subsided and the son of the Shah, Muhammad Ali Mirza, invaded Iraq in 1818, but his troops were held in check by the outbreak of a cholera epidemic.

In Istanbul, Sultan Mahmud decided to reform the army. The move was accompanied by an instruction to abolish the local Janissaries (Christian children trained for service in the palace). The fact that Daud Pasha of Baghdad had not supported the sultan in Turkey's war with Russia soon became a major issue and an envoy was sent to Baghdad to demand his voluntary retirement. The envoy did not return alive and a new successor, Ali Rudha Pasha, was appointed. Daud was declared an outlaw.

The bubonic plague and devastating floods of 1831, which washed away two-thirds of East Baghdad (Rusafa) and much of West Baghdad (Karkh), followed. The population of the city dropped from 150,000 during the days of Daud Pasha to 50,000.

Ali Rudha, the governor of Baghdad during the 1830s, summoned the military slave class (Mamluks) to the reading of an imperial decree abolishing their colleges and grades of officials. The reading of the decree was a pretext to gather this class in one place so they could be slaughtered (see page 60).

The city recovered slowly from disease, natural disasters and horrendous internal disputes. Mehmet Rashid Pasha (1847) was one of the more enlightened rulers who tried to introduce economic reforms. His successors abolished taxes on produce brought into the city, established the first publishing house and laid the foundations for a modern education system.

This was the age of the railway, the steamboat and the telegraph.

Increasing numbers of European travellers started visiting the city during the 19th century. Felix Jones, a British official who surveyed Baghdad in 1853, noted that conditions had improved and that much of the city, which had been washed away by floods, had been rebuilt. Jones refers to 63 quarters in East Baghdad and 25 in West Baghdad. Other visitors commented on the variety of races and creeds that co-existed and noted that the non-Muslims were well integrated into the life of the country. Three thousand Jews lived in the city and there were nine synagogues. People who shared a common creed, racial or tribal origin tended to live in the same quarter.

The city was governed by the beladiyah system of Midhat Pasha. Its functions were similar to those of city councils in Western cities. There were 12 council members and a president who was elected by the citizens for a four-year term.

THE 20TH CENTURY In the last decade of the 19th century the city's bazaars became prosperous once again, and its inhabitants were ready to welcome Western ways. Trade, largely imports and re-exports, amounted to US$4 million annually. World War I brought increased activity as Baghdad became the base of operations against the British. The Turks finally left the city in 1917, but not before the military commandant destroyed as many official records as he could. The Talisman Gate was blown up as a parting gesture. General Maude entered the city and delivered a famous speech (see page 68) in which he urged the people:

> through your nobles and elders and representatives, to participate in the management of your own civil affairs in collaboration with the political representatives of Great Britain, who accompany the British Army.

10

The army did not leave immediately, even though the threatened Turkish return never took place. A new city administration took over the running of Baghdad, electricity was introduced and improvements were made to the streets and water supply. When the plague broke out again in 1919, a large scale inoculation programme was organised by British doctors and nurses. The country's first constitutional assembly met in 1924 after the women's hospital in Karkh was renovated and turned into the Parliament House of Iraq.

Until the 1920s the city maintained its largely medieval appearance. But after independence (1932) it started to expand. Attention was paid to the construction of schools and hospitals, the infrastructure, and a system of bunds (embankments) to protect the city from floods. The dismemberment of the traditional central districts (Karkh and Rusafa) began. Most of old Baghdad had been 'modernised', but as the city underwent the agonies of urban renewal some of its most important areas of traditional housing were conserved and revitalised. According to John Warren and Ihsan Fethi, authors of *Traditional Houses in Baghdad*:

> Flood, decay and the city planners together destroyed almost all parts of the city which were over 50 years old. With the exception of a scattering of old mosques and of two much-restored 13th century structures (the Abbasid Palace and Mustansiriyah School), the city of Baghdad dates from the end of the First World War (1918) when its first two metalled roads – Rashid Street and River Street – were constructed by German engineers to ease the passage of the Ottoman army in its retreat before the advancing British forces.

During the time of the monarchy Qasr Al-Rehab was the king's first official residence. The construction of a new republican palace was completed during the time of Abdul Karim Qasim, but due to his modest nature Qasim chose not to live there. Saddam Hussein has constructed another republican palace.

Freya Stark, who took up residence in Baghdad during the 1930s, fell in love with life near the river, which she described in *Baghdad Sketches*:

> The width of the Tigris in Baghdad is about four hundred yards, a noble stream. It is the only sweet and fresh thoroughfare of the town: not clear water, but lion-coloured, like the Tiber or Arno. Its broad flowing surface is dyed by the same earth of which the houses and minarets on its banks are built, so that all is one tawny harmony. Its low winter mists in early morning, or yellow slabs of sunset shallows when the water buffaloes come down to drink after the day; its many craft, evolved through the centuries so that one looks as it were upon an epitome of the history of ships from the earliest days of mankind; the barefoot traffic of its banks, where the women come with jars upon their shoulders and boatmen tow their vessels against the current; all this was perpetual joy in my new home.

Baghdad slowly became an industrial centre. The first large-scale factory was a woolen textile factory, followed by a number of cigarette factories and a brewery. Plants for making bricks and other construction materials also sprang up, along with factories for cement, soap-making, tanning and leather goods, soft drinks and confectionery. Other early industries included flour mills, print shops and car repair shops.

The construction sector in the city, small machine shops and the service industries provided employment for peasants who converged on Baghdad from the rural areas. Squatters lived in hastily erected reed and mud huts on the outskirts of the city, where one of the squatter settlements was turned into Ath Thawra township (renamed Saddam City in 1980 and again renamed Sadr City in 2003 – see pages 209–11). Squatters also congregated in the An Nur district.

The city, and its population, has grown dramatically since the end of World War II. From a mere built-up area of around 6km^2 in the first decade of the 20th century it mushroomed to around 240km^2 in 1970. In 1900, 140,000 people lived in Baghdad. Between 1957 and 1987, the population grew by 73% and in the mid-1970s Baghdad had 3.5 million inhabitants. Today over six million people live in Iraq's capital.

The new wealth of the 1970s, generated by a four-fold increase in oil prices, led to a growth spurt that saw the construction of motorways, new residential areas and an upgrading of the sewage and water supply systems. Several bridges connected the two sides of Baghdad along the east and west banks of the Tigris. The main streets are Rashid Street (the financial district, the copper, textile and gold bazaars, cheap hotels and restaurants), Al-Jammouri Street (historical mosques, government offices), Sadoun Street (a commercial area with expensive hotels and cinemas) and Abu Nawas Street (with many outdoor cafés). Al Mansour suburb can be compared to London's Park Lane. The rich live near the race-track in magnificent villas. It was also the venue of the Baghdad Fair and a popular area for foreign embassies.

Baghdad became a city of contrasts, where minarets and skyscrapers competed for attention and traditional craftsmen co-existed with businessmen in Western suits clutching mobile phones. Once the capital of the Muslim world, Baghdad became a modern 20th-century metropolis: a city of the future that would never forget its past.

THE 2003 WAR

Baghdad was the jewel in the crown during the 26-day war in 2003. For the Iraqi regime, defending Baghdad was of utmost importance. 'In the end, the invaders will have to enter the city,' said Defence Minister Sultan Hashim Ahmed. 'We inherited it from our forefathers, and history will see how we defend it.'

Everyone seemed convinced there would be a major battle for Baghdad: Saddam, the Coalition and the media. But there was no 'Stalingrad siege'; the Special Republican Guard melted away. Through secret contacts Iraqi exiles working with the Americans convinced them it was futile to resist (see page 108).

As Al Shabab Television fed the hapless residents a daily diet of patriotic songs, foreign correspondents watched Baathist ministries disappear in cauldrons of fire and ash, debris was hurled 100m into the air and the deafening noise echoed through every narrow alleyway.

The most famous image from the fall of Baghdad was the toppling of Saddam's statue in Fardous Square. *The Financial Times* correspondent, Paul Eedle, noted that it did not fall without a struggle.

> A rope failed to pull him down. But once US soldiers had thrown a steel hawser round his neck and hooked it to their hulking armored vehicle, he toppled and finally crashed to the ground in a cloud of dust. Dozens of cheering Iraqis, delirious with sudden, unaccustomed freedom, surged forward to dance on the wreckage of their former ruler.

An orgy of looting followed and Lieutenant Colonel Michael Belcher of the US Marines admitted his force could not stop it – even though the Americans were able to protect the Ministry of Oil building. Nothing was beyond the pale: foreign embassies, hotels, the Central Bank, the National Museum, and the National Library and Theatre were ransacked. Even hospital equipment was stolen. One Baghdad resident said that the American army seemed happy with the chaos.

The rebuilding of Baghdad and the restoration of the authority of a central government proved a daunting task. The Coalition had no local army or police force to rely on. The army was disbanded and a new army and police force had to be established from scratch. Many Iraqis wanted the Americans as little as they wanted Saddam. The suicide bombings, which started the day the war ended, have continued. Targets included the US headquarters, the UN headquarters (leading to the withdrawal of the organisation), the Red Cross Building, police stations, the Jordanian Embassy, and Nabil's Restaurant, a favourite among foreigners.

Thousands of cars have flooded the Iraqi market, there is scant regard for traffic regulations, and for many democracy means they can drive as they please. The Americans are known for their 'tactical driving' when traffic jams pose a threat. In practice this means driving on footpaths, jumping the medians of divided boulevards, swearing and brandishing their guns. Rory McCarthy, author of *Nobody Told Us We Are Defeated: Stories from the New Iraq*, described how:

> It wasn't all bad at first. Internet cafés, once heavily restricted under Saddam, had sprung up everywhere. Satellite television dishes rose from the rooftops for the first time. As I drove around Baghdad in the mornings I would listen to the BBC World Service broadcasting in English a daily reading from *Animal Farm*, a book banned in the Saddam days. Some shopkeepers and Iraqi businessmen were making quick profits. Parts of the telephone networks destroyed during the war were up and working again and old signposts had been replaced with freshly painted noticeboards. Some people, particularly teachers, were getting paid much more than they ever had under Saddam, and they were spending their new wages. The main high street in outer Karrada, a shopping district round the corner from the hotel, was lined with shops selling fridges, televisions, cookers and washing machines stacked several rows deep across the pavement. More Iraqi policemen appeared to be on the streets, directing traffic or standing at busy junctions, but richer families were already employing squads of heavily armed bodyguards outside their villas. Some neighbours, anticipating the worst, had simply cordoned off their streets with lumps of concrete or fallen tree trunks. Almost every home still had a gun.

Baghdad today is a divided city drenched in blood. Nearly every day there are fatalities from car bombs, clashes between Iraqis and Coalition forces, attacks by Sunnis on Shias and Shias on Sunnis as the sectarian cleansing continues, along with mortar attacks, revenge killings and robberies. 'During Saddam's days killings were silent. Now the killing is done openly and loudly,' said one resident. A city of approximately five million in a country of 25 million, the capital continues to suffer half of all the attacks and deaths (see *Chronology*, pages 185–8).

Iraq Body Count, a voluntary organisation that records civilian deaths attributable to Coalition and insurgent military action, sectarian violence and criminal violence in Iraq, reported that Baghdad, the most populous region of the country, continues to be one of its most pervasively violent, experiencing about five times more deaths per capita than the rest of the country. By the end of year four of the occupation, approximately 1 in 160 of its residents had been violently killed. Up to 592 unidentified bodies were found dumped in different parts of Baghdad between 18 June and 18 July 2007.

The face of Baghdad, once Iraq's magnificent, modern capital, has been scarred by checkpoints, roadblocks, concrete blast walls, burned-out buildings, sandbags and concertina wire.

There are two cities within the city of Baghdad: the Green Zone (now the International Zone) set up to protect first American's Coalition Provisional Authority, then the Iraqi government; and Sadr City, a poverty-stricken Shia suburb, hotbed of Islamic militancy and home to many of the perpetrators of sectarian attacks and murders.

Sectarian cleansing has divided the city into the Sunni west and the Shia east and north (see maps on pages 204–5). The vicious 'Iraqi apartheid' is intensifying. Christians and Palestinians are also targeted, and the surge – America's dispatch of more than 30,000 additional troops to Iraq to seize control of the lawless capital and surrounding areas – is having limited success.

The fragments of yesterday – museums, mosques, historic buildings and palaces – are shadows of their former selves, as if in a deep coma, longing to wake up to a dawn of peace when their glory will be restored.

THE SUNNI WEST, THE SHIA EAST AND NORTH

The sectarian cleansing of Baghdad is creating a city of Sunni and Shia neighbourhoods. Mixed neighbourhoods are rapidly becoming a phenomenon of the past as the Sunnis intensify their hold on the west of the city and Shias dominate the east and north. Ten previously mixed neighbourhoods are now exclusively Shia.

During the 1970s there was no talk of Sunni or Shia. The Iran–Iraq War increased awareness of sects and it became more of an issue during the 1990s. After the 2003 war it became a matter of life and death: Baghdad's residents are being killed at impromptu checkpoints for being 'the wrong type of Muslim' and the city is fragmenting into hostile townships.

When Saddam exercised an iron hold on power, animosities between the two sects were suppressed, as was all dissent. The Sunnis were the mainstay of Saddam's government and the Shias were systematically discriminated against.

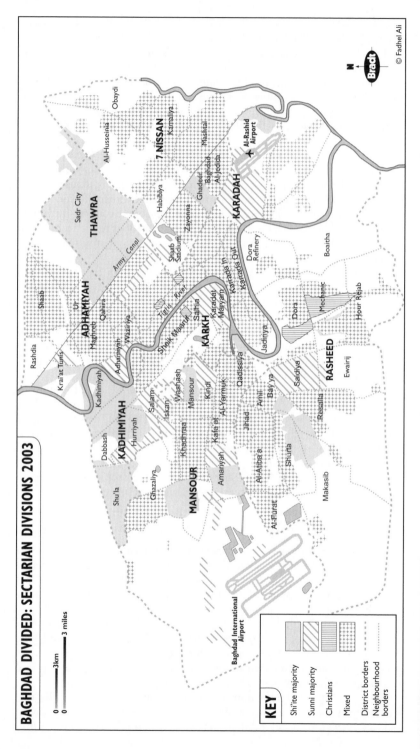

BAGHDAD DIVIDED: SECTARIAN DIVISIONS 2003

© Fadhel Ali

0 3km
0 3 miles

KEY

Shi'ite majority

Sunni majority

Christians

Mixed

District borders

Neighbourhood borders

204

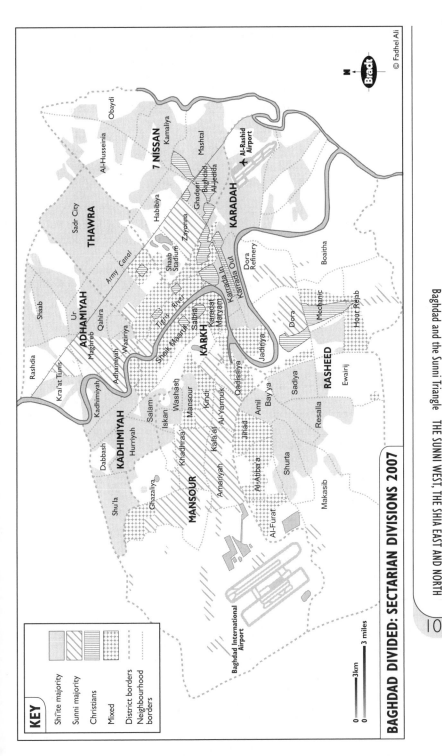

KEY

- Shi'ite majority
- Sunni majority
- Christians
- Mixed
- - - - District borders
- · · · · · Neighbourhood borders

BAGHDAD DIVIDED: SECTARIAN DIVISIONS 2007

0 ——— 3km
0 ——— 3 miles

© Fadhel Ali

Baghdad International Airport

Al-Rashid Airport

7 NISSAN
- Obaydi
- Al-Husseinia
- Kamaliya
- Mashtal
- Baghdad Al-Jedida
- Ghadeer

THAWRA
- Sadr City
- Ur
- Habibiya
- Zayona
- Shaab Stadium
- Shaab

ADHAMIYAH
- Rashdia
- Krai'at Tunis
- Qahira
- Maghreb
- Waziriya
- Adhamiyah
- Sheik Maaruf
- Army Canal
- Tigris River

KARADAH
- Al-Rashid Airport
- Dora Refinery
- Boaitha
- Karrada In
- Karrada Out
- Karradat Maryam
- Salhia
- Jadiriya

KADHIMIYAH
- Dabbash
- Shu'la
- Ghazaliya
- Hurriyah
- Salam
- Iskan
- Kadhimiyah

KARKH

MANSOUR
- Amariyah
- Khadhraa
- Washash
- Mansour
- Kindi
- Kafa'at
- Al-Yarmuk
- Jihad
- Al-Furat
- Al-Atiba'e

RASHEED
- Qadissiya
- Amil
- Bay'ya
- Sadiya
- Resalla
- Shurta
- Makasib
- Ewairij
- Dora
- Mechanic
- Hour Rejab

When the Baathist regime was overthrown in 2003 the Sunnis made up the bulk of the resistance. They also engaged in a sectarian war against the Shias to stop the Shia majority and the Kurds from dominating the government and holding on to power. The Shia were restrained in their retaliation to sectarian attacks until the destruction of one of their holiest shrines on 22 February 2006 (see page 239). They responded firecely with 'The Battle of Baghdad' and ended up controlling 75% of the city.

In October 2005, 22 Sunnis were killed in the predominantly Shia district of Iskan in old Baghdad. All the Sunni victims were married to Shia women.

The government condemns violence against the Sunnis, but the attacks are continuing and neither the Iraqi police, the security forces nor the Americans seem capable of stopping it.

Washash, nicknamed Little Sadr City by the Americans, has been cleansed of its Sunni inhabitants. In a raid in October 2006 a US patrol found a list of 65 houses where Shia families have replaced the former Sunni residents. There was also a roster of 'virtuous families', which were not harassed. Sunni families have received threatening letters with deadlines for leaving and DVD images of houses exploding. A male member of the family may be murdered to ensure the rest of the family leaves.

Baghdad's residents accuse the police and masked members of the Badr Brigade (the armed wing of the Islamic Council of Iraq) of collaborating in the raids, killings and evictions. This has been rejected by Major-General Adnan Thabit, commander of the Interior Ministry's special forces, who says that fighters are dressing in police uniforms to inflame sectarian divisions.

The Shias have been driven out of Amariyah and the outlawed Baath Party is making a comeback with slogans such as 'Saddam Hussein will live for ever, the symbol of the Arab nation'. Shias have also been killed in the Sunni districts of Al Doura, Ghaziliyah and Sadiya. Abandoned houses with smashed windows covered by layers of sand stand among busy, occupied residences.

The mortuary classifies victims by their injuries: beheaded victims are Shias killed by Sunnis, victims killed by a power drill to the head are Sunnis murdered by Shias. Bodies are dumped by the side of the road, many with horrific torture marks.

The Sunni plan seems to be to split Baghdad in half before Iraq itself is divided into three separate regions. The Shias seem to be motivated by revenge.

Writing in *The Times* on 29 October 2006, Marie Colvin reported that the spirit of resistance has not been crushed. At an Eid celebration at the end of Ramadan in the Hunting Club in Mansour, the Mayfair of Baghdad:

> The skirts were low on the girls' hips, there was barely a *hijab* in sight and Abir the DJ spun western and Arabic discs. And then there is the bravest ice cream seller in Baghdad, a Sunni. When Sunni militants demanded he close because there had been no ice cream in the time of the Prophet Mohammed, he told them that he would stop selling ice cream when they rode up on camels to threaten him. There were no BMWs in the time of Prophet Mohammed either.

'BAGHDAD IS A SMASHED CITY'

Abu Talat fled from Baghdad with his family and is now a refugee in Syria. He returned in May 2007 to salvage what is left of his former life.

Habibi (My dear),

Baghdad is a smashed city...no roads to drive on...most of them are closed off by concrete obstacles with concertina wire. In addition the Iraqi military cover their faces with black masks and hold their guns in such a way that when you see them you are definitely afraid that they will shoot you.

When I returned to my neighborhood of al-Adhamiya, I couldn't get in unless the soldiers checked my ID and my car, even though the guards are from the same neighbourhood and they know me personally. But they had to check it to ensure that no car bombs might go off. Nevertheless, daily mortars shell my neighbourhood and those are out of control, despite this concrete wall placed by the Americans which now surrounds our neighbourhood.

Baghdad has been changed into the city of garbage. You can find it everywhere. You can smell the stench of dead bodies wherever you go.

With regard to electricity, there is now only one hour daily. That's it. From where we're staying in the city centre, in Bab al-Muadham, I can see from the balcony that people sleep nearly naked on their rooftops because it is so hot and there is no electricity to run fans or air conditioners. Thank God that there are two large generators that maintain electricity in our building.

I found my car ruined, so I had to repair it. For that I called the mechanic to come to my home and repair it, since I couldn't take the car to him as all the mechanics' shops are closed and there is no place to have a car repaired. All of those shops are totally closed.

When I saw the mechanic he said, 'We cannot live anymore, and there is no job we can find.'

Dahar Jamail's weblog, www.dahrjamailiraq.com

THE GREEN ZONE – A FORTRESS IN THE CENTRE OF BAGHDAD

After the fall of Baghdad, Saddam's 258-room republican palace became the base for the Coalition Provisional Authority, the American administration that ruled Iraq from April 2003 to June 2004. A 1,450ha area around the palace, including the conference centre and Al-Rasheed Hotel, was closed off and became a heavily fortified area known as the Green Zone. The name green was a reference to the supposedly safe area, as opposed to the rest of the country referred to as the Red Zone.

After the hand-over of power to the Iraqi Interim Government, the Green Zone (renamed the International Zone) remained the seat of government and the administrative centre of Baghdad.

The first significant attack on the zone was launched on 26 October 2003 when rockets were fired at the Al Rasheed Hotel during the visit of the US Deputy Defence Secretary, Paul Wolfowitz. Since then the zone has been attacked regularly. In October 2004 the bazaar and café were destroyed. On 12 April 2007 a bomb in the parliament cafeteria killed one person and injured 22 others, including the vice-president.

Baghdad and the Sunni Triangle   THE GREEN ZONE – A FORTRESS IN THE CENTRE OF BAGHDAD

10

207

Few changes have been made to the over-the-top architecture. Only the busts of Saddam have been removed from the palace building. The Tomb of the Unknown Soldier, the Victory Arch modelled on Saddam's hands, and the Military History Museum are now in the Green Zone. Saddam's man-eating lions have been moved to the national zoo.

The zone is home to some 3,000 Iraqis who help keep the wheels of the administration turning, and 7,000 others living in flats or large houses. Rents paid by foreigners rival those of Mayfair or Manhattan. Edinburgh Risk and Security Management, which facilitates business operations in high-risk environments, has rented a whole street from Iraqis, many of whom have moved abroad.

Around 5,000 squatters took up residence in properties abandoned by the Baath Party elite. Some do manual work while others sell trinkets and soft drinks from roadside stalls. Their district is the Green Zone's slum, referred to as '215 apartments'.

In his book *Imperial Life in the Emerald City: Inside Baghdad's Green Zone*, Rajiv Chandrasekaran observed that:

> It was Saddam who first decided to turn Baghdad's prime riverfront real estate into a gated city, with posh villas, bungalows, government buildings, shops and even a hospital. He didn't want his aides and bodyguards to mingle with the masses. The homes were bigger, the trees greener, the streets wider than in the rest of Baghdad. There were more palms and fewer people.
>
> It was the ideal place for the Americans to pitch their tents. Saddam surrounded the area with a tall brick wall. There were only three points of entry. All the military had to do was park tanks at the gates. One of the gates was named Assassins Gate in reference to an American tank company which won a battle near the gate in April 2003.
>
> The Americans expanded Saddam's neighbourhood by a few blocks to encompass the gargantuan Convention Centre and the al-Rasheed, a once-luxurious establishment made famous by CNN's live broadcasts during the 1991 Persian Gulf War. They fortified the perimeter with seventeen-foot-high blast barriers made of foot-thick concrete topped with coils of razor wire.

The Green Zone became little America in the heart of Baghdad. The Americans lived in prefabricated housing, ate imported American food, watched satellite TV and made frequent calls home on telephones with US area codes. The Ibn Sina hospital was taken over to treat wounded soldiers and civilians. One of the palaces of Saddam's notorious son Uday was transformed into a dry-cleaners. The zone had its own taxi service, local shops and an Iraqi flea market. In its heyday in 2003, the Green Zone had six bars, a disco, a café, two Chinese restaurants and an outdoor shopping arcade. The foreign residents went jogging and chilled out in the garden behind the Republican Palace.

The 18-storey Al-Rasheed Hotel was the place for parties. Halliburton re-opened the disco, and a sports bar was opened in the basement bunker.

The protective walls of the Green Zone hemmed in its inhabitants and isolated them from the Iraqi people. Few made the effort to communicate with the locals. Chandrasekaran pointed out that a few thousand Iraqis lived inside the Green Zone. They travelled outside the walls all the time to work and to see relatives. Many of them spoke English and had Americans in the palace offered to listen to them, they would have heard an unvarnished description of life in the real Baghdad. But except for the odd, adventurous CPA staffer, most Americans didn't seek out their Iraqi neighbours.

Iraqi politicians, cut off from the reality of everyday life, bickered as they tried to grab power and re-arrange the deck chairs on a sinking ship.

Since the handover to the Iraqis, the Green Zone is still the base of Western private military contractors and home to the British and American embassies. The largest and most expensive (US$592 million) US embassy in the world, with 21 buildings spread across 42ha, is being built here. It will have its own power station and probably the largest swimming pool in Iraq, plus a surface-to-air missile station.

Richard Houghton, a former Capitol Hill staffer who worked in the Green Zone for 19 months, felt it even deserved its own guidebook and produced a 41-page work: *A Visitor's Guide To Baghdad's International Zone*.

For the Iraqis the zone is a forbidden city inside a city, viewed with suspicion and hatred. Signs in English and Arabic at the entrances warn 'Do Not Enter or You Will Be Shot'. In the words of Iraqi artist Rashad Salim:

> Every person and grain of Iraq is touched by the trauma of war, sanctions, more war, occupation and sectarian strife. Concrete barriers are sown in the middle of the streets separating the palaces of the new them from the same old us.

Describing the Green Zone in a *Washington Post* article on 7 January 2008, Karen DeYoung said:

> The zone feels more gray than green. At the end of Iraq's long dry season, scattered palm trees limp under the dust that covers every surface. Head-high walls of sandbags wrapped in a gray canvas line the walls and pathways: they are used as protection against mortar attacks. The clusters of metal boxes that provide embassy housing, whimsically signposted with such names as 'The Oasis' and 'The Palms' are surrounded with stacks of the fat, gray bags, worn with age and dripping sand.

SADR CITY – A SHIA WORLD IN THE HEART OF BAGHDAD

Life is hard in Sadr City (Saddam City before the 2003 war), home to more than two million Shias. It is a place of urchins, pickpockets, dirt, rubble, crushing unemployment and 20-to-a house poverty. The houses are so close together that the Mehdi Army (the militia under the control of firebrand cleric Moqtada Al-Sadr (see pages 254–5), who treats the city like his personal fiefdom) can jump from one roof to another for kilometres. The city has retained a degree of autonomy: the Mehdi Army acts as the unofficial police force and the Sadr movement has provided social services and assisted in food distribution. People queue for hours outside Sadr's office to ask for help with employment, education and medical bills. Typhoid and other waterborne diseases are endemic.

'We're fighting a war to cleanse the world of evil. It starts here but will spread everywhere,' said Sheikh Saadi, one of the commanders in the authoritarian Mehdi Army. He believes that Mohammed Al-Mehdi, who disappeared in AD874 (see page 234) will return to herald a just world, and that his time is near:

Saddam's fall was a sign, the US occupation was a sign, our job is to prepare the way for the Mehdi's return. One way to think of the Mehdi Army is as a *mukhabarat* (intelligence service) for souls.

The Mehdi Army patrols the warren of side streets. It has killed drug dealers and kidnappers, and it co-operates with the local police. Liquor stores and video stores accused of selling pornography have been firebombed.

The city is 50 years old. Its perfect street grid system put in place in 1959 was the brainchild of the then Iraqi Prime Minister, Abdul Karim Qasim, who constructed the square city to provide housing for the urban poor who had migrated from the countryside. The area is separated from the rest of Baghdad by the wide Army Canal and highway that run alongside it. The Communist Party exerted its influence and the residents resisted the Baathist-led coup of 1963. In 1999 there were riots bordering on a public uprising when Saddam's regime assassinated Ayatollah Mohammad Mohammad Sadiqu Alsadr, Moqtada's father. The police put them down brutally. It was a perfect place for a revolution.

Saddam Hussein ordered the construction of a municipal building, gave a single speech from the balcony and never returned. The building was looted down to the wiring, plumbing and marble stairs, and torched in the mayhem after the fall of Baghdad in 2003. It was repaired at a cost of US$30,000 by US soldiers and is now used by Sadr City's 30-member advisory council.

There have been frequent clashes in the city between American forces and the Mehdi Army. In 2003 a temporary US base Camp Marlboro was set up in a cigarette factory to try and quell the violence. On 4 April 2004 the Mehdi Army ambushed a US Army Patrol and killed eight American soldiers. As a result, fighting between the army and units of the 1st Brigade Combat team 1st Cavalry Division lasted until June. The son of the anti-war activist Cindy Sheehan was killed in the fighting on 4 April.

In August 2005, the city was locked down for three days, death squad leaders were arrested and hostages were freed. In October 2006, US forces put a security cordon around the city as they searched for an abducted American soldier. The measures angered the Iraqi prime minister, who ordered the lifting of all checkpoints. But when the cordon was in place the daily murder rate in Baghdad fell by around 50%. According to some estimates half of the daily sectarian attacks in the capital come out of Sadr City.

The city itself has suffered from car-bomb attacks. The most deadly occurred on 23 November 2006, when six car bombs and two mortar rounds killed 215 people and injured 257 in the single deadliest sectarian attack of the war.

The Americans have set aside US$350m for infrastructure improvements. Much of the money has been spent on sewage and water systems, which have been upgraded, transforming some of the squalid neighborhoods. The US Army Corps of Engineers has played an important role in the reconstruction efforts in Sadr City, covering all sectors, electricity, water, sewage, schools,

IS THE MEHDI ARMY THE ONLY INSTITUTION TO SERVE THE PEOPLE?

Abbas, a driver who lives in the Sadr City district of Baghdad, describes his daily battle against rubbish, rats and the fear of explosions and gunfire.

'I live in a house in Sadr City, in the east of Baghdad. I work as a driver. The entire house has three rooms, in which myself, my wife, 11 children, and my son's wife and children live.

Most of us in Sadr City feel that the only institution which has ever really served the people here is the Mehdi Army. In the first month of chaos after the war they brought people food and drinking water and protected hospitals from looters.

More recently they drove away criminal street gangs, kidnappers and drug dealers, and kept watch against terrorists.

In Sadr City, rubbish is piled high in the gutters and in the central reservations between streets. Rats live in it. Many are the size of small cats.

One of the biggest decisions that every family in Sadr City needs to make is whether to sleep outside on the roof [to avoid the oppressive summer heat] or inside in the house. Sleeping outside can get you killed. At around midnight, every night, we hear the sound of explosions and gunfire as the Americans hunt for the Mehdi Army.

The Mehdi Army sometimes fights from the roofs against US vehicles in the streets, and this means that American soldiers and helicopters will fire at anything they see moving on the roof.

About a week ago three women in my district were killed this way. At another house, less than a kilometre away, another five roof-sleepers died when aircraft fired rockets at them.

Every morning on my way to work, I stop by the nearby hospital which is right outside my home. When I see a number of people waiting by the door of the morgue, I know it was a particularly bad night.'

The Financial Times, *19 June 2007*

clinics and surfacing roads with asphalt. The corps' website echoes the views of satisfied Iraqis, 'Al hamdu liAllah (Thank God),' said Yass:

> After a period of time we started to see our hopes getting closer and closer to reality, such as drinking water, cleaner streets and better sewage thanks to those who participated in the reconstruction process; including the government and the multi-national forces.

In June 2007 the Sadr City Municipal Council rejected a proposal to open a joint security centre with US troops. Council chairman Abdul Hussein Al-Ka'abi said the residents demanded the withdrawal of US troops. 'The citizens of the city reject American participation in security because they feel the city is stable and is one of the safest areas in Baghdad,' he said under the watchful eye of turbaned clerics who look down from hundreds of posters. Back to the future seems to be the motto in this Shia stronghold.

10

The Baghdad Security Plan, commonly known as 'the troop surge', refers to reinforcements of more than 30,000 additional soldiers and marines (five brigades) to Iraq, deployed mostly in Baghdad to bring sectarian violence to an end. It was announced in a live broadcast given by President Bush on 10 January 2007.

The new initiative began in February 2007. Troop levels reached their peak in June, with the number of American troops reaching 160,000.

The plan had two phases. Phase one from February to June was based on securing central Baghdad and stopping the sectarian cleansing of Sunnis (see pages 203–6), which intensified following the attack on the Al-Askari Mosque (see page 239).

The number of detainees held by the USA in August 2007 had increased by 50% since the US administration announced the surge, bringing the detainee population to at least 24,500. Many claim they were arbitrarily arrested and have nothing to do with terrorism.

To the dismay of many local residents, the Americans replaced makeshift blockades built by the people with concrete barriers to stop the movement of death squads and suicide bombers.

In *Ending the War in Iraq*, Tom Hayden referred to the new model proposed by Bush, which involved subdividing Baghdad into what was promoted as 'gated communities':

> After sweeping all suspected insurgents out of the areas, the military would create controlled neighbourhoods with mini bases, barriers, checkpoints, and identity cards. Having failed to crush the resistance from the top down, the US strategy was now to cut the people off from the insurgents. The model was based on the 'new villages' built in Malaysia by the British and the 'strategic hamlets' tried by the Americans in Vietnam.

'Don't say the Americans have not built anything in Baghdad,' quipped Iraqi bloggers. These measures temporarily reduced sectarian killings and some displaced Sunnis began returning to their abandoned homes. After securing an area the Americans focused on the restoration of local councils and funds for street cleaning, the refurbishment of schools, etc. The Iraqi government will have to overcome its institutional and political incapacity and follow up these measures with long-term development.

In April, the third month of the surge, Al-Qaeda in Iraq (AQI), which had been driven out of its stronghold in Haifa Street and the Al-Karkh area, began launching car-bomb attacks in mainly Shia areas.

The second phase of the surge, from June 2007 until its end, probably in April 2008, aims to send the final wave of US troops to Baghdad's outer suburbs from where much of the violence originates. It will mean confronting the Shia Mehdi Army. On 21 October 2007 the Americans claimed they killed 49 criminals in three separate raids on Sadr City, but Sadr's representatives said that most of those killed were women, children and elderly men.

The Americans will also have to control the turbulent areas surrounding Baghdad, known as the triangle of death, to prevent Al-Qaeda using them as a

I increased the number of patrols in [Amariyah], gained the confidence of the local sheiks and imams, picked garbage off of the streets, and conducted more raids to capture insurgents. Early perceived results appeared encouraging: the number of dead bodies on the streets declined significantly.

I came to realise [however] that the reduction of bodies was due not so much to my unit's military actions but to the simple fact that most of the minority Shias who had lived in Amariyah had either been killed or had fled. Fewer Shia bodies were showing up on the streets because there were fewer Shia for the local Sunnis to kill.

There were thousands of unemployed young men in Amariyah. I had commander's emergency reconstruction money to spend on endeavors like trash [rubbish collection]. But the young men [who lived in Amariyah] were the Sunni children of the former Baathist elite. They wanted to go to college and become computer engineers, college teachers, doctors or lawyers.

They could not do this, however, out of fear of leaving Amariyah and being kidnapped or killed at the checkpoints run by the Shiite militia and Iraqi security forces that surrounded their district. I would have needed the wisdom of Solomon and the power of Franklin D. Roosevelt to solve the economic and employment problems of Amariyah.

I learned that there was only so much that I could do in the middle of a civil war.

Abridged from an article by Gian P Gentile, a lieutenant colonel in the US Army and professor of history at the US Military Academy at West Point, International Herald Tribune, *27 September 2007*

base from which to launch attacks on the capital (see pages 217–26). The experience of Baquba suggests that American tactics leave a lot to be desired. They complain that the insurgents leave the area and the civilian population suffers from American military action. When the Americans leave, the insurgents return.

The surge has brought a lull in the violence: in October and November 2007, Coalition forces suffered 40 fatalities, and in December only 23, compared to well over 100 a month in April, May and June. Civilian deaths have also dropped by more than 50% since the summer of 2007.

The declining death rate from sectarian violence is also due to the standing down of the Mehdi Army and the activities of neighbourhood security groups, which have been growing during 2007. Three hundred groups funded by the Americans in 12 of Iraq's 18 provinces have around 72,000 members who are focusing on eliminating Al-Qaeda. Shia neighbourhood security groups are trying to counter the influence of the Mehdi Army. The fact that alcohol is being sold openly once again on the streets of Baghdad illustrates their success. The legal trade, driven underground by illegal militias, has resumed.

The surge can limit the activities of death squads and militias in the short term, but it cannot provide a lasting solution: only a political reconciliation between the Shias, Sunnis and their warring militias can bring the elusive peace

Baghdad and the Sunni Triangle THE SURGE – A FORMULA FOR CURBING VIOLENCE

10

Iraqis have been longing for since the American invasion. Reform of the government and sustained Sunni participation in the political process is vital. Thomas Pickering, a veteran of US foreign policy, pointed out that there is a civil war in Iraq and the Americans are 'partners, players and victims'. He has criticised both the Demorats and the Republicans for focusing on troop numbers rather than the real issue: Iraqi governance.

LIFE GOES ON

Writing in the *Washington Post* on 24 June 2007, John Ward Anderson concluded that:

> the military might focus on a new security plan, but in the streets and homes of Baghdad, the demands are more elemental – to flick a switch and get some light on, to turn a faucet and get some water. The lack of such necessities breeds discontent, and lofty talk of more elections and constitutional reforms seems like a twisted joke from a government that cannot walk, yet alone run.

The Iraqi capital is a shadow of its former self. In Al Mansour, Baghdad's Mayfair, the shopkeepers close their shops in the afternoon. Al-Karrada is now the place for shopping, but throughout the city local merchants complain that the new security measures are driving away customers. 'These concrete barriers hurt our businesses as much as they help us,' Ahmed Yas, a shopkeeper on Palestine Street in eastern Baghdad told AFP:

> They prevent customers from approaching our shops because they completely cover the shopfronts, and customers cannot park their cars anywhere close because there is no parking.

Among the most recent reconstruction is the market in Abu Nuwas Street, famous for its *mazgouf* fish restaurants. *Mazgouf* is a flatfish native to the Tigris. It is split open and roasted on stakes around a fire. Many of the restaurants have been completely rebuilt with the assistance of the 2nd Infantry Brigade Combat Team based out of Fort Carson, Colorado, and the 1st Battallion, 504th Parachute Infantry Regiment from Fort Bragg, North Carolina. A three-story art gallery may also re-open shortly.

Ice cream shops have become the place for meeting and socialising and there are long queues as children and adults wait for their favourite cones.

Baghdad's museums stand closed. The entrance to the famous Iraq Museum has been sealed (see page 297). The Natural History Museum, part of Baghdad University, was reconstructed from May 2005 until January 2006. It has not opened to visitors because it is in a dangerous area. Only 10% of the 260,000 volumes in the magnificent library were destroyed. The exhibition hall was not so lucky. During the looting rare fish fossils and insect, mammal, reptile and amphibian collections were destroyed, and now there is no exhibition hall.

The Ministry of State Tourism and the Baghdad Municipality is co-operating in the restoration of the Khan Marjan, a unique historical museum built in AD738.

The Marjan Mosque next to the museum, dating back to 1356, is famous for its ornamental brickwork and reference library. Its location in the centre of the city on Rashed Street makes it a target for attacks, but to date it has only suffered from minor damage, which has been repaired.

Many of the capital's mosques have been damaged. The famous Sheikh Abdul Kader Al-Gailiani Mosque, burial place of a 10th-century Muslim saint, was hit by a car bomb, as was the new minaret that was under construction. Development of the shrine, with four inner mosques, has stopped, and will not resume unless the complex is surrounded by high concrete blocks.

In August 2007, arms and ammunition were discovered at the Al-Imam Al-Adham Mosque in Adhamiya, a strong-hold of Sunni extremists and the scene of frequent armed clashes.

The security situation is preventing visits to the magnificent Sitt Zumurrud Khatun's Tomb, with a dome that transforms itself from an octagon into a 16-sided figure and back again.

Mustansiriyah University, one of the most impressive reminders of the Abbasid Age, with its stunning Islamic architecture, closes from time to time because of the security situaiton.

In a city where areas of regeneration and new developments are few and far between, the new garden around the most famous monument, Jawad Salim's Nasb Al-Hurriyah (Freedom Monument) makes a refreshing change. The monument consists of 14 separate bronze castings averaging 8m in height providing a visual narrative of the 1958 revolution, and reflecting on Iraqi history through Assyrian and Babylonian wall-reliefs. Baghdad municipality is constructing a resthouse, internet café and other accommodation behind the monument.

Vendors are returning to Mutanabi Street, home of the famous book market, which was ripped apart by a car bomb on 5 March 2007. A plan to restore the street's historic buildings has been launched and the Shahbandar coffee house is being completely rebuilt. Despite death threats and the murder of some of its staff, librarians at Iraq's National Library and Archive (Inia) are doing their best to rebuild it: 60% of the archive materials and 95% of the rare book collection were either destroyed or went missing during the looting that followed the capture of Baghdad in 2003.

The biggest green expanse in the city, Al-Zawra Park and its zoo, is one of the safe public places in Baghdad. During the 2003 war, 650 of the zoo's animals escaped, while others were looted or eaten by hungry civilians. The zoo was rescued by two South Africans: zoologist Brendan Whittington-Jones and conservationist Lawrence Anthony. It re-opened in July 2003.

A group of lions reared by Saddam's son Uday were transferred from a Baghdad palace and 17 of Saddam's prized Arabian horses were brought back from secret stables in Abu Ghraib.

During the rescue of the animals former Republican Guards worked with American soldiers. Not a single animal died.

The story of the rescue of the zoo has been told in *Babylon's Ark: The Incredible Wartime Rescue of the Baghdad Zoo* by Lawrence Anthony. It is also the subject of a Disney film, *Good Luck Mr Anthony*.

Today there are around 100 animals in the zoo, including ostriches, camels, wolves, lions, a cheetah, brown bears, antelopes and giraffes. When the

Americans killed a tiger that attacked a soldier, it was not possible for them to replace the animal so they made a large donation to the zoo.

An Iraqi heritage garden is being constructed in Zawra Park. There is a waterfall characteristic of the Kurdish north, a reed guesthouse from the south, and a tent from central and western Iraq. Date-producing palms have been planted in the palm garden and a resthouse is planned.

Baghdad is a city of monuments and statues, some commemorating events in Mesopotamian times, others recalling more recent historical developments – quite an extraordinary achievement for a city where in 1958 there were only three public sculptures: General Maude, the British officer; King Faisal, Iraq's first king, installed by the British; and Muhsin Sadoun, a former prime minister.

On 30 May 2003 a 7m sculpture by Basim Hamad replaced the statue of Saddam demolished when American troops entered Baghdad. Hamad is part of an artistic group called Najin – the survivors – who prided themselves on their ability to evade Saddam's authorities. The new sculpture reflects optimism about the future of the country. It is a symbolic representation of an Iraqi family holding a crescent moon and a sun.

Once again the names of the streets are changing as they changed when the monarchy was overthrown and the Baathists seized power. Anything and everything named after Saddam has a new name and the Americans are making up their own street names: Canal Road, Virginia Avenue, etc. Saddam's 'Big Bridge' has been renamed Mohammed Baqir Al-Hakim Bridge, after one of the foremost Shia Muslim leaders in Iraq, until his assassination in a bombing in Najaf on 29 August 2003.

Catherine Arnold, author of Bradt's Baghdad city guide, observed an overwhelming desire to consign the past and the degeneracy of Saddam's regime to history and to focus on an international future – as soon as there is money and stability to do so. But no-one knows when that will be. The people of Baghdad have many plans but they do not have a timetable. In Baghdad, as throughout the country, the magnificence of historical, old Iraq is only a step away from the present-day chaos. 'We all have guns but we don't want them,' said one Baghdad resident. 'All we want is peace and stability.'

Iraqi artist Rashad Selim proposes a memorial to the war on Iraq:

To do justice to the devastation of the ongoing war I suggest that every concrete slab, sand bag and stretch of barbed wire used to segregate,

My father used to walk all around Baghdad with my brother and me. He introduced us to the great history of our country. I wish that I could bequeath to my son what we inherited, but they have killed this dream. We stand here in silence, remembering the people we loved now buried in the ashes of the books and manuscripts. Here we stand where they left us – Adnan, Ghanim, Kutaiba, Bilal, Bariq and many others whose names we don't know.

RAYA, www.openshutters.org

imprison, create blast walls and wreak havoc on civil society be gathered together to construct a ziggurat, using the heavy military equipment that supported the destruction. A hanging garden should then be created by the five million orphans of Iraq, all of which will be paid for by the coalition of the willing.

BEYOND BAGHDAD – THE SUNNI TRIANGLE

The Sunni Triangle, the most dangerous area for American soldiers, is an inhospitable place, with hundreds of small no-name, one-camel towns. Most of the inhabitants are Sunni Muslims, strong supporters of Saddam Hussein, who drew many government workers, politicians and military leaders from the area. Saddam was captured in the triangle in the village of ad-Dawr, 15km south of Tikrit on 13 December 2003 (see page 202).

The triangle's corners (see map) consist of Baghdad on the eastern side, Ramadi on the west, and Tikrit on the north. Each side is 200km long. The main cities are Tikrit (Saddam's hometown), Samarra, Baqubah, Habbaniyah, Fallujah and Ramadi.

The area has been a hotbed of resistance to the occupation forces. It is home to just 2% of Iraq's population, but roughly two-thirds of all attacks on US troops occur there. Towns like Fallujah became 'independent Islamic city states' under the control of the insurgents. American soldiers have tried to pacify the area and bring it under the control of the Iraqi army and security forces, but attacks on Coalition forces continue.

There are plenty of horror stories coming out of the Sunni Triangle, but it is also a place of success in the face of formidable challenges. Vincent Foulk, author of *The Battle for Fallujah: Occupation, Resistance and Stalemate in the War in Iraq*, described the work of the 1st Infantry's 3rd BCT commander, Colonel Dana Petard, in Baqubah:

He developed a reputation for reaching out to the community. He established a neighbourhood watch. He met regularly with three groups of local leaders, the government officials, the Sheikh's Council and an advisory council made up of local community leaders. He also turned to his civil affairs team and told them to get out there and find out what was going on. The insurgents became so alarmed at his success that they placed a US$60,000 bounty on his head.

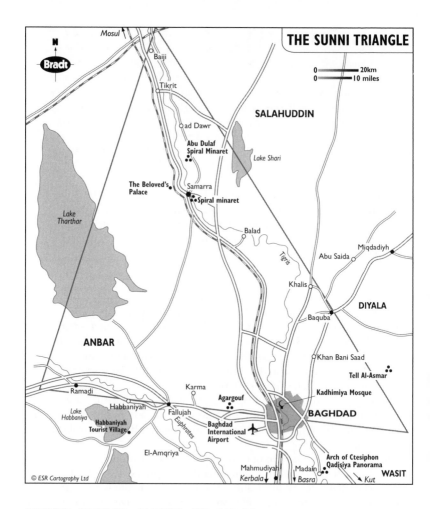

FALLUJAH: BATTERED, BLOODIED AND BRUISED Fallujah, once a city of 200 mosques, was the scene of one of the bloodiest battles in the continuing hostilities between American forces and the insurgents.

The city, with a population of 350,000, is on the Euphrates, 70km west of Baghdad. It dates back to Babylonian times and was home to an important Jewish academy, the Pumbedita Academy, from AD258–1038. During the Sassanid era (AD227–636) the region served as a warehouse for Persian troops. In Ottoman times it was a resting place on one of the main roads across the desert. The discovery of oil changed the fortunes of the city. It increased in importance due to its location on one of the main roads out of Baghdad.

Saddam's era was a time of heavy industrialisation for the city, which saw the construction of several large factories, including one closed down by the weapons inspectors, as it was suspected of manufacturing chemical weapons. More than 3,000 Fallujah residents were Saddam's intelligence officers, while others held high ranks in the army.

He is, even by Iraqi standards, an unlikely leader – a dentist from Manchester whose only previous cause was supporting Liverpool FC.

Yet Abdallah Al Jibouri, 45, an exiled Iraqi who spent more than 20 years in Stockport, has turned his back on drilling and filling to become the reluctant saviour of one of the Sunni Triangle's most violence-prone trouble spots. (Jibouri is from one of Iraq's largest, mostly Sunni tribes, the Al Jibour, with members throughout Iraq. Many leaders of the extremists come from this tribe and some of the influential clerics have links to Saddam's former intelligence agents. Some of the clerics urged the people to resist the new Shia-dominated government, which they claimed would crush the Sunnis.)

He had originally planned merely to check up on his elderly mother when he visited his home town of Al-Miqdadia, 60 miles north of Baghdad, shortly after Saddam Hussein's fall.

His Mancunian-accented English, however, ensured that he was pressed into service as an unofficial negotiator between American troops and Iraqis, who elected him mayor.

Much to his astonishment – and, he says, to the dismay of his British wife, Sharon – he also became governor of the province of Diyala, whose population is 1.8 million.

Local insurgents have paid his leadership the ultimate backhanded compliment: they have tried to kill him 14 times, and have put a US$10,000 bounty on his head.

'I came for a visit two weeks after the liberation because I have got my mum and other family here,' said Mr Al Jibouri:

I just wanted to make sure that they were all right. But I found the whole place was really a mess, with weapons everywhere, even little kids with machine guns.

I began talking to the local sheiks and the US army and we hired some police. I thought I'd go home then but they said, 'No, you've got to stay and help us.' Of course it's dangerous, and the wife back in Manchester worries, but there are a lot of good people out here and they are worth it.

By agreeing to become governor of Diyala in August 2003, Mr Al Jibouri unwittingly walked into one of the toughest jobs in post-war Iraq. Sunni-led uprisings culminated in pitched battles outside his offices in the provincial capital, Baquba.

Mr Al Jibouri has helped recruit a 5,000-strong police force and new Iraqi army units, and organised the construction of schools, houses, roads, courts and jails.

Locals, including those who initially dubbed him a 'traitor who rode in on a British tank', now visit his house to seek help and favours.

'He opens his house to all – common people, farmers, taxi drivers,' said Sheikh Ibrahim al Jibouri, a neighbour:

He did not need to stay, he has a home in England and is well off. But hard circumstances improve people: when you melt the gold, you get rid of all the blemishes.

Colin Freeman, www.telegraph.co.uk

During the 1991 Gulf War the city suffered one of the highest numbers of civilian casualties: two attempts to bomb its bridges hit crowded markets and killed 200 people.

At the beginning of the 2003 war the city was not damaged. The Iraqi army stationed in the area abandoned its positions and looters quickly targeted government sites, including the Dreamland compound, a Baathist resort. The city was not always hostile to Coalition forces. In 2003 the new mayor, Taha Bidaywi Hamed, was strongly pro-American.

Vincent Foulk, author of *The Battle for Fallujah: Occupation, Resistance and Stalemate in the War in Iraq*, described Fallujah as:

> a dingy city sprawling across the desert to the Euphrates River. Mostly of cinder block buildings, it was a colourless sea of gray stretching from Highway 10, the road coming up past Baghdad some 45 minutes away. From the houses, low-hanging power lines bowed haphazardly across the streets in an amateurish tap for electricity. On a good day they gave power for only twelve hours. In the heat, along roadsides, vendors set up stands made of woven reeds and scrap wood. Upon them a carcass of sheep dangled, butchered and dressed, ready to have a piece cut off for a buyer. Around each stand grazed several other live candidates should sales be good that day. This was a common person's town, not easily taken to new ideas.

Especially galling to the Iraqis were the humiliating house searches, during which furniture was broken, men and women frisked and cash and jewellery stolen. They told the soldiers that they were never humiliated like this during Saddam's time.

The real problems started on 28 April 2003, when a crowd gathered outside a local school to protest against the presence of foreign forces. US troops were fired on from the crowd and their return fire killed 17 Iraqis. In March 2004 the killing of four US contractors, whose bodies were mutilated, resulted in a three-week siege by the marines. The operation was named 'Vigilant Resolve'. After five days of intense fighting a truce was declared to allow two hospitals to re-open, after they were shut down when the marines took up positions on the roads leading to them. According to hospital officials 600 Iraqis were killed and 1,250 were injured. More than half of the dead were reportedly women and children. US military spokesman Brigadier General Mark Kimmitt claimed the insurgents were using the civilians as human shields and fired on the troops from schools, mosques and hospitals.

Foulk described some of the scenes of horror during the first battle of Fallujah:

> Upon returning to his house, one resident spoke to the press of finding by the front gate of his home the body of his sixteen-year-old son. The boy had the back of his skull torn away. It was said that he was standing by the gate when a bomb landed nearby. At the house was the owner's missing and now confirmed-dead nephew. He had left his own home to check on his fiancée's family. The family retrieved the young man's body from where it lay in the street. He had been hit once by a bullet

These are the stories that will continue to emerge from the rubble of Fallujah for years. No, for generations…

Speaking on condition of anonymity, the doctor sits with me in a hotel room in Amman, where he is now a refugee. He'd spoken about what he saw in Fallujah in the UK, and now is under threat from the US military if he returns to Iraq.

'I started speaking about what happened in Fallujah during both sieges in order to raise awareness, and the Americans raided my house three times,' he says, talking so fast I can barely keep up. He is driven to tell what he's witnessed, and as a doctor working inside Fallujah, he has video and photographic proof of all that he tells me.

'I entered Fallujah with a British medical and humanitarian convoy at the end of December, and stayed until the end of January,' he explains, 'but I was in Fallujah before that to work with people and see what their needs were, so I was in there since the beginning of December.'

When I ask him to explain what he saw when he first entered Fallujah in December he says it was like a tsunami had struck the city.

'Fallujah is surrounded by refugee camps where people are living in tents and old cars,' he explains. 'It reminded me of Palestinian refugees. I saw children coughing because of the cold, and there are no medicines. Almost everyone left their houses with nothing, and no money, so how can they live depending only on humanitarian aid?'

The doctor says that in one refugee camp in the northern area of Fallujah there were 1,200 students living in seven tents.

'The disaster caused by this siege is so much worse than the first one, which I witnessed first hand,' he says, and then tells me he'll use one story as an example.

'One story is of a young girl who is 16 years old,' he says of one of the testimonies he video-taped recently. 'She stayed for three days with the bodies of her family who were killed in their home. When the American soldiers entered she was in her home with her father, mother, 12-year-old brother and two sisters. She watched the soldiers enter and shoot her mother and father directly, without saying anything.'

The girl managed to hide behind the refrigerator with her brother and witnessed the war crimes first-hand.

'They beat her two sisters, then shot them in the head,' he said. After this her brother was enraged and ran at the soldiers while shouting at them, so they shot him dead.

'She continued hiding after the soldiers left and stayed with her sisters because they were bleeding, but still alive. She was too afraid to call for help because she feared the soldiers would come back and kill her as well. She stayed for three days, with no water and no food. Eventually one of the American snipers saw her and took her to the hospital,' he added before reminding me again that he had all of her testimony documented on film.

Dahar Jamail's weblog, 8 February 2005

Baghdad and the Sunni Triangle **BEYOND BAGHDAD – THE SUNNI TRIANGLE** 10

through the heart. Since it was too dangerous to go to the cemetery, they buried him in a patch of ground. Later they would take out his body and bury it properly.

The US Navy is investigating 'credible allegations' of wrongdoing by US marines in the city of Fallujah in 2004. The inquiry centres on claims that members of a marine unit killed several unarmed Iraqi captives.

The first battle ended with an agreement that the locals would not allow resistance-fighters into the city. Security was handed over to the Fallujah Protection Force. In September 2004 the UK-based charity Islamic Relief began a tree-planting project and local labourers created a small park.

The protection force was ineffective and the city soon fell under total insurgent control. It was fortified, defensive positions were built and preparations were made for a major offensive.

The Americans launched Operation Phantom Fury on 8 November 2004, after the interim government's efforts to reach a negotiated settlement with the insurgents failed. There were enough arms in the city to launch a nationwide rebellion. According to the American military 1,200 insurgents were killed in 11 days of fighting. International public opinion reacted strongly to the fatal shooting of a wounded, apparently unarmed, man in a mosque by a marine, and the International Red Cross expressed concern at the apparent failures by all sides to respect humanitarian laws. The American government denied that it used white phosphorus against civilians but admitted its use against 'enemy combatants'. The Italian state broadcaster RAI made a documentary *Fallujah: the Hidden Massacre*, alleging that both insurgents and civilians were killed or injured by chemical burns due to the use of white phosphorus.

Much of Fallujah was reduced to rubble. Some 60% of the buildings were damaged and 20%, including 60 mosques, were completely destroyed.

Not all the residents of Fallujah were unhappy about the military action. Foulk described the experiences of an elderly man who was detained by militants and held for four days before being freed:

We suffered from the bombings. Innocent people died or were wounded by the bombings, but we were happy you did what you did because the Mujahadeen had suffocated Fallujah. Anyone considered suspicious would be slaughtered. We would see unknown corpses around the city all the time.

A serious blow had been dealt to a stronghold of the local insurgents, but foreign fighters fled from the city before Operation Phantom Fury.

Reconstruction progressed slowly and focused on clearing rubble and restoring basic services. NBC reported that 9,000 homes were destroyed. Fallujah's compensation commissioner reported that 36,000 of the city's 50,000 homes were destroyed, along with 60 schools and 65 mosques and shrines. Of the 32,000 compensation claims, only 2,500 had been paid by April 2005. It is difficult to rebuild as it is too dangerous for American contractors to leave their compound. They sub-contract to Iraqis who are faced with demands for some of the money, or kidnapped or killed for working with the Americans. The British hostage, Kenneth Bigley, was held and beheaded in Fallujah. Sub-contractors working at American bases would pass on information about the facilities to the insurgents and their teams of mortar men.

Residents who fled from the fighting were allowed to return in mid-December 2004. They had to agree to biometric identification and wear their ID cards all the time. On 6 May 2005 a group of Shia Muslims called the Muslim Peacemaker Team (MPT) travelled to Fallujah from as far away as Kerbala and Najaf to help their Sunni counterparts clean up rubble. In a symbolic act of solidarity, members of MPT sought to counter the growing reports of Sunni–Shia sectarian violence and to demonstrate unity in a tense time.

Reconstruction continues to take a back seat to security, and police, soldiers, marines and the city's residents are still the victims of insurgents. Four of the city council's chairmen have been killed. Speaking to AFP in May 2007 Staff Sergeant Mauricio Piedrahita emphasised that the main need in Fallujah is still essential services.

By December 2006 control of the city had been transferred to the Iraqi army. In May 2007 Coalition forces were supporting the Iraqi security forces in the city, which has been segmented, and Iraqi police and Coalition forces are setting up police district headquarters to localise law enforcement. Hundreds of locals, many who fought in the insurgency, have joined the police.

Reporting from Fallujah on 5 September 2007, Ali Al-Fadhily, of the Inter Press Service, described deserted streets, closed shops and people with sullen faces. There is a ban on vehicles and people are back to riding donkeys. Unemployment is high, there are problems with electricity and water, and the price of basic goods is very high. 'They [the police and the American army] should not be proud of having the city quiet in a way that kills everybody with hunger and disease,' a lawyer, Ahmed Hammad, told IPS.

But not all the news from Fallujah is negative. At the beginning of 2008 Boston travel agent Roxana von Kraus printed 100 posters of Iraq's football team, which won the Asian Cup in July 2007. Her son, Captain Brian Von Kraus, gave these posters to children he met patrolling Anbar province. The sheikhs from the Abu Issa tribe were so impressed they invited the marines for a meal and Brian decided to set up a football league. His mother hopes the Iraqi teams will come to the USA and play with local teams.

TIKRIT Tikrit dates back to Babylonian times. The Babylonian king Naboholasar took refuge there when he was attacking the city of Assur in 615BC. Interestingly in view of its late history, Tikrit flourished as a Christian centre during the final three centuries of Arab rule. There was a cathedral (later destroyed in 1089) and many Syrian Orthodox churches. In 1036 it was the stronghold of the Uqaylid Dynasty, descended from the Bedouin. Saladin was born in Tikrit (see page 56). Like much of Iraq, it was devastated during the Mongol invasion of the 14th century.

The city will always be associated with Saddam Hussein. The dictator gave the town closest to the village of Al-Awja, where he was born, a facelift. 'It was a different town from the one I passed through in 1991' John Simpson recalls in *The Wars Against Saddam*:

Then it had seemed like just another untidy, backward little place; now real money had been spent on it. Several of the buildings were faced with marble. A statue of Saddam on horseback stood at the junction where the road from the bridge met the main street which ran through the town.

The Saddam Mosque in the centre of the city is one of the cleanest, best lit and best air-conditioned in the country. The town was not a victim of the post-war orgy of looting, as Saddam's government had looked after its people. It got its first privately owned internet café, courtesy of the 4th Infantry, in August 2003. There is an American version of a truck stop, the Mashallah restaurant, on a highway in upper Tikrit. The courthouse was renovated by the US Army Corps of Engineers (USACE). The Americans also set up an industrial vocational training school. It is a self-supporting institution, which owns a textile mill and employs many of its graduates in uniform production.

In the 1990s Saddam built a huge palace complex in the town overlooking the Tigris. It was not a place for happy families: his wife and mistress resented each other. Extravagance was the name of the game: the hillside had nine palaces, the one with the best view reserved for Saddam. Maybe he wished he had paid the contractors what they were owed – they exacted their revenge by linking the sewage system to the air conditioning.

The palace complex was the scene of the famous film clip of Saddam firing a rifle into the air from a balcony overlooking his troops. It was occupied by American troops until 22 November 2005, when it was handed over to the governor of Salahuddin province. It is now being used by the Iraqi police and army for its headquarters.

Saddam's anticipated 'last stand' in Tikrit never transpired. When several thousand marines converged on the town on 13 April 2003 with 300 armoured vehicles they met little resistance.

Before his capture on 13 December 2003, Saddam sheltered in and around Tikrit for six months. The 'spider hole' from which he was ingloriously extracted just outside ad-Dawr is 15km south of Tikrit.

A number of insurgent attacks against occupation forces have taken place in Tikrit at the northern end of the Sunni Triangle. As in most of Salahuddin province the real power is in the hands of the sheikhs, who co-operate with the insurgents, referred to as 'former regime elements' by the Americans.

Al-Awja, Saddam's birthplace, is an ugly, dusty little village. Most of it was flattened in 1987 after a shot was fired at Saddam's motorcade.

Saddam was buried here in 'Martyrs Hall' after he was hanged in December 2006. The grave site is simple, with a wooden eagle from which his prayer beads hang.

Saddam's two sons, Uday and Qsay, are also buried in the village of Al-Awja. They were killed after a gunfight with American forces in Mosul on 22 July 2003.

Habbaniyah Tourist Village, 84km west of Baghdad between Ramadi and Fallujah, has been transformed from Iraq's top luxury resort with fashionable holiday chalets into a shelter for refugees – mostly Sunnis driven from the capital due to death threats from Shia militias and refugees from the American offensive against Fallujah.

A tourist guide published by the Iraqi government in 1982 described a six-storey four-star hotel, three restaurants, bars, a night club, 500 chalets, two large swimming pools, a sailing club, a horse-riding arena, four tennis courts, a supermarket, an open-air theatre and an Arab tent casino.

The lakeside beach is now used as a laundry and if the refugees can't catch fish they have only bread to eat.

The largest Middle East base for British forces was located in the area during World War II. Prior to that it was a major base for Turkish forces.

The towns of **Yusufiyah**, **Latifiyah**, **Iskandariyah** and **Mahmudiyah** in the area immediately south of Baghdad were among the most treacherous in Iraq. According to the residents, draconian Islamic laws had been imposed and there was a price on the heads of police, national guardsmen, Shiite pilgrims and foreigners. The most radical Sunni Muslims believe the Shias are apostates and the penalty for apostasy is death. Extensive campaigns by American and Iraqi forces have largely pacified these towns.

The main problem areas as this book went to press were **Al-Buhairat** north of Iskandariyah, and a group of villages belonging to Iskandariyah 50km south of Baghdad, both major insurgent bases where the date palms, orchards and eucalyptus trees provide cover for the insurgents.

In a classic case of poacher turned game-keeper, some of the Sunni tribes began co-operating with the Americans against Al-Qaeda. The change of heart was sparked by Sheikh Abdul Sattar Abu Risha from the Al Burisha tribe in Anbar province, whose brothers and relatives were killed by Al-Qaeda. Other tribal leaders followed his example.

On 3 September 2007 President Bush made a surprise visit to Anbar, where he met Abu Risha and local sheikhs who have received millions of dollars from America, in addition to training to help fight Al-Qaeda. Ten days after the meeting Abu Risha, leader of the Anbar Salvation Council, was killed by a car bomb. He had in fact reduced his number of bodyguards because of the perceived improving security.

President Bush and Abu Risha

The new American strategy, which in 2007 has seen US$125m given directly to local leaders in Anbar for reconstruction projects and security, is a ground-up approach, as opposed to the top-down approach of supporting the central government. Some US$17 million has been paid to groups known as 'Concerned Local Citizens' or 'Awakening Forces', whose members are paid US$300 a month. Many were resistance fighters who attacked American forces. The new forces number more than 76,000; 82% are Sunni and the USA hopes to add another 10,000. They have successfully chased foreign fighters out of Anbar province but accusations of extortion, corruption and brutal tactics have been levelled against them. 'We will behead anyone who carries a gun,' Wussam Hardan, a senior leader in the Awakening Forces, told Inter Press Service on 29 November 2007. 'No courts, no lawyers. We have our own ways to get those criminals to confess.'

America is riding a tiger that may or may not take it where it wants to go. If this strategy is continued Iraq may emerge with a weak central government and largely self-governing autonomous regions – a soft partition rather than the dramatic break-up of the country based on the north/south/centre division.

Dr Ayad Allawi, the first prime minister in post-Saddam Iraq, warned that:

> we don't know what the post-conflict Al-Qaeda policy is going to be. The ultimate goal is to bring these people [tribal leaders] into the political process. If this does not happen there will be lot of problems.

Al Shaheed Mosque

11

The South

It is related that the commander of the faithful, Ali, once sought solitude and went to a place on the edge of the city of Najaf for seclusion. One day, while Ali was glancing at Najaf, he suddenly saw a man approaching from the desert, riding a camel and transporting a corpse. When the man saw Ali, he walked up to him and greeted him. Ali returned the greeting and asked the man: where are you from? The man answered: from Yemen. And what is this corpse? It is my father's corpse: I came to bury it in this land. Why do you not bury him in your own land? It is my father who ordered me to do so, and he said one day there will be buried a man in Najaf whose intercession with God was far reaching. Do you know who this man is? asked Ali. No said the man. Ali then said: by God, I am that man. Go and bury your father.

Ibrahim al-Musawi al-Zanjani
Quoted in *The Shi'is of Iraq* by Yitzhak Nakash

If the Prophet Mohammed came to Basra today he would be killed because he doesn't have a militia. There is no state of law, the only law is the militia law.

Basra law professor

Tragic events in the early history of Islam led to the construction of magnificent shrines in the desert cities of Najaf and Kerbala (referred to as the holy cities, or Atabat) in southern Iraq. Every year, thousands of pilgrims flock to these sites of Islamic splendour, where a tragic massacre that occurred some 14 centuries ago led to the Sunni–Shia divide in the Islamic religion, a divide that still evokes strong emotions (see pages 233–4).

Like the rest of Iraq, the south has a long history. The first artificial stone was made in Mashkan-Shapir, a city dating back 4,000 years in what is now southern Iraq. The city's artisans heated fine-grained alluvial silt to melting temperatures, then slowly cooled it to produce a rock-hard slab resembling a type of volcanic rock called basalt. Maskhan-Shapir seems to have vanished without trace.

Iraq is a land of contrasts: fine golden domes from opulent times are only a few hours' drive from the simple reed huts of the Marsh Arabs, whose lifestyle has changed little since the Sumerian era. Their homes in the reed beds contrasted sharply with the mainly desert environment of the rest of Iraq and the Middle East. The port city of Basra, from which Sinbad the sailor set off on his adventures, is also in the south of the country.

HISTORICAL BACKGROUND: THE SHIAS AND THE HOLY CITIES

CHRONOLOGY

2000BC	Ancient city of Mashkan-Shapir founded in what is now southern Iraq.
1900BC	Babylon emerged from the union of the Sumerian and Akkadian kingdoms.
1400BC	Assyrian Empire.
606–539BC	Neo-Babylonian kingdom.
539–330BC	Rule of Persian Achaemenid dynasty.
331–129BC	Kingdom of Seleucid ruled Mesopotamia and Persia.
130BC–AD226	Parthian Persians ruled ancient Iraq.
AD227–636	Rule of Sassanian Persian dynasty.
632	Death of Prophet Mohammed.
637	Defeat of Persians by Arab forces at the battle of Qadasiyah.
661–750	Muslim world ruled from Damascus by Ummayad caliphs.
680	Battle of Kerbala led to Sunni–Shia divide in Islam.
750–1280	Muslim world ruled from Baghdad by Abbasid caliphs.
836	Capital of Abbasid Caliphate moved to Samarra for 56 years.
1261	Caliphate moved from Baghdad to Cairo
1509–33	Ismail Shah, founder of Persian Safavid Dynasty, conquered Iraq. The Persians favoured the Shia religious establishment.
1534–1918	Iraq ruled by the Ottoman Turks, who favoured the Sunni religious establishment.
16th century	Iranians converted to Shi'ism in large numbers.
18th century	Southern Iraq became a magnet for Persian religious scholars and their students after the Sunni Afghans captured Isfahan in Persia.
1737	Kerbala replaced Isfahan as the main centre of Shia scholarship.
1801	Kerbala sacked by Wahhabis.
1803	Construction of Hindiyya canal alleviated Najaf's water problems.
1805	Wahhabis laid siege to Najaf.
1843	Najib Pasha occupied Kerbala, which was functioning like a self-governing republic, and returned it to Ottoman control.
1860s	Indians from the Awadh kingdom migrated to Najaf and Kerbala in large numbers.
1875	Iranians accorded special status under a law that made them answerable to the Iranian consul and exempted them from paying taxes. Famous Shia *mujtahid* (Islamic scholar) Muhammad Hasan Shirazi, left Najaf for Samarra, increasing the city's status as a Shia religious centre.

19th century	Large-scale conversion of Iraqi tribes to Shi'ism, most of whom settled down and started farming.
1900s	Increased Shia political activism.
1918	Religious scholars filled power vacuum created by the departure of the Ottomans.
1920	Revolt against British rule supported both by the mujtahids and the sayyids (descendants of the Prophet Mohammed), whose position was threatened by the colonialists.
1924	Fatwa issued against any Muslims who took part in the elections to the constituent assembly. Influence of mujtahids and sayyids started to decline.
1930	Pilgrims began arriving by train, rather than camel train. Their stay in the holy cities was limited to three months.
1935	Shia lawyers in Baghdad and mujtahids presented a manifesto to the government calling for greater participation in parliament, government and civil service, and greater investment in Shia areas.
1938	Holy cities (Najaf and Kerbala) failed to develop alternative sources of income. Declining revenues from pilgrims and fees for the transportation of bodies to be buried in the holy cemeteries caused economic problems. Around half of Najaf's population unemployed.
1940s &1950s	Shias increased their demands to secure government and civil service posts.
1946	Leadership of the Shias shifted from the southern Iraqi city of Najaf to the Iranian city of Qum after the death of Abu al-Hassan Ishahani. Post-World War II, Shias attracted to Baghdad, where they accounted for more than 50% of the inhabitants.
1960s	Shias' support for the communists declined as they saw little change in the Sunni-dominated power structures. The Baath Party's pan-Arab ideology, which is identified with Sunnism, alienated the Shias. Revival of interest in Islam.
1970s	Thousands of Shias expelled to Iran under the pretext of their Iranian origin.
1980	Execution of renowned Shia scholar Muhammad Baqir Al-Sadr and his sister Bint Huda.
1980–88	Iranian pilgrims banned from Iraq during the Iran–Iraq war. Economy of the holy cities suffered.
Feb 1991	Protests in the city of Diwaniyya against Saddam's refusal to leave Kuwait.
Mar 1991	Popular uprising throughout southern Iraq. Crushed by Saddam's regime by the end of March. Repression of Shia religious establishment continued. Leading Shia scholar Abol Qasim Al Khoei forced to make media appearances not long before his death.

11

1998	Assassination of Ayatollah Ali Al-Gharavi.
1999	Assassination of Mohammed Sadiq Al-Sadr.
Mar 2001	Tribal leaders and mayors in the south ordered to sign undertaking to ensure Saddam's pictures and statues cleaned after acts of vandalism.
	Death in suspicious circumstances of Shia scholar Hussain Bahr al-Uloom. More than four million pilgrims in Kerbala.

2003

24 Mar	Stronger than expected resistance in Basra and Nasiriyah to invading forces.
25 Mar	Port city of Um Qasr captured. Fierce battle between American and Iraqi forces left 700 Iraqis dead.
28 Mar	*Sir Galahad* docked in Um Qasr with 1,000 tonnes of food and humanitarian aid.
30 Mar	Some 600 British commandos launched an assault to capture a suburb southeast of Basra.
2 Apr	Kerbala secured by American forces. In Najaf the Iraqis fired at the Americans from the Imam Ali Mosque but the Americans did not return fire out of respect for the religious site.
21 Apr	Thousands of Shia pilgrims celebrated Ashura in Kerbala and delighted in the performance of rituals banned by Saddam's regime.
15 May	Management of the port of Um Qasr handed back to the Iraqis.
24 Jun	Six British military policemen killed in Majar Al-Kabir.
29 Aug	The head of the Supreme Islamic Council and 79 others killed by a car bomb in Najaf.

2004

5 Jan	Prime Minister Blair visited British troops in Basra.
3 Mar	Explosions in Kerbala and Kazimiya killed around 180 Shia pilgrims celebrating Ashura.
Apr	Moqtada Al-Sadr's Shia militia occupied Najaf.
22 Apr	Seventy people killed in a series of suicide bombings in Basra.
Aug	Al-Sadr's Shia militia left Najaf following American bombardment and mediation by Ayatollah Sistani. Twenty-five Shias killed when Iraqi national guardsmen fired at thousands of supporters of Al-Sadr who were marching on Najaf in response to a call by Ayatollah Sistani for a mass march on Najaf to save it.
3 Oct	Samarra freed from the control of the insurgents after one of the biggest offensives since the invasion of Iraq.
4 Oct	The expansion of the courtyard of the Imam Ali shrine in Najaf by 120m started.

| 19 Dec | A car bomb in Najaf, near the Imam Ali shrine, killed 48 people. In Kerbala a blast at a bus station killed 13. |

2005

19 Sep	British troops used tanks to break down the walls of a prison in Basra and free two undercover British soldiers who were seized earlier in the day by local police. Major demonstration against the British followed and Basra's provincial council voted unanimously 'to stop dealing with the British forces'.
20 Sep	The governor of Basra condemned the 'barbaric aggression' of the British forces used to free the SAS soldiers held at a police station.
21 Sep	Hundreds of police officers in Basra demonstrated, calling for the withdrawal of British troops. Senior Iraqi officials admitted that up to 60% of the police in Basra may have been infiltrated by members of radical Shia militias.
6 Oct	Tony Blair accused Iran of involvement in passing sophisticated roadside bombs to insurgents in southern Iraq in retaliation for Britain's stance on Tehran's nuclear weapons programme. The bombs are thought to have been responsible for the deaths of eight British troops.
22 Dec	Tony Blair visited Basra, where he hinted British troops could begin being withdrawn inside six months.

2006

12 Jan	Two aides to Iraq's most senior Shia cleric, Grand Ayatollah Ali Al-Sistani, assassinated.
31 Jan	100th British solider killed in Iraq, dying from injuries suffered in an explosion at Um Qasr
22 Feb	A bomb badly damaged the Al-Askari shrine in Samarra.
26 Feb	Two British soldiers killed when their Land Rover was blown up by a roadside bomb while on patrol in the town of Amarah. The attacks took the number of British soldiers killed in Iraq to 103.
26 Feb	'Operation Corrode' in Basra to 'reform the reformable' policemen and 'detain the rest'.
16 Mar	More than 50 US aircraft launched the biggest air assault in Iraq since 2003. The aircraft, along with 1,500 US and Iraqi troops, targeted insurgents near the city of Samarra.
31 May	Month-long state of emergency in the southern city of Basra followed sectarian clashes.
13 Jul	Iraqi authorities in Al Muthanna, southeast Iraq, officially took over responsibility for security in their province.
Sep	Dhi Qar handed over to Iraqi authorities.

11

2007

27 Feb	Tony Blair announced partial military withdrawal from southern Iraq.
23 Mar	Eight sailors along with seven marines arrested by Iranian Revolutionary Guards for illegally entering Iranian territorial waters. They were subsequently pardoned by Iran's president and returned home.
Apr	Two bombings in Kerbala, one at the bus station, another at the Abbas Shrine.
May	Maysan handed over to Iraqi control.
16 May	Decision not to deploy Prince Harry with the British army in Iraq due to 'unacceptable risks'.
19 May	Abdul-Aziz Al-Hakim, the leader of the largest and most powerful Shiite party, travelled to Iran for urgent medical attention for lung cancer.
25 May	Moqtada Al-Sadr returned after four months in Iran and called for Sunni–Shia co-operation to end the occupation.
28 May	The USA and Iran held the first bilateral talks for 30 years on ending the violence in Iraq.
30 May	A top aide of radical Shia cleric Moqtada Al-Sadr said the Mehdi Army was not involved in the kidnapping of five Britons in Baghdad on 29 May.
8 Jun	Some 600 members of the Iraqi Federation of Oil Unions (IFOU) who work for the Oil Pipeline Company went on strike in Basra over non-payment of a bonus.
13 Jun	Two minarets of Al-Askari Mosque in Samarra destroyed in near-simultaneous blasts.
28 Jul	Clashes between the Mehdi Army and a joint US-Iraqi force left nine people dead in Iraqi holy city of Kerbala.
11 Aug	A roadside bomb killed the governor and police chief of the southern Iraqi province of Diwaniya.
28 Aug	David Miliband, the foreign secretary, declared that future decisions about British troop deployments in Basra would be taken on the basis of the situation on the ground in that city, not on the basis of US military operations in Baghdad.
	Hundreds of pilgrims ordered to leave Kerbala during a Shia festival after shooting in the city.
3 Sep	British forces pulled out of Basra Palace.
6 Oct	Al-Sadr and the Supreme Islamic Council signed a deal to end violence between their two groups.
9 Oct	Prime Minister Gordon Brown announced that Britain would halve its troop contingent in Iraq in spring 2008. A British official later said they could not guarantee that any troops would remain in Iraq by the end of 2008.
17 Dec	The British officially transferred control of Basra to the Iraqis.

A RELIGIOUS DIVIDE Muslims believe the Prophet Mohammed was the last of the ancient monotheistic prophets who passed on the wisdom of one God. Mohammed's teachings are found in the holy book the Koran. The religion is centred around five duties known as 'pillars': recital of the creed (*shahadah*), which states 'there is no God but Allah and Mohammed is his prophet'; prayers five times a day; the giving of alms (money) to the poor; fasting during the month of Ramadan, the month in which the Koran was revealed to Prophet Mohammed; and a pilgrimage to Mecca, the Prophet's birthplace in Saudi Arabia, where the Grand Mosque houses the holy sanctuary (the Kaaba). Social life is governed by Islamic canon law, called the Sharia, the Prophet's traditions (Hadith and Sunna) and local traditions and customs.

The Sunni–Shia (orthodox–heterodox) schism in the first half of the 7th century occurred due to differences over the leadership of the Islamic community after the Prophet's death in AD632. Some of the Prophet's followers believed that the successor should be an elected member of the Prophet's tribe (the Quraysh) while others believed that the Prophet's cousin (Ali ibn Abu Talib, AD600–61) was the legitimate successor, and insisted that the successor had to come from the Prophet's family.

Ali was strongly opposed to this division in the Muslim community. He decided to send a message from his residence in Kufa to Muawiyah, his rival in Damascus, proposing a negotiated solution: the two 'leaders' would nominate a caliph (successor to the Prophet) to lead the Muslims. The nominees would subsequently resign and a third man, acceptable to both sides, would be chosen. Ali's nominee resigned as agreed but Muawiyah was not a man of his word and his appointee declared himself caliph. Muawiyah subsequently instigated the murder of Ali, who was stabbed to death while praying in the mosque at Kufa, and persuaded Hassan, Ali's eldest son, to renounce his claim to the caliphate.

The followers of Ali (Shias) carried out their master's instructions regarding his burial place. They tied his body to a camel and let it roam in the desert. The camel finally stopped to rest in Najaf. Ali was buried there and a mosque, one of the most famous shrines in the Muslim world, was built over his tomb.

The struggle between Ali and Muawiyah was continued by their sons. Hussein, Ali's second son, refused to submit to the rule of Yazid I, Muawiyah's son, who succeeded his father in AD680. The people of Medina, where the Prophet had established a base in AD622 after the inhabitants of Mecca rejected his teachings, urged Hussein to claim his rightful place as head of the Muslim community. He began the trek across the desert to confront Yazid in Damascus, with 72 companions, men and women, expecting thousands to join them, but no-one came to their assistance. Near Kerbala they were confronted by a force of some 4,000 troops loyal to Yazid. For eight days the commander of Yazid's forces tried to persuade Hussein to surrender, but he refused.

The massacre that changed the course of Islamic history by splitting the religion into Sunnis and Shias took place on the tenth day, when Hussein and his followers were mercilessly killed. Hussein, defiant to the end, died with a sword in one hand and a Koran in the other. His brave words, 'Death with dignity is better than a life of humiliation', have never been forgotten by the Shias, who believe that to die as a martyr in the fight for a noble cause is a great honour that guarantees a place in paradise. The martyrs at the battle of Kerbala

11

embodied the ideal of manhood and remain popular role models, both in Iraq and throughout the Muslim world.

Events at Najaf and Kerbala had a profound effect on Shia thinking. The Shias have traditionally been the downtrodden, the poor and the weak, who stand in opposition to privilege and power, obliged to struggle for social, political and economic equality and overthrow illegitimate, tyrannical rulers.

Ali was succeeded by 12 imams (hence the name 'twelvers sect'), the 12th being Muhammad al-Mahdi, who disappeared in AD874 and is said to have gone into a state of occultation (a non-corporeal existence). The Shias believe he will return one day heralding a just world.

In the 20th century the Shias acquired a reputation for radicalism and fanaticism, yet many of their traditional beliefs are incredibly liberal. Through interpretation (*idjtihad*), scholars (*mujtahids*) can interpret the law in the light of different circumstances. Temporary marriage (*zawaj mut'a*) for a specified period of years, months or even hours is also an option, although disapproved of by Sunnis.

Of the total global population of about one billion Muslims (in 1998), between 15% and 20% are Shias. In Iraq, they are found mainly in central and southern areas, where they make up at least 65% of the total population. According to Yitzhak Nakash, author of *The Shi'is of Iraq*, the Iraqi Shias are:

> by and large recent converts to Shi'ism, a result of a development which took place mainly during the 19th century as the bulk of Iraq's Arab nomadic tribes settled down and took up agriculture

(See pages 13–17 for further information on the Sunni–Shia divide.)

THE 19TH CENTURY Southern Iraq became a magnet for Persian religious scholars (*ulama*) and their students during the 18th century after the Sunni Afghans captured Isfahan. The Shia centres of learning moved from Persia to Kerbala and Najaf, where the Persian language was widely used.

During the 1860s Indians from the Shia state of Awadh also flocked to the holy cities, prompted by the British annexation of the Awadh kingdom and the Indian Mutiny. Najaf and Kerbala benefited greatly from the donations of their co-religionists in Awadh. By the 20th century some 5,000 Indians had settled in the holy cities. The first migrants were well-to-do members of the royal Nawwabs family who arrived with their subjects. When their munificence decreased, the number of poor Indians in southern Iraq increased to the point where a 1929 report by the Protector of British Indian Pilgrims described Kerbala as 'a sink of Indian pauperism'.

The Persian community, numbering some 80,000, exerted the greatest influence in the holy cities. Under an 1875 agreement they were accorded special status, made answerable to the Iranian consul and exempted from taxes. Ottoman subjects living in Iran were granted the same privileges.

The religious activities of Najaf and Kerbala had a profound influence on the Arab tribes of central and southern Iraq, made up of camel and sheep breeders and the inhabitants of the marshlands (see pages 256–8). Their large-scale conversion from Sunni to Shia Islam took place during the 19th century, which also saw the migration of a number of tribes from Arabia keen to escape

BADRA

The tomb of Ali al-Yathribi, a son of the seventh imam, near the town of Badra.

BAGHDAD

The tombs of the four representatives of the 12th imam.

BALAD

The tomb of Sayyid Muhammad, a son of the tenth imam, is near the city of Balad.

HILLA

The site of the tombs of the sons of Muslim ibn 'Aqil, his brother (and son-in-law of Imam Ali) Muhammad, and those of Hamza and Jasim, a son and grandson, respectively, of the seventh imam.

KADHIMAIN

The shrines of Musa al-Kazim (the seventh imam) and his grandson Muhammad al-Jawad (the ninth imam), situated 5km northwest of Baghdad.

KERBALA

The famous shrines of Imam Hussein and his half-brother Abbas.

KHAYMAGAH

The site of Hussein's tent before the battle of Kerbala is in the city. About 6.5km outside Kerbala are the tombs of Hurr ibn Yazid al Riyahi (a military commander sent to intercept Hussein who defected and joined him) and Awn ibn Abdallah ibn Jafar who fought with Hussein at the battle of Kerbala.

KUFA ALI

He was fatally wounded in the mosque at Kufa. The tombs of Muslim ibn Aqil (Hussein's cousin) and Hani ibn Urwa, who gave refuge to Muslim ibn Aqil, are also in the city.

KUMAYYIT

A brother of the eighth imam, Ali al-Rida, is buried here.

MUSAYYIB

The tombs of the sons of the seventh and 11th imams.

NAJAF

Famous throughout the Muslim world for the shrine of Imam Ali. The tomb of Banat al-Hasan is frequently visited by Muslim women.

QALAT SALIH

The tomb of one of Imam Ali's sons is near the town.

SALMAN PARK

Tombs of three followers of Muhammed.

SAMARRA

The hiding place of the 12th imam, Muhammad al-Mahdi, 106km north of Baghdad.

TUWAYRIJ

The tombs of the children of the 11th imam and the tomb of a grandchild of the seventh imam.

The South HISTORICAL BACKGROUND: THE SHIAS AND THE HOLY CITIES

11

Wahhabi influence. The Shia religious scholars (*ulama*) in Najaf were aware there was no force strong enough to resist the Wahhabis, followers of Abdul Wahhab (1703–87), who declared a holy war (*jihad*) against anyone who rejected their puritanical interpretation of Islam. The Shias and the holy cities of Najaf and Kerbala were considered fair game.

The *ulama* were keen for the tribes to convert to Shi'ism because they used Najaf and Kerbala as convenient desert market towns without any regard for their spiritual significance. The tribesmen did not contribute to the upkeep of the shrines and could easily disrupt pilgrimages and the corpse traffic (the bodies of thousands of Muslims have been transported to the cemeteries in the holy cities for burial) on which the economic life of the cities depended.

Tribal resettlement was encouraged by the Ottomans, who wanted to undermine the power of the sheikhs and increase the revenue from taxes. It was facilitated by the increase in cultivatable land made possible largely by the Hindiyya canal. As the tribesmen became cultivators the traditional tribal structure was disrupted and they needed a new identity, which Shi'ism provided. As Shias their status increased in the eyes of the townspeople. The appeal to the downtrodden fell on receptive ears due to the oppression of the Ottomans and the gap between the rich and poor: the sheikhs who had become landed aristocrats and the tribesmen who cultivated their land. Conversion to Shi'ism was also a way of escaping conscription.

Most of the tribes settled down and started farming in the 19th century. The land was now identified as their tribal home and disputes over land and water rights inevitably followed. New towns sprang up throughout central and southern Iraq and existing towns expanded. The beginning of the 20th century was a time of increased Shia political activism: the mujtahids cultivated the image of the leaders of the Muslim opposition. It was also the time of the introduction of a Shia secular education, a major departure from the curricula of the religious schools (*madrassas*) of the holy cities.

The first defensive holy war (*jihad*) was fought against the Wahhabis, who laid siege to Najaf in 1805. When the British landed in Iraq during World War I a jihad was declared against them. It failed and the country was occupied in 1918, but the mujtahids filled the power vacuum created by the departure of the Ottomans.

THE 20TH CENTURY

The 1920 revolt (see page 70) against British rule was supported by both the mujtahids and the sayyids (descendants of Prophet Mohammed) whose position was threatened by the 'colonisers: Christian occupiers of a Muslim land'. As a poem by Muhammad Habib Al-Ubaydi shows, Sunnis and Shias were incited to revolt against the British mandate:

Do not talk of a Ja'fari or Hanafi
Do not talk of a Shafi'i or Zaydi
For the shari'a of Muhammad has united us
And it rejects the Western mandate

The revolt was crushed but, as Yitzhak Nakash, author of *The Shi'is of Iraq*, pointed out:

The Shia religious establishment could compete with any government in Iraq over the influence and mobilisation of the local population. The existence of such a highly autonomous and politically active religious establishment posed a danger to the authority of the nascent Iraqi state. Successive Sunni governments would therefore seek to eradicate the power of Shia mujtahids and institutions in the country and to reduce the links between Najaf and Kerbala and Iran.

While the Sunni ex-Ottoman officers and the royal family installed by the British (see pages 70–2) had their differences, they were united in their desire to keep the Shias firmly under their thumb. The religious establishment struck back and a fatwa was issued stating that any Muslim who took part in the elections to the constituent assembly in 1924 would be shunned by his fellow Muslims and forbidden from going to the public bath.

But the influence of the mujtahids and the sayyids started to decline. The Shias did not have a strong leadership, the Persian language presented a communication barrier between the mujtahids and the Arab masses, and the spread of secular education undermined the role of the madrassas. A modern legal system was established and the sayyids lost their traditional role as mediators. The government put an end to preaching about the Shia faith and arrested Shia emissaries who tried to convert the Turcomans. The leadership of the Shias shifted from Najaf to the Iranian city of Qom after Abu al-Hassan Ishahani died in 1946.

While the mujtahids were crushed with the stick the Shia sheikhs were assimilated into the ruling establishment through the carrot. They were rewarded by the British for keeping order in the countryside and ensuring the steady flow of tax revenues to the government. The army officers threatened both the sheikhs and the monarchists. They formed a strong alliance, which lasted until the revolution of Abdul Karim Qasim overthrew the monarchy in 1958.

The holy cities declined in importance. They failed to develop alternative sources of income and continued to rely on the money brought in by pilgrims and the corpse traffic (see page 251). Government investment was negligible and in 1938 around half of Najaf's population was unemployed. The government also made life difficult by placing restrictions on the amount of rice that could be sold to Saudi tribes. In 1951 the quota was set at 3,000 tons for Najaf and 500 tons for Kerbala. There was also competition with Samawa and Zubair, two other granary centres.

Baghdad, the city of bright lights and economic opportunities, became the focus of Shia migration. Before World War I the Shias accounted for 20% of the capital's population; after the war more than 50% of the city's inhabitants were Shias, who brought their clan and tribal affiliations with them. But they were also influenced by the urban environment, changed their style of dress, re-evaluated their religious beliefs and were attracted by the ideology of the Iraqi Communist Party (ICP). Kadhimain and Samarra benefited from Baghdad's growth and developed rapidly.

Despite the fatwa on participating in elections, which alarmed many Shias, they were eager to secure employment in government service. In 1930 the Kurds, who made up 17% of the population, held 22% of important government posts while the Shias only held 15%.

Kadhimain's and Samarra's claim to fame is derived from Shia imams: Musa al-Kazim, the seventh imam, and his grandson Muhammed al-Jawad, the ninth imam, are buried at Kadhimain, while Samarra is the resting place of the tenth and 11th imams, Ali al-Hadi and his son Hasan al-Askari. Muhammad al-Mahdi, the 12th imam, who the Shias believe will return as the saviour of the world, was reportedly born in Samarra.

Kadhimain is now part of greater Baghdad, while Samarra lies 100km north of the capital. Their proximity to Baghdad ensured they were under the control of the Ottomans and unlike Najaf and Kerbala did not acquire an independent life of their own. Both the Ottomans and the Iranians were eager to win the favour of the local people and renovations to the shrine started by Shah Isma'il in the 16th century were completed by Sultan Suleiman (1520–66). In Kadhimain it was easy for the government to control religious rituals performed during Muharram, and in 20th-century Iraq it lost its attraction as a place of Shia celebrations.

Samarra, on the left bank of the Tigris, has a glorious past. Between the 3rd and 7th century AD it was the site of a small Sassanian Persian town with a Christian monastery. The city blossomed in the 8th century AD when it became the capital of the Abassid Empire (see pages 49–55).

The Caliph Al-Mutasim, who came to power in AD833, was eager to isolate the Turkish bodyguards who usurped their status and alienated the local people. It was also important for him to create a new environment of which he was master and he spared no efforts to build a new, splendid city: the palm trees came from Basra, the marble from the churches of Egypt, including the church of St Menas near Alexandria. Even though Mutasim paid the Christian monks of Samarra he felt justified in looting the treasures of antiquity. A Friday mosque and three palaces were constructed. The Turks were housed in an area to the north of the town.

Mutasim's son, Al-Mutawakkil, followed in his father's footsteps and built another new city known as Al-Ja'fariya. The Great Street (Shari'al-Azam) ran parallel with the Tigris. On completing his palace Al-Mutawakkil commented, 'Now I know that I am indeed king for I have built myself a city and live in it.' In Samarra itself he constructed The Great Mosque, with its 52m-high spiral minaret (*malwiya*), a synthesis of Babylonian ziggurat and Islamic architecture.

In the words of British archaeologist Sir Mortimer Wheeler:

> What matters most about the Samarra minaret is not its formal origin but its startling originality. Strikingly bold and simple in design, functional, elemental, finely proportioned, comfortable to the eye. Here we have in the 9th century many qualities which bridge the centuries. The malwiya is truly a great and rather lonely masterpiece.

Mosques and palaces sprang up all over Samarra, a city that had a short but eventful 56-year life. Today the main sites are the ruins of the caliph's palace with numerous

In 1935 Shia lawyers in Baghdad and the Arab mujtahids drafted a manifesto in an attempt to unite rival Shia sheikhs and force the government to accept their demands. These included Shia participation in parliament, government and the civil service in accordance with their numbers, government investment

arches and cellars; the Al Ma'shooq Palace; the Great Mosque built by Al-Mutasim with its spiral minaret; the Abu Dalaf Mosque built 20km to the north of Samarra by one of Al-Mutawakkil's commanders; and the Al-Rawdha Al-Askari (Ali El Hadi) Mosque in the centre of the modern city, with its great shining golden dome and the tombs of the tenth and 11th imams.

The Al Ma'shooq Palace, some 10km northwest of Samarra, is a monumental building, left untouched apart from some restoration on the outer walls. It is a very large brick construction on a high platform with many rooms.

In 1875, the famous Shia mujtahid Muhammad Hasan Shirazi left Najaf for Samarra and gave the city a new lease of life; his presence attracted students, exposed the mainly Sunni region to Shia influences and alarmed the Ottomans to the extent that they established two new religious schools. When Shirazi died Samarra's importance decreased once again. The shrine is popular with Shia pilgrims.

Since the occupation Samarra has been the scene of insurgent violence. In October 2004, after a two-day assault, a 5,000-strong joint US-Iraqi force regained control of the city from insurgents. In one of the biggest offensives since the invasion, 125 insurgents were killed and 88 detained. The then Iraqi defence minister, Hazem Shaalan, said up to US$40 million was being allocated for reconstruction and compensation. The operation was part of similar operations conducted against other cities held by insurgents, including Falluja (see pages 220–3). The Iraqi government cited Samarra as an example of how they were able to restore order to areas formerly controlled by rebels, but on 6 November 2004 more than 33 people were killed by a car bomb there.

Disaster struck on 22 February 2006 when armed groups bombed the Al-Askari Mosque. There were no casualties but the golden dome was badly damaged. Following the bombing Sunni and Shia clerics and mosques were attacked and random mortar firing and bomb attacks claimed many lives. Sectarian violence and sectarian cleansing increased and the incident was described by some analysts as the beginning of the much-feared civil war. Commemorating 100 days since the bombing, Al-Sayyid Hazim al-A'raji, imam and preacher at the Al-Rawdhah al-Kazimiyah Mosque, strongly criticised the Iraqi government for stalling the reconstruction of the holy dome of the Al-Askari Mosque and for failing to produce any investigation results. Both Prime Minister Blair and President Bush said they were ready to contribute to the rebuilding of the mosque. Traditionally the Shia shrine has been cared for by the Sunnis. On 13 June 2007 two near simultaneous blasts destroyed the mosque's two minarets. A number of Iraqi police were detained, suggesting it was an insider job.

In July 2007 the UN's Educational, Scientific and Cultural Organisation (UNESCO) announced that the shrine city of Samarra had been declared a world heritage site. Reconstruction of the Al-Askari Mosque will be financed by the EU (US$8m), UNESCO (US$5m) and the Iraqi government (US$5m).

in health and education in Shia areas, inclusion of Shia teachings in the law school and the distribution of religious endowments (*waqf*) to all Muslim institutions. The government did not respond to calls for negotiations over these demands and the conflict between the government and the tribes of the middle Euphrates intensified: railway lines were torn up, martial law was declared, the villages of rebellious tribes were bombed. In the end the representation of Shia tribal sheikhs in parliament was increased.

During the 1940s and 1950s the power struggle between the Shias and Sunnis intensified as young, educated Shias were eager to secure government and civil service posts. They also resented their under-representation in the army and police force. State education in rural areas and Shia access to state education was largely the achievement of two main figures in the Ministry of Education: Abd al-Karim al-Uzri and Muhammad Fadil al-Jamali. The government bureaucracy expanded, the number of Shia employees increased, but the Sunnis remained dominant in the state's institutions, pushing the Shias either towards the Iraqi Communist Party or the Islamic opposition. The Shias' support for the communists declined during the 1960s when they saw little change in the power structures.

The Baathists failed to attract the Shias in large numbers as they advocated pan-Arabism, which the Shias equated with Sunnism. When it became clear that the Baath Party was controlled by the Sunni Takritis (Saddam Hussein's tribe) many Shias shifted their allegiance to the Islamic Dawa Party under the leadership of Muhammad Baqir Al-Sadr. His books – *Our Philosophy* (published in 1959) and *Our Economic System* (1960) – presented an alternative political and economic ideology.

Even though the Baathists executed Baqir Al-Sadr and his sister Bint Huda, a renowned female Islamic scholar, in 1980 and expelled thousands of Shias to Iran under the pretext of their 'Persian connection' in the late 1970s, their identity as Iraqis prompted them to fight for Iraq during the Iran–Iraq War, when the Shias made up the bulk of the Iraqi army's infantry.

THE SOUTH DURING THE WARS After the invasion of Kuwait and Iraq's defeat, the Shias (encouraged by outside influences), and the Kurds in the north, revolted against Saddam's regime. On 10 February 1991, Iraqis in the southern city of Diwaniya, encouraged by southern and outside political forces and the seeming weakness of Saddam after the invasion of Kuwait, rose up and protested, resulting in much bloodshed.

But no strong Islamic figure emerged to lead the resistance, which was mercilessly crushed by the regime's troops. The regime did not hesitate to shell the shrines and mosques in Najaf and Kerbala where the rebels hid. Tanks were painted with the slogan 'no more Shias after today'. By the end of March 1991 resistance was confined to guerrilla attacks, mainly in the marshlands.

In an attempt to secure the loyalty of the Shia inhabitants of the south, Saddam found it necessary to appoint a Shia from Kerbala, Sa'dun Hamadi, as prime minister, and to hold meetings with important religious and tribal leaders from the south. In a gesture of reconciliation the damage to the shrines was repaired.

But despite these gestures aimed at appeasing the Shias, the regime was determined to eliminate the influence of the religious establishment. A number of religious scholars, including Hussain Bahr al-Uloom, died in suspicious circumstances.

The Third River Project (see page 257) also undermined the holy cities as it reduced the water supply to some of Iraq's finest rice fields. Unable to make a living, many of the farmers moved to other areas.

The south did not recover economically after the 1991 war when Allied bombing damaged the infrastructure, especially sewage and desalination plants. Sanctions resulted in further impoverishment and the small towns and villages had an air of decrepitude. Despite attempts to foster economic growth after the 2003 war, development has been relatively slow and hampered by the sabotage of infrastructure projects implemented by the Coalition and NGOs.

The bitter memories of the allies' betrayal of the 1991 uprising dampened the welcome extended to the Coalition forces throughout much of southern Iraq. Many people feared that Saddam would be allowed to return and the cycle of fear was not broken until his capture on 13 December 2003. Many of the Shias who received the worst treatment from Saddam's regime also suffered disproportionately during the 13 years of sanctions when the south was left to decay and disintegrate and, partially due to Iranian influence, adopted a viciously anti-Western stance.

The Coalition forces encountered some of the heaviest resistance in Nasiriyah and Najaf (see pages 107–9). The south was guarded by troops loyal to Saddam who fought fiercely. The ordinary people, fearful of a re-run of the slaughter that followed the 1991 uprising, watched. Hundreds of Iraqi soldiers surrendered across the frontline between Kuwait and Basra.

After the towns of the south came under Coalition control, the British, responsible for much of the south (notably Basra), began patrolling in berets rather than helmets and built up a rapport with the people. First the curious children came to talk to the soldiers, who handed out sweets and ration packs. A steady stream of locals then gathered around the bases in Um Qasr and Zubair, some curious, some friendly and some opportunistic.

The south, historically more lawless, proved a nightmare for the enforcement of law and order. The police force disappeared after towns fell to the Coalition forces and armed men (almost everyone in Iraq has a gun) pillaged houses and held up cars. The streets of southern towns like Zubair and Um Qasr became menacing at night when the Coalition soldiers were not on patrol and the kidnapping of women spread fear throughout the female population and increased their reluctance to return to work and play an active role in society.

THE BRITISH ARMY IN SOUTHERN IRAQ UK military operations in Iraq are conducted under the name Operation Telic. UK forces are a part of the US-led Multi-National Force – Iraq (or MNF-I).

Since the end of major combat operations in April 2003, the UK has been playing a full role in rebuilding the country, both in terms of restoring essential infrastructure and services, and through attempts to establish conditions for a stable Iraqi government.

The overwhelming majority of UK personnel in Iraq are based in the southeast, with a small number in Baghdad and around the country to liaise and co-ordinate with other Coalition and Iraqi forces. At the time of writing there were 4,200 British troops in the country. The remaining troop contingent will be halved by the spring of 2008. The cost of British military operations for 2005/06 was £958m. As at 1 March 2008, a total of 175 British Armed Forces personnel have died serving in Iraq.

Transition from the MNF to Iraqi Security Forces control has already occurred in Muthanna, Dhi Qhar, Najaf and Basra. The four provinces within

A British soldier who served in Iraq has made a film documenting his time there. It is the first time a reservist has produced a diary of this kind.

Private Joshua Fortune, 22, was posted to Basra as part of Operation Telic in October 2005.

One of the hardest things I witnessed was one day when we were on the main gate and some Iraqi civilians turned up. They brought a lady in an ambulance who had been caught in a gas explosion inside her house. She had been cooking with a canister and it had caught alight and exploded. She had 98% secondary burns so she was in a very bad way.

Obviously seeing the suffering, both of soldiers and Iraqi civilians, was never pleasant. And there were some sights that my colleagues and I saw that I'm sure will stay with us forever.

Iraqis are quite an amazing people. One of the things that struck me was the discipline that they have. I'd have difficulties waking up in the morning, but whenever I was awake, they were already out there, having done their prayers, and they were working for the day.

A lot of them were farmers and the ground wasn't the most fertile, so they had to do what they could. A lot of the time, when they saw our convoys coming, the children would come out and either just wave at us or beg for food.

In my opinion it's a country that's improving. When we first got there, there was a lot of poverty, but at the end of my six months things had improved. Obviously it's hard to tell from a private soldier's perspective, but from what I could see we were doing a good job out there.

www.bbc.co.uk

MNF (South East) control – Maysan, Basra, Dhi Qar, and Al Muthanna – account for less than 10% of the overall violence in Iraq. Unlike in Baghdad, there is very little sectarian conflict here; the challenges are criminality, infighting between Shia factions, and the corrosive influence of the militias.

In conjunction with security training and operations by MNF and Iraqi Forces, Operation Sinbad has completed around 550 projects to improve the local environment, including neighbourhood and infrastructure projects and agricultural development. As of March 2007 these included: 212km of new water pipe laid in an US$18 million project which employed 2,310 people at its peak; five medium-level electrical distribution projects worth US$9.8million; 140,000 date palm offshoots planted in a US$12 million project to reinvigorate the regionally-significant date palm industry; 336 schools refurbished and basic supplies delivered; 51 football pitches and other sporting facilities built or refurbished; 41 projects to supply equipment to refurbish medical facilities completed; and six footbridges refurbished.

But despite their laudable development efforts, the overall performance of the British army in southern Iraq is under a cloud, as indeed is the performance of the whole Coalition throughout Iraq. In a comment entitled 'The British Defeat in Iraq', the eminent American analyst on Iraq, Anthony Cordesman of the Center for Strategic and International Studies, in Washington, asserts that British forces had lost control of the situation in and around Basra by the second half of 2005.

Mr Cordesman's gloomy conclusions about British failure are confirmed by a study called *The Calm before the Storm: The British Experience in Southern Iraq* by Michael Knights and Ed Williams, published by the Washington Institute for Near East Policy. Comparing the original British ambitions with present reality the paper concludes that:

> instead of a stable, united, law-abiding region with a representative government and police primacy, the deep south is unstable, factionalised, lawless, ruled as a kleptocracy and subject to militia primacy.

Local militias are often not only beyond the control of the Iraqi government, but of their supposed leaders in Baghdad. The big money earner for local factions is the diversion of oil (priced at US$100 a barrel at the beginning of 2008) and oil products, with the profits a continual source of rivalry and a cause of armed clashes. Mr Knights and Mr Williams say that control in the south is with a 'well-armed political-criminal Mafiosi [who] have locked both the central government and the people out of power.'

Some of the local people are also criticising what they describe as the 'Iraqified' occupation. Residents of Maysan province told Jo Wilding, author of *Don't Shoot the Clowns: Taking a Circus to the Children of Iraq*, that – as throughout their colonial history – the British found a power on the ground that was amenable to them, in this case a local militia, legitimised them in that position and left them to exercise authority, denying responsibility for any atrocities committed by the proxy and saving themselves the effort of actually running the place themselves. It meant those who had power and privilege before had it again, but now without the strong control from the centre.

Colonel Andrew Williams, the senior British commander at Abu Naji in Maysan province, suggests the army's presence is self-defeating:

> You can't have an insurgency without an occupier to fight. And if you justify your occupation as an effort to combat insurgency then you're chasing your own tail.

An opinion poll for BBC's *Newsnight* conducted in mid-December 2007 showed that only 2% of Basra residents believed that the British presence had had a positive effect on their province. The day after the British handed control of Basra back to the Iraqis (17 December 2007) a Ministry of Defence report said that Iraq was still beset by 'violence and instability'. A report published by the Commons Defence Committee at the beginning of December 2007 admitted that the UK was handing over control of Basra despite failing in its goal to establish security. It explained that:

> the relative security of Basra is said to owe more to the dominance of militias and criminal gangs, who have achieved a fragile balance in the city, than to the success of the multinational and Iraqi security forces in tackling the root causes of the violence.

Toby Dodge, an Iraq expert at London University, said that British policy in Basra had been doomed from the start. 'We never had anything like enough troops or resources on the ground. Since we were never able to help the ordinary people of Basra, we simply set the policy to fit the resources.'

THE ISLAMISATION OF SOUTHERN IRAQ

'Welcome to Tehran.' This comment from a senior Iraqi general in Basra's interior ministry summarised the influence of the Islamists in southern Iraq. In his article about the city published in *The Guardian* on 19 May 2007, Ghaith Abdul-Ahad asked the general about British claims that the security situation was improving. His reply was withering:

> The British came here as military tourists. They committed huge mistakes when they formed the security forces. They appointed militiamen as police officers and chose not to confront the militias. We have reached a point where the militias are a legitimate force in the street.

After 30 years of neglect and repression by Saddam's government, which culminated in the draining of the marshlands and the displacement of thousands of people (see page 257), the towns and cities of the south are dusty, cranky and impoverished, the inhabitants tough, self-reliant and traditionally suspicious of outsiders, hence the ever-increasing growth of the grass roots insurgency against foreign forces.

The people, made over-expectant by Western promises and media hype, are frustrated by the snail's pace of reconstruction. The Coalition has invested US$140m in Maysan Province, but the whole infrastructure needs replacing, rather than applying 'quick patches'. The billions of dollars that must be provided for new powerplants and water treatment facilities is not there, and protests against the occupation are continuing.

Samawah, 271km southeast of Baghdad, with a population of 600,000, is a success story. There have been no serious incidents in the town, where Japanese troops are assisting with water purification, rebuilding of schools and hospitals, and other humanitarian projects.

The first reports of impoverished southern farmers growing opium emerged in May 2007 from Diwaniya, where the drug started to replace rice cultivation on well- irrigated land around towns like Ash Shamiyan, Al Ghammas and Ash Shinafiyah. Local gangs have been financing the new cash crop, which was once grown in 3,400BC by the ancient Sumerians, who called it *hul gil* (joy plant). Writing in *The Independent* on 23 May 2007 Patrick Cockburn noted that as in Afghanistan after the fall of the Taliban in 2001, conditions of primal anarchy are ideal for criminal gangs and drug smugglers and producers. The smugglers are also using Iraq, and especially its porous border with Iran, as a transit point to send heroin to markets in Saudi Arabia and the Gulf.

Gangs, religious parties and militias have filled the gap resulting from the collapse of the Baath Party and Saddam's government. They are not united in their vision of the kind of society they want to create, but they all oppose the presence of foreign forces just as they were all opposed to the previous regime.

The Shias do not have one leader. Grand Ayatollah Ali Al-Sistani is the highest ranking religious leader of Iraq's Shia majority (see page 248). Moqtada Al-Sadr (see pages 254–5) and Abdul Aziz Al-Hakim, leader of the Supreme Islamic Council Iraq (previously known as the Supreme Council for the Islamic Revolution in Iraq, or SCIRI) are among the most influential religious figures.

The United Iraqi Alliance (al-Itilaf) is the main Shia coalition grouping, which won the largest number of votes in the two elections held in 2005 (see pages 130–2, 134). This coalition is led by the **Supreme Islamic Council of Iraq** (which converted its armed wing, the Badr Brigade, into a civilian organisation, even though the militia is still active) and one of the factions of the Islamic Dawa Party. Other UIA members include the **Islamic Virtue Party (al-Fadhila)**, a branch of the Sadrist movement which has a number of parliamentary seats. The Sadrist movement is also represented by **Al-Risaliyun** (Upholders of the Message) and the **National Independent Cadres and Elites**.

Other Islamic parties include:

- The **Hizbullah Movement**, founded in the marshes during the first Gulf War to fight Saddam's regime. It is now very influential in southern Iraq, especially Maysan province, and has a popular weekly newspaper, *Al-Baynaa*.
- The **Islamic Action Organisation**, aligned to the Dawa Party. It was formed in 1961 in Kerbala and played a part in the 1991 uprising.
- **Revenge of God**, a radical Shia movement led by Khaled Hassan Chiyad. Dozens of similar movements have sprung up in Basra, Amarah and Nasiriyah, headed by radical clerics who advocate Sharia law, including the amputation of hands for theft.
- The **Islamic Movement for Kurdish Shias** led by Sheikh Assad al-Faeli, a senior Shia cleric who returned to Iraq after two decades of exile in Iran.

The Shia movements are hierarchical and authoritarian, yet they appeal to the people who have traditionally given obedience to jurisprudents.

The inhabitants of the heartland of Shia Islam have welcomed the ousting of Saddam's regime as a signal for the end of oppression and a chance to gain political power from which they had been excluded since the days of the Ottoman Empire. But this new-found freedom is viewed with concern by moderate Shias and intellectuals. In the words of Iraqi writer Nabil Yunis Damman: 'We do not wish to emerge from the cloak of fanatical nationalism only to enter into the cloak of religious extremism.'

In his book *Occupational Hazards: My Time Governing in Iraq*, Rory Stewart creates an insight into the views of radical clerics:

I asked him [a young cleric] what he thought about the current situation. He answered that he was sorry that we were not cutting the hands off thieves. It was ordained in the Koran.

'But even Imam Khomeini did not encourage people in Iran to cut off hands,' I said.

'Imam Khomeini has his opinion and I have mine,' the cleric replied.

The South THE ISLAMISATION OF SOUTHERN IRAQ

11

I asked which Grand Ayatollah he had followed.
'I followed myself,' he replied.

Violence seems to be part of the way of life in the south, whose inhabitants have been the victims of suicide bombings and bloody rivalry in the religious establishment. On 10 May 2003 the spiritual leader and head of the Supreme Islamic Council Iraq, Mohammed Baqir Al-Hakim, returned to his country after 23 years spent in exile in Iran. He was killed, along with 79 others, by a car bomb in Najaf on August 29. Majid Al Khoei, a Shia moderate with close ties to the British government, was killed in inter-Shia rivalry on 11 April – just ten days after he set foot in his country following more than a decade in exile.

Moqtada Al-Sadr's Mehdi Army and the Coalition clashed in Najaf and in other cities in the south – Hilla, Samarra, Diwaniya, Kut, Al Hayy, Nasiriyah, Amarah and Basra – between June and August 2004. There were also violent clashes in Baghdad's Sadr City (see pages 209–11). The violence was sparked off by the closing of Sadr's newspaper and was finally resolved after the intervention of Grand Ayatollah Al Sistani. US Defense Secretary Donald Rumsfeld claimed that US forces had killed between 1,500 and 2,500 insurgents, while an Iraqi health ministry official estimated that 400 civilians had been killed and 2,500 wounded during the fighting in Najaf.

Some of the strongest criticism of the central government, although led by a Shia coalition, the United Iraqi Alliance, has come from southerners who feel marginalised. They claim most of the government jobs have been given to Shias from Baghdad, Najaf and Kerbala, and returning exiles. In 2005 the people of Basra went on strike due to grievances about the oil industry, petrol prices and relations with British forces.

In an article *The Maliki Government: what it could mean to Southern Iraq*, Reidar Visser, research fellow at the Norwegian Institute of International Affairs, points out that several of the southern demands appear to be eminently negotiable: southern under-representation in government bureaucracy and in Iraqi diplomatic missions abroad could be remedied and southern demands for regional oil quotas could be addressed in a 'softer' manner through long-term development funds set aside to address regional under-development.

The central government in Baghdad is concerned about Iran's substantial influence in Iraq through political parties, like the Supreme Islamic Council, that have been sponsored by Iran and given arms. A missile that shot down a helicopter over Basra on 26 May 2006 came from Iran. 'The only thing that I've seen get any better here is the weapons they're using against us,' quipped Corporal Patrick Owens. Iraqi Vice President Tareq Al Hashemi said on 20 May 2007: 'Iran should not be tempted to interfere in my country. At the end of the day I would like the Iranians to end their interference.'

In May 2007 Iran and the USA held the first public bilateral talks in 30 years. The USA called for Iran to stop arming Iraqi militants and the Iranians proposed setting up of a regular 'trilateral security mechanism' incorporating Iraq, Iran and the USA.

Iran-friendly clerical rule seems inevitable, especially after the British withdrawal, probably some time in 2008. For Furat Al Shara, the head of the Supreme Islamic Council, peace will come:

above **Dohuk in winter** (CK) page 338

below **The walls of Erbil's UNESCO-listed Citadel** (CK) page 339

Carpet and antiques seller in
Baghdad's bazaar (GH) page 215

top **Market in Suleimaniyah**
(ML) page 181

above **Tea stall outside the Great Mosque, Kufa**
(GH) page 255

right **Antiques in Baghdad's Green Zone**
(CS) page 207

top left   **Kurdish men in traditional costume** (GH) page 144
top right   **Lady in Kurdish traditional dress** (GH) page 144
above left   **School girls, Baghdad** (CS) page 215
above right   **Kurdish men play the ancient game of the north, similar to draughts, Erbil** (GH) page 177

top Water buffalo cool themselves while women pole through the marsh waters
(AB) page 259

above A *muddhi* – traditional reed-built meeting house, Houta Basra province
(AB) page 260

left Women returning to their village, Houta Basra province
(AB) page 265

above left **Man working on a date plantation, northwest of Qurnah**
(AB) page 271

above right **Fishing on the Euphrates**
(AB) page 266

right **View across the Euphrates to the town of Chibayish in Basra Province**
(AB) pages 256–7

top   Iraq National Museum, Baghdad. Two galleries are set to re-open in 2008. (GH) Page 344

above   Artists paint the bomb-blasted walls of Baghdad, 2007 (CS) page 280

left   Maysaloun Faraj is determined that Iraqi art should be brought to the fore. *Blind man in Market* (Hafidh al-Drobi) is displayed in her gallery. (MF) Page 281

Just accept that there will be an Islamist government that will fall short of Iranian theocracy, but that will be nothing like Western-style democracy.

A strict code of Islamic law is being imposed. The women are clad in black, none venturing outside without a headscarf, posters of Islamic clerics decorate the streets, Iranian goods are in the shops, Iranian currency can be used in the holy cities and Farsi is spoken as well as Arabic. Like the Kurds in the north, the Islamists in the south are creating a separate state, which may one day sever its links with the rest of the country.

THE HOLY CITIES

NAJAF AND KERBALA Daniel Bates and Amal Rassam, authors of *Peoples and Cultures of the Middle East*, described how:

Shahs, sultans, emperors and other rulers have all made gifts in demonstration of piety and perhaps in pursuit of legitimacy. Even quite recently the former Empress of Iran, Farah Pahlavi, donated two massive gold and jewel-encrusted doors to the sanctuary of Kerbala. The cupolas of leading shrines are leafed in gold and coloured mosaics, and mirrors and gold and silver calligraphy embellish the walls.

Every year thousands of pilgrims flock to Najaf and Kerbala, some with donations of gold and expensive jewellery. Ashura, the tenth day of the Islamic month of Muharram (the Islamic calendar is based on the lunar cycle), when the massacre at Kerbala occurred in AD680 (see page 233), is one of the most popular times of pilgrimage. Events surrounding the death of Hussein are recounted in Shia mosques throughout the world and acted out as a passion play (*shabih*) accompanied by frenzied grief and tears, wailing and even self-flagellation in public. At the beginning of the 20th century, the shabih was so popular that in some villages in southern Iraq as many as 60 'actors' took part. As in the battle of Kerbala, they were divided into two rival camps. During the play actors on horseback were cheered by the audience who handed them rifles. The play ended when bullets were shot over the heads of the actors. In Najaf even Ottoman soldiers took part in the shabih.

Throughout the 19th century the Iraqi Shias were united during the procession in Kerbala. Sometimes it was difficult to distinguish where religion ended and politics began as the processions in Kerbala and other cities often turned into anti-government protests. From 1930 successive Iraqi regimes struck back by banning the processions, the people protested and the cycle of resistance and oppression continued until the overthrow of Saddam. Shia pilgrims are now being targeted by suicide bombers.

Both Najaf and Kerbala made their money from the steady flow of pilgrims, mainly from Iran and India. The pilgrims had to be housed, fed, taken to the shrines and even provided with a 'temporary wife'.

Things started to change during the 1920s and 1930s. The pilgrims began arriving by train, rather than on camels and mules, and they needed passports and visas, and could only stay in the holy cities for three months. The Iranian

Constantly referred to in the media as the most influential man in the country, Grand Ayatollah Ali Sistani is the most senior Shia cleric in Iraq and the prime *marja*, or spiritual reference, for Shia Muslims everywhere. He is thought of as a peaceful and wise religious leader.

He, and only he, was able to derail American plans for the drafting of a constitution before elections, and he brought a halt to three weeks of fighting in Najaf between Moqtada Al-Sadr's Mehdi Army and American forces in 2004.

The grand ayatollah is totally opposed to violence: he has urged his followers not to fight the occupation forces. When terrorists set off suicide car bombs killing hundreds of Shia pilgrims he ordered no retribution.

Now a frail man (he was in the UK for treatment of a heart complaint in 2004) with a black turban and snow-white beard, Sistani was born in Mashhad, Iran, on 4 August 1930. He began his religious education in the holy city of Qom. In 1951 he travelled to Iraq to study in Najaf under the late Grand Ayatollah Abul-Qassim Khoei. When Khoei died in 1992 he ascended to the rank of grand ayatollah and made Najaf his permanent home.

Keeping a low profile and living in virtual seclusion in a decrepit alley in Najaf enabled Sistani to survive the persecution that killed many other Shia clerics in Saddam's Iraq. After the American invasion he never gave speeches or preached at Friday prayers. His influence is exerted through an extensive network of junior clerics who convey his teachings to every Shia neighbourhood in Iraq, and through an internet company with 66 employees in the Iranian holy city of Qom. He regularly answers questions emailed to him by followers.

In his fatwas Sistani has urged Shia clerics to get involved in politics. He supported the elections, but when the United Iraqi Alliance, a mixture of Shia religious parties, secular groups, independents and a few Sunnis and Kurds, won he said: 'You were elected so it's up to you now. Don't drag me into it.' He has refused to meet American officials, fearful that such contacts could be interpreted as an endorsement of the occupation. He has also kept his distance from Iranian officials.

Austerity is the hallmark of his lifestyle. When his air conditioner broke down he had it repaired and gave the new one purchased by his staff to a poor family. Yet he is responsible for a multi-million dollar network of charities and religious foundations throughout the world.

In September 2006, the grand ayatollah gave up trying to restrain his followers and conceded that there was nothing he could do to prevent Iraq sliding towards civil war, especially after his calls for an end to the fighting between the Mehdi Army and American forces in Nasiriyah were ignored. In September 2006, his spokesman Ali Al-Jaberi commented that after the war politicians visited Sistani every month. But no-one has visited him for two or three months. He is very angry that this is happening.

To date Sistani has not appointed a successor. Moderate Shias fear that the vacuum he leaves will be filled by radicals eager to see the Shia south split from the rest of Iraq.

government made life difficult for its citizens (and for the Iraqis) by stopping the pilgrimage under the pretext that it was an obsolete Shia tradition that wasted money outside the country. Inside Iraq itself the wealthy Shias did not support religious activity to any great extent and were not noted for their generosity in caring for the poor and needy. Religious schools were on a downward spiral; Iraq was no longer the Shia seat of learning; Iranian students who did not receive allowances from home left Iraq; the secular education system competed with the religious establishment; the mujtahids did not always use the funds they received for the benefit of their students; and the previously independent religious establishment began to rely on the state, through the Ministry of Education and Awqaf Directorate, for funds. The Iranian city of Qom replaced Najaf as the centre of Shia learning.

During the Iran–Iraq War (1980–88) Iranian pilgrims were not allowed to visit the holy cities, whose economy suffered greatly. Today Iranian pilgrims and Shia pilgrims from all over the world are once again making their way to Najaf and Kerbala.

After the imposition of sanctions in 1990 the majority of tourists who visited Iraq were pilgrims. This is still the case. Thousands of Iranian pilgrims are braving bandits, minefields, border guards and a barren, sun-baked no-man's land *en route* to the holy cities. As many as 10,000 religious tourists a day have been seen in the holy cities, bringing in revenue of around US$2 billion a year.

Najaf Najaf, 190km south of Baghdad and 80km from Kerbala, was the power centre of Shia Islam, referred to as a world within a city. It had a life independent of Iraq's Ottoman rulers, with around 20 religious schools at the end of the 19th century. The Wahhabis placed the city under siege towards the end of the 18th century.

During Ottoman times, the city was plagued by two main problems that discouraged pilgrims: raids by Arab tribes and the lack of a reliable water supply. At the beginning of the 17th century the number of inhabited houses in the city dropped from 3,000 to 30. The water problems continued until 1803, when the Hindiyya canal was built. The pilgrims returned and doubled the city's population from 30,000 to 60,000.

The city on the edge of the desert was basically an Arab city influenced by tribes. The Zuqurt and the Shumurt expelled the Ottomans from Najaf in 1915 and ruled until the arrival of the British. They did not relinquish power without a struggle. The city's four quarters were then controlled by the heads of the Zuqurt and the Shumurt, who received an allowance from the British.

In 1918 the British tried to increase their control of the city and Captain Marshall was put in charge of Najaf. Yitzak Nakash, author of *The Shi'is of Iraq*, described how Marshall took up residence in a house just outside the city walls:

> He attempted to organise a police force in the city not subject to the authority of the four sheikhs and sought to regulate the payment of municipal taxes. At his suggestion the allowance that had been paid to the four sheikhs was discontinued. Faced with a serious threat to their authority the sheikhs rebelled and had Marshall murdered.

But the city's problems were not over. Its inability to supply the Anaza, a tribe allied to the British, with grain, ignited a rebellion supported by the junior *ulama* (scholars) and *mujtahids* (scholars who can make legal decisions based on their interpretation of legal sources and the Koran). It ended with a siege of the city, the cutting off of its water supply and the end of the rule of the Zuqurt and Shumurt.

When they next came to Iraq, foreign forces received more of a welcome in Najaf, where they were greeted as liberators rather than occupiers. Grand Ayatollah Sistani told his followers not to interfere with the Americans and they were cheered as they drove through the city. But the ayatollah refused the protection of the Americans and did not meet them.

Some of the city's residents provided information about the remnants of the Iraqi army, while others approached the Americans with 'to do' lists – turn on the electricity, provide water, etc. The Baath Party headquarters was looted with chants of 'Bush, Bush' as gasoline cans, telephones and weapons disappeared.

The steady flow of pilgrims into the city resulted in a commercial boom and the rapid construction of hotels started along the thoroughfare leading to Imam Ali's shrine.

Najaf is a city of alleyways, markets and squares, the most famous being the large market that starts at the eastern wall of the city and ends at the shrine of Imam Ali. Everything is available here, from satellite phones to religious texts and souvenirs, including brightly coloured paintings of imams and mosques – Najaf is a city where religious, political and commercial ambitions meet.

The army of the Shia firebrand cleric Moqtada Al-Sadr occupied the city in April 2004 and were finally ousted in August by a combination of American bombardment and mediation by Ayatollah Al-Sistani. The fighting resulted in an estimated US$550 million-worth of damage: while the shrine itself was not damaged, the old city and the markets suffered extensively. Many graves in the old and new cemetery were completely destroyed. In October 2004, 1,500 of 9,000 claims involving death or injury had been paid.

The expansion of the shrine by 120m started on 4 October 2004 at an estimated cost of US$50m. The Ministry of Municipalities and Housing, in consultation with the clergy, is organising a competition for international companies to prepare plans for rebuilding the old city. This will give the thousands of pilgrims who visit the shrine more room.

Large scale development projects have been undertaken in Najaf: three new electrical substations were completed in April 2006 at a cost of US$4.8 million each. A new road is being built from Kerbala to the old city in Najaf. Ambitious plans have been made for the construction of parks, gardens, resthouses and a housing complex (Al-Najaf Sea). The Imam Ali International Airport is currently under construction in the eastern side of the city.

Najaf, a major seminary centre for the training of Shiite clergymen (*al-Hawzah al-`Ilmiyyah*), is a city of mosques and shrines. The most famous is the shrine of Imam Ali and the Wadi Al Salam cemetery. The tomb is covered with windows of gold and silver and the courtyard has four gates with arches. The golden dome of the tomb has 7,777 gold bricks and two golden minarets about 35m high made of 40,000 gold bricks about half a centimetre thick. Visitors have adorned the shrine with magnificent gifts, including a pearl-covered crown and a purple velvet carpet embroidered with diamonds, pearls and other precious stones.

A US tank veered hard right, smashing a tombstone; a mortar slammed into a catacomb with an ear-shattering roar and Iraqi snipers dodged amongst the graves; it was hard to imagine that the hallowed cemetery at Najaf is also known as 'The Valley of Peace'.

But this was August 2004 and the sacred burial site – the biggest in the world – became a battleground after followers of the radical Shia cleric Moqtada Al-Sadr occupied the nearby Imam Ali Mosque, a site so holy Imam Ali himself declared it: 'the gates to paradise.'

I was working for the US television network Fox News and we were the first Western crew to set up a live link from the graveyard, to cover the unfolding Najaf conflict.

It was mid-summer and the 45°C temperature was overwhelming; so hot the heat from the blistered earth burned my soles through my shoes.

As far as the eye could see: thousands of graves, mausoleums and catacombs; quite literally a city of the dead. More than five million people have been buried in this hallowed graveyard since the 7th century AD, and, covering five square miles, it's the biggest on the planet.

Some family vaults were topped with adobe-style homes, made from a mixture of what appeared to be ochre-coloured mud and rocks. Entering the ground floor, here was where the body was prepared for internment, and set in the floor a kind of trap-door through which you could see the coffins on shelves.

We interviewed one of Al-Sadr's supporters, Abdul Zahra Hadi, who had been sniping at US soldiers.

'We ambush their patrols and the Americans cannot get into the area, because it's full of winding lanes and underground mausoleums.' he said. 'We can hit and run and hide inside the many tombs.'

Incredibly, despite heavy fighting the graveyard was still functioning, and we met the Ansari family from Tehran, Iran who had brought a grandfather for burial. The head of the family, Ali, 52, told me his father's dearest wish was to be buried there. So, despite the dangers from flying bullets and mortar rounds in the graveyard, they had come.

The stand-off at Najaf by Moqtada Al-Sadr and his followers had ended by September 2004 and once again the graveyard returned to tranquility.

But the damage to hundreds of graves and mausoleums was immense; human remains, buried for centuries, had been disturbed. Even the dead did not sleep in the so-called Valley of Peace.

John Cookson, former Baghdad correspondent for Fox News

Mosques are found on almost every street and in every square. Prominent scholars from well known Najafi families have their own mosques, the most famous being Al-Tusi, Al-Hindi, Al-Hannanah Al-Shakiry and Kashif Al-Ghita.

Najaf is also a city of religious seminaries, libraries and cultural centres. It is the home of Ayatollah Al-Sistani (see page 248). The religious university, known as Hawza Ailmiah, is the focal point of religious movements and has produced many well known poets and religious intellectuals.

The South **THE HOLY CITIES**

The shining golden dome of the mosque in Najaf is visible from a distance of 75km. In *Iraq: Land of Two Rivers*, Gavin Young recalls:

> The façade of Ali's tomb, seen from the northern gateway, is richly beautiful – the gold tiles have darkened handsomely with age. And through the doorway to the tomb itself you can see the glistening stalactite effect of mirrors and the harsh neon lights that are features of all major shrines of Iraq. Pink, blue and yellow patterns of birds and flowers bedeck the archways into the courtyard. Heavy wooden doors lead in from the street opposite the covered *suq* (market) where you can buy worry-beads (*sibhas*), finely worked gold ornaments, or ankle-length cloaks for winter or summer, some hemmed with gold braid.

Ali's burial place was not revealed during the time of the Umayyads and the first mosque was not built until AD791 by Harun Al Rashid. The tomb is said to have been built by Azud ed Dowleh in AD977. The monument was destroyed by fire and rebuilt before the visit of Malik Shah in 1086, and continual reconstruction and renovation has been carried out over succeeding centuries.

The famous religious public libraries are Imam Al-Hakin in Al-Rasoul Street, Al-Alameen Library in Al-Tusi Mosque, Al-Haidary Library and Ameer Al-Muminin Library, which contains a Koran written in Kufic style by Imam Ali himself. Some Korans have been written on snake skins. The prominent families also have great libraries.

The repression of Shia intellectual and religious life, a hallmark of Saddam's regime, has ended, and cultural establishments are restoring ancient manuscripts and saving them on CDs. The Kashif Al-Ghita religious school has saved more than 1,800 religious manuscripts on 74 CDs.

The city's heritage is in the old city around the shrine of Imam Ali. Most of the traditional houses have a cool basement know as a *sardab*, where people sleep during the hot summer months. The modern city, with its wide streets and large buildings, is far from the shrine.

Kerbala The name Kerbala is derived from the Babylonian word *kerb* (a prayer room) and *El*, Aramaic for God – hence God's temple. The city, 80km southwest of Baghdad, was strongly influenced by the Persians, who were the dominant community, making up 75% of the population at the turn of the 20th century, when there were around 50,000 people in the city.

Like Najaf, Kerbala also suffered from severe water shortage, which reduced the number of pilgrims. The water problems were largely solved by the building of a dam at the head of the Husayniya Canal, and in 1737 the city replaced Isfahan as the main centre of Shia scholarship. The Ottoman governor Hassan Pasha (1704–23) made life easier for pilgrims by building and renovating inns *en route* from Baghdad. In 1801 the city was sacked by the Wahhabis.

In Ottoman times, when Kerbala began functioning as what the British described as 'a self-governing, semi-alien republic', Najib Pasha occupied the city in 1843 and returned it to Ottoman control. Many students and mujtahids moved to Najaf, which became the main Shia religious centre.

Kerbala maintained strong links with Iran. The Kammuna family, related to the Shahs, were custodians of the shrines and practically ran the city until the time of the British mandate. The most influential figures were two brothers, Fakhr al-Din and Muhammad Ali Kammuna, who were both deported, the former for organising supplies to the Turkish forces and the latter for spreading anti-British propaganda. The control of the city passed to seven mukhtars, who started receiving a salary from the municipality. They were succeeded by Iraqi government employees.

The influence of the Persians was curbed both by British attempts to establish an Arab character for the city and a series of nationality laws, including a law that made it illegal for foreigners to occupy government posts. Arabic became the language of administration. By 1957, Persians accounted for only 12% of the city's population. Those who remained accepted Iraqi nationality.

After the popular uprising in 1991 (see pages 240–1) the Persian-looking bazaars of Kerbala were not rebuilt, but the pilgrimage continued. In March 2004 thousands of pilgrims converged on Kerbala, beating their breasts with their fists and symbolically whipping their backs with chains. A film, *The Road to Kerbala*, was made by Katia Jarjoura, who accompanied the pilgrims on the 100km trek from Baghdad to mourn the killing of the Prophet's grandson (see page 247). The ritual was banned for 30 years under Saddam. The excessive bloodletting of 2004 has been quietly discouraged. It is also discouraged in Iran.

The 3 March 2004 was the Shias' September 11: Iraq was plunged into rivers of blood when suicide bombs and mortars fell among the crowds at Kerbala and Kazimiya, killing 180. A heavy presence of police and Iraqi troops enabled three million people to gather for a ritual in Kerbala on 9 September 2006, to be addressed by the head of the Supreme Islamic Council Abd al-Aziz Al Hakim, who called for an autonomous federal region in the south.

In January 2007, guerrillas posing as Americans entered a government compound, killing a soldier and driving away with four others, who were later killed. In April 2007 suicide bombers struck twice in Kerbala: a car bomb exploded in front of the Abbas Ali shrine killing 68 people and a suicide bomber killed 42 people at the bus station.

The piety and unshakeable belief of the Muslims who visit the sanctuaries is illustrated by heart-rending acts of devotion, such as kissing the grails that surround the shrines. The atmosphere in this oasis of spirituality, in a country often characterised by violence, disaster and suffering, can be overwhelming.

The mosques of Hussein and Abbas stand out on their own as islands in the middle of a city whose activities are centred around the needs of pilgrims. In May 2007 final approvals were completed for the establishment of Kerbala International Airport. The town is split into two: Old Kerbala, famous for its shrines, and New Kerbala, the residential district containing Islamic schools and government buildings. There are more than 100 mosques and 23 religious schools in the city.

Hussein's mosque and shrine have been built on the site of the Battle of Kerbala, fought in AD680 (see pages 233–4). It has a gilded dome surrounded by two golden minarets. The date of the construction of the first sanctuary is unknown. In AD850, Mutawakkil ordered its destruction. In AD979 Azud el Dowleh, a Persian governor, built a mosque on the site, which was burned down in 1016 and subsequently rebuilt.

The shrine consists of the mausoleum, galleries, hall and courtyard measuring 95m by 75m. There are ten gates, each with an archway and decorated with tiles and Arabesque. The Mecca gate is also known as 'The Golden Gate' as it is covered in gold and silver. The shrine has 65 galleries, with rooms specially reserved for religious students, which later became graves for the *ulama* (scholars).

The second major shrine in Kerbala is that of Abbas, Hussein's half brother, who died with him at the battle of Kerbala. The shrine, with nine gates, is 4,370m square. On the sides of the courtyard are several galleries and rooms in which several ulama, sultans, emirs and ministers have been buried.

In the middle of the shrine is the tomb of Abbas, over which there is a huge dome with Koranic verses and the Prophet's sayings inscribed in gold. The dome is flanked by two tall minarets. The mausoleum is made of pure gold and silver, with inlays of mina (blue stones) and precious stones.

The vault of Abbas stores treasures and antiques that cannot be valued. It has more than 16 Korans, one of which is written in Kufic style, plus gold, golden lamps and Persian carpets, gold crowns, and chains inlayed with precious stones.

MOQTADA AL-SADR: FIREBRAND CLERIC OF THE DOWNTRODDEN SHIA

The presence of Moqtada Al-Sadr and his 70,000-strong Mehdi Army (officially stood down in May 2007) has been felt in Iraq since the overthrow of Saddam. He is extremely popular among the poor Shia masses, numbering between three and five million, and many Iraqis see him as a heroic symbol of resistance to the occupation.

He identifies Iraq's main enemies as the occupation and its forces, the Saddamists (Baathists) and the Nawasib (radical Sunni Muslims who see the Shias as heretics who have to be exterminated. He is also opposed to Al-Qaeda). Despite his anti-American stance he has participated in the political process and his followers have 32 out of 275 seats in parliament, with the power of veto over the choice of prime minister. They also have six ministers running the health and transport departments.

Al-Sadr's appeal comes from the mixture of religion (he calls for an Islamic democracy) and nationalism, which he espouses. His background has also proved invaluable. Even though he is only in his 30s, his followers have elevated him to the rank of *hujjat al-Islam* (Sign of Islam, the third highest rank in the Shia clerical hierarchy). He is the youngest son of Muhammad Sadiq Baqr al-Sadr, a senior cleric assassinated in 1999 by Saddam's agents after trying to counter secularism in Iraqi society, opposing the Iraqi Communist Party and the Baath Party, and helping set up the religious Dawa Party. When Saddam's regime was ousted, Al-Sadr, from his power base of a network of charitable institutions, instructed his followers to distribute food and patrol the streets in the poor Shia suburbs of Baghdad.

His ability to mobilise the Shia masses was clearly illustrated in April 2007 when an estimated 1.5m people turned up for a massive rally in Najaf demanding that the government agree to a timetable for the withdrawal of foreign troops. The Mehdi Army now controls Sadr City, the Baghdad shanty town with a population of two million, much of Baghdad and some areas in southern Iraq.

KUFA Kufa, 10km north of Najaf, was founded in AD618 by Saad bin Abi Waqqas, the Commander-in-Chief of the Arab forces. It was the first capital of the Abbasid Empire (see pages 49–55). Before Baghdad became established as the capital, Kufa, Basra and Wasit were the most important towns in the country. In the early days of Islam, Kufa was the bastion of support for Ali in his struggle against Muawiyah (see page 233).

From an important political-military centre, its role changed to that of a cultural centre where one of Islam's main codes of law (the Hanifa code) was developed.

Today, it is a pleasant, if somewhat fly-blown, town with the second oldest mosque in Iraq, containing the tombs of many pious men of religion, including Aqeel Bin Talib and Hani bin Urwa, and the pulpit of Ali, where he was murdered while praying (see page 233). The mosque area has been heavily restored with new walls around the mosque. The shrines have also been rebuilt and embellished.

In August 2004 two mortar shells fell on the mosque compound, which had been taken over by Al-Sadr's militia (see below). Al-Sadr used this mosque for a major speech in May 2007 when he returned to Iraq after four months in Iran.

The House of the Caliphate (Dar Al-Imara) has been reconstructed. It has an outer square wall, each side 170m long, 4m thick, with six semicircular

---

The Shias rely increasingly on the Mehdi Army to protect them from sectarian violence and suicide bombers, but Al-Sadr denies that death squads, who are killing Sunnis, are really members of the Mehdi Army. His followers have clashed regularly with American troops, the Iraqi army and police and members of rival Shia militias.

He has been a thorn in the side of the Americans who have put him on top of their hit list. But, as Patrick Cockburn writing in *The Independent* on 15 February 2007 pointed out:

> President Bush shows no sign of learning from his failures in Iraq since 2003. For almost four years he has been fighting the Sunni community. Now, by confronting Moqtada, he is moving towards armed conflict with the Shia as well.

An attempt to assassinate Al-Sadr has been revealed in the book *The Occupation of Iraq: Winning the War, Losing the Peace* by Ali Allawi, the former finance minister. The Iraqi National Security Adviser, Dr Mowaffaq Al-Ruabie, negotiated an end to fighting with Al-Sadr in Najaf in August 2004. Al-Sadr wanted the old city of Najaf to have special status like the Vatican. Al-Ruabie was due to meet Al-Sadr in a house in Najaf to finalise the agreement, but as he headed for the house marines bombarded it. Al-Sadr had not arrived yet and managed to escape.

Fearing for his life, Al-Sadr left Iraq in January 2007 ahead of a joint US-Iraqi security sweep in Baghdad and members of the Mehdi Army were stood down. He returned in May, and in a characteristically fiery sermon in Kufa to 6,000 worshippers called for Sunni–Shia co-operation to end the occupation. During his absence he withdrew six ministers loyal to him from the cabinet to pressure the prime minister into setting a timetable for the withdrawal of US troops.

towers punctuating each side, with the exception of the northern side, which has only two towers.

The first mosque at Kufa was marked out by Al Waqqas in AD638. Its boundaries were fixed by a man who shot an arrow towards the south, then another towards the north, another to the west and a fourth to the east. It was almost square in plan and enclosed by a ditch only. Its sole architectural feature was a covered colonnade, which ran the whole length of the south side. Little changed until AD670 when it was enlarged and rebuilt by Ziyard ibn Abini. The mosque underwent some restoration in the Umayyad period. An interesting account written in 1187 notes high marble columns supporting a flat roof. Almost nothing remains from this time. The present mosque, which is of quite recent construction, still retains several ancient architectural features and has an additional monument constructed during the 14th century.

A brick-built monument, Safina (The Ship) in the court of the Kufa Mosque, is partly below ground level. Its important features are *iwans* (entrance arches) and a unique mihrab, the niche indicating the direction of Mecca, which believers must face when praying. The monument is shaped like a boat. Local tradition identifies the site with the ship of the Prophet Noah that was made by the order of God shortly before the flood. This is allegedly the place from where the ship departed. The Sufis consider it a monument worth visiting.

In **Kifal** near Kufa is the shrine of the Jewish prophet Ezekiel, from the 6th century BC, who lived among the Jews exiled to Babylon (see pages 41–2). He warned of the destruction of Jerusalem and foretold the restoration of Israel.

UKHAIDHER   About 50km southwest of Kerbala, on the edge of the desert, lies Ukhaidher (Small Green Place) Castle, dating back to the 8th century, the beginning of the Abbasid era (see pages 49–55). An impressive monument to early Islam, the majestic structure is nearly 21m high with vaulted rooms surrounded by fortified walls.

The historical city of Ain Al-Tamr is not far away, in the midst of a large oasis. Mineral waters from numerous springs make it a very attractive place for visitors. Ain Al-Tamr was built in the pre-Christian era, but did not acquire any particular importance until the Arab conquest, when it became a flourishing military and trade centre, and birthplace of Musa Ibn Nusair, the Arab general who conquered Spain in the 8th century.

THE MARSHLANDS

> Reed-house, reed-house! Wall, O Wall, harken reed-house. O man
> of Shuruppak, son of Ubaru-Tutu: tear down your house and build a
> boat -
> abandon possessions and look for life ... and take up into the boat the
> seed of all living creatures.
>
> Epic of Gilgamesh, *The story of the flood*

A trip to the marshlands of southern Iraq was once a journey in time to the era of the Sumerians (4500–1900BC). In 1991 there were 250,000 Marsh Arabs in their ancestral homelands. In 2003 the number was 40,000. With the return of displaced persons, the total population could reach half a million. The inhabitants of this sea of reeds, which covered 15,500km² and formed a triangle between Basra, Amarah and Nasiriyah, are the ancestors of Sumerian fisher folk who lived in the area 6,000 years ago.

The Sumerians were the first inhabitants of the marshlands. According to legend, the Babylonian God Marduk, who lived in a primordial universe where 'all the lands were sea', built the first reed platform, similar to the floating reed platforms once found in Hor il-Hammar and Hor il–Hawazia. Qurnah, 72km north of Basra, where the Tigris joins the Euphrates, is said to be the site of the legendary biblical Garden of Eden and Adam's Tree, the tree of the knowledge of good and evil.

Until the intensification of drainage through the Third River Project during the late 1980s and throughout the 1990s, the Marsh Arabs, like the Sumerians, built cathedral-shaped reed houses and bitumen-covered boats and caught fish using spears. The region's thin-grained rice, introduced in around 1000BC, was considered one of the finest and most nutritious in the world.

But during the Iran–Iraq War (1980–88) the watery haven of the Marsh Arabs became a launch pad for attacks by Iranian armed forces. Iraqi army deserters and the regime's opponents also hid in the area, prompting the central government to accelerate a land reclamation project started decades earlier to drain saline water from waterlogged farmland north and west of the marshes. This idea was later modified to drain the marshes themselves. Massive engineering works, consisting of a series of dams hundreds of kilometres in length, were constructed to drain the waters of the Euphrates away from the area.

This threatened a unique culture. The poetic words of a refugee who fled from the region tell us that: 'The birds died, the animals died, the people died, the world died. There is no water, there is no life, we are naked in our misery.'

But the tragic story, summarised in this poignant poem, has a happy ending. As the former regime ended, people began to open floodgates and break down embankments that had been built to drain the marshlands. By mid-2004, the marsh dwellers had re-flooded many of the areas that were drained.

In 2003 Basra Marsh was linked with the central marsh when the Iraqi army blew up a road leading to Basra to stop the advance of the British army. The Huwaiza Marsh on the Iran–Iraq border was re-flooded with the assistance of Iranian engineers.

Satellite images and analysis by the United Nations Environment Pro-gramme (UNEP) show that almost 50% of the total marshlands area has been re-flooded, with seasonal fluctuations – a stark positive contrast to 2001, when 90% of the marshlands had been lost.

Writing in *The Independent* on 5 January 2004 from the Sahel River, southern Iraq, Robert Fisk pointed out that many Marsh Arabs had long ago exchanged the water buffalo for the Mercedes and become traders:

> Other tribes moved in and planted crops in newly irrigated land. But Thesiger's people have survived and Saddam's regime has not. A small tide of dark-blue water was seeping back into the desert, creeping around Mahamar, Manzan, Meshal and all the lost villages of the marshes. It is a beautiful, enchanting, peaceful sight, a place where, centuries ago, the legendary Sumerian hero Gilgamesh fell asleep and let the plant of life slip from his grasp [see page 30].

11

The UNEP reported that thousands of people living in the area are now getting access to safe drinking water, and that approximately 300 Iraqis have been trained in marshland management techniques and policies. A series of community-led environmental awareness campaigns have been organised by local leaders and residents, and an internet-based Marshland Information Network (MIN) has been set up. By the middle of 2006, 23km of water distribution pipes and 86 common distribution taps had been installed. A sanitation system pilot project is being implemented in the community of Al-Chibayish, where inhabitants are facing health hazards from discharges of untreated waste-water to a nearby canal.

HISTORICAL BACKGROUND
Chronology

4500–1900BC	Sumerians pioneered the building of reed houses and the domestication of water buffalo.
AD635	Caliph Omar decreed the founding of two cities, Basra and Kufa, in the south of Iraq.
8th century	The Abbasid Caliph Harun Al Rashid succeeded in re-opening the water courses of the Babylonians.
883	Ali the Abominable, leader of a slave rebellion, who captured Basra and threatened Baghdad, was executed.
1533	The tribes of the Gharraf and the central Hawazia marshes of Basra made obeisance to the Turkish sultan, Suleiman the Magnificent, who captured Baghdad.
1865	The Ottomans who ruled Iraq paid increasing attention to the marshlands and tried to persuade the tribes to settle and cultivate land and their sheikhs to become Turkish officials.
1914–18	Struggle between the British and Ottomans for control of Iraq. The tribes in the marshlands often changed allegiances as they wanted to back the winner.
1920–30	Thousands of marshlands inhabitants left to join the newly formed Iraqi army and police force, and to work in the towns as porters, night watchmen, building workers and servants.
1950–70	Services improved in the marshlands, land reforms reduced the estates of absentee landlords, clinics and schools opened, ice factories aided fishing industry. Earlier scheme to drain saline waters from waterlogged farmland north and west of the marshlands modified to drain the marshlands themselves, with the construction of Saddam's canal.
2001	Satellite images from the US space agency NASA showed that 90% of the marshlands no longer exist.
Apr 2003	Marsh Arabs began demolishing dams that restricted water flow to the marshes.

2004

May	Some 50% of marshes already re-flooded.

Aug	United Nations Environmental Programme (UNEP) began extensive marshlands restoration project.
1 Aug	US-led troops raised the level of the river running alongside Al-Jamha village 110km north of Basra.
24 Aug	Death of Sir Wilfred Thesiger, legendary British explorer, who lived with the Marsh Arabs for several periods between 1951 and 1958.

2006

Jul	The Government of Japan carried out the second phase support for UNEP's Iraqi Marshlands restoration project.

Early history Geologists theorise that the Persian Gulf once covered the area, leaving a swamp as river sediment built up the land. The marshes are fed by the spring floods of the Tigris and Euphrates.

The Sumerians introduced the ancestors of the water buffalo from India and domesticated them in around 4000BC. The reeds, up to 6m in height, provided house-building material, the birds and fish a ready supply of food, and the self-sufficient, simple life of the marshland's inhabitants remained unchanged for centuries. Birds like duck and heron bred in the reeds and there was also a plentiful supply of carp and eel. Fishing had its own ethics. Nets were taboo and were only used by a low caste known as the berbera. The Marsh Arabs, excellent swimmers, displayed remarkable skill with a spear and could kill a fish from a moving canoe. They also laid poison bait as an aid to catching fish.

Gavin Young, author of *Return to the Marshes*, points out that life was good in those remote times:

> The green, well-watered gardens, orchards and seemingly endless date
> forests of Sumer; the gloriously intricate cobweb of canals and dykes
> that made Mesopotamia the granary of the Near East; prosperous
> farmers with their thousands upon thousands of sheep and cattle;
> singing boatmen in the giant reeds fishing and hunting undisturbed:
> such was the golden prospect when southern Iraq was young. A
> paradise – to be lost later through conflict and neglect.

The buffalo and fisher-people of the marshes could not lead their idyllic life without becoming involved in the battles of Mesopotamian history and the tooth and claw struggles between its rulers (see pages 22–43).

During the reign of the Assyrian King Sennacherib, the tribes of the marshlands rebelled and the king sent his troops into the area in canoes. His victory in the 6th century BC has been immortalised in a bas-relief that is now in the British Museum.

With the coming of Islam the pure Arab camel-breeders from the Arabian Peninsula met the marshmen, learned their ways, intermarried and introduced the Islamic faith.

After defeating the Persians in AD635, Caliph Omar decreed the founding of two cities in the south of Iraq: Basra and Kufa. Both were military bases. The houses in the two cities were at first made of reeds: the first mosques were built of reeds and clay, and then clay and brick. The two cities became major Islamic centres and Basra soon emerged as an important port due to its strategic location between East and West.

These momentous political developments proved almost fatal to the agricultural economy on which Iraq depended. The dykes, which the Sumerians had kept in immaculate condition, were left to decay until a conservation-oriented Sassanid king tried to rebuild them. Even the public execution of 40 dyke-builders who were not up to the job failed to halt the decline.

During the 8th century, the Abbasid Caliph Harun Al Rashid (see page 49) succeeded in re-opening the water courses of the Babylonians. But the perfect system of dykes with which Rashid reclaimed tracts of the marshes was destroyed by the Mongols.

Arab refugees fleeing from the Mongol hordes sought sanctuary in the marshlands. They were joined by the survivors of the great slave uprising. The black slaves, forced to drain the marshes, revolted against their inhuman treatment. Led by Ali the Abominable, they rebelled against the caliph, and from the shelter of the reed-beds carried on a guerrilla war of ambushes and night raids. Ali the Abominable captured Basra and came within 30km of Baghdad itself, but his luck ran out in AD883, 14 years after the start of the rebellion, and his head was sent to the caliph.

This insurrection established the marshes as a place of refuge for political rebels, revolutionaries and criminals. The famous 14th-century Arab explorer and historian Ibn Battuta described the region as 'a waterlogged jungle of reeds, inhabited by Arabs noted for their predatory habits. They are brigands.'

The Turkish Empire After the devastating Mongol invasion, Iraqi history became the history of the struggle between Persia and Turkey (see pages 58–9). When Baghdad fell to the Turkish Sultan Suleiman the Magnificent in 1533, the tribes of the Gharraf and the central and Hawazia marshes of Basra quickly made obeisance to him. But their rebellious nature could not be subdued until the Turkish expedition of 1546, when 300 ships were sent to the marshes. In 1549 they were up in arms again. Even after their defeat at the hands of Ali Pasha on the Euphrates, they still threatened the approaches to Basra.

Ali Pasha's enlightened rule, however, saw the establishment of a humane and liberal government within the Ottoman Empire. The arts flourished and even the Marsh Arabs were mollified for a time. But Ali Pasha's graceless successor, Hussein, infuriated the marshmen through the imposition of a buffalo tax.

The tribes of southern Iraq developed into a force to be reckoned with. The most powerful confederation was on the lower Euphrates. After a long period of feuds and bloodshed, the main tribes – the Beni Malik, the Ajwad and the Beni Said, in the area between Samawa and the Hor Al-Hammar – were united under the famous grouping known as the Muntafiq Confederation.

In *Return to the Marshes*, Gavin Young comments that during the 16th century, when the tribes in the marshlands paid nominal obeisance to the Turkish Sultan, the obscure children of the reeds had grown up:

> What were they originally but peaceful spear-fishers of Sumer, then sanctuary-givers to refugees from Assyrian 'kings of the Universe' and from Mongolian horsemen. Later the intrusive Shahs and Khans of Persia found a different sort of population. Centuries of unwelcome arrivals – foreign soldiers, tax-gatherers, cattle-rustlers, the predatory henchmen of tyrannical over-lords – had bequeathed them an intense suspicion of visitors … Transformed by constant infusions of the fiery blood of the Arabian tribes, the Medan [Marsh Arabs] still fished, kept buffaloes and grew rice, but they had become fighters, too. Pashas learned to think twice before sending expensive armies to put them in their place. The marsh people had become the Marsh Arabs, with the shrewd will-o'-the-wisp spirit of their desert kinsmen. Seba lion, they call a brave man; but they say cunning people are mithel firan – like mice, cautiously, silently, living on their wits under the ground. And so, the beau ideal of the Marsh Arabs is half-mouse, half-lion: an odd creature but, in its special habitat, not an easy one to snare.

During the four centuries of the Ottoman occupation of Iraq, there was no effective administration of the marsh region. Only during the last 50 years of Turkish rule, especially from the reign of Midhat Pasha, the Wali of Baghdad (1869–72), onwards, did the Turks establish a few gendarmeries here and there, along with administrative centres in the towns and bigger villages.

For the previous seven centuries all of Iraq's tribesmen had lived under feudal sheikdoms, with a tendency towards despotic rule. During the days of the Ottomans hardship and insecurity grew because of the destruction of irrigation works, poor communication and the lack of organised administration and law and order. The tribes lived in a state of constant hostility, which strengthened feudalism.

From 1865 onwards the Turks paid increasing attention to the marshlands. They adopted a policy of trying to induce the tribes to settle and cultivate land and their sheiks to become Turkish officials. Under Midhat Pasha, Nasir Pasha Ahl Sadun, the paramount sheikh of the Muntafiq tribal confederation, became the pasha's chosen and willing tool to tame the confederation. Midhat Pasha was even prepared to appoint him governor of Basra.

Through the long period of Ottoman rule the majority of the Shia population were dominated by Sunni Turks, so, at first, many welcomed the British occupation in 1918 at the end of World War I.

British rule During the struggle for Iraq between the British and the Ottoman Turks, some of the marsh tribes fought with the Turks, while others sided with the British. The sheiks were shrewd enough to realise that their status, power and land holdings depended on whoever won and they frequently changed allegiances. The war was a great time for replenishing the supply of rifles – again from both sides.

surrounded by smaller gods and kings. The two forces came into conflict and their infighting created the world. Man was a product of the forces of darkness, but the soul (*adam*) has its origin in the world of light. Death is the day of deliverance when the soul leaves the body and starts on a dangerous journey to the realms of light.

The Mandeans have their own language, part of the East Aramaic group with its own script related to Nabataean writing. The holy book, The Treasure (*ginza*), deals with mythological, cosmological and moral treatises and hymns and songs that focus on the fate of the soul.

The Mandeans used to live in the marshes, where they earned a reputation as the best canoe-makers and most talented carpenters. But the majority left for Baghdad during the 1950s, where they became Iraq's renowned silversmiths and goldsmiths who, in the words of the legendary British explorer Wilfred Thesiger, 'were satisfied with no less than perfection in their work.'

The Mandeans are proud of their heritage, but recruitment to the priesthood is difficult. The sect is having trouble maintaining its traditions as many of the priests have little knowledge of the old language and scriptures.

In Saddam's Iraq the Mandeans were used as a showcase to demonstrate before the glare of the international media that he was a tolerant man. Today they are worse off than under the dictator. According to the Sabian Mandean Association in Australia (SMAA), attacks by Muslims against Mandeans commenced within days of the overthrow of Saddam Hussein. Before he was assassinated, Ayatollah al-Hakim, head of the Supreme Islamic Council, decreed that Mandeans are not 'people of the Book'. In practical terms this means they can be forced to convert to Islam or be killed if they do not. Their religious classification as outcasts makes it difficult for them to find work or live in a society which is becoming rapidly Islamicised (see page 247). The SMAA continues to receive reports of forced conversion to Islam. Mandean women are often raped and murdered, their places of worship are confiscated and the police offer little protection.

The ancient sect is threatened with extinction: converts are not allowed and one is only considered a Mandean if both one's parents were Mandeans.

Under the British Mandate (1920–32) and the period of monarchic rule (1932–58), public services began to be introduced into the marshes, starting with police posts and administrative centres in the 1920s, and a few tiny schools in the 1930s.

Frequent contact between the marsh dwellers and the neighbouring towns and villages began only after World War I, with the penetration of the marshes by the Iraqi administration and the growth of law and order in the region.

The marsh dwellers began to realise that the markets of the neighbouring villages and towns were profitable places in which to sell their produce. Women began to make daily visits carrying reed mats, usually 8ft by 4ft (2.4m by 1.2m) – a major source of income and an essential house covering – buffalo and cattle dung for fuel, dairy products, fish, birds and other produce.

When this trade proved profitable, they began to spend some of the money earned on luxury articles such as sugar, tea, tobacco and cloth. Contact increased steadily until eventually townsmen started opening shops in the marsh region. Later the Marsh Arabs themselves became shopkeepers selling sugar, tea, tobacco and later aspirin, pencils and safety razors. Shops were designated by a white cloth, resembling a flag. Trade at first was by barter, according to the convenience of the shopkeepers. Canoes fitted up as floating shops also began to tour the remote parts of the marshes.

This trade and constant contact between villagers and neighbouring towns encouraged the marsh dwellers to consider leaving the marshes temporarily or even permanently. The main inducement was the readiness of the Iraqi government in the early 1920s to enlist an enormous number of young men in its newly formed army and police force. Men and women from the marshes also worked in towns as porters, night-watchmen, building workers and servants.

The slump in cereal prices during the 1920s and early 1930s compelled the government to raise taxes on produce. The sheiks passed these demands on to the peasants. In the marshlands the cruelty of the sheiks coupled with the low prices offered for their crops prompted thousands to leave. After 1931 the difficulty of finding employment in the urban areas checked the migration tide.

Iraqi independence When they first came under the direct rule of the central government in Baghdad, most of the marshlands' tribes welcomed the new regime because of the hope it gave them of throwing off the yoke of many corrupt despots and absentee landlords and of enjoying justice and security. But not all the sheiks were tyrants and the people voted for those who were genuinely concerned about their welfare to remain.

In the field of law and order the government accomplished a great deal. Blood feuds were checked, since the wronged party in a dispute was compelled to accept compensation in money and not to take any unlawful action. As the British explorer Wilfred Thesiger, who lived in the marshes of southern Iraq from 1951 until 1958, notes in *The Marsh Arabs*, the settlement of feuds was a complex affair and the truce was only negotiated for a year:

> No sheikh, however powerful, and no sayyid (a holy man who claims descent from the Prophet Mohammed), however revered, could finally settle a blood feud. Only the headman (*qalit*) could seal the pact by binding the head cloth round the reed and handing one end to either party.

Compensation in the form of women, a traditional tribal practice, was not paid in disputes settled by the government. The British paid blood money for Iraqis shot accidentally when the army tried to maintain security in the south after the 2003 war. Some locals complained they were too generous.

S M Salim, author of *Marsh Dwellers of the Euphrates Delta*, commented that during the 1920s, when the government accomplished more than the people expected, the villagers were particularly disposed to co-operate with the new regime, which promised improved living standards and an end to old extortions.

The atmosphere cooled somewhat through three decades of increasing administrative corruption, but the Minority Rights Group points out in its report *The Marsh Arabs of Iraq* that the period from the 1950s to the end of the

In his book *Occupational Hazards, My Time Governing in Iraq*, Rory Stewart, the Coalition Provisional Authority's deputy governorate co-ordinator of Maysan and Dhi Qar provinces from 2003–04, provides a penetrating insight into life in a marshlands village:

Once the old men had shaken hands and seen us depart their day was largely over. They would walk slowly back to huts or small reed shelters in mud courtyards. There they would wait out the day until the evening meal, which might be little more than bread and perhaps rice with no meat or fruit or vegetables. Some would listen to religious sermons and the news on the radio. The older men did not and often could not read and there was no electricity in the village to power a television.

At dusk the water buffalo would return to the compound, thrusting out their hairy lips and loose, bristled necks, lowing for fodder, their horns grey, cracked and mud-caked like ancient pottery. The women would push them towards the corners of the yards and squat beside them, running their fingers down each teat in turn and sometimes dropping a little of the milk on the cow's flat black nose as a reward. Families now had only one or two buffalo each. But that was enough for a glass of the strong sweet milk for dinner.

The women did much of the work: operated a loom if they had one, fetched water, washed, cared for the children and swept the thick layer of sand that accumulated daily in their huts into the street. But they were almost entirely excluded from education and the political life of the village. Often they were not welcome in the mosque. They were frequently the victims of honor killings, forced marriages and domestic violence. I never met them. But when not looking after buffalo they were known for composing and reciting poetry – oral poetry, because almost all the women were illiterate. Shortly after dark it was time to sleep, since everyone would wake early for ablutions and the dawn prayers.

Perhaps a quarter of the province lived in this fashion – though in many cases growing wheat and keeping sheep rather then relying on fish and buffalo. They did not pay taxes and they received little from the state. Legal punishments were meted out by the elders in the mudhif: people seldom used courts or the police.

I visited the community in order to learn about their political influence. I concluded they had next to none. They were too poor and too remote.

1970s was one of gradually improving, state-provided public services and land reforms. More schools were opened, small clinics were established in larger villages, and mobile health services reached into the heart of the marshes by motor boat. Doctors treated the most common diseases such as dysentery, bilharzia, skin diseases, tuberculosis and trachoma, as well as horrific injuries caused by wild pigs. Explorer Wilfred Thesiger always carried a medicine chest and treated a variety of ailments from cataracts to swollen genitals. Personal charms were also used as a protection against sickness.

A marshland village

The introduction of ice factories in the 1960s made fishing much more commercially viable and helped change attitudes to the practice of net as opposed to spear fishing.

The abolition of the sheikhs during the 1950s had the most disruptive effect on the traditional marshland social structure. Clan heads, known as *mukhtar*, who acted on behalf of the sheikh, were installed as sirkals, appointed by the governor of the province with the approval of the Interior Ministry in Baghdad.

As Gavin Young pointed out in *Return to the Marshes*, just as the post-Raj British disappeared, so did the sheikh landlords of the marsh world. After the imposition of the monarchy by the British in 1920, nationalism proliferated in the kingdom like a strong creeper grappling a wall:

> By 1958 the wall collapsed, burying not only the royal family and those close to the palace, but merchants, politicians and land-owners as well. Pompous sheiks were banished from their lands to easy exile in Baghdad, where they lived comfortably but without power.

After depriving the traditional tribal leaders, many of whom were served by slaves, of their power and status, the Iraqi authorities realised that they were having trouble controlling the marsh tribes. At first they thought they would be able to rely on the sirkals, but these government surrogates did not have the same authority as the traditional, well-respected tribal leaders. The government tried to provide public services for the marshlands' inhabitants but it remained wary and suspicious of the people, realising the difficulty of controlling an intractable area with a history of challenging government authority and providing refuge to dissidents.

The 30 years between 1950 and 1980 were a time of relative prosperity and beneficial land reform. The giant land-holdings of the tyrannical absentee landlords, who lived in stone fortresses on the edges of the marshlands, were broken down into one-and-a-half acre plots. The government provided social services such as schools and clinics. The introduction of ice factories during the 1960s made fishing more of a commercially viable proposition. Barbel, carp and binny were eagerly sought as far away as Baghdad. In the 1970s, the boat-building business was booming in Al Huwayr, a town near the junction of the Tigris and Euphrates, where 200 small canoes (*mashhufs*) were constructed every month.

During the Iran–Iraq War (1980–88) the Marsh Arabs were generally patriotic, but the army made numerous incursions into the marshlands to seek out deserters.

Saddam's regime was determined to destroy the marshlands to make military movements easier, to gain access to 50% of Iraq's oil reserves in the area, and to teach the Shias a lesson for using the region as a hideout during the 1991 uprising.

Commencing in the summer of 1991 Baghdad's plans to quell any remaining opposition to the regime resulted in the systematic destruction, which shrank the original marshlands from 15,000–20,000km² to 1,500–2,000km².

But after the toppling of Saddam's regime the UNEP launched a major restoration project (see pages 257–8).

Rania Dagash of the International Organisation for Migration in Basra, who carried out an assessment of Marsh Arab communities, discovered that they want both worlds:

> Those close to town centres have tasted the modern world and they don't really want to let go of it. Their farming is quite stable and it is probably the only stability they have seen. They want their children to know the other world, but at the same time to have the benefits of services in the urban world.

As in the rest of southern Iraq, opposition to the occupation has cast a shadow over developments in the marshlands. Rory Stewart, in *Occupational Hazards: My Time Governing in Iraq*, notes that:

> by the beginning of 2006, the Sadrists, the Dawa Party and the Iranian-linked parties had taken almost all the votes across the south and the majority of seats in the new national parliaments. Southern Iraq was under Coalition occupation but not Coalition control. Most people in the south believed the occupation was illegal. They only tolerated it because they believed the presence of the troops in bases might deter civil war. Iraqis were reluctant to trust us or work with us. Because of this lack of cooperation, it had been difficult for the Coalition to achieve as much as it hoped with its billions of dollars in development aid, and it had received almost no credit for its efforts. Despite thousands of troops and tens of millions invested in essential services, despite a number of impressive reconstruction projects, despite ambitious programmes in police training and in developing 'good governance and civil society', the Coalition has had only a minimal political impact in southern Iraq.

The new Basra Development Commission is trying to develop a plan for economic development involving both public and private sectors and regional and international stakeholders.

11

The southern cities of Amarah, Nasiriyah and Basra form the marshlands triangle.

Amarah (population 420,000) lies on a low ridge beside the Tigris, and Nasiriyah (population 560,200) lies on the Euphrates in a flat, date-growing area. Both cities, like most of southern Iraq, have been known for their turbulent inclinations; both Amarah and Nasiriyah were captured by the British during the 1915 Mesopotamia campaign. They are important trading centres, known for their silverware. Nasiriyah, founded in 1879, is a city largely of sun-dried brick. The ruins of the ancient Sumerian city of Ur are 18km to the southwest of the city.

AMARAH Approximately 365km from Baghdad and 185km north of Basra, this modern town was built in 1866 as an Ottoman military outpost from which the empire tried to control the warring Banu Lam and Al Bu Muhammad tribes. As the river steamer traffic developed, the Turks settled in the area.

Before World War I the area was the stronghold of tyrannical tribal sheiks with their own armies. They owned massive estates in the rice-growing areas until Abdul Karim Qasim overthrew the monarchy, introduced a more equitable system of land distribution, and put an end to most of the internecine tribal warfare connected with the marshlands. As the river steamer traffic developed, the Turks settled in the area.

During the eight year Iran–Iraq War, Amarah and its surrounding province became the site of several battles, notably Operation Before Dawn launched by

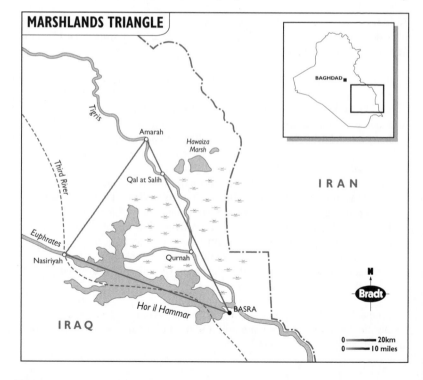

MARSHLANDS TRIANGLE

Tigris

Amarah

Hawaiza Marsh

Third River

Qal at Salih

I R A N

BAGHDAD

Euphrates

Nasiriyah

Qurnah

N

Bradt

Hor il Hammar

BASRA

I R A Q

0 — 20km
0 — 10 miles

Iraq. Iran targeted Amarah due to the strategically significant Baghdad–Basra highway, which cut through the province.

In 1991 the city's residents took part in an uprising against Saddam Hussein and the insurgents retreated to safe havens near Amarah. Many were killed and crudely buried in a mass grave outside the city. Saddam Hussein also resorted to a crude tactic of draining the marshes surrounding Amarah. Furthermore, Saddam constructed a number of dams in an effort to cut off the water supply to the area.

Throughout the 1990s, the town's population swelled with refugees from the marshes. Saddam Hussein occasionally neglected services to the city in retribution for its role in the uprising. The city also supported Moqtada Al-Sadr, whose father was killed by Saddam. In May 1999, Baath Party militias and

PRINCE OF THE MARSHES TRIES TO RECONCILE SHIAS

For 13 years Abd al-Karim al-Mahmud Muhamedawi (aka Abu Hatem) was a defiant symbol of Iraqi resistance. Hunted in vain by Saddam Hussein's militia, the legendary guerrilla fighter fought an extraordinary campaign against the Iraqi regime from his secluded bases in the marshlands. After the marshes were drained his men dug bunkers in dried up water courses. Known as the Prince of the Marshes, his exploits earned him a reputation that is a cross between Robin Hood and Lawrence of Arabia, with tales of suicide missions and narrow escapes. *The Guardian* correspondent Ewen MacAskill, writing from Amarah in April 2003, described him as a striking figure, tall and thin, part politician, part brigand, dressed in white robes and traditional Arab head dress.

Apart from the Kurdish resistance, he was the only indigenous resistance fighter to confront Saddam's forces. Abu Hatem is now spending his time mediating between various Shia factions in the south (see page 273). His militia, which once numbered up to 8,000 men, has been stood down, but members of his tribe, Albu Mohamed, can be mobilised immediately.

His 'career' as a guerrilla fighter began after he was released from Abu Ghraib Prison, where he spent seven years after being jailed in 1980 for anti-regime activities. The name of his guerrilla group is Hezbollah (no relation to the Lebanese Hezbollah).

Abu Hatem had a post in the interim government, which he temporarily resigned in protest against the Fallujah siege (see pages 220–3). The coalition led by Ahmed Chelabi, of which he was a member, did not win enough votes to secure a parliamentary seat in the 2005 elections and he is now focusing on local politics. He heads a civic Council of Notables, with representatives from Maysan, Nasiriyah and Basra, and tries to play a conciliatory role, as intra-Shia and sectarian violence hinders development.

In 2003 he helped dispel tensions after six British soldiers were killed in Majar al-Kabir when they tried to disarm the local population. The tribesmen initially co-operated with the British and saw the attempt to render them defenceless as a dishonour.

Abu Hatem is a vehement opponent of Iranian interference in Iraqi affairs. He has close links with Moqtada Al-Sadr and many members of his tribe are now in Sadr City in Baghdad.

11

units of the Special Republican Guard conducted operations in the region. Local resistance fighters reportedly repelled the operation.

The city was a centre of resistance to Saddam's regime. Like the rest of Maysan province it liberated itself before the Coalition arrived, but it has been caught up in inter-Shia rivalries and was seized by the Mehdi Army on 26 October 2006 when police stations and state facilities, largely under the control of the Badr Militia, the military wing of the Supreme Islamic Council, were attacked, leaving 15 dead. On 12 December 2007, three car bombs in Amarah killed 39 people and injured more than 100. No one claimed responsibility for the attacks, but it is likely they were related to a power struggle between Shia factions.

The power of the sheikhs, once the wealthiest and most powerful men in the province, has been declining steadily and they often asked the Coalition for contracts to raise money – in addition to theft, kidnapping, smuggling and looting.

Some sheikhs, like the legendary Abu Hatem, are reinventing themselves as 21st-century politicians and power brokers, and are playing an important role in the current administration.

NASIRIYAH   Nasiriyah, on the Euphrates, 362km southeast of Baghdad, is near the ruins of the ancient cities of Ur and Larsa (see page 311).

The city, which dates back to 1870, was named after its founder Sheikh Nasir Sadun. In July 1915 around 400 British and Indian soldiers were killed in the battle for Nasiriyah, fought against the Turks who controlled the city.

During the 1991 Gulf War Coalition forces decided not to proceed further into Iraq after liberating Kuwait.

The local people took part in the uprising against Saddam Hussein, which he subdued with heavy loss of life and destruction (see pages 240–1).

The tranquility of life by the river was severely disrupted once again on 23 March 2003, when the Americans tried to capture a bridge over the Euphrates near Nasiriyah. They fought one of the longest battles of the war and reacted to snipers with house searches and arrests. Sniper Alley was almost completely demolished as the Coalition advanced towards Baghdad. In addition to the official American losses and an unknown number of Iraqi troops lost, 250 civilians died of their injuries.

Nasiriyah was the backdrop to the modern America war myth of Jessica Lynch, a 19-year-old supply clerk with the 507th Maintenance Company. She was injured and captured by Iraqi forces after her group made a wrong turn and was subsequently ambushed on 23 March 2003 near Nasiriyah. The propaganda version of the story referred to her 'detention' in an Iraqi hospital, where she was set on by vicious Iraqi guards and rescued by elite teams of US Army Rangers and US Navy SEALs. Nurses, doctors and eyewitnesses at the hospital said the Fedayeen guards (composed of young soldiers recruited from regions loyal to Saddam) fled the day before the 'rescue' and there was no resistance. Lynch was well cared for by the Iraqi hospital staff. Dr Al-Houssona reportedly tried to arrange for her to be delivered to the US forces but the Americans fired on the ambulance and she was returned to the hospital. On 24 April 2007, Lynch testified in front of Congress that she never fired her weapon and was knocked unconscious when her vehicle crashed. 'They should have found out the facts before they spread the word like wildfire,' she said.

According to the Iraqi Ministry of Irrigation, 400 square miles (1,035km²) (0.7%) of the marsh around Nasiriyah has been flooded. The US Agency for International Development budgeted US$4 million for the restoration of the marshes, focusing on healthcare and re-introducing fish into the ecosystem. The marshlands once provided up to 70% of the country's fish and dairy products, but today there is only enough for local consumption.

AL AZAIR Al Azair is notable as the home of the alleged tomb of Ezra, the 4th-century Old Testament prophet, priest and scribe who led the Jews returning from exile in Babylon, and who came to be known as the father of Judaism.

Ezra's work involved the reconstitution of the Jewish community based on the Torah, and his influence on Jewish law, tradition and family life cannot be underestimated. At a time when Iraq was ruled by the Persians, Ezra could be described as the Minister of Jewish Affairs.

During the Mesopotamian campaign of World War I, the green-blue dome of his shrine was preserved, even amidst the most intense fighting. Attached to this Islamic building is a remarkably well-preserved synagogue.

QURNAH Continuing south approximately 65km from Basra, on the confluence of the Tigris and Euphrates, lies Al Qurnah, where Eve's tree of the knowledge of good and evil allegedly stands in the grounds of a hotel.

The town, on the crossroads of the western road to Al Chibayish and the marshes, has a very busy market and a pleasant, congenial atmosphere.

Originally built by Seleucus Nicator I under Alexander the Great, it has always had a strategic importance: a fort was constructed in the 17th century by the Turks, who regarded Al Qurnah as an important customs post. Under the British a small garrisoned administration was established. During the Iran–Iraq War it was shelled many times.

In June 2003, the Coalition's Danish contingent set up Camp Eden 8km east of Qurnah on a previously destroyed military installation of Saddam Hussein. The locals nicknamed it Desert Fortress. The camp was disassembled in August–September 2004, when the contingent expanded and moved further south.

BASRA Basra, known for hundreds of years as the Venice and Amsterdam of the East because of its network of canals and spectacular architecture, competes with Mosul for the classification of Iraq's second-largest city (see pages 162–7). The traditional leisurely lifestyle that accompanies a waterborne existence is now a distant memory.

11

THE GARDEN OF EDEN TODAY

The Garden of Eden is now covered in concrete crazy paving and the tree of life is dead. If you want an apple you have to buy it from the market nearby!
Lindsay Fulcher, British tourist, who visited Qurnah in 2002

The city's strategic location at the mouth of the Shatt Al Arab, one of the Middle East's busiest marine trade routes, and its proximity to Iran and Kuwait, has made Basra one of the most fought-over areas in history. It is a region of contrasts, where the cries of camels blend with the sirens of passing ships. In summer the temperature soars to 40°C or higher, and the humidity is unbearable.

The area was also one of the world's most important date-producing centres. Considered a dessert in the West, dates are a staple food in some parts of the Middle East, especially among the Bedouin. Products intended for export are sometimes stuffed with walnuts or almonds.

Basra, from whose shores Sinbad the Sailor's adventures began, is a city steeped in history. Sinbad's island in the middle of the Shatt Al Arab once had attractive gardens, fountains and refreshment kiosks. Among the recent constructions in Basra is a mosque with a green dome built in the last ten years. At night it resembles a Christmas tree.

The city was also the home of the Sassoons, a wealthy Iraqi-Jewish family who had substantial property-holdings in London's Park Lane and who dabbled in the arts. Siegfried Sassoon, for example, became a celebrated poet in the 19th century. Baghdadi Jews Saatchi & Saatchi set up the famous British advertising company.

Caliph Omar bin Khattab founded the city in AD637. During the time of the Abbasids it gained importance both as the focal point of the Arab sea trade, which extended as far as China, and as a cultural centre and a centre of learning, where discoveries in optics and mechanics were made.

When the Abbasid caliphate declined in importance, the city was still valued for its strategic importance and the Turks and Persians did not hesitate to fight for it. When the Turks finally gained control in 1668 they turned it into a province (*vilayet*) of the Ottoman Empire. While the Turks annoyed the native inhabitants by imposing a buffalo tax (see page 272), the city's next occupiers, the British, encouraged the expansion of the port, built new wharfs and provided electricity and steam cranes.

The British returned in large numbers in 2003 and once again tried to encourage development and ease the suffering of the city and its people, but their noble efforts were overshadowed by the pervasive influence of the Shia militias and attacks by insurgents targeting foreign troops. Projects are often deliberately sabotaged and British soldiers painstakingly return time and time and again to repair the damage – a mirror image of the situation throughout much of Iraq.

The towering bronze figures along the waterfront, which once pointed accusingly towards Iran, suffered the same fate as Saddam's statute in Ferdous Square (see page 202). During the Iran–Iraq war Basra's losses were enormous. It was bombed during the 1991 and the 2003 wars. Iraqi Airways has been slow to resume flights. The plaque on the memorial to Iraqi Airways, which was restricted to internal flights when sanctions were imposed in 1990, reads 'Iraqi Airways, 1947–1990'. The airline resumed flights in September 2004.

During the latest war Basra became a main prize once again. In his book, *The War We Could Not Stop*, author Randeep Ramesh drew attention to the fact that through Arab eyes, as portrayed by the satellite channel Al-Jazeera, in the battle for Basra it was Iraqi tanks, artillery and rocket-propelled grenades that were repelling invaders – as Arabs had done for centuries.

The city's residents were terrified. One of the regime's most notorious criminals, Ali Hassan Al Majid (nicknamed Chemical Ali after he ordered the use of chemical weapons against the Kurds in 1988 – see page 182) was put in charge of the southern region, where the Fedayeen and the ruthless Special Republican Guard were cowing the people into submission.

Reports of an uprising in the city proved to be unfounded. Before the city finally came under the control of the British on 8 April 2003, over a million people had to survive without fresh water or electricity. The bombing was heavier than during the Iran–Iraq War and the residents were terrified as civilian casualties grew.

A dispatch from Tim Butcher describing Saddam's palace in Basra that was published in *The Daily Telegraph*'s compendium *War on Saddam* provided an insight into the tyrant's psychology:

> Only one man in Iraq is powerful enough to afford such a palace and that man is Saddam Hussein. Dripping with dictator kitsch was everything a megalomaniac could wish for, from gold-plated lavatory brushes to French-made ornate lamp posts entwined with climbing ivy. Outside the opulent palace lay suburbs full of very poor people. Hundreds of them began to gather outside the gates after the Royal Marines had checked all the rooms for booby traps. But their caution appeared unfounded, as the pink palace, made from a pale rose-coloured stone, was occupied only by a flock of doves, a powerful symbol of what Basra needed most – peace.

The battle for hearts and minds of local people is being fought by Al-Sadr's Mehdi Army (which controls the police, the ports and customs); the armed wing of the Supreme Islamic Council, the Badr Brigade (which controls the intelligence commandos); the Fadhila Party, a branch of the Sadrist Movement (which controls the tactical support unit); and about 20 tribes, which have their own smuggling businesses. Loyalties are a moveable feast, with the militiamen switching sides depending on who pays most. Tribes like the Gramsha have been known to charge protection money on the roads around Basra.

In December 2007 the leaders of 25 factions in Basra signed an agreement stating they would co-operate with the security services to maintain law and order. General Mohan Al-Furayji, the Iraqi commander in Basra, is emerging as a new strongman who is helping to contain the violence.

Abu Ammar, once an important politician, emphasised that the city is calm not because it is under the control of the police, but because all the militias have interests and want to maintain the status quo. The moment their interests are under threat the whole city can burn. The police are also allied to these groups and take sides in serious confrontations.

A senior Iraqi general interviewed by *The Guardian* correspondent Ghaith Abdul-Ahad predicted:

> Ahead of us we have years of fighting and murder, a militia will be toppled by another militia and those will split so day after day we are

witnessing the formations of new groups. And the British withdrawal [the British officially transferred control of Basra to the Iraqis on 17 December 2007] is leading to a power struggle between the different factions.

But there is light at the end of every tunnel – the light of the oncoming train! In February 2008 the first rail passenger service resumed with a service from Baghdad to Basra. The 500km journey takes 12 hours because the line leaves a lot to be desired.

The Islamic influence has changed the character and appearance of the city. Gone are the liquor shops in the streets behind the Sheraton hotel, some of their Christian owners murdered. The area was once lively with local restaurants. The record shops are now selling Koranic recordings, and there are no chess or backgammon sets on sale, as these games are frowned on by the religious establishment.

Near Basra Zubair is a traditional picnic spot just outside Basra. Zubair Bin Awwam was one of the earliest converts to Islam, who embraced the religion when he was just 15 years old. He fought for the cause of Islam and was martyred in the battle of Al-Jamal in AD656.

Other Islamic sites include the shrines of Ibn Sirin and Hassan Al Basri, and Imam Ali's Mosque. Al Basri, born in AD642, was a Sufi scholar who had a great impact on Islamic thought. His shrine has been restored. The Imam Ali

Mosque was the first mosque to be built in Iraq at the beginning of the Arab conquest in AD635. It is an important place for pilgrimage as Imam Ali personally prayed there. The mosque has been rebuilt many times, the latest incarnation being completed under Saddam's rule. All that is left of the first structure is a remnant of the original minaret, and the column and slabs of the original courtyard, which faithfully reflect the very first mosques of Mohammed in Medina.

Zubair was the scene of a more recent intrigue. On 23 March 2003 two members of a specialist bomb disposal unit of the Royal Engineers went missing after an attack on their vehicles near the town. Their bodies were shown on the controversial Arab satellite channel Al-Jazeera and a British army chief claimed they had been executed in cold blood. But sources in the men's regiment were adamant they were killed in action. Tony Blair apologised for any offence that may have been caused to the family, but the execution claim was never withdrawn.

Abul Khasib, 26km south of Basra, has a strange claim to fame: the highest density of palm trees in the world. It is also the birthplace of the famous Iraqi poet, the late Badr Shakir Al-Sayyab.

Um Qasr, Iraq's largest deepwater port (population 45,000), just across the Kuwaiti border and reputed to be a smugglers' haven, had its 15 minutes of fame in March 2005 when fewer than 50 guerrillas held out for six days against overwhelming American firepower. In so doing, they became a symbol of defiance for the Iraqis.

Once the minesweepers had finished their job the first humanitarian aid was brought in by the *Sir Galahad* on 28 March – the good news story the Coalition's propagandists dreamed of became a reality. But the dream soon turned into a nightmare. Iraq was too dangerous for the civilian aid workers, so food, water and medical supplies were piling up in warehouses in neighbouring countries and the military were not good at delivering aid. To make matters worse, they came under fire from Iraqi militias.

Um Qasr was the first population centre to be 'liberated' by the invading forces. It was also the first town to be handed over to self-government, on 15 May 2003, in what military commanders hailed as a huge success story. Yet *The Daily Telegraph* reported that British soldiers who had worked closely with the 12-member, all-male council in the run-up to the handover described it as a 'joke' and 'a bloody disaster'. 'They're almost all of them on the make.' One soldier, from 23 Pioneer Regiment, said: 'We've worked hard to get where we are today, but there is concern as to just what we're leaving ordinary people with.' Given £6,000 to start up the administration and to begin paying public servants, 'they came back to us and said they still needed money to pay the wages, saying they had lost the original amount.'

The American overseas development agency USAID has spent US$30m upgrading the port, removing sunken ships from the harbour, which had been there since the Iran–Iraq War, and dredging a deepwater channel, giving access to large vessels.

Operation of the ports at Um Qasr and Zubair has been returned to the Iraqis after bitter fights with the Stevedoring Services of America and the Maersk Shipping Company. The south has also witnessed intense labour activity and the creation of trade unions, such as the Iraqi Longshoremens Union in Um Qasr.

11

At the end of the 1991 Gulf War the ceasefire agreement was signed in **Safwan** near Basra, on the Iraq–Kuwait border. Relations between the two countries improved remarkably following the overthrow of Saddam's regime, which invaded Kuwait in 1990. In October 2003 the Interim Iraqi President Ghazi Al Yawer visited Kuwait to press for improved ties and to discuss Baghdad's multibillion-dollar debt. It was the first such visit by an Iraqi president in decades. On 3 August 2004 Iraq and Kuwait agreed to restore full diplomatic relations. Kuwait and Iraq have subsequently signed economic co-operation protocols and Kuwait has donated money to assist Iraqi refugees.

12

Culture

While violence might appear to predominate on the television news and in newspapers, beneath the surface there is a vibrant culture struggling to reassert itself. Despite the violence and 35 years of totalitarian Baathist rule, Iraqi artists, poets and writers continue to produce a full measure of artistic work both inside and outside Iraq. The struggle for cultural survival remains, perhaps as intensive as the violence directed against it. And one can hope that the Iraqis' pride in their cultural heritage will prevail over attempts to obliterate it.

Nimrod Raphaeli, *Middle East Quarterly*, Summer 2007

IRAQI ART: STROKES OF GENIUS

The story of Iraqi art starts with the splendid Mesopotamian civilisation and its Sumerian glazed-brick architecture with colourful designs dating back to 4500BC.

Throughout the centuries, art has reflected the values and taste of the society from which it has emerged. When the Assyrian kings of ancient times ruled in 1400BC, art was an official profession that ensured the rulers' exploits were glorified and immortalised. The 'professional' Assyrian artists created statues of winged bulls that once guarded the palace portals and city gates, and recorded the life of their kings in magnificent, larger-than-life murals showing hunting, wars and battles.

In the words of one of the most famous 20th-century Iraqi artists, Jewad Selim:

Art in Mesopotamia has always been like its people, who have been the product of the land and the climate. They have never reached decadence and never achieved perfection; for them perfection of craftsmanship has been a limitation on their self-expression. Their work has been crude but inventive, has had a vigour and boldness which would not have been possible with a more refined technique. The artist has always been free to express himself, even amid the state art of Assyria, where the true artist speaks through the drama of the wounded beast.

ISLAMIC ART During the Abbasid period (AD750–1258), Islamic art with a unique spiritual dimension emerged. It was enhanced rather than stifled by the prohibition on portraying living forms. Calligraphy, script embellishment, floral and geometric design and miniature painting characterised Islamic art, which was also influenced by Chinese ceramics, paintings and textiles brought back to Iraq by traders. The first Islamic art school was established in Baghdad in the 12th century AD, where artisan and craft guilds flourished.

Kings, aristocrats and intellectuals generously rewarded calligraphers who decorated their houses and palaces with ornamental designs based on Arabic letters. Mubarak Al-Makki perfected the Kufic (square block) lettering style, while Yahya Al-Wasiti was the most famous figure in 13th-century book illuminations, whose drawings provide a rich source of historical information. Architecture, furnishing, weapons and national costumes were all depicted.

Throughout the Abbasid era (AD750–1258), Baghdad was the intellectual centre of the Islamic world, where art, science and philosophy flourished. When Baghdad was sacked by the Mongols art was also dealt a devastating blow. It did not fully recover until the beginning of the 20th century, when an amalgam of the ancient and the contemporary became a recurring feature.

MODERN ART The first generation of painters, the 'early pioneer artists' – Abdul Qadir al-Rassam, Mohammed Salih Zeki, Asim Hafidh and Haj Mohammed Selim – belonged to a class of officers or officials of the Ottoman Empire who saw a promise of regeneration in European culture and science in the early years of the 20th century. In tune with the disaffection towards the old regime of the Young Turks and Kemal Ataturk, they also nurtured an avid patriotism towards their homeland. It was men like these, claiming a rational scientific perspective to guide the hands of the future, who first breached the traditions and forms of identity. Significantly, the early pioneers were the only ones who portrayed what they saw; landscapes both urban and rural, images of people in daily social contexts, portraits and self portraits.

During World War II the military once again made a contribution to Iraqi art when a group of Polish officers, who came to Baghdad with the Allied troops, joined in the country's cultural life. One Iraqi artist commented that after discussions with the Poles he came to know what colour was and how it should be employed.

The 1930s and 1940s launched a generation on scholarships abroad, among them a handful of talented young artists collectively known as *Al-Ruwad*, 'The Pioneers' or the 'fifties generation', including Faiq Hassan, Jewad Selim, Ismail al-Sheikhli, Kamil Chadirji and Nadhim Ramzi. Between the late 1930s and 1950s they bridged the gap between modernity and heritage.

The Pioneers were a mixture of art-school graduates and self-taught artists who left their studios to paint scenes from the country and city streets. They

Monument for Freedom by Jawad Selim

were led by Faik Hassan, the father of Iraq's modern art movement. After graduating from the Académie Nationale des Beaux Arts in Paris, he became a teacher at the Baghdad Institute of Fine Arts.

In 1951, Jawad Salim (1921–61) formed The Baghdad Group of Modern Art, eager to establish an Iraqi artistic identity. He believed that a new trend in painting would solve the artistic identity problem in the contemporary awakening by following in the footsteps of 13th-century Iraqi painters. After gaining an appreciation of the aesthetic values of ancient art while working at the Directorate of Antiquities in Baghdad, Salim studied in Rome and England before abandoning painting to concentrate on sculpture. His most famous work is the Monument for Freedom, in Baghdad (see page 215).

The Impressionists emerged in 1953 and gravitated around Hafid Al-Drubi, who opened the first independent painting studio in Iraq. After training at Goldsmith's College in London he turned to Impressionism, then Cubism, which he used to depict landscapes and city scenes.

Two artist groups captured the spirit of the decade that would define the sixties generation. They were *Al-Mujadidin*, 'The Innovationists' (1965), including Ali Talib, Salim al-Dabbagh, Salman Abbas, Amer al-Obaidi, Salih al-Jumai'e, Faiq Hussain, Nida Kadhim and Talib Makki. *Al-Ru'yah al-Jadida*, 'The New Vision' (1968), included Ismail Fattah, Mohammed Muhriddin, Hashim al-Samarchi, Salih al-Jumai'e, Rafa al-Nasiri and Dia Azzawi. They exhibited a distinct individualism – an essential component of the artist's identity. The Arab identity in the works of some of these artists dealt with issues such as the shock of the Six Day War of June 1967, the Palestinian cause, and the Lebanese civil war, which inspired a creative response of powerful empathy.

The 1960s began with the establishment of the Institute of Higher Education, which became the Arts College. The well-known architect Rifa'at Chaderji opened the Aya Gallery, while Mohamed Makiya opened the Wasiti Gallery with two other architects. Makiya later moved to Britain and set up the Kufa Gallery (see pages 36–7).

Amatzia Baram, who analysed the culture, history and ideology in the formation of Baathist Iraq, concluded that the country's rich cultural heritage was used to foster the theme of the unity of the Iraqi people. The cult surrounding Saddam Hussein resulted in the 'art of veneration', which became a pervasive art form in Iraqi society while Saddam was in power. He was portrayed as a benevolent 'uncle' in a variety of costumes and was depicted on numerous posters throughout the country.

GROWTH AND PROSPERITY The prosperous decades of the 1970s and 1980s were the years of 'cultural exports' and the staging of numerous international art exhibitions, festivals and symposia in Iraq. Iraqi artists took their works to North Africa, Egypt, Syria and Lebanon. The Iraqi Cultural Centre in London published the high-quality cultural magazine *Ur*. Exhibitions were held on the ground floor while intelligence activities were conducted on other floors.

Iraq hosted the first international arts gathering, the Al-Wasiti Festival, in 1972. Then came the meetings of the First Congress of Arab Artists, which led to the formation of the Union of Arab Artists. Exhibitions in Baghdad included the Arab Graphic Art Exhibition, held in London in July 1980 then transferred to Baghdad in September, and the Baghdad International Exhibition of Posters held in the early 1980s. The Saddam Arts Centre, opened in 1986, had halls where the works of artists from all over the world were featured. In 1988 it was the venue for an International Calligraphy Festival. The Babylon Festival became an international cultural event, which has not been revived in post-Saddam Iraq.

The works of the 1980s, especially the eight years of the Iran–Iraq War (1980–88), were characterised by challenge and cynicism. There was a marked shift in the work of the eighties generation towards a form of abstraction, which artist Rashad Salim described as:

> a pictorial language leached from the debris of civilization, as if in search of missing clues and principles to an essential forgotten code… One recurring compositional construct symbolic in itself is the grid or squared-off plane dear to many of the artists from this generation, including myself.

Iraq's creative output could not be stifled by war or life under sanctions. Despite the complex tribulations of sanctions and oppression, a few of the best established artists, as well as a significant number of dynamic young artists, chose to stay in Iraq. In 1997 Britain's Arab Club organised a fundraising exhibition of contemporary art. The money raised was spent on paints and other artists' supplies, which were sent to Iraq. According to Hani Muthir, one of the exhibition's organisers, the real wealth of Iraq is embodied in its civilisation and human resources, not only in its oil reserves:

> Today's children of Iraq are tomorrow's creative artists. They should have the right to draw a rainbow and to expel the ghost of illiteracy if the blockade is there to stay.

ART IN IRAQ TODAY The story of contemporary art post-occupation has narrowed over the past four years to one of absence, chaos and ever-increasing loss in the country, mirrored by growing activity and interest abroad. Today there is a better chance of experiencing Iraqi art (or art dealing with Iraq) in a capital close to Iraq, especially Jordan. Amman's Café Al-Ofreli is a favourite meeting place for poets and artists.

The lack of security and deteriorating living conditions have led to a mass exodus of Iraqi intellectuals and artists who now live and work in the diaspora, joining previous waves of exile. Naturally the situation has become a major influence on artistic output as many artists address the plight of their people with their creativity.

Of the artists remaining in Iraq there are practically none of international repute left in Baghdad. Iraqi Kurdistan, on the other hand, has seen some growth, with artists such as Ali Mandalawi, a renowned painter/illustrator, joining the regional government in Erbil, and the activist painter Rabwar setting up an arts centre in Suleimaniyah. Those artists who would have painted portraits and posters of Saddam now paint portraits of the US military and Green Zone inhabitants! They recently began to paint murals on security and bomb-blast walls and barriers.

The Iraqi Museum of Modern Art in Baghdad was damaged by fire and looting after suffering bombings in 2003. The museum contained thousands of works

Maysaloun Faraj is an artist with a mission: as well as developing her painting and ceramic work she is determined to ensure that Iraqi art is brought to the fore on an international scale.

'I will not rest until I see the works of our deserved artists being sought after by every serious art collector, museum and international auction house.'

Her dream started to come true in March 1995 when she began collecting information about Iraqi artists and established a unique and expanding database and archive, which she is constantly developing and updating. She was assisted by Edinburgh-based curator Ulrike Al-Khamis, formerly Curator of Islamic Art and Culture in the Glasgow Museums, and artist Rashad Selim, whose extensive knowledge of and links with many Iraqi artists, particularly in the diaspora, was pivotal in moving the project forward. Baghdad artist Hana Mal Allah provided essential links with artists inside Iraq. These endeavours culminated in the ground-breaking website and exhibition and publication of the book *Strokes of Genius: Contemporary Iraqi Art*. The project was eventually renamed iNCia (The International Network for Contemporary Iraqi Artists, www.incia.co.uk). It is the foremost source of reference for valuable, up-to-date information on Iraqi art today.

In 2002 Maysaloun and her husband Ali established the Aya Gallery in West London, whose *raison d'être* is to communicate peace through art. Nine major exhibitions have been held at the gallery, including *Expressions of Hope*, a collective exhibition showcasing the work of Iraqi artists to highlight the role and responsibility of the artist to motivate and inspire people with much-needed hope for a more promising future in response to the chaos and confusion in Iraq.

'If there is any chance for humanity, it will be in the hands of artists,' Maysaloun said. 'The human spirit is resilient and as long as there is soul, there will always be inspiration ... there will always be art.'

Reflecting on the past 12 years of carrying the torch for Iraqi art, Maysaloun is now concentrating on her own work. But she has no regrets:

> In fostering cultural and educational dialogue between East and West we are able to expand our horizons and enrich our humanity. Being surrounded by inspiring artwork and working closely with artists has been a challenging and exhilarating experience, which in itself has become for me an art form in the making and a true source of enlightenment.

Of Iraqi parentage, and born in the USA in 1955, Maysaloun returned to Baghdad in 1968 where she continued her studies and obtained a BSc in architecture from the College of Architectural Engineering, Baghdad University, in 1978. She later pursued a career in the arts, developing her skills in painting and ceramics in London, where she trained with the Inner London Education Authority (ILEA). Over a period of 25 years, Maysaloun has contributed to more than 50 group exhibitions at local and international level, won numerous awards and held 15 one-woman shows to date. Her artwork is in private collections worldwide, as well as important public collections, including the British Museum London; the National Museum for Women in the Arts, Washington; the Wereldmuseum, Rotterdam; the United Nations, Geneva; and numerous art institutions throughout the Middle East.

Culture **IRAQI ART: STROKES OF GENIUS**

12

from the late 19th century to the early months of 2003, including paintings, sculptures, ceramics, calligraphy and other priceless pieces. So far, about 1,500–1,600 of the 8,000 missing originals have been retrieved. Though the museum has reportedly been rebuilt, at the time of writing it remains closed.

The College of Arts at the University of Baghdad was trashed and looted, the library and extensive archives (some 7,000 manuscripts) and its theatre burnt. Students and staff have worked to save and clean up the college, but with inadequate funding, loss of teachers, lack of water and electricity, plus the entry of sectarian politics, attendance and tuition is patchy. Night classes and adult education, once a very important and much loved facility, has become impossible to maintain without light and under curfews.

The Association of Iraqi Artists and the Iraqi Artists Union in Damascus Street, opposite the Zawra Park, were likewise looted. After changing hands between different parties laying claim to the building, it was returned to the Iraqi Artists Union.

Qassim Sebti renovated and developed the Huwaar Gallery but it was closed at the time of writing. Art in Iraq is dying as the artists are fleeing, while those in the diaspora are keeping Iraqi art and culture alive until their homeland once again becomes a centre of creativity and a beacon for artists throughout the Arab world and further afield.

IRAQI POETS: THE SOUL AND CONSCIENCE OF THE ARAB WORLD

Throughout the Middle East, poetry is held in the highest esteem. In Iraq the mosques, religious schools and traditional institutions were custodians of traditional verse. Formal poetic composition is a speciality of the towns and cities.

Poetry was very important in pre-Islamic times, with poets acting as historians, soothsayers and propagandists. The early poems were collected in the 8th century. They were referred to as Mu'allaqat or hung poems, as they were hung in the most sacred place in Islam, the Kaaba, the large cuboidal building located inside the mosque known as al-Masjid al-Haram in Mecca, now in Saudi Arabia.

The Abbasids introduced the preoccupations of court into poetic themes. Arab poetry was influenced by Persian civilisation as seen in romantic and heroic epics, and poems with mystical themes, while Sufism (Islam's mystical tradition) is characterised by unique verse written to incite a state of ecstasy.

At the turn of the 20th century, Iraqi poetry followed traditional form and restricted itself to verses for formal occasions such as weddings, and poems venerating the Prophet and high-ranking religious and tribal leaders.

The two pioneers of modern Iraqi verse (Ar-Rasafi, 1875–1945 and Az-Zahawi, 1863–1936) worked on the principle that content was much more important than form. They used language to inform; social and political topics replaced idealised Bedouin themes such as courage.

During the World War I period, poetry charged with patriotic emotion and the revival of Arab heritage emerged in the Holy Shia city of Najaf, a traditional centre of Islamic scholarship.

The post-World War II period was characterised by the influence of Western forms, among them the works of T S Elliot. It is largely the poetry of rebellion and rejection. The poets of the 1940s and 1950s experimented with new, untried forms. Buland Al-Haidari, Mahmoud Al-Brekan, Nazik Almakaeka, Badr Shakir Al-Sayyab and Saadi Yousif are regarded in the Middle East as the soul and conscience of the Arab world. Haidari's constant self-searching takes on a menacing, perturbing note when he describes the superficiality of society, from which the artist cannot escape:

> You have repeated
> A thousand times
> That we are hollow men ... our days are hollow
> Our god is counterfeit
> That the keyhole of our door
> Has no key to it
> That neither the sun, nor any adulterous
> wind will bear a key for it.

Today Iraqi poets are no longer obliged to praise 'the great leader Saddam'. Religious poetry commemorating the martyrdom of Imam Hussein (see page 233) is making a comeback. The themes of violence and loss are still dominant. Popular poets inside Iraq include Kazim Al-Hajaj, Muwafak Mohamed, Hasan Sheikh Jafar, Hussain Abdulatif, Alfrid Saman, Sami Mahdi, Abdul Razzaq, Abdul Wahid and the late Yousof Alsayg. Today's poetry is written in local dialect rather than literary Arabic, and is published by hundreds of writers who make extensive use of internet sites.

Among the well-known poets who have made their homes in exile are Fawzi Karim, Sadeq Al-Saygh, Hashim Shafiq, Fadil Azzawi, Nusayf Nasiri, Karim Kadim, Lamia Abbas Umara and Abdulkareen Kasid, a renowned poet, critic and author of 16 books, including short stories and collections of poems. His most recent work is a French-to-Arabic translation and adaptation of the play *Soldiers Tale* by Ramouz. Kasid introduced the experiences of an Arab soldier into the anti-war play, which deals with the universal theme of the plight of soldiers returning home after war. The play was staged at London's Old Vic in 2007. He also translated the Japanese poet Santyoka into Arabic for the first time.

Like many Arab intellectuals, Kasid escaped from Iraq in 1978 after being pressured to join the Baath Party. With his friend, another poet Mahdi Mohammed Ali, he arranged for a smuggler to take him to Kuwait. Most of the seven-day journey through the desert was by camel and ended with a ride in an empty water tanker with 20 other people, Palestinians and Syrians who were trying to get into Kuwait to work. After living and working in South Yemen, Syria and Lebanon, Kasid arrived in Britain in late 1990, where he completed an MA in translation at Westminster University. He has since visited Iraq three times. In June 2007 he was the only poet from exile who attended the Al-Marbid Poetry Festival in Basra, organised by the Iraqi Writers Union. Two years ago he was honoured at the festival.

'A poet deals with everyday life, ordinary things and the sublime – anything can be dealt with in a poem,' Kasid said. He was inspired by the famous Lion of Babylon statue seen by thousands of visitors to Iraq:

12

Lion of Babylon

A metre or two from the river
sits the Lion of Babylon.
No bench,
no child,
no garden,
nor tower in the vicinity.
As people pass
not noticing him
he shakes his head regretfully
repeating the same thing.
No-one hears a thing, or
if they do, they ignore it:
'I am the Lion of Babylon,
the Lion of Babylon,
the Lion…'

Dr Nabeel Yasin has been promoting modern Arab poetry in the English-speaking world through translations of his prolific work, and through poetry readings at festivals in the UK, Holland, New York, Germany, Cairo, Beirut, Budapest and Sofia.

His story, lovingly told by Jo Tatchell in her book *Nabeel's Song*, is a fascinating one. In 1994, in exile, he published a volume of poetry including *Brother Yasin*, written in 1974 and published to great acclaim in Egypt and Lebanon, and its follow-up work, which reflected the experience of exile. The following year, a single copy of the work was smuggled into Iraq. The poems spread by stealth, requiring considerable courage on behalf of those involved and become part of a body of work that represented the silent fight against the regime.

Yasin is sad that poets in exile are still using political parties, such as the Communist Party, as a plaftorm to market their work:

I am one of the few Iraqi poets outside the political parties. They tried to kick me out of the cultural circles. They don't like independent thought and poetry. For five decades Iraqi culture was ideological culture, but that dosen't mean there wern't two or three birds flying outside that group.

Reflecting on his return to Baghdad in 2007 after 27 years in exile, Yasin said he was a stranger. 'It was very difficult to see my family as their home is in a dangerous area of Baghdad. I tried to find myself in the city.'

In *Brother Yasin*, he reflects on the plight of the poet:

And Baghdad is the last of places
At the Apocalypse, when the dead rise up before God
And the noise becomes deafening
I will be the last wise man – a man of sorrows –
In a time when wisdom is despised
I will be the last to grab smoldering embers
Before being consumed by fire

In total contrast to stylised poetry, Iraqi music is informal and largely improvised. The life of a song is marked by changes introduced by succeeding generations, and the ability to improvise and embellish a melody still constitutes one of the standards by which a performer is judged.

The most well known traditional instruments are the *oud* (similar to a lute), the *rebab* (similar to a fiddle), the *riqq* (a type of tambourine) and the *darbuka* (a hand drum). Well-known *oud* players include Munir Bashir, Salem Abdul Karim, Nasir Shamaa, Ai Emam and Riad Hoshabr.

TRADITIONAL MUSIC Iraqi *maqamat*, a system of melodic modes used in traditional Arabic music, dates back to Abbasid times. Its modern form descends from the 19th-century Turcoman composer Rahmat Allah Shiltegh (1798–1872). The *pesteh*, a light song which concluded *maqamat* performances, was popularised in the later 20th century.

Arabic folksongs in Iraq can be classified into Bedouin songs, Bedouin-rural songs, the songs of southern Iraq and the songs of the towns. Bedouin songs can be further subdivided into heroic or love poems, which are usually sung to the accompaniment of a one-string fiddle, sung poetry, which usually accompanies the march of the camel caravan, war songs and women's songs.

A new society, half-Bedouin and half-rural, was created by the tribes who settled on the banks of the rivers and cultivated land. They performed Bedouin songs and also developed dance songs with different patterns of rhymes. The songs of southern Iraq are based on four-line stanzas. The singer is accompanied by a drum, clapping, clicking fingers, large cans or trays! The towns are the places for folksongs. The singer typically sings the whole stanza and the chorus repeats the last word of the refrain.

20TH-CENTURY PERFORMERS At the beginning of the 20th century Iraq's most prominent musicians were Jewish. Iraq Radio, established in 1936, had an ensemble made up entirely of Jews except for the percussion player. The most famous singer of the 1930s and 1940s was Salima Pasha.

In the early 1920s, Iraq's most famous composer was Ezra Aharon, an *oud* player, and the most prominent instrumentalist was Duwad el-Kuwaiti.

Iraqi singer Kazem Al Saher, whose mournful songs about life in the good old days are juxtaposed with lyrics describing the state of Iraq today, has become a household name throughout the Arab world. In the words of Nabil Adbel Fattah, of the Al Ahram Strategic and Political Studies Centre in Cairo, 'Iraq is a very fragmented society and he has managed to unite them. He has become a national symbol.'

Musician Aws Nayeb has composed a song in English as a message to the world about sanctions: 'You're sitting here all alone, and the tears fill up your eyes. You've got no legs to walk, you've got no wings to fly.'

Nasser Shamma, who performed in London's Queen Elizabeth Hall in 2001, is an Iraqi *oud* maestro whose overriding passion is to revive the solo *oud* tradition, which was lost after the medieval Kurd Ziryab introduced a brass string to the instrument.

Culture MUSIC: INFORMAL AND IMPROVISED

12

ACADEMIES AND INSTITUTES The Iraqi Fine Arts Institute was opened in 1936 under the directorship of Al Sharif Muhaidin Haider, an *oud* master.

The Institute of Musical Studies was established by the Ministry of Culture in the late 1960s, to revive traditional Iraqi music and songs. In 1973, the Ministry of Culture and Arts set up a Musical Arts Advisory Board to supervise its School of Music and Ballet, the Institute of Musical Studies and the National Symphony Orchestra, first established in the 1940s, which became increasingly popular after it was re-organised in 1971.

Today the Baghdad Symphony Orchestra plays Bach, Beethoven, Brahms, Gershwin and American jazz. Like many musicians, its director, American-educated Karim Wasfi, has received many death threats, as religious extremists are convinced that music is wicked, dangerous and against the Koran. But he is determined to stage a concert for all of Iraq's warring religious groups, and sees music and art as a source of unity.

Baghdad's School of Music and Ballet, which opened in 1968, has achieved considerable cultural and artistic standing since its early years. Ballets presented have included *The Magic Wings* by the Iraqi choreographer Abd Al Amir Al Sarraf, and *The Birth and the Journey*, a one-act ballet choreographed by Sa'd Mahmud Hikmat. After the 2003 war UNESCO provided equipment for the school.

The National Troupe of Popular Arts was set up in 1971 to preserve Iraq's traditional folk songs and dances. Five months after its debut in 1972, it won the first prize at the Arab Youth Festival in Algeria. It has also taken part in international folklore festivals.

The Iraqi Traditional Music Group, which performed in a number of European and Asian capitals, was formed in 1973. It consisted mainly of young artists performing traditional, rural, Bedouin and Arabian songs. They also performed on string instruments such as the lute, canon, zither and wind instruments, including the flute and double-pipe. In 1977, a musical instruments workshop was set up for the making of traditional instruments, to ensure that this craft was passed on to the younger generation by a rapidly disappearing generation of master craftsmen.

A LAND WITHOUT MUSIC Post-Saddam Iraq is an Iraq virtually without music. Professional musician Ehsan Emam, a graduate of the famous Iraqi Institute of Music Studies and an *oud* specialist, has joined the exodus of Iraqi musicians who are now scattered around the Middle East, Europe, Afric, Canada and Australasia. Emam said:

Ehsan Emam

The decline started during the 1980s when all the main teachers were drafted into the army [to fight in the Iran–Iraq War]. Iraq once had music academies in the north, south, east and west, but now it's all 'Allah Akhbar', and music is seen as a big threat. Iraqi songs today all have the same tune, the same melody, the same tempo – there was variety before.

Since arriving in London in 1997, Emam has given many concerts across the whole of the UK, including recitals in Edinburgh, Cambridge and Kingston universities. Currently he is teaching the *oud* privately, and music and Arabic song theory at London University's School of Oriental and African Studies (SOAS).

Emam believes Iraqis in exile have to preserve the cultural traditions as the country passes through a period where 'everything is destroyed'.

WESTERN MUSIC Western music is popular with the younger generation. Before the 2003 war there was no shortage of discos in Baghdad. The lighting and sound were definitely well over the top. The most popular radio station, which kept young people up to date with Western music, was *Voice of Youth FM*, owned by Saddam's oldest son, Uday.

There were a number of bands in the 1970s playing Western pop music in clubs. Ilham el Madfaii adapted some traditional tunes and composed new ones with Iraqi Baghdadi characteristics to be played on electric guitars and organs, ie: for a rock or pop band ensemble.

Acrassicauda is Iraq's only heavy metal band. Like 80% of the country's singers, they have fled into exile and are now in Syria. They have only managed three live performances in Baghdad, one in 2005 in the Fanar Hotel surrounded by private armies, American forces and the police. The future seems bleak for the band's members Firas Al Taleef, Tony Aziz, Marwan Riyak and Faisal Talal, who are between a rock and a hard place. In Baghdad their rehearsal rooms of six years were destroyed by a bomb, and in Damascus the authorities are reluctant to renew their visas.

The group Akhlad came out after the occupation with a song called 'Al-Watheeya', meaning the situation. It is a superb description of life in Baghdad, which is full of irony.

FILMS: A FEW HOMEGROWN 'MAGIC TRICKS'

The first Iraqi films were shown at the Al-Shafa House on the banks of the Tigris in 1909. Nobody knew where these films, or 'magic tricks' as they were termed by the Baghdadis, had come from.

But after the screening of the first eight films, which included *Leopard Hunting*, *The Agitated Sea*, *The Industrialist* and *The Funeral of Edward VII*, the daily papers urged everyone to see the 'magic tricks' for themselves.

The first attempt at making local films failed miserably: in 1938 Hafidh Al Qadhi dispatched his brother to England to import the necessary equipment and materials to start producing a film. This proved over-ambitious and beyond the capabilities of the new industry.

Until financiers and war profiteers started setting up film companies such as the Baghdad Company for Film Production, licensed in 1942, the Iraqis could only manage to appear in Egyptian films as extras.

In 1946, an Iraqi-Egyptian company produced *Son of the East*, in which a number of Iraqi actors and actresses made their debut, and the film industry was born. Shortly after its inception the industry suffered from an acute attack of sluggishness, which lasted until the Art World Company brought it out of the doldrums in 1953 with the production of *Fetna and Hassan*. A number of poor quality, amateurish films followed, namely *Who is Responsible?*, *The Watchman* and *Saied Effendy*, filmed in the streets of Baghdad.

The state appeared on the scene during the 1960s and commenced its feature film production with *The Collector*. The most sophisticated equipment was made available to the film industry, which excelled in documentaries and prompted Iraq to take part in international film festivals. The productions included *The Long Days*, a highly propagandistic account of Saddam Hussein's life, *Another Day*, a film about feudal life, and the *Battle of Al Qadisiya* (fought in AD636, when the Arabs defeated the Persians). Egyptian films, especially romances, were very popular in Iraq, as were Indian films.

During the years of sanctions the production of Iraqi films virtually stopped.

Film and photography are the two fields of creative activity that developed after the occupation despite the collapse of the state. As the security situation has worsened, foreign filmmakers and photographers have become rather thin on the ground: Iraq under occupation has seen the largest casualty count of media workers and journalists of any recent conflict. A mixture of self-interest (mainly by news agencies) and the sincere good will of NGO's and individuals to allow Iraqis to at least find expression and documentation, has opened up new opportunities and markets.

Though much of the imagery reaching Western audiences is seen as news footage, there have been works of an artistic nature as young Iraqi filmmakers start concentrating on documentaries. One of the first was Uday Rashid's *Underexposure*, filmed with out-of-date Kodak film stock (hence its name) between October 2003 and April 2004. The film poignantly captures the feeling of the city under occupation. Hay-dar Daffair's documentary *Dreams of Sparrows* shows how dreams of liberation are shattered on the rocks of occupation. Hadi Mahood's film *The Office* deals with Saddam's security office, where thousands of people were tortured. Two young Iraqi filmmakers have made a film about the history of Iraqi cinema as seen through the eyes of young filmmakers. *Just Playing* shows children enjoying a football game next to a minefield. The film *Contradiction* is a about nectar-eating bee and a bee-eating hornet. In 2005, Iraqi director Laith Abdul Amir travelled throughout Iraq and produced *Songs of Absence*. In 2005 Baghdad staged the First International Iraq Short Film Festival. But there are still many problems to be overcome. An erratic electricity supply makes it difficult to screen films and pressure from Islamists has led to the closure of a number of film theatres.

The Independent Film and Television College was set up in Baghdad by filmmakers Kasim Abid and Maysoon Pachachi in 2004 to provide – free of charge – intensive short courses in film and television technique, theory and production. It has trained Iraqi filmmakers and has also supported their filmmaking by providing production facilities and information about funding and further training. Since the beginning of 2007, the students' films have been shown at various international film festivals.

In 2006 the continuing violence made it impossible for the college to remain open in Baghdad. There were explosions near the school, which blew out every pane of glass in the building, and with increasing roadblocks, closures and curfews, it became virtually impossible for students to even get in to the college for classes. They have, however, managed to complete shooting their documentary projects, and these were edited in Damascus. The college will

Emad was working on his film about the Shabandar Café, a meeting place for poets, writers and artists since the 1920s and the only literary café left in Baghdad. In early March, there was a massive explosion there, which demolished the Shabandar and much of the street, dealing a death-blow to the cultural life and identity of the city. Emad went to film on several occasions.

The last time, he was walking to get a taxi after filming when he was attacked by two armed men, who grabbed the small camera he was using and attempted to abduct him. Emad saw an opportunity to escape and made a run for it. He got about four metres away before he was shot in the leg. The men walked up to him, shot him in the chest and drove away, leaving him for dead. Luckily, the chest wound was just a surface one, but his leg was seriously damaged. Emad lay on the pavement for 20 minutes bleeding; no-one went to help him – they were too frightened. Finally a woman passer-by stopped a car and took him to hospital. He stayed there for some weeks while doctors tried to patch up his leg with bone grafts. He is now home, not yet able to walk. A doctor goes to see him every other day and the college is helping to pay for these expenses.

www.iftvc.org

have to relocate temporarily, at least for the next course/workshop – probably to Damascus.

Four years after the start of the war, Hollywood responded with two films: *Grace is Gone* (about a husband whose wife dies during military service in Iraq) and *Valley of Elah* (parents search for their awol son after he returns from Iraq). *Redacted* by US director Brian DePalma, deals with the rape and killing of a 14-year-old Iraqi girl by US soldiers, who also murdered her family.

British director Nick Broomfield produced *Battle for Haditha*, dealing with an incident on 19 November 2005 when a group of marines were patrolling a town in western Iraq. After a roadside bomb under a Humvee killed one of its occupants, the marines killed 19 civilians. Broomfield recreates the event using Iraqis, who had witnessed similar killings, as actors.

As in poetry, violence has become a predominant theme in the **theatre**, which is now highlighting the problems of Iraqi society. Mithal Gahza'i's play *The Day After The Seventh* deals with the plight of an Iraqi man who survives wars and violence only to discover he has developed cancer and has only seven days to live. It was produced under the auspices of the Ministry of Culture's Department for Cinema and Theatre. In the National Theatre the National Acting Group staged Qadim Al-Sumari's *What if?*, in which the poet is depicted as a hero because his life represents hope. Hassan Abdulrazzak's play *Baghdad Wedding*, focuses on the everyday life of ordinary Iraqis as the war rages.

Western playwrights have also been influenced by the Iraqi quagmire. *Fallujah* is based on interviews with people involved in the siege of the city. In *Called To Account – The Indictment of Anthony Charles Lynton Blair For The Crimes of Aggression Against Iraq – A Hearing*, diplomats, politicians and members of parliament are called as witnesses. *What Andrew Heard* deals with a report on the BBC's *Today* programme, which claimed that the British government knew that one of the claims about Iraq's WMD-threat was not true.

In ancient Iraq an artist would produce a pot, a cup or the image of a god without stopping to think about the nature of creativity. He worked spontaneously. In the 6th millennium BC, artists would mould clay into human forms without making a single preliminary sketch. During the Islamic period new values came into prominence. The art of ceramics was influenced by calligraphy and ornamentation.

After a break of several centuries, ceramics became an art form once again. In 1954 the first furnace for the production of ceramics was set up in the Baghdad Institute of Fine Arts. Its foundations were strengthened in 1967, when the Academy of Fine Arts was established, and it was later incorporated into Baghdad University.

The country's leading ceramicists have been influenced by rich traditions and Western techniques, which have been absorbed into the Arab context. Sa'ad Shakir's works consist of fantastical shapes modelled on plants, shells, fungi and rocks. Abla Al-Azzawi often abandons the potter's wheel and works with her hands. The late Nuha Al-Radhi specialised in folkloric themes, while the work of Muqbil Al-Zawi has a link to the Sumerian past.

David Kanikanian produces vases and other decorative pieces from his workshop in West London's Gallery Tavid. His work is enhanced by the lustre of the glazes in which he specialises.

FOOD

Arab hospitality is inseparable from sharing a meal with friends. The Iraqis feel duty-bound to make sure a guest is welcomed even in the most adverse circumstances. When thousands of Iraqi Kurds escaped to neighbouring Turkey at the end of the Gulf War (1991) fearing retribution for their three-week uprising against the regime, the refugees offered embarrassed aid workers tea.

Iraqi cuisine has been influenced by the ancient spice routes, when spices were brought to the Middle East from India and Persia more than 3,500 years ago. Poets lauded the creations of Abbasid chefs, which included various goat meat dishes and spit-roasted gazelles.

Iraqi dishes are extremely varied, ranging from meat and chicken kebabs to *quzi*, a whole lamb stuffed with rice, almonds, raisins and spices. The Bedouin speciality is sheep's head cooked in an enormous pot. The most famous Iraqi dish is *mazgouf*, redolent of the biblical Tigris River: as night falls a glittering necklace of lights illuminates the water, fishermen return with their fresh catch to the open-air restaurants along the river bank. Split and hung to smoke lightly over a charcoal fire, the fish is laid above the glowing ashes and filled with peppers, spices, onions and tomatoes. Each restaurant and family has its own secret recipe.

Religious festivals are times for feasts. Eid al Fitr, at the end of Ramadan, when Muslims fast from dawn to dusk, is one of the most significant celebrations in the religious calendar. Before the imposition of sanctions in August 1990, neighbours and friends would take elaborate dishes to each other's homes, and for many, Iraq being largely secular, there would be wine and arak, but this is changing as Islamists increase their grip on society.

A spread of food might include *tabouleh*, crushed bulgur wheat with sweet, chopped, broad-leaf parsley (very heavy on the parsley, which lingers on the tastebuds). There are also imaginative salads with dressings of fresh lime or lemon, yoghurt and/or oil, again with an abundance of parsley or mint. Iraqis can create magic with aubergines. One dish, which looks misleadingly like thinly fried, crisp slices of aubergines topped with tiny dots of buffalo yoghurt, actually reveals an explosion of subtle flavours: garlic, sesame, sweetened baby peppers and other unidentified, scented excursions.

Cooling, wafer-sliced cucumber with dill and yoghurt, lamb, beef and chicken (always cooked in an array of vegetables mixed with sweet, thick, natural fresh tomato paste) are essential to every great celebration and must be served for honoured guests.

Lavish meals are always served at births, weddings and circumcisions. On Eid al Adha, which commemorates the end of the pilgrimage to Mecca (*haj*), a lamb is roasted and food is offered to the poor.

Tea is the national Arab hot drink: there are few problems that cannot be solved over a cup of tea. Iraq's café society, the home of armchair politicians, has been transplanted into the major cities of the Middle East and Europe by expats and exiles. As Felicity Arbuthnot, a British journalist specialising in Iraqi affairs, has said:

> Not all Iraqis are good Muslims but most follow the Prophet's
> injunction to:
> Eat together and do not eat separately,
> for the blessing is with the company.

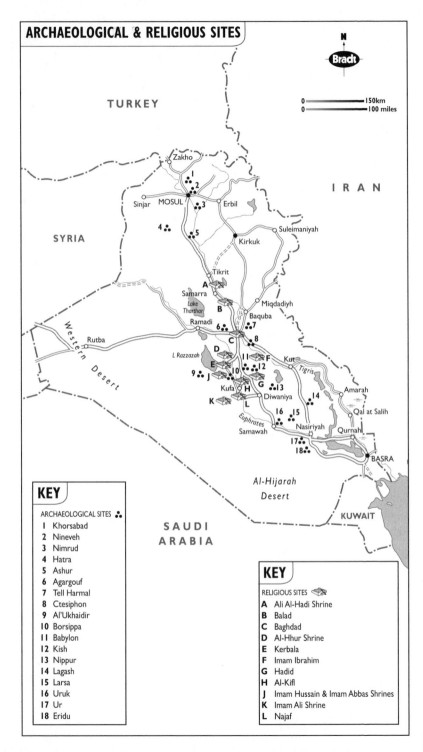

ARCHAEOLOGICAL & RELIGIOUS SITES

N

Bradt

TURKEY

0   150km
0   100 miles

Zakho

1
2

I R A N

Sinjar   MOSUL   3   Erbil

4   5   Suleimaniyah

SYRIA   Kirkuk

Tikrit

A

Samarra
Lake Tharthar

B

Ramadi   Miqdadiyh

6   Baquba

C   7

Rutba   8

W e s t e r n   *L Razzazah*

D   11   F   Kut

E   12   *Tigris*

D e s e r t   9   J   10

Kufa   H   G   Amarah

K   13   Diwaniya   14   Qal at Salih

L

Euphrates   16   15

Samawah   Nasiriyah   Qurnah

17   **BASRA**

18

Al-Hijarah Desert

KUWAIT

KEY

ARCHAEOLOGICAL SITES

1   Khorsabad
2   Nineveh
3   Nimrud
4   Hatra
5   Ashur
6   Agargouf
7   Tell Harmal
8   Ctesiphon
9   Al'Ukhaidir
10   Borsippa
11   Babylon
12   Kish
13   Nippur
14   Lagash
15   Larsa
16   Uruk
17   Ur
18   Eridu

SAUDI ARABIA

KEY

RELIGIOUS SITES

A   Ali Al-Hadi Shrine
B   Balad
C   Baghdad
D   Al-Hhur Shrine
E   Kerbala
F   Imam Ibrahim
G   Hadid
H   Al-Kifl
J   Imam Hussain & Imam Abbas Shrines
K   Imam Ali Shrine
L   Najaf

Archaeological Sites

There is a hall in Bloomsbury that
no more dare I tread,
For all the stone men shout at me
and swear they are not dead.
And once I touched a broken girl and
knew that marble bled.

Elroy Flecker, from the poem *Oak and Pine*
www.poets-corner.org

More than 100 Sumerian tells have been destroyed by looters since the beginning of the war. It's a disaster that we all keep watching but about which we can do little. We are incapable of stopping the looting. We are five archaeologists, some hundred guards and occasionally a couple of policemen – and they are a million armed looters, backed by their tribes and the dealers.

Abdul Amir Hamadani
Archaeologist, Nasiriyah

The way of life evolved by the Mesopotamians of ancient Iraq was a way of life guided by a sense of moderation and balance. In the words of Samuel Noah Kramer, author of *Cradle of Civilisation*:

Materially and spiritually – in religion and ethics, in politics and economics – they struck a viable mean between reason and fancy, freedom and authority, the knowable and the mysterious.

MANKIND'S CULTURAL CHAIN IN MESOPOTAMIA

4500BC	Sumer and Akkad
1900BC	Babylon
1400BC	Assyria
606–539BC	Neo-Babylonians
539–330BC	Achaemanid Persians
331–129BC	Seleucid Greeks
130BC–AD226	Parthian Persians
AD226–636	Sassanid Persians

The remains of their civilisation lay buried under the sands of Iraq for 2,000 years. Despite the scramble for antiques and the archaeological boom of the 19th century, thousands of tells (artificial mounds, which are formed by the accumulated remains of ancient settlements) are still waiting for excavation.

Iraq's magnificent, ancient archaeological sites have acted as a magnet for visitors to the country throughout the centuries. It is a land where clay tablets, cylinder seals, painted murals, ziggurats and ruins of temples and palaces shed light on life in ancient times.

EARLY ARCHAEOLOGY

The Western world first became interested in the antiquities of the east in the 16th century. One of the earliest visitors was a Dutch plant-collector, Dr Leonhardt Rauwolff, who combined his botanical work with a visit to the Tower of Babel in 1574. The Portuguese traveller Pedro Teixeira set sail for Basra in 1604, and visited Kerbala and Baghdad before travelling north to Aleppo in present-day Syria. The Italian Pietro della Valle wrote about his journeys in *Travels into East India and Desert Arabia* and described the cuneiform inscriptions he saw on bricks and black marble. In 1625, he brought back bricks from Ur to Europe. The embalmed body of his dead wife, a Nestorian Christian, accompanied him on his journeys for more than ten years. In 1761 the King of Denmark commissioned the first scientific mission to the area.

In the early 19th century travellers crossed Iraq on the overland route from India to England and visited the ruins of Babylon and Nineveh. Thomas Cook's first world tour of 1872 included Mesopotamia. The great desert route between Aleppo in Syria and Basra in southern Iraq was also described in the journals of William Beawes, Gaylard Roberts, Bartholomew Plaisted and John Carmichael, who were amongst the first travellers to describe the antiquities in the region.

Orientalists and archaeologists started arriving at the beginning of the 19th century. They included Constance M Alexander, who travelled throughout the country between 1816 and 1821, collecting Oriental manuscripts and antiquities. Between 1816 and 1821 Claudius James Rich took up residence in

THE LATEST DISCOVERY

One of the most recent discoveries was made in June 2000 in Wasit, south of Baghdad, at the archaeological site of Tel Al-Willia, dating back to 3000BC. The Iraqi Archaeological and Heritage Department announced the discovery of terracotta figurines from the Akkadian era and the earliest versions of *harshasha*, a pebble game still popular today. Models of boats and chisels were also unearthed.

In July 2001, a team of archaeologists working in Nimrud uncovered the remains of an Assyrian temple and statues of winged bulls dating back to the 8th century BC. There were a number of excavations in the south from around 1997 until the outbreak of the war at sites such as Umma and Umm Al-Aqarib, where an important Sumerian temple and a large number of tablets were discovered. No official excavations have taken place in post-Saddam Iraq due to the ongoing violence.

northern Iraq, near Nineveh, and spent his time collecting manuscripts and antiquities. Lady Blunt accompanied the Bedouin on their journeys towards the end of the 19th century, while Ely Bannister Soane visited both the north and south of the country in 1909.

Twentieth-century travellers with an intimate knowledge of the country included Freya Stark and Gertrude Bell (see page 69), both prolific writers.

Colonial officers and businessmen combined their official duties with an interest in antiquities. Claudius James Rich, a resident of the East India company at the Court of the Pasha of Baghdad, published *A Memoir on the Ruins of Babylon* in 1818. The British government subsidised the Tigris Euphrates Expedition of F R Chesney in 1835.

Henry Creswicke Rawlinson, a British political agent in Baghdad, was also a philologist of unsurpassed intellect. He spoke an enormous number of Indian dialects, which he learned very quickly, and decoded a trilingual (Old Persian, Elamite and Babylonian) inscription containing a message from King Darius, immortalised on a 122m rock-face at Behistun in western Iran. An account of his work was published by the Royal Asiatic Society in 1852.

Archaeological excavations began in the 1800s when Paul Emile Botta, the French consul in Mosul, unearthed Assyrian artefacts in Khorsabad. Remnants of the Sumerian civilisation were discovered near Nasiriyah by Ernest de Sarzec, the French consul in Basra. The early archaeologists were mainly interested in augmenting the display cabinets of their museums back home and the period was characterised by a scramble for antiquities. In Europe there was also a strong interest in biblical connections; anything that authenticated the Old Testament was of great interest.

The most important finds included Austen Henry Layard's unearthing of the Assyrian palaces of Nimrud. *The Illustrated London News* of 1840 publicised the finds, which heralded an Assyrian revival in Victorian England.

Layard and his exploits inevitably evoke controversy. The Iraqis, correctly, say that he plundered their country, but when the local people found ancient remains they often burned them for limestone to dress their fields. During most of its time under the Ottomans, Iraq was a backwater of ignorance, sloth and corruption, and looters inspired competition between European countries to create their collections of antiquities, to prove to the world that this ancient, almost lost, past was there. One of the best-preserved remains of Sennacherib's palace is now safely in the British Museum, while the site in Iraq was attacked and some carvings were taken. They later turned up in Switzerland.

THE MESSAGE FROM DARIUS, THE PERSIAN KING

Saith Darius the King:
Thou who shalt hereafter
Behold this inscription
Or these sculptures,
Do thou not destroy them
[But] thence onward
Protect them as long
As thou shalt be in good strength

13

At the beginning of the 20th century, German archaeologists succeeded in introducing new discipline and meticulous recording techniques into a field previously governed by luck or intuition. The *laisser-faire* attitude of the Ottoman government and then the British administration, followed by the Kingdom of Iraq, allowed foreign archaeologists – British, German, French, Japanese, Russians and Polish – to dig up the past. Restoration work was undertaken at Nimrud, Nineveh, Babylon, Ur and Hatra.

The period between World Wars I and II, when the British archaeologist Sir Leonard Woolley unearthed the royal cemetery at Ur, turned out to be the golden age of archaeology in Iraq. It also reignited public interest in such projects and assisted funding for museums and universities worldwide.

Excavations continued after World War II and young Iraqi archaeologists were keen to, and were encouraged to, train in the new discipline.

The Directorate General of Antiquities assumed responsibility for research and technical activities connected with archaeology, including the administration of museums and archaeological exhibits, and the excavation and protection of sites and antiquities.

The sanctions period from 1990 saw a deterioration in maintenance of sites and buildings. Today the Ministry of Culture presides over all such matters. On a positive note a growing co-operation and understanding is emerging between all parties, Iraq and the world of archaeology. Training and study programmes are being offered by many institutions worldwide to Iraqi archaeologists and conservators (see pages 300–2).

The Iraq Museum in Baghdad, originally founded and inspired by Gertrude Bell (see page 69), contained an impressive record of the peoples and cultures that flourished in Mesopotamia from time immemorial up to the time of the Arab conquest. Display halls were chronologically arranged, starting with the civilisation of the Sumerians. Despite the destruction of the 2003 war, there is no doubt that it will one day re-emerge as a great museum.

The Mosul Museum in northern Iraq had a large collection of finds from successive civilisations, from the Palaeolithic age up to Islamic times, with an emphasis on archaeological finds in the Nineveh governorate. It was looted in the first days of the war, but not as badly as the Iraq Museum. The antiquities from small museums around the country were stored in the Iraq Museum before the 2003 war broke out.

In Saddam's time the State Board of Antiquities was responsible for the restoration and preservation of antiquities and historic buildings throughout the country. The most notable restoration work took place in Babylon. Numerous buildings and main temples in the ancient city of Hatra have also been restored.

During the 1970s the construction of dams on the Euphrates, including the Hamrin basin project, prompted salvage excavations, which led to the discovery of relics ranging from prehistoric to Islamic times.

The 1991 Gulf War dampened further exploration and left a tragic legacy of looting and theft. In its issue of January 1997, *Trace*, a magazine that liaises with international police forces and the art world to find stolen art works and antiques, estimated 4,000 items were looted during the Gulf War in 1991. Black marketeers have been encouraged by legitimate deals. On the legal market an Assyrian stone carving sold for £2.7 million to a Japanese collector.

The looting of the Iraq Museum was the story of a cultural genocide. If a country's civilisation is looted its history ends, commented Riad Mohammed, an Iraqi archaeologist.

The museum, which first opened in 1923, occupies an area of 4,700m². It was expanded continually until 1983, culminating in 28 large exhibition halls, with displays pre-dating 9000BC and reaching right up to the Islamic era. The museum's collections included some of the earliest tools ever made, gold from the famous Royal Cemetery at Ur, and Assyrian bull figures and reliefs from the ancient Assyrian capitals of Nimrud, Nineveh and Khorsabad.

The former president of Iraq's State Board of Antiquities, Donny George, recalled in the introduction to *The Looting of the Iraq Museum Baghdad: The Lost Legacy of Ancient Mesopotamia*:

As I walked through the museum, I passed gigantic Assyrian wall carvings, some 15 metres long and about five metres tall, showing ceremonies in ancient Nimrud and Khorsabad. Giant human-headed winged bulls that had once guarded the gates of the Assyrian capitals loomed overhead. Buried for thousands of years they blazoned forth as though carved only yesterday, to proclaim the majesty of the greatest empire in the ancient world. In other cases were some of the earliest known pieces of elaborate pottery, jewelry and statues from Ur, Babylon, Nineveh, Nimrud, Ashur and the score of cities scattered along the Tigris and Euphrates Rivers. All in all, the Iraq Museum was one of the greatest collections of cultural treasures in our world. And today it is no more.

After the capture of Baghdad by American troops in April 2003 the museum was looted, and an estimated 15,000 items were stolen, including Abbasid wooden doors and Sumerian, Akkadian and Hatraean statues, gold and silver materials, necklaces, pendants and pottery. Several famous pieces, such as the Warka vase, were returned, but the collection of 4,800 cylinder seals is still missing, along with 10,000 other looted artefacts. By June 2005 antiquities from looted sites had been intercepted from Kuwait to Japan and Italy.

On 4 July 2003 the American authorities displayed the fabulous golden treasure of Nimrud (see page 312) for two hours, in an attempt to salvage their reputation after they failed to protect the museum from looters.

No-one is quite sure when the museum will re-open. Much of the extensive damage has been repaired but the precarious security situation in Baghdad makes it impossible for the museum to function normally. In June 2006, 50 people were kidnapped near the museum building. Donny George had the museum's doors plugged with concrete as he feared looters would see the building as a soft target and plan another raid. Two galleries displaying Assyrian slabs from Khorsabad and Hatra sculptures are due to open in 2008.

Archaeological Sites THE 20TH CENTURY

13

In leaflets dropped from the air on 27 March 2003 the Coalition said it did not wish to destroy Iraqi landmarks. None of Iraq's historic sites were damaged during military action.

The problems started after the war: rampant looting and long-term neglect. Simon Jenkins pointed out in a *Guardian* article on 8 June 2007:

> Under Saddam you were likely to be tortured and shot if you let someone steal an antiquity: in today's Iraq you are likely to be tortured and shot if you don't.

Soon after Saddam's statue was dragged to the ground and smashed in Fardous Square the looting of the museum began. Witnesses and antiquities experts believe that the first looters were insiders who knew what they were looking for and stole the most valuable items by unlocking display cases and vaults. They were followed by thieves who embarked on an orgy of looting characterised by brute force and ignorance.

It took three days to vandalise the museum. American patrols watched as vases, jewellery, pots and anything that could be carried 'walked'. It was not a choice between protecting civilians or guarding the museum's exhibits. There were enough military personnel on hand to remove the mural of former President George Bush from the floor of the Al Rashid Hotel.

Both the National Library and the Ministry of Religious Affairs were burned almost to the ground. Antique manuscripts and thousands of illuminated and handwritten Korans turned to ashes. Employees of the National Library have been forced to work in a burned-out shell. The Ottoman archive was soaked by flooding in 2003 and affected by mould. It was placed in the freezer of an abandoned Baathist officers' building. If the archive thaws – which is very likely with the intermittent electricity supply – the documents will perish and a record of Iraqi history from the 16th to the early 20th century will be destroyed.

Iraq is a country of 10,000 archaeological sites, of which only 1,500 have been researched. Most are unprotected and as such it is open season for looters.

Even when a site is guarded the guards are no match for looters, who have organised themselves into armed gangs. Sites in the remote desert of the south, such as Dahaileh, are especially vulnerable. Umma, a famous Sumerian city in the desert north of Nasiriya, has been ravaged, and what the city could have revealed about pre-Akkadian times is probably in the dustbin of history. Nothing remains of the 2000BC cities of Isin and Shurnpak situated in the south of Iraq. The looters have left a desert full of holes.

In their contribution to *The Looting of the Iraq Museum*, Micah Caren and Marie-Helene Carleton describe the farming of antiquities in southern Iraq as 'erasing the past'.

In the Kurdistan region, which has more than 3,000 archaeological sites, artefacts are disappearing or disintegrating. Some sites have been damaged by the expansion of agriculture and the construction of buildings, trenches built in preparation for war and 'looting to order' from the sites and museums. The sites have been neglected due to a lack of experience, equipment and money.

A new bridge has been erected on the remains of the ancient Dalal Bridge over the Khabir River to the east of Zakho. The old bridge was constructed by the Greeks, Romans, Alexander the Great or the Badinan Kurdish sultans, depending on whose theory you subscribe to.

Sadly everything is up for grabs: castles, ziggurats, old cities, ancient minarets and mosques. Muslim shrines from the 10th and 11th centuries have been bombed by radical Muslim groups who are opposed to shrines.

The illicit antiquities trade is third in international monetary terms after drug dealing and arms sales. Collectors are willing to pay hundreds of thousands of dollars for carved seals and cuneiform tablets depicting historical events. The criminals have connections with dealers who in turn have links with the international antiquities market. An antiquities bazaar has been set up in Rifa'i north of Nasiriyah.

Colonel Matthew Bogdanos, a former assistant district attorney from Manhattan who led the American multi-agency task force assigned with investigating the looting, declared an amnesty on looted items. Around 4,000 objects were returned to the museum by Iraqis, the Iraqi police and customs and the Coalition MP units, among them the Uruk alabaster vase carved 5,000 years ago, known as the Warka vase. Islamist leaders in Sadr City suggested that wives should refuse to sleep with their husbands until looted items were returned.

Many antiquities were recovered in neighbouring countries: 1,054 in Jordan, 200 in Syria, 35 in Kuwait, a number in Saudi Arabia and Lebanon, more than 300 in Italy and over 600 in the USA.

In a lecture delivered in London on 7 June 2007, Dr Abbas Al-Hussaini, head of the State Board of Antiquities and Heritage, said that one of the major threats to Iraq's heritage is the bombing of Islamic sites by Islamists and Al-Qaeda. The severely damaged sites include Samarra Mosque, Ana Minaret, Hidir Mosque in Anbar, the Abdul-Qadir Al-Gailani mosque (in Baghdad), the tomb of Yahya Bin Qasim (in Mosul) and ten shrines in the Diyala region.

Dr Al-Hussaini also described sites damaged by neglect and the security situation: the minaret of the Imam Ali mosque in Basra, Basra's heritage houses, the tomb of Ezekiel at Al Kifil, Assyrian Ashur which is being eroded by the River Tigris, and Qasr Al-Atshan in Kerbala. The late Abbasid caravanserai at Khan-Al-Rub'a near Kerbala has been badly damaged through an accidental explosion of ammunition stored in a well by Coalition forces.

Among the board's conservation projects for 2008 are the synagogue and the tomb of Prophet Nahum, situated in the northern Christian Iraqi town of al-Qoush, 40km north of Mosul. The Prophet is venerated by all sects.

Some activities of the coalition have also damaged archaeological sites. A military camp has been built on the site of Babylon, and the pre-war Saddam airbase at Ur continues to be occupied by allied forces. The Americans have been blamed for setting up their own airbase on this ancient site, when in actual fact it was there long before they came on the scene.

Excavation and conservation work in Iraq came to an end in 2002, and all foreign archaeologists, fearful for their lives, left. On 7 August 2006 Donny George, the Board of Antiquities' president, resigned and followed in their footsteps. Ending a 30-year career with the board, George said he resigned because the board was inceasingly influenced by the militant Al-Sadr Shia movement; the staff were adopting an Islamist stance and showed scant regard for Iraq's earlier cultures; contact with foreigners was discouraged; and the

13

money for the 1,400-member police force to protect the ancient sites had run out. George is now teaching a course in archaeology at Stony Brook University east of New York City.

There has been some good news, however: in the last week of November 2007, for example, 594 looted antiquities were returned to the Ministry of Culture and Antiquities. The Minister of Culture and Antiquities has made the recovery of looted antiquities his priority and has instituted a reward system – people are paid anything from US$8 to US$4,000 for turning in antiquities. Special police task forces have been formed to patrol the routes that smugglers are using to neighbouring countries and are achieving some success.

SAVING THE CRADLE OF CIVILISATION

Prevention would have been better than cure. Having failed to stop the looting, not only of museum artefacts but also art works, the border guards could have prevented them from leaving the country. Tragically the porous borders were a smugglers' dream come true. Interpol has set up a task force to trace Iraq's stolen treasures.

On 22 May 2003 the United Nations passed Security Resolution 1483 banning trade in Iraqi cultural property. A further resolution, 1546, was passed on 8 June 2004 stressing the need for site protection. But little has been done to enforce these resolutions as the establishment of law and order continues to be a priority.

The British Museum, UNESCO, The University of Chicago and the World Monuments Fund are among the organisations assisting with the preservation of Iraq's cultural heritage.

THE BRITISH MUSEUM In 2003 the Director of the British Museum, Neil MacGregor, emphasised that the museum stands ready to offer to the Iraq Museum, if it is wanted, as much conservation and curatorial assistance as it can reasonably provide. 'We will also continue to draw attention to ongoing problems at every opportunity.'

The deteriorating security situation has forced the museum to abandon a number of projects in Iraq, such as sending an international team of conservators to carry out work on damaged objects in the Iraq Museum.

The museum is one of the main institutions in Britain providing information about Iraq's archaeological heritage through lectures and information programmes. Before the war, the museum, in conjunction with the London Middle East Institute of the School of Oriental and African Studies, wrote to the Defence Minister warning about the consequences of military action to archaeological sites.

On 15 April 2003, the main topic for discussion at a press conference at the museum's 250th birthday celebrations was the looting of the Iraq Museum. During the conference Neil MacGregor said the British Museum would adopt a leading role in assisting the Iraq Museum and would co-ordinate the activities of other museums. A subsequent conference entitled 'International Support for Museums and Archaeological Sites in Iraq' was held at the British Museum on 29 April and attended by Donny George of the Iraq Museum.

For three months in 2003, Sarah Collins, Assistant Keeper, Early Mesopotamia Collections, was seconded to the CPA (Coalition Provisional Authority) to work with the Ministry of Culture in Iraq.

To date the British Museum has provided training for two or three Department of Antiquities staff each year since 2003, including museum curators and conservators and staff from the archaeological site of Babylon. A co-operation protocol has also been signed with the Iraqi State Board of Antiquities and Heritage.

John Curtis, Keeper of the Middle East Department, with special interests in Iraq and Iran, produced a report on damage to the archaeological site in Babylon (see page 306) and on damage to Ur (see page 316) as military bases have been situated on both sites.

UNESCO UNESCO acted quickly to assess, the damage to Iraq's heritage. In 2003 three major meetings were held in Paris, London and Tokyo, bringing together experts on the cultural heritage of Iraq. Subsequent assistance was based on the recommendations from these meetings.

On 24 September 2003 the establishment of an International Co-ordination Committee for the Safeguarding of Iraqi Cultural Heritage was approved. The committee continues to meet and UNESCO participates in international fora and conferences on Iraqi heritage and culture.

It has many projects in Iraq, among them the development of a database on stolen Iraqi cultural property; assisting the Iraq National Museum by restoring and upgrading storage spaces and providing literature on conservation theories and practices; repairing the fences at the Nineveh site (see pages 302–4); training courses for Iraqi professionals in the field of documentation, including photogrammetrical techniques; preparing a proposal to stabilise the arch at Ctesiphon and the Nouri Minaret in Mosul; and providing a lighting system for the exhibition spaces in the Ottoman building in Baghdad known as Dar Al Wali.

UNESCO has rebuilt Baghdad's National Heritage Institute and supplied a generator and air conditioning equipment, provided equipment for the School of Music and Ballet in Baghdad, and trained archaeological site guards and those engaged in border patrols.

It is also active in education and training courses. At the end of January 2005, it financed a training course on 'First Aid Conservation' for 15 Iraqi trainees from the Iraq National Museum in Baghdad and six Jordanian trainees from the Department of Antiquities of Jordan. The focus of the course was to rescue archaeological artefacts on sites endangered by illicit excavations.

Three Iraqi sites, Ashur, Hatra and Samarra, are on UNESCO's World Heritage List. UNESCO is also active in the rehabilitation of the Erbil Citadel, Kirkuk Museum, Suleimaniyah Museum, and the historic quarters of Basra, and in the conservation of mud-brick architecture.

LOST TREASURES FROM IRAQ: ORIENTAL INSTITUTE, UNIVERSITY OF CHICAGO
The University of Chicago has set up a website to provide information about looted Iraqi antiquities from the Iraq Museum. When the Iraq Museum re-opens, it will be the headquarters of the database.

The site is constantly updated with information about recovered artefacts and descriptions of missing artefacts. It has a facility for information to be added by visitors.

The University of Michigan, the University of Southern California, Harvard University, the University of California at Berkeley, the British Museum and the

13

British Institute for the Study of Iraq (formerly the British School of Archaeology in Iraq) are among the institutions assisting with the website and providing information. It is hoped the site will deter potential buyers of looted artefacts.

WORLD MONUMENTS FUND (WMF)   The Iraq Cultural Heritage Conservation Initiative was created in 2003 to address the urgent threats facing Iraqi cultural heritage sites. The programme aims to build the capacity of Iraqi professionals from the Iraq State Board of Antiquities and Heritage to protect and manage their cultural heritage after decades of isolation and conflict.

Through training and the development of technical tools and expertise, the initiative is helping local stewards prepare for a time when active on-site conservation work will again take place. This initiative is made possible through a partnership with the Getty Conservation Institute (GCI) in coordination with UNESCO, and with support from the J M Kaplan Fund and the National Endowment for the Humanities.

The training is undertaken in Amman and the Jordanian Department of Antiquities is a partner with the GCI and the WMF.

The initiative also involves the development of a national database/GIS (Geographic Information System) of archaeological sites and monuments.

WMF and Iraq's State Board of Antiquities are also developing a management plan for Babylon.

Above all, existing sites must be given adequate protection from further looting and destruction. If this is done, further catastrophies could be prevented.

ARCHAEOLOGY CARDS FOR AMERICAN TROOPS

American troops in Iraq are being sent another deck of playing cards, this time showing some of the country's most precious archaeological sites, and giving advice on how to respect them.

The Pentagon sent 40,000 new decks to units in Iraq, four years after it issued soldiers with a more gung-ho pack containing pictures and information about the most-wanted former members of Saddam Hussein's regime.

The cards are part of an archaeology awareness programme designed to make troops aware of the damage they can cause to sites and to discourage the illegal trade in artefacts.

Archaeologists working at Ford Drum, New York, where troops are trained for deployment in Iraq, hope soldiers will know what to avoid when it comes to bivouacking or setting up gun installations.

The suits have different themes: diamonds for artefacts, spades for digs, hearts for 'winning hearts and minds' and clubs for heritage preservation. The seven of clubs carries a picture of the Ctesiphon Arch in Iraq and a caption which asks: 'This site has survived 17 centuries. Will it and others survive you?'

In another Defense Department programme, US pilots have received training in recognising and identifying ruins, cemeteries and other sites so they don't accidentally bomb them. A third involves soldiers in simulating incidents, such as practising what they would do if they were taking hostile fire from an archaeological ruin.

Tom Leonard, www.telegraph.co.uk

It is imperative that the American and British governments recognise the damage the war has done to Iraq's heritage. Little is being done to stop the 'farming of antiquities' even though the Geneva Convention states that an occupying army should 'use all means within its power' to guard the cultural heritage of a defeated state.

Writing in the *Herald Tribune* on 6 March 2007, Matthew Bogdanos, author, with William Patrick, of *Thieves Of Baghdad*, pointed out that:

> In the past, most archaeological digs in Iraq have had foreign sponsorship – the Germans at Babylon and Uruk, the British at Ur and Nimrud, the French at Kish and Lagash, the Italians at Hatra, and the Americans at Nippur. Given that background, it would make sense for each of these countries to 'adopt' the sites its scholars have been studying. Each of the foreign nations would provide guards around the perimeter and around the clock. Ideally, these foreign forces would also be assigned a group of Iraqi recruits to train. Once the Iraqis were mission-capable – it should take only six months or so if the Baghdad government supplied the manpower – the donor nation would recall its forces.

A–Z OF ARCHAEOLOGICAL SITES

Iraq's archaeological sites have been damaged by wars, sanctions, the collapse of infrastructure, looting, military bases stationed within the sites themselves, accelerated decay, and questionable reconstruction methods, such as those used in Babylon in the 1980s. The seriousness of conditions in Iraq prompted the World Monuments Fund (WMF), for the first time, to put the entire country on its biannual list of the One Hundred Most Endangered Sites. Most of the major sites described in this section have been looted and damaged during or since the 2003 war.

Due to neglect there is nothing left at Jarmo, one of the earliest villages where seeds were first planted 100,000 years ago, and Tel al Suwan, where household paintings dating back 8,000 years were found. But while some sites vanish into the mists of time, others are unearthed in an endless journey of discovery. In February 1997, Iraqi archaeologists reported the discovery of Nimrik, an ancient farming village in Kurdistan dating back to between 8000 and 9000BC.

AGARGOUF (*Location: approximately 33km from the city centre in Baghdad on the Damascus Road. The site is on the right bank of the Saklawiyeh Canal. Date: 15th century BC.*) The most stunning feature is the ziggurat, which has been restored up to its platform, the remainder giving a very good idea of what the original site was like. The temple buildings have been heavily restored.

The site dates back to the beginning of the 3rd millennium BC when it may have been a border fortress of Babylonia. In the 15th century BC the ancient town of Dur Kurigalzu was founded here by the Kassite King, Kurigalzu. The Kassites, like the Babylonians and the Sumerians, built large ziggurats and a group of sacred buildings, among which were several temples. The temples and palaces were used until the end of the 2nd millennium BC, when the Kassites ceased to be a dominant power in the region.

13

The ziggurat, made from unbaked bricks with a coffering of baked bricks measuring 81m by 67m, rises to a height of 57m. Its corners correspond to the four points of the compass. In front of the ziggurat one room in the religious precinct has been restored and is being used as a museum.

The remains of a religious building are found 100m west of the ziggurat. Originally this structure, which formed a huge terrace 650m by 28m, was built of unbaked bricks, but it was later covered by a coffering of baked bricks. A temple dedicated to the god Enlil took up most of the terrace. The remains of the paving of the esplanade are visible.

The palaces of the Kassite kings were built about a kilometre southwest of the ziggurat in the artificial hillocks grouped together under the name of Tel El Abiad. The royal storehouse and treasury was the place for Kassite art: a lifelike terracotta figurine of a lioness, a gold bracelet with paste inlay and a decorated ceremonial macehead were found on the site.

ASHUR (QALA'AT SHARQAT) *(Location: 112km south of Mosul, on a stony hill overlooking the Tigris on the east, near the Himrin mountains. Date: from 1200BC.)* Ashur was the first capital of the Assyrians, who named their city after their major god and built a vast empire that included Iraq, Syria, Anatolia, Iran, Egypt and parts of Arabia.

The latest excavations, early in 2002, revealed some small houses and religious buildings, a very sophisticated drainage system and new tombs. The inner part of the city with the Parthian graves and palaces is fenced off.

King Kikkia built a wall around the city in 2300BC, but the city's exposure to invaders from the west prompted the resiting of the Assyrian capital to Nimrud at the end of the 11th century BC. The city's temples ensured it did not decline in importance until the fall of the Assyrian Empire in 612BC. The city was resurrected during the reign of the Parthians, but after being sacked by Trajan (AD116), Septimius Severus (AD198) and Shapur I (AD257), the exact location of Ashur remained uncertain until the excavations carried out by German archaeologists between 1903 and 1914.

The most striking feature of the site today is the ziggurat and temple devoted to the god Ashur, called the Temple of the Universe.

The temples on the site include the temple of Anu-Adad, with two ziggurats from the 12th century BC, completed during the reign of Tiglath-Pileser I. A palace was built between the great ziggurat and the temple of Anu-Adad. Its basement was converted into a royal necropolis. Another double temple dedicated to the gods Sin and Shamash was built in the 16th century BC and continually modified until the 7th century BC. The Ishtar Temple dates back to the 3rd millennium BC.

The city had great religious significance and the Assyrian kings were buried there. Their tombs were robbed in ancient times. Erosion by the waters of the Tigris is damaging the site.

BABYLON *(Location: 90km south of Baghdad; 10km north of Hilla. Date: from 2350BC.)* In Akkadian times, in around 2350BC, Babylon was a small village. During the next six centuries it grew in size and importance until it became the capital of the famous king, law-giver and social reformer Hammarubi (1792–1750BC) (see pages 31–2). In the next thousand years or so it was surpassed by other Mesopotamian cities in power and influence, until it

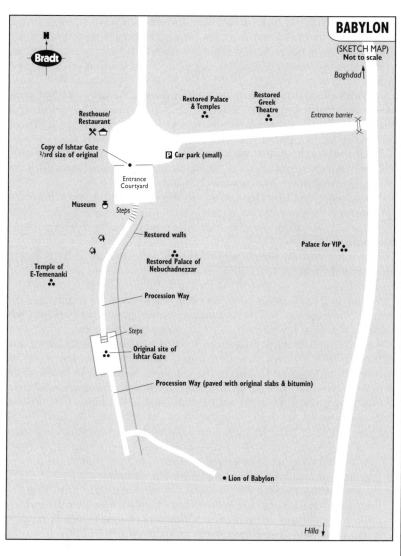

BABYLON

(SKETCH MAP)
Not to scale

N

Bradt

Baghdad↑

Restored Palace & Temples

Restored Greek Theatre

Entrance barrier

Resthouse/ Restaurant

Copy of Ishtar Gate ⅔rd size of original

P Car park (small)

Entrance Courtyard

Museum

Steps

Restored walls

Palace for VIP

Temple of E-Temenanki

Restored Palace of Nebuchadnezzar

Procession Way

Steps

Original site of Ishtar Gate

Procession Way (paved with original slabs & bitumin)

• Lion of Babylon

Hilla ↓

13

flourished again under King Nebuchadnezzar (605–603BC) who rebuilt it according to a new plan (see pages 39–41). The Babylon that has left its imprint on the history of the world is the Babylon from the time of Nebuchadnezzar onwards – two centuries of glory and decadence when the arts and sciences flourished and when there was an unprecedented boom of prosperity.

The site is a mixture of the remains of Nebuchadnezzar's Babylon, from which nothing tangible has survived, and extensive restoration. Saddam reconstructed parts of Babylon until it became the most restored site in Iraq. Bricks inscribed with Saddam's name adorn the site. He reconstructed Nebuchadnezzar's palace and built his own palace on the site.

Today little remains above ground of the famous Processional Way (just road slabs and asphalt covering can be seen) or of the ziggurat and the temple of

Marduk. The ruins of Nebuchadnezzar's summer palace are no more than a great mass of bricks. The palace was identified by excavators through the inscriptions on the bricks. Some vaulted structures are thought to be the remains of the Hanging Gardens of Babylon, one of the Seven Wonders of the Ancient World.

As Processional Way descends, the foundations of the original Ishtar Gate merge with the original decorations of bulls and dragons.The dragon is a composite animal with the physical attributes of a snake, lion and eagle. These brick reliefs are not glazed. The gate with beautiful glazed-brick panels with bulls, dragons and lions (the symbol of Ishtar) was taken in thousands of pieces and painstakingly reconstructed in the Berlin Museum before World War I, by the German expedition that excavated Babylon.

The magnificent Lion of Babylon is carved in basalt. The marks on the lion's back indicate that it was meant for a precious saddle on which the goddess Ishtar would stand. Ninmakh Temple, Alexander's amphitheatre and storerooms have been restored.

American troops are now living in Saddam's former palace in Babylon and Major David Giolleran speculated it could become a Marriott with a five-star restaurant.

Writing in *The Guardian* on 8 June 2007, Simon Jenkins commented on America's conversion of Nebuchadnezzar's great city of Babylon into the hanging gardens of Halliburton – a 150ha camp for 2,000 troops.

Archaeological grounds have been levelled to build a landing zone for helicopters and a dozen 170m trenches. The continuous movement of helicopters has destroyed a wall in the temple of Nabu and the roof of the Temple of Ninmah. Both date back to the 6th century BC. English and Arabic graffiti scrawled on some of the walls in Babylon does not appear to have done extensive harm.

In his report of 2006, Dr John Curtis of the British Museum noted that:

> substantial damage has been caused to Ishtar Gate, one of the most
> famous monuments from antiquity [...] US military vehicles have
> crushed 2,600-year-old brick pavements, archaeological fragments have
> been scattered across the site, more than 12 trenches have been driven
> into ancient deposits and military earth-moving projects have
> contaminated the site for future generations of scientists. [...]

Add to all that the damage caused to nine of the moulded brick figures of dragons in the Ishtar Gate by looters trying to remove the bricks from the wall.

Between November 2003 and February 2005, the Polish military contingent financed a number of projects at the Babylon site from the Commanders Emergency Resource Programme, including the construction and repair of the roof at the gallery shop at Babylon's Archaeological Museum; providing an electricity supply to the museum; purchasing computer hardware and providing training for Iraqi antiquity service staff in Babil province; and providing equipment for the archaeological police and refurbishing their office.

The World Monuments Fund and the Iraqi State Board of Antiquities and Heritage are producing a site management and protection plan.

BORSIPPA (BIRS NIMRUD) *(Location: 15km south of Babylon. Date: from 1900BC.)* These are ruins at their best. If seen at dusk they resemble a science-fiction landscape. Borsippa was the place of worship of Nabu, son of the great Babylonian god Marduk.

The seven-level ziggurat contains dark green lumps of molten bricks, which scholars believe melted when it was hit by a meteorite. Nebuchadnezzar II's personal foundation cylinders were discovered in the ziggurat's foundations. (Note that when a King restored, rebuilt or built a temple or palace, then at each corner of the building would be placed large foundation cylinders describing the date.)

On another ancient mound, almost opposite the ziggurat and still part of the ancient city, is a small mosque and shrine. It is believed that Abraham was born here. In the depths of the shrine is a door socket on which he is said to have rested.

CTESIPHON (AL-MADA'IN) *(Location: on the east bank of the Tigris, 30km south of Baghdad. Date: from the 2nd century BC.)* Two ancient cities were once located near this site. A ship canal, the Nahr Al-Malik, linked the Tigris with the Euphrates. Seleucia was established by Seleucus, a successor of Alexander the Great, in 301BC on the west or right bank of the Tigris, while their successors the Parthians set up the town of Ctesiphon on the east or left bank. The two cities, one Greek and the other Oriental, tolerated each other's presence until Avidius Cassius razed Seleucia in AD165. Ctesiphon survived and turned into a cluster of small towns rather than a single city, hence the name The Cities (Al-Mada'in) adopted by the Arab conquerors in AD636. After the Arab conquest Ctesiphon declined in importance. The river changed its course and now cuts through the site.

Amid the ruins of the city of Ctesiphon stands the largest single-span brick arch in the world, built in the 3rd century AD under the Parthians. A descendant of Ancient Mesopotamian structures in style, it embodied a skilful development of temples and palaces where the front part of great buildings would consist of large halls topped by high arches, as seen in the entrances to Assyrian cities.

The museum at Ctesiphon was among the completely looted museums following the 2003 war. The gardens, once lovingly tended by the Department of Antiquities, have been turned into a soccer field by local children.

The small town of Ctesiphon (Salman Park) has a friendly atmosphere. The small mosque incorporating the tomb of one of the Prophet's barbers is a pleasant, cool place.

A panorama, which once stood near Ctesiphon, covering an area of 1,640m², has vanished. It depicted the Battle of Qadissiya in AD637, when the Muslims were victorious over the forces of the Persian Yezdegird.

ERBIL *(Location: halfway between Mosul and Kirkuk: 86km from Mosul, 93km from Kirkuk. Date: from 35,000 years ago.)* This part of Iraq is one of the most important places in the world for the study of the culture of Neanderthal man, 35,000–70,000 years ago. Cuneiform (wedge-shaped) inscriptions suggest that Erbil was very well known towards the end of the 3rd millennium BC. Syrian inscriptions of the 2nd millennium refer to it as

13

Urbilum or Erbilum. In Assyrian and Babylonian texts it is called Arba Ilu (the four gods).

Erbil was a centre for the worship of Ishtar, whose temple was called E-kshan-klama, or House of the Lady of the Regions. There was also a temple devoted to the god Assur. A stela (a stone slab with inscriptions) of Ashur-banipal (668–627BC) was unearthed here, together with images of other Assyrian kings. Sennacherib (705–681BC) built an irrigation canal that carried water down to the city from the Bastura valley, 20km away.

At Bastura where the canal starts there is a well-built stone wall with a cuneiform transcription that reads:

> I, Sennacherib, King of Assyria, have dug three rivers in the Khani mountains above Erbil, home of the venerated Lady Goddess Ishtar, and made their courses straight.

(Also see page 39.)

ERIDU (TELL ABU SHAREIN) (*Location: 315km southeast of Baghdad. Date: from first half of the 4th millennium BC.*) According to Sumerian legends, Eridu was one of the five cities built before the great flood. Its exact origins are lost in the mists of antiquity but it could be one of the most ancient settled places on earth, and one of the earliest examples of a palace separate from temples and religious buildings. The city was a focal point for the worship of the god of sweet waters, Enki, and an important religious centre from 5000BC to the early 3rd millennium BC. It began as a village and evolved into a large city, as the remains of 16 superimposed temples show. Fishing was a vital part of the economy and fish bones, the remains of offerings to the gods, have been found in the ruins of the city's shrines. Ur-Nammu began constructing a ziggurat in 2100BC but it was never completed. The Elamites destroyed the city at the end of the 3rd millennium BC.

Nothing is left of the city except mounds and the ruins of Ur – Nammu's ziggurat. Inscribed bricks are scattered throughout the site. Excavations began here in 1850 but the excavated buildings are covered by sand. A cemetery dating back to the Ubaid period (4th century BC) has been discovered.

Looters tried their luck at the old excavation house of the Iraq Museum's team and found only a few old sardine cans.

HATRA (*Location: 100km southwest of Mosul. The site is approximately 20km off the highway into desert terrain. Date: from the 1st century AD.*) Like India's Taj Mahal, photographs cannot do justice to the wonder of Hatra. During the rule of the Parthian Empire, Hatra became the capital of a client kingdom under Arab rulers. It served as a religious centre for the Bedouin and a bulwark against the aggressive Roman armies. It was abandoned after the Sassanians overthrew the Parthian Dynasty and destroyed the city in AD258.

The town, with its seven gates, was surrounded by walls reinforced by round towers. Its administrative sector was isolated from the rest of the buildings.

The ruins of the temple of the Sun and a temple dedicated to the goddess Shahiro are the most impressive. The remains of a temple dedicated to the goddess Allath are also visible. Another temple has not been identified yet, but the sanctuary next to it was probably consecrated to Mithras, whose cult spread throughout the whole Roman world from the 2nd century AD onwards. The remains of 12 small temples have also been unearthed, along with a Hellenistic temple and several statues of Apollo, Poseidon, Eros and Hermes. Statues of princes, high priests and important figures in the history of Hatra were discovered on the site in 1961 and transferred to the museums of Baghdad and Mosul. There are also ruins of several funeral towers and stone wells.

The classical folklorist Adrienne Mayor believes that Hatra's inhabitants used naphtha bombs and jars of desert scorpions to repel Roman invaders.

This site now has a round-the-clock American and Iraqi military guard. One of the figures in the temple complex lost a head before the soldiers arrived. They are now conducting controlled explosions of recovered munitions and mines at a nearby military base. The constant seismic activity is damaging the stone arches in the main temple and the outer wall of the city and this may cause the collapse of parts of this site, listed as a World Heritage Monument.

Sadly, a mass grave containing the bodies of executed Kurdish mothers and their children, victims of the Anfal campaign (see page 182), was found in a trench 3km south of Hatra.

KHORSABAD (DAR SHARRUKIN) *(Location: 20km northeast of Mosul, a region of tells, monasteries and churches. Date: from 721BC.)* The city was built by the Assyrian King Sargon II as his capital. Unlike other ancient cities it was not an important centre of communications and was constructed solely for Sargon's benefit.

The city wall enclosed an area 1.75km square and was pierced by seven gates, now visible as seven mounds. Little remains of the royal palace, temples and ziggurat.

During the 19th century many of the stone reliefs were removed. The Sibitti Temple near the Palace of Sargon has been excavated and its foundations restored.

The area is full of mounds, monasteries and restored churches, such as the Monastery of St Matti (Matthew) clinging to the cliff side on Mt Maqloub. The views from the monastery, which dates from the 4th century AD, are magnificent. Five monks live in the building, which is also used as a religious retreat. Several small villages and a new church have been recently built in the slopes leading to the monastery for Christians fleeing persecution from Baghdad and Mosul.

The Iraqi army has dug many pits at this site and in the neighboring Tell Billa. Unexploded bombs are a major problem and could hinder future archaeological work.

KISH (AL-UHAIMIR) *(Location: 85km south of Baghdad, 15km east of Babylon, in the northern alluvial plain of Mesopotamia. Date: from 2500BC.)* This was the city of the magnificent Akkadian King Sargon, founder of Agade, the first empire in history. The city's red ziggurat is the main attraction. The site stretches over 4km from Uhaimir in the west to Ingharra in the east.

Kish was referred to as the first seat of kingship after the flood and the title King of Kish signified hegemony in Sumer. After the foundation of Agade, Kish declined in importance and in the 6th century BC it was merely a suburb of Babylon. Hammurabi (1792–1750BC) rebuilt the temples of Zababa and Ishtar

13

and the ziggurat, and Nebuchadnezzar (605–562BC) restored the temples. On the eve of the collapse of the Babylonian Empire (c 550BC), Nabonidus took the statue of Zababa to Babylon, but Cyrus the Great returned it to Kish in 539BC.

Excavations started at the site in 1818. Further excavations were carried out by a team from Oxford University in 1925 and by the Field Museum of Chicago in 1933.

A large number of tablets were found on the site in the scribes quarter. In Tell Inghara, the façade and the courtyard of a Sumerian palace were discovered, along with the remains of two temples from the Babylonian period (6th century BC), which were rebuilt by Nebuchadnezzar and Nabonidus.

To the east of Tell Inghara are the remains of several richly decorated Sassanid villas from the 5th century AD, and to the northeast is Tell El Bender, with the remains of a Parthian fortress.

The ziggurat of Zababa, in an advanced state of decay, is in the northwest group of ruins. Nearby is a city from the time of Hammurabi (1792–1750BC), where many texts in the Sumerian language have been unearthed. Some damage has been done to the site by the Iraqi military digging gun pits.

LAGASH (TELLOH) (*Location: midway between the Tigris and Euphrates. Date: from the beginning of the 3rd millennium BC.*) The ancient Sumerian city of Lagash was founded at the beginning of the 3rd millennium. It was one of the most important capital cities in Sumer and had many temples, including the House of the Fifty (Eninnu). During the reign of Gudea (2130BC), Sumerian sculpture reached its zenith. Important discoveries on this site included the Stele of Vultures, a slab of sculptured stone, and thousands of Sumerian tablets dating back to the 3rd millennium BC, which the French dug up between 1877 and 1933. The stele marks the victory of King Eannatum over the state of Umma in around 2580–2560BC.

The remains of a temple built before the Neo-Sumerian period (22nd–21st century BC) have also been found on the site.

LARSA (*Location: 30km east of Samawa near Uruk. Date: from the end of the 3rd millennium BC.*) The Larsa Dynasty was founded towards the end of the 3rd millennium BC after a conqueror from the Syrian hinterland overthrew Ibi-Sin, King of Ur. The rulers of Larsa were involved in struggles with other dynasties and the city finally came under the control of Babylon and shared the same destiny as other provincial Babylonian cities.

A ziggurat rises 18m above the plain and the remains of the city are still visible.

Some tablets with the name of Ur-Nammu, the founder of the 3rd Dynasty of Ur, were discovered on this site by Austen Henry Layard, who also unearthed the Assyrian palaces of Nimrud in the 1840s (see page 295). It is believed this site has been extensively looted.

NIMRUD (*Location: 37km southeast of Mosul, overlooking the east bank of the Tigris. Date: from 1100BC.*) The second capital of Assyria had been a well-settled place for a thousand years before it became the focal point of the kingdom of Shalmaneser I (1273–1244BC). In the Old Testament it is referred to as Caleh. Ashurnasirpal II (883–859BC), the founder of Nimrud, was responsible for a large-scale building programme that included the building of a new city wall, a palace and nine temples, three of which have been identified. Shalmaneser III (858–824BC) constructed a ziggurat and a temple. In 707BC Khorsabad replaced Nimrud as the capital of Assyria, but Nimrud remained an important city, which was renovated by Esarhaddon (699–680BC) before it was sacked by the Medes and the Babylonians in 614–612BC.

This famous Assyrian site, where Layard carried out the first large-scale excavations from 1841 to 1851, was originally surrounded by a 7km city wall enclosing an area of approximately 360ha. The British queen of crime writing, Agatha Christie, spent some time in Nimrud during the early 1950s with her husband, the famous archaeologist Max Mallowan. Her stay in Iraq provided the inspiration for *Murder in Mesopotamia* and *They Came to Baghdad*. It is possible to visit Agatha Christie's house in Mosul. Her murder-mystery writing in Iraq is documented in *The 8.55 to Baghdad*.

The restored south façade of the Palace of Ashurnasirpal II is decorated with reliefs, and the two doorways flanked by winged lions and bulls lead into the throne room. A few slabs were stolen from the wall of the palace during the post-2003 war looting, and the site has been the scene of exchanges of gunfire between looters and guards.

The Nimrud ivories, a cache of Iraq's greatest and most valuable antiquities, is in storage in the vaults of Baghdad's Central Bank and the Iraq Museum's storerooms. Some fragmentation has been caused by mould and treasures from the 8th century BC are under threat. A throne base from Fort Shalmaneser, Nimrud and the banquet scene stele from the Northwest Palace are in the Mosul Museum.

Tombs of Assyrian queens, containing a wonderful hoard of more than 60kg of gold and jewellery, were found beneath the palace in the late 1980s and are now housed in the Baghdad Museum.

One of the greatest and most mysterious treasures to have been found in Iraq in recent times is the hoard of gold jewellery found in tombs below the floor of the Assyrian palace of Ashurnasirpal II at Nimrud.

The story of the 'Nimrud Gold' weaves together both the drama that is the political history of modern Iraq and the splendour and enigma of ancient Assyria.

The treasure rivals Tutankhamun's in terms of splendour and similarly involves an undisturbed royal tomb.

In the 1950s, the famed British archaeologist Max Mallowan excavated at Nimrud in the Northwest Palace, clearing a room in what had been the harem. He did not notice a modification of the floor-tile pattern, which was only later seen by the Iraqi archaeologist Sayid Muzahim in 1988.

Subsequent excavations under the floor revealed four tombs in the south wing of the Northwest Palace of King Ashurnasirpal II (883–859BC). A number of skeletons and bone fragments were found in the tombs and a sarcophagus identified one occupant, of Tomb III, as Mulissu, queen of Ashurnasirpal II.

More than 23kg of gold (157 items) were found, along with a stone tablet naming one of the occupants as Queen Yaba, wife of Tiglath-Pileser III (744–727BC). The inscription on this tablet even included a 'curse of restlessness' on the spirit of those who would disturb the tomb, also translated as a warning that those 'who lay hands on my jewellery with evil intent, or whoever breaks open the seal of this tomb, let his spirit wander in thirst.' Ironically, this very jewellery was retrieved from a flooded vault.

The Central Bank vaults in Baghdad, where the precious finds were stored, were flooded during the 2003 war, some believe deliberately, in order to prevent Saddam Hussein's sons or henchmen from making off with the gold.

A National Geographic team organised the draining of half-a-million gallons of water, which took three weeks. Three boxes containing the treasure were then found, undisturbed since being placed there.

Abridged from an article by Diana McDonald in The Looting of the Iraq Museum, Baghdad *edited by Milbry Polk and Angela Schuster*

The remains of the Temple of Nabu, dedicated to the God of writing, are another interesting feature of this site. The temple's archive contained many magical texts and the last will and testament of Esarhaddon, king of Assyria (699–680BC).

A gate north of the Temple of Nabu leads to Shalmaneser's arsenal. Another stone gate built in about 675BC can also be seen. Just prior to the outbreak of the 2003 war, the archaeologist Sayid Muzahim had begun excavating the Ishtar Temple adjacent to the ziggurat and uncovered two bulls – uniquely small for these guardians of the temple gates.

NINEVEH (*Location: 400km north of Baghdad, just across the Tigris from Mosul. Date: from 721BC.*) The city of Nineveh has a glorious history, which prompted the governorate to assume its name. It was the third Assyrian capital after Ashur and Nimrud and its location in the centre of the Assyrian lands between the

Tigris and Zab gave it an added administrative and religious importance. It was a cultural settlement during the Sumerian and Babylonian periods. The name of Nineveh is of Sumerian origin.

Impressive collections of Assyrian sculptures from the sites of Nineveh, Khorsabad and Nimrud are found in all the major museums of the world. Some were bought, some were given away by the Ottoman rulers, and excavators received permission to remove others. Post 2003, a number were looted.

Attempts have been made to remove valuable gold and ivory artefacts. Would-be looters have not managed to get through the locked doors at the Nergal Gate Museum in Nineveh and the storage facility and excavation house have not been damaged. While the danger from looters has been eliminated, Nineveh is still threatened by the expansion of new suburbs, and the reliefs are decaying due to a shortage of conservation materials.

Nineveh was ruled by a number of great Assyrian kings, such as Sargon II (721–705BC). Successive rulers built up the city and made it the centre of the civilised world from 705BC onwards. Sennacherib brought water via an 80km-long canal from the River Gomel, built a dam (the remains of which are still visible near the eastern wall), and filled the city and the surrounding countryside with gardens and orchards to which he brought some rare trees. Sennacherib's successors lived in the city until it was destroyed by the Medes in 612BC.

One of the most astonishing features of this site is its size: the city wall has a circumference of over 12km. There are 11 gates in all, and five have been excavated. The original statues of giant bulls still flank the entrance to Nergal Gate, but the towers are a modern reconstruction. Inside Nergal Gate is a small museum where models of leading Assyrian towns are on display. The east wall on either side of Shamash Gate by the Erbil road has also been rebuilt. On Koyunjuk Hill are the remains of two magnificent Assyrian palaces: Sennacherib's palace and Ashurbanipal's palace built between 690 and 650BC.

The throne room of Sennacherib's palace has been re-excavated and roofed. Some of the relief slabs depicting the king's victories have been left at the site. Some were looted in the 1990s and later appeared on the antiquities market in Europe. Most of the sculptures are now in the British Museum and the Louvre. While he was working at the site in the mid-19th century, Layard described the palace in a letter:

In the magnificent edifice I opened no less than 71 halls, chambers and passages, whose walls had almost without exception been panelled with sculptured slabs of alabaster. By a rough calculation, about 9,880ft or nearly two miles of bas-reliefs, with 27 portals formed by colossal winged bulls and lion-sphinxes.

Ashurbanipal's palace had a library of 25,000 texts in cuneiform, which preserved much of the lore and knowledge of ancient Mesopotamia. This is one of the most depressing sites in Iraq. The protective overhead coverings of tin have been stolen and the remnants of panels have been destroyed by the sun and robbers. One great palace mound that has not been excavated is the site of an ancient church, now converted to the mosque of the Prophet Jonah (mosque of Nebi Yunis). The mosque has been totally renovated with a new courtyard.

13

In Mosul, as in the whole of northern Iraq, an immense amount of reconstruction work has been carried out on mosques, churches and tombs. In 2007 attempts were made to blow up some of the churches and some destruction has taken place.

NIPPUR (*Location: 150km south of Baghdad, close to the modern town of Afak. Date: from 4000BC.*) Nippur, the northernmost of Sumer's main religious cities, dates back to the early 3rd millennium BC. The Temple of Enlil, the chief god of the Sumerian pantheon, was the major religious site and all the city's rulers ensured it was well maintained. The earliest temple and ziggurat were built by Ur-Nammu of Ur in 2100BC. Thousands of clay tablets dealing with commerce and the records of a banking house are testimony to the city's prosperity. After the Babylonian period (7th–6th century BC), Nippur was ruled by the Achaemenians and the Seleucids. The Parthians (2nd century BC to the mid-3rd century AD) built a palace on the site. The city was finally abandoned during the Muslim period in the 10th century AD.

Each civilisation left its mark on the site: superimposed on the tablets from the Sumerian school of scribes are buildings from the Achaemenian and Seleucid periods, with an Arab cemetery on top of the tell.

The remains of Nippur consist of massive mounds divided by the ancient course of the Euphrates, known as the Shatt al Nil. Excavations have been conducted northeast of the watercourse on the site of the religious quarter and scribes' district. The remains of the ziggurat, no more than a mass of unbaked bricks in an area of ruins, are in this quarter, and the Enlil Temple is found to the north. The Temple of Inanna, queen of heaven, is close by in a southwesterly direction. Several bricks with her name stamped by Shulgi, King of Ur, were found in the area, along with a bronze figurine of Shulgi.

The city wall has been reconstructed from a map dating back to 1900BC. It is one of the rare maps from antiquity that can still be related to the area it depicts.

Tribal guards saved this site from looters. Tragically they were not on hand in the nearby sites of Umm al Hafriyat, Umma (also known as Jokka) and Umm Al Aqarib. Looters had a field day digging pits at these sites. They were armed and dangerous. In 2004 more than 200 looters descended on Umma alone.

TELL HARMAL (*Location: in a southeastern suburb of Baghdad known as Baghdad Jadida, just south of the modern road leading to Baquba. Date: from the 2nd millennium BC.*) This small town, a centre for priests and scribes, was part of the kingdom of Eshnunna, on the Diyala plain east of Baghdad. One of the most famous Babylonian mathematical texts, which anticipates the theorem of Pythagoras, was found on this site, along with tablets dealing with literature, the law and economics.

Tell Harmal gives a good idea of what an ancient Babylonian town would have been like. The priest's house has been restored and the whole site can be viewed from the roof of this two-storey building. It has a parapet and ventilation shafts that are still found in many of Baghdad's old houses. The main temple foundations have been restored, with copies of the guardian lions at the entrance. The remains of dwelling houses, characterised by an internal courtyard, have been preserved on this site.

Tell Harmal and the neighbouring site of Tell Mohammed were not looted. Unexploded ordnance and wild dogs are a problem.

UKHAIDER *(Location: 145km southwest of Kerbala, 120km from Baghdad. Date: from AD600.)* The palace-fortress of Ukhaider (A Little Green Place), located in the desert far from civilisation, is one of the most impressive and well-preserved sites in Iraq, and comes into view from a considerable distance.

There is some disagreement among archaeologists as to when Al'Ukhaidir was actually built. Some say it dates back to the time of the Lakhmid Dynasty of Arab princes, who built several palaces as sanatoria for ageing princes, while others believe it was a Syrian hunting palace on the road from Mecca to Damascus. It could have been the retreat of the Baghdad Caliph Mansour, who became a millionaire recluse in his twilight years, or it could have been built by a Christian Arab known as Ukhaidir, who was expelled from Arabia in AD635.

Gertrude Bell made a detailed study of Ukhaider in 1909:

I have sometimes found myself longing for an hour out of a remote
century, wherein I might look my fill on the walls that have fallen and
stamp the image of a dead world indelibly upon my mind.

Her dream must have come true at this site. The cool interior of the castle gives the impression of what living in the early Islamic period was like. During the past 20 years the castle has been heavily restored to over-perfection from the crumbling deserted desert ruin seen by Bell.

The mosque mihrab, which faces in the direction of Jerusalem rather than Mecca, has generated considerable controversy. To the right of the castle is a small, partly reconstructed mosque with fragmented marble columns of different origins, taken from Byzantine churches.

UR *(Location: 15km south of Nasiriyah, 300km southeast of Baghdad beside an ancient bed of the Euphrates. Date: from 2142BC.)* Ur, along with Uruk and Eridu, was one of the leading old religious Sumerian cities of Mesopotamia. Its earliest dwellings go back 6,000 years. It was prominent during Early Dynastic periods 4,800–4,300 years ago, and was (later, in the Bible) referred to as Ur of the Chaldees, Abraham's native city. Even when political leadership shifted to other Babylonian and Assyrian centres, Ur maintained its importance and kings continued to lavish their care on its temples and institutions. The city was finally abandoned around the time of Alexander the Great (356–323BC).

During the third dynasty of Ur (2124–2015BC) it is likely that the Euphrates separated Ur from the plain and flowed to the west of the ziggurat. The city had two harbours and large official and residential quarters.

Ur has the best preserved ziggurat in Iraq. It was first constructed by Ur-Nammu, the founder of the third dynasty, and was restored in the 6th century BC by Nebuchadnezzar II. The remains of several temples, including a temple to Ur's favourite god, the moon god, and the great oval-shaped city wall, are other prominent features on the site.

As well as the magnificent ziggurat, Ur is also the site of a royal cemetery dating back 4,500 years. The British archaeologist Sir Leonard Woolley, and his

13

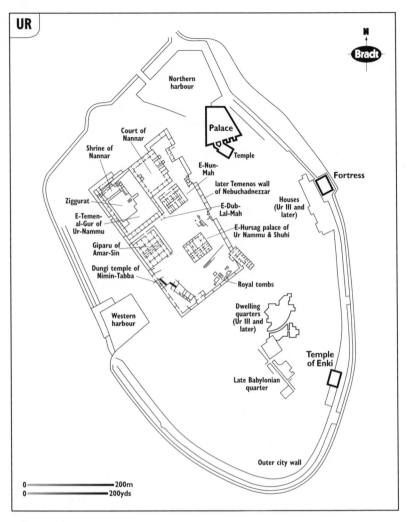

UR

N

Bradt

Northern harbour

Palace

Temple

Court of Nannar

E-Nun-Mah

Shrine of Nannar

later Temenos wall of Nebuchadnezzar

Fortress

Ziggurat

E-Dub-Lal-Mah

Houses (Ur III and later)

E-Temen-al-Gur of Ur-Nammu

E-Hursag palace of Ur Nammu & Shuhi

Giparu of Amar-Sin

Dungi temple of Nimin-Tabba

Royal tombs

Western harbour

Dwelling quarters (Ur III and later)

Temple of Enki

Late Babylonian quarter

Outer city wall

0 ——— 200m
0 ——— 200yds

team from the British Museum, conducted extensive excavations at the site between 1923 and 1924. They uncovered over 2,000 graves, which yielded thousands of rare objects that have enriched the display halls of the Iraq musum and museums abroad. They range from musical instruments such as the lyre of Ur, gold and silver ornaments, and precious jewellery.

The ziggurat, which has survived thousands of years of Middle East turmoil, has some slight marks, left by strafing of the Saddam-built airfield by UK and US planes, which patrolled the southern safe haven.

Ur, always inside the perimeter of the Talil airbase under Saddam although separate from the actual airfield, is under the protection of American forces, who have not allowed the head of Iraq's supposedly sovereign Board of Antiquities and Heritage to inspect the ziggurat, which is in the flight path of aircraft using the base. Some reconstruction has been undertaken in the area of the House of Abraham, but it has not remained faithful to the original design.

Ubaid, a prehistoric village near Ur, was surrounded by a barbed-wire fence, which deterred looters. Another nearby historic village with no protection was pitted, as was Dahaileh, a town west of Ur from the Old Babylonian period.

URUK (WARKA) *(Location: 20km east of Samawa. Date: from 4000BC.)* One of the most famous Sumerian cities of ancient Iraq, Uruk was continuously inhabited from about 4000BC up to the 5th century AD. Some of the earliest Sumerian pottery was found here. In the bible Uruk was referred to as Erech. Tablets dug up from this site date back to the invention of writing, in which Uruk played a major part. It was also the centre of worship of the goddess Inanna, or Ishtar. The Greeks and the Romans knew her as Aphrodite and Venus, respectively.

Uruk was renowned for its walls, which ancient texts say were first built 4,700 years ago by the Sumerian king Gilgamesh, hero of the epic named after him (see page 30). The city limits and traces of the walls can still be seen today.

Among the major remains is the ziggurat of Inanna, which rises to a height of 16m. It dates back to the time of Ur-Nammu, 4,000 years ago. Numerous rulers, down to Cyrus of Persia in the 6th century BC, restored this structure. Nearby are the ruins of a temple where thousands of coloured clay cones were used for ornamentation. The ruins of a temple devoted to the sky god Anu, built with mud-bricks some 5,000 years ago, are also visible. There is a temple to his wife, Anu-Antim, built in Seleucid times about 2,200 years ago.

A more recent structure is the brick temple, whose façade is ornamented with arches and columns, together with decorative brickwork of animals and geometrical patterns. It was built around AD110. The remains of the 2nd-millennium palace of Sinkashid, along with Parthian ruins, can also be found on this site.

The ancient sites of Lagash and Larsa in the neighbourhood of Uruk have been turned into lunar landscapes by extensive looting. Looters have dug 5m craters and removed portable antiquities. It was also open season on Isin (Ihsan al-Bahriyat), where as many as 300 looters caused extensive damage. Uruk was protected by the neighbouring tribe who had good relations with German excavators.

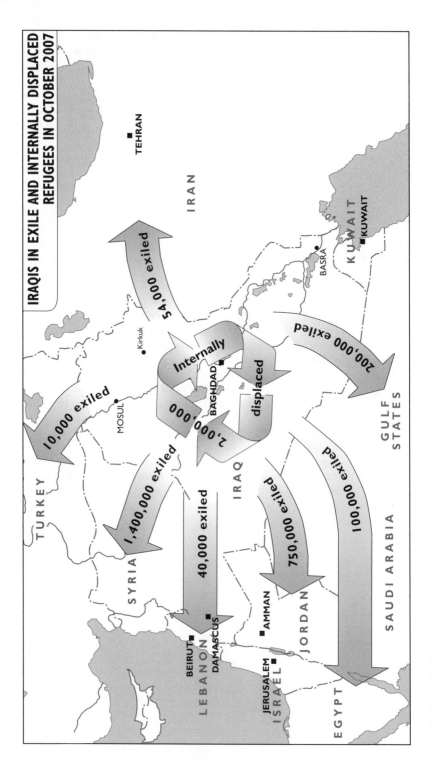

IRAQIS IN EXILE AND INTERNALLY DISPLACED REFUGEES IN OCTOBER 2007

54,000 exiled

10,000 exiled

200,000 exiled

Internally

displaced

2,000,000

1,400,000 exiled

40,000 exiled

750,000 exiled

100,000 exiled

IRAN

TEHRAN

KUWAIT

KUWAIT

BASRA

Kirkuk

MOSUL

BAGHDAD

IRAQ

GULF STATES

TURKEY

SYRIA

BEIRUT

DAMASCUS

LEBANON

AMMAN

JERUSALEM

ISRAEL

JORDAN

SAUDI ARABIA

EGYPT

14

Iraqis in Exile

Four million Iraqis have been forced to flee from their homes in fear –
the biggest mass Exodus since the Second World War.

The Independent

For the refugees the change in Iraq was a bittersweet honey.

Dr Bayan Alaraji, Chairperson, World Wide Welfare

The aftermath of the Iraq war and invasion has displaced 4.2 million Iraqis since
2003. Two million have fled abroad while the remainder are internally displaced
persons.

In August 2007 the latest figures from the United Nations High
Commission for Refugees showed that 60,000 Iraqis per month were fleeing
the country. The decision to leave is often made after they have been threatened
by letter, or by an envelope containing a bullet telling them to go immediately.
The killing of relatives or friends also prompts people to leave.

INTRODUCTION

Iraq, with its almost daily car bombings, kidnappings and sectarian killings, is a
country where no-one feels safe. Kurds are being forced out of Mosul (see
pages 166–7) and Baghdad has broken up into Shia and Sunni neighbourhoods
(see pages 203–6). In towns near Baghdad, Shias are fleeing from
Mahmoudiyah to Suwaira and Kut. Shias from Diyala are fleeing to Najaf and
Karbala, and Shias from Salman Pak are fleeing to Kut. Around 70,000 Kurds
have left Mosul, 50,000 Arab settlers have left Kurdish land, and Kurds from
Diyala have moved to Kurdistan, along with 50,000 Kurds and Arabs. Sunnis
fled from Fallujah during two American offensives in 2004 (see pages 220–3)
and have been displaced from Shia areas of Baghdad.

Many of the Shia refugees forced out of Baghdad are living in tents in the
Abu Skhair camp near Najaf.

There is hardly any response to their plight from international aid
organisations who believe the Iraqi government has money and is duty-
bound to assist these people,

said Dr Bayan Alaraji, Chairperson of World Wide Welfare, a British-based
charity set up 14 years ago to assist Iraqi refugees in Iran:

We've decided to leave our home. The only other option is extending the nightmare of life in Iraq.

I guess I've known we would be leaving for a while now. We discussed it as a family dozens of times.

Since last summer we had been discussing it more and more. What began as a suggestion – a last resort – soon took on solidity and developed into a plan. For the last couple of months it has only been a matter of logistics. Plane or car? Jordan or Syria? Will we all leave together as a family? Or will it be only my brother and I at first? After Jordan or Syria, where then? Obviously either of those is going to be a transit. They are both overflowing with Iraqi refugees, and every single Iraqi living in either is complaining about the fact that work is difficult to come by, and getting a residency is even more difficult. There is also the little problem of being turned back at the border. Thousands of Iraqis aren't being let into Syria or Jordan – and there are no definite criteria for entry; the decision is based on the whim of the border guard. I know starting a new life somewhere else is such a huge thing that it should dwarf every trivial concern. The funny thing is that it's the trivial that seems to occupy our lives. We discuss whether to take photo albums. Can I bring along a stuffed animal I've had since the age of four? The problem is that we don't know if we'll ever see this stuff again.

We don't know if whatever we leave, including the house, will be available when and if we come back. There are moments when the injustice of having to leave your country, simply because an imbecile got it into his head to invade it, is overwhelming. It is unfair that in order to survive and live normally, we have to leave our home and what remains of family and friends. And to what?

It's difficult to decide which is more frightening: car bombs and militias or having to leave everything you know and love, to go to some unspecified place for a future where nothing is certain.

Riverbend, 11 May 2007. Riverbend is the blogging name of a young Iraqi woman posting at riverbendblog.blogspot.com. Her blogs are published in Baghdad Burning: Girl Blog from Iraq

But the government is pre-occupied with security. Some refugees have been living in tents for more than a year. The government could rent a house for them or accommodate them in a hotel until they solve their problem.

Most of the Shias who fled to Iran after the 1991 uprising have returned home and World Wide Welfare is now focusing on obtaining sponsorship for widows and orphans, whose number is increasing daily due to the continuing violence.

Dr Al Alaraji, who has lived in Britain since 1982, was hoping to return to Najaf, her hometown, set up a clinic and initiate poverty-alleviation projects. 'All my dreams have been shattered. It is very dangerous for me to travel and continue my work. I am waiting for another change.'

Although they have received additional funds for this crisis in 2007, the UN High Commissioner for Refugees can't provide adequate protection and assistance to Iraqis. The agency lacks the resources to process refugees' documentation adequately. Without staff to monitor borders, UNHCR depends on national governments for updated information on new arrivals. UNHCR is also unable to provide significant assistance to Iraqis, and receives very little support from other UN agencies that seem slow to acknowledge the extent of the crisis. The fact that Lebanon, Syria and Jordan are not state parties to the 1951 Refugees Convention further reduces UNHCR's ability to protect Iraqi refugees.

www.refugeesinternational.org

In his paper to the Cross Party Commission on Iraq (15 June 2007), *Iraq's Lost Generation: Impact and Implications*, Ismail Jalili reports that over 833 assassinations have been documented among Iraq's professionals: 380 university academics and doctors, 210 lawyers and judges, and 243 journalists and media workers. The reported incidents are only the tip of the iceberg: many cases go unreported. Statistics from the US-based Brookings Institute reveal that some 40% of Iraq's professional class has fled abroad.

The New York-based Institute of International Education has set up the Iraq Scholar Research project to assist more than 150 senior Iraqi scholars whose lives and work are threatened. A one-year fellowship is being offered to scholars in institutions of higher learning in the Middle East and North Africa.

Syria and Jordan have taken in the majority of refugees from the 2003 exodus. Iran, Saudi Arabia and Kuwait, Iraq's other neighbours, have closed their borders. In the West, the largest Iraqi communities are found in the USA and the UK, but persecution throughout Saddam's rule has scattered Iraqis all over the world, some even settling in Antigua, Argentina and New Zealand. Writing in *The Independent* on 30 July 2007, Patrick Cockburn commented that:

Governments and media crudely evaluate human suffering in Iraq in terms of the number killed. A broader and better barometer would include those who have escaped death only by fleeing their homes, their jobs and their country to go and live, destitute and unwanted, in places like Kalawar [a refugee camp in Suleimaniyah]. The US administration has 18 benchmarks to measure progress in Iraq, but the return of four million people to their homes is not among them.

The President of Refugees International, Kenneth Bacon, described the international response to the Iraqi refugee crisis as 'dismal'. Despite numbers that

Iraqis in Exile **INTRODUCTION**

14

rival the displacement in Darfur, there has been scant media attention and even less political concern.

Human Rights Watch has stated that 'generally, Iraqis throughout the Middle East remain unregistered, uncounted, unassisted and unprotected.'

Around 40,000 refugees and 60,000 internally displaced persons chose to return to Iraq during October and November of 2007, some because they believed the situation in Iraq had improved, but many because they had run out of money and were not able to survive in exile or educate their children. Most refugees in Syria, Jordan, Lebanon, Egypt and many other countries stay on as illegal residents facing threats of deportation or imprisonment.

The United Nations senior representative in Iraq, Dr Staffan De Mistura, emphasised that Iraq should clarify its policy regarding those who return voluntarily and the settlement of property disputes. A survey by the United Nations High Commission for Refugees (UNHCR) revealed that two-thirds of returnees found their houses were occupied and were once again displaced. The UNHCR is not encouraging refugees to return mainly due to a lack of security and the absence of services. Most of the returnees go to a district where a single community, either Sunni or Shia, dominate, and are afraid to venture outside this district.

IRAQIS IN SYRIA

During the day the road from Damascus to the convent in Seidnayya is a place for pilgrims. At night prostitutes, mostly destitute Iraqi women, many the heads of households, look for clients. They also work in nightclubs on the outskirts of Damascus. Even hard-nosed club managers are sympathetic to their plight and when business is bad try to give some extra help to those with children.

Syria is now home to 1.5 million Iraqi refugees. The locals joke that two Iraqis walking down the street in Damascus were complaining about the large number of Syrians taking over the city. Qudsiya, an hour's drive from Damascus, is an Iraqi neighbourhood with a travel agency and a 'Baghdad barber shop'.

Another Iraqi neighbourhood is near the shrine of Zeinab, Prophet Mohammed's granddaughter, where one of the streets has been nicknamed 'Iraqi street'.

In Saddam's days, Damascus was home to many of the regime's opponents – the Patriotic Union of Kurdistan was formed in a Damascus restaurant. Today Syria accommodates refugees and former high-ranking Baathists, and recognises the government in Baghdad, believing contact with every side best serves its interests.

According to Syria's deputy foreign minister, Fayssal Mekdad, Syria spent US$160m on the refugees in 2006. Unable to cope with one of the world's fastest growing refugee populations, the government introduced visas on 10 September 2007.

'When the Iraqis first came, Syrians were happy to help them but now that is no longer the case,' explained Ammar Qurabi of the National Organisation for Human Rights (NOHR). 'Now most people hate the refugees.'

They are making increasing demands on Syria's subsidised services, especially education and health. More than 75,000 Iraqi children are registered in Syrian schools, doubling class sizes and pushing the system to its limits.

Other than recent initiatives led by the UNHCR to build three new schools and one hospital, there has been little infrastructure growth to meet the additional pressures.

According to the Syrian Consulting Bureau for Development and Investment (SCB), the Iraqi influx, which began in 2005, has resulted in a 35% increase in demand for bread, 27% for electricity, 20% for water and 17% for kerosene.

The head of the bureau, Nabil Sukkar, pointed out that the Iraqis have brought in money, invested in real estate and opened shops. This has increased spending in the economy, contributing towards the increase in the government's expected GDP growth of 7%, from 5.6% in 2006. But they are also blamed for kidnapping, blackmail, rape and prostitution.

On 27 November 2007, 800 Iraqi refugees returned home on the first official convoy organised by the Iraqi government. A survey conducted by the UNHCR at the end of November 2007 showed that only 14% believed security was better, 46% could not afford to stay in Syria, and 25% said their visas had expired and they were forced to leave.

IRAQIS IN JORDAN

Jordan is experiencing similar problems to Syria in coping with a refugee influx of some 750,000 people, costing the government US$1 billion a year. Many are Sunnis from Baghdad and Western Iraq.

Even though it has signed a memorandum of understanding with the UN High Commissioner for Refugees regarding the treatment of refugees and asylum seekers, Refugees International reported that Jordan refused to grant Iraqis temporary protected status after the 2003 invasion. Currently, it applies standard immigration law to Iraqis, which is based in part on an individual's ability to demonstrate economic self-sufficiency. As a result, anecdotal reports suggest that up to 50% of Iraqis are being turned away at the border – especially men and boys aged between 17 and 35. Attitudes towards admitting refugees hardened after Iraqis bombed three hotels in Amman in 2005.

CHILDREN WHO CAN DREAM AGAIN

The Jordanian government's decision to allow Iraqi refugee children into state schools transformed the life of Flora and her family. In her first year in Jordan, Flora and her two brothers had attended a private school, which was permitted by the government. But with fees of around US$490 a term (compared with US$85 per term for state school), the family's savings quickly ran out and now they are in debt. Without a residency permit, her parents can't work, and Flora and her brothers had been forced to leave school.

'My children used to cry all the time,' Flora's mother recalls. 'All our money went on education. There was not enough for food. We were all physically ill. Thank God they are now in state school.'

An enormous smile spreads across Flora's face. 'I want to be a doctor or a teacher,' she says.

Natasha Gilbert, The Guardian, 5 February 2008

14

Though Iraqis allowed to enter the country must demonstrate economic self-sufficiency, the prolonged nature of the conflict in their home country has seriously strained the resources of many. Without the ability to work they are facing an increasingly precarious situation. Those who undertake illegal employment can be subjected to exploitation and abuse.

On 26 January 2007, The Jordanian government announced that State schools would open to Iraqi refugees.

A fact-finding mission to Jordan by the Women's Commission for Refugee Women and Children in mid-2007 discovered that domestic violence was getting worse in refugee families. Many women were traumatised by violence before escaping, but psychological assistance was rarely available.

Iraqis can only get a Jordanian residency card if they have more than US$100,000 in a special account. This is not a problem for the well-heeled who are buying apartments and villas with maids in Amman's Umm Udhaina district. Some of the rich fled with money they stole after the war. Abdoun, another smart area, is jokingly referred to as Adhamiya, a Sunni area in Baghdad. Former high-ranking ex-Baathists, Saddam's daughters among them, keep a low profile in this district.

For the majority, international support is extremely limited. UNHCR's budget for Iraqi refugees in the entire region has been slashed from a high of US$150 million in 2003 to US$29 million in 2006, seriously decreasing the agency's ability to provide for the needs of the growing refugee community. As a result, most Iraqi refugees in Jordan have turned to family networks to provide basic support.

Many families are selling their assets as their savings run out. They were hoping Jordan would be a stop-over on the way to a third country, but most countries are reluctant to accept them.

In Jordan, Iraqis make up 10% of the population. Speaking in June 2007, the Secretary General of Jordan's Interior Ministry, Mukhaimer Abu Jamous said: 'We need international political will to support UNHCR to relocate recognised and registered refugees to third countries.' Few have been deported but the resources, and good will, of a country that absorbed thousands of Palestinians in 1948, 1967 and 1990, and has the highest refugee population in the world, are limited.

IRAQIS IN BRITAIN

For two decades London was a focal point of Iraqi opposition activities. In mid-December 2002 the largest ever meeting of opposition leaders was held in London's Metropole Hotel, to discuss the future of Iraq after the overthrow of the government.

'This time the Americans are serious,' delegates said in hushed optimistic voices, reflecting on years of US support that achieved little. The conference revealed the divisions and antagonisms between the diverse parties. 'Just wait until we have democracy and I'll throw you in jail,' one delegate yelled at another. Most of the men, and a few women, who ruled Iraq in the post-Gulf War years were present at the conference, one of many held in London since the 1990s. *Iraq 2020*, held in 1996, was the most forward-looking, and totally mistaken in its rosy vision of the future set out by intellectuals and academics.

As well as engaging in opposition politics with varying degrees of enthusiasm, Iraqis in London from all walks of life held a weekly picket every Saturday from January 1997 until March 2003. They called the gathering in London's Trafalgar Square 'Suq Ikath' after a regular gathering in Mecca held in pre-Islamic times for tribes to discuss important matters. The London picket called for Saddam and his henchmen to be put on trial for war crimes and crimes against humanity. It was also a social event, a venue for animated political discussions and gossip.

Until its closure in 2006, the Kufa Gallery in west London was another magnet for Iraqis from all walks of life. They regarded it as a home away from home and attended the monthly lectures and exhibitions, where catching up with friends was an added attraction.

Iraqis, mainly businessmen and students, started arriving in Britain during the 1930s after the British installed a constitutional monarchy in Iraq and

ONE MAKIYA: ONE KUFA GALLERY

London's Kufa Gallery was established in 1986 by well-known Iraqi architect Dr Mohamed Makiya, now 91. It was his vision and dream. Back in the 1960s he and a few other academic and professional people in Iraq worked towards the establishment of a private university in Iraq, in al-Kufa, a district of Najaf. It was built on a new concept which went beyond the boundaries of the teaching environment to spur the regeneration of the south of Iraq. The coming of the Ba'ath regime in 1968 put an end to this dream.

However, Makiya, who initially came to Britain in 1935 and married an English woman, kept the dream in his mind and in the mid 1980s, when he finally settled in the UK, made an attempt to establish such a university on the Thames.

The university did not materialise, but a positive development was the establishment of the Kufa Gallery in Westbourne Grove in central London. Dr Makiya envisaged a 'diwaniya' (venue for social gatherings) for Arab culture. For 20 years he kept it above any clash of loyalties due to religion, race, personal taste etc. It provided a platform for lecturers, poets, musicians and artists. Wednesday evenings, for two decades, were always a special event. I went there as many times as I could to meet Makiya and other friends, have a free cup of tea and biscuits, and listen to whoever was delivering a talk or a reading, or to tour an art exhibition.

Al-Kufa was not only a house for culture, a unique institution, but a home to Iraqi, Arab and many other intellectuals. It had an international outlook and aimed to bridge the cultural divide between east and west.

Since its closure in the summer of 2006, London has lost one of its vibrant cultural centres and Iraqi intellectuals in particular struggled to find a meeting place. They are to be found in a coffee shop or small gallery situated far from the centre. There were attempts to revive the spirit of Al-Kufa but to no avail. Neither the Iraqi embassy in London nor the Ministry of Culture in Baghdad came to the rescue when the gallery faced financial problems.

My friend, the sociologist Dr Ibrahim Al-Haidari, summed it up nicely: 'There was only one Kufa Gallarey and there is only one Dr Makyia.' This says a lot for the place, and the person who had the vision and turned the dream into reality.

Dr Abdul-Rahim Hassan

14

London now has another 'Mr Iraqi Culture', artist Yousif Naser, who holds a weekly 'Poem in a Studio' meeting. It began in February 2007 as an informal gathering where friends sit, talk and read poems. The meetings, characterised by a homely, cordial atmosphere, have moved on to screenings of rare and contemporary Iraqi films and philosophical lectures, including a presentation by Dr Ibrahim Al-Haidari on the famous Iraqi sociologist Ali Al Wardi. There has been a discussion about the work of members of the Iraqi Writers' Union, a musical night featuring an *oud* player, and Yousif has spoken about his trip to China. The studio, known as the Ark, is also used for rehearsals by an Iraqi theatre group.

'Ours is the only Iraqi meeting that starts on time, eight o'clock sharp,' Yousif said with a mischievous grin. In his less optimistic moments he complains that he can't continue as the only person who organises the evenings:

> I have to arrange the studio, send out the emails, welcome the people, sort out the topic for every event. And then they say bad things about me.

The events at the Ark are now the only regular cultural forum for the community in London. The Iraqi Community Association organises monthly social and cultural events and interest groups campaign for specific issues. There is also the Committee for the Defence of Democracy in Iraq, and charities such as the Iraq Child Appeal.

scholarships were awarded to promising students. By the 1980s there were around 6,000 Iraqi students in the country. The first Iraqi refugees who started to arrive in Britain in large numbers were Kurds. They came in 1975 after the collapse of their rebellion (see pages 152–4), when both America and the Shah of Iran withdrew their support. During the 1970s, when Saddam was consolidating his power, the Baath Party's opponents, especially members of the Iraqi Communist Party and the Islamic Dawa Party, started to flee. The Iran–Iraq War (1980–88) brought the next wave of refugees, including Feyli (Shia) Kurds who were expelled because of their alleged Iranian origins. The biggest influx occurred in 1991 following the liberation of Kuwait. These refugees included Kurds from the areas controlled by the Kurdistan Regional Government, where lack of economic development and constant fear of the regime's wrath prompted many young people to emigrate.

Today there are between 300,000–450,000 Iraqis in Britain. In 2002, 15,000 Iraqis applied for political asylum in Britain. In 2006 the number had dropped to 950. The Director of the Iraqi Association in Britain, Jabbar Hasan, said:

> It is getting more and more difficult for asylum seekers to get into Britain. The smugglers are charging US$15,000 per person, border controls are improving and EU countries are co-operating in controlling the movement of people,

He pointed out that on the one hand Britain promised to bring democracy and respect for human rights to Iraq, but now people are fleeing because of violence and scant regard for human rights. Yet they are received in a harsh way by the authorities, even though most of those who apply for asylum have a genuine case.

Mr Hasan is especially concerned about Iraqis who worked for the British in Basra and are now targeted by the terrorists:

> We are not witnessing any measures by the British to help them out of their misery. There are ways of helping these people to get out of the threat under which they are living.

(On 10 October 2007, after extensive lobbying and pressure, the British government announced that more than a thousand interpreters and other civilians who worked for at least a year for British troops and diplomats could apply for 'exceptional leave to remain' to enter Britain or be given money to resettle elsewhere. By December 2007, 600 had applied to settle in the UK but 230 had their cases turned down, often because of 'non-attendance' at work, even though they were advised by an army liaison officer not to turn up after receiving death threats. Hundreds of applicants had to travel to Jordan or Syria to apply and faced months of bureaucratic delays.)

Adding insult to injury, the British Government decided in mid-March 2008 that 1,400 Iraqis, who had had their applications for asylum rejected, must sign up for voluntary return to Iraq or lose all state support. The UNHCR said return of asylum seekers to central and southern Iraq and for some categories to the north was not advisable due to the continuing conflict.

Returning home was a dream for the exiles, but now people have woken up and realised it was only a dream. Very few go back, for obvious reasons. Events back home have contributed to uniting the community more than ever before. When Iraq won the Asian Football Cup in July 2007, the Kurds, Assyrians and Jews all celebrated together.

While the first Iraqi ambassador after the overthrow of Saddam, Dr Salah Al-Shaikhly, was universally respected for reaching out to all Iraqis, the services of the consulate has been severely criticised – especially the provision of services such as arranging power of attorney, assisting with pension claims for retired people, acquiring official documents such as death certificates, etc.

'We need experts to deal with these problems,' Mr Hasan pointed out. 'The consular section in the embassy is not functioning well but we can't isolate it from the situation in Iraq.'

Communicating with Baghdad is almost impossible and getting information to help secure aid for needy women and children is difficult. But Mr Hasan remains optimistic. 'I have to stay hopeful for the sake of my people – otherwise I would just give up.'

Yousif Naser is also working hard for his people but seems low on optimism. His brother in Basra, a great supporter of the British, is now claiming compensation for the shooting of his son by a British soldier in April 2007.

The walls of Yousif's studio are decorated with a series of paintings entitled *Black Rain*, comprising over 300 multi- and single-media works ranging from haunting, gigantic canvases to smaller drawings and paintings, all inspired by the horrors of the 2003 war. The theme is the suffering and consequences of armed conflict and its tragic impact on the lives of innocent people.

14

An Iraqi in Britain, Yousif can never escape from the anguish of being removed from the country of his birth and now witnessing from a distance the events that are unfolding in his homeland.

Commenting on the paintings, Alex Rotas, a lecturer in Visual Culture at the University of the West of England, said they invite us into an uncomfortable space that challenges us not to look away, and in looking, to feel something of the suffering of those involved in the war in Iraq. In the process, we share our common humanity with the Iraqi people and with the combatants, recognising our own involvement and accepting that, in a world of globalised politics, we are all implicated. Yousif's *Black Rain*, to a greater or lesser extent, falls on us all.

IRAQIS IN AMERICA By Julia Duin

The small number of recent Iraqi refugees in America became quite a scandal in 2007, when it became clear the US government was not serious about helping to clean up a problem they began by invading the country in 2003. Stung by media reports of two million refugees clogging up Syria and Jordan, in February 2007 the US government promised that they would take in 7,000 people. By the end of September, they had only allowed in 1,608; a paltry amount compared to countries like Sweden, which was taking in 1,000 refugees a month. Worst off were the Iraqis who had worked for the Americans. They – along with their families – were in great personal danger, and were clamouring to be allowed refuge in the United States. These were not idle concerns; more than 250 Iraqi translators working for the US military had been killed in four years.

'We can take hundreds of thousands of people if we want,' Amelia Templeton of the Washington-based Lifeline for Iraqi Refugees at Human Rights First, said in late 2007:

It's a lack of political will. This is the worst refugee crisis in the Middle East since 1948 and the president has not even mentioned it. It's embarrassing to them, and the Democrats don't have a plan for it, either.

The American government promised it would admit 12,000 Iraqis from September 2007 to September 2008, but as of January 2007 only 1,057 had been admitted, spurring further criticism of the Bush administration for its poor performance in rescuing its friends from Iraq.

Iraqi immigrants are no strangers to the American melting pot. The earliest arrivals were the Christians in the late 19th century, starting with a Chaldean Assyrian migrant worker from Telkaif in northern Iraq, who arrived in 1889 to work in a Philadelphia hotel. More Assyrian labourers arrived to work in factories in Chicago. Communities also sprung up in Connecticut, New York, Philadelphia, Turlock in central California, and Flint, Michigan. More Assyrians were uprooted from their homelands after World War II, causing their US numbers to swell. By 2001, the USA was home to 350,000 persons of Assyrian descent, mostly living in Chicago, Detroit and Turlock.

Iraqi Jews were next. Settled in Mesopotamia since 597BC, more than 124,000 Jews left Iraq between 1948 and 1952. Those who did not move to the new state of Israel headed for California and New York, Connecticut, Florida, Massachusetts and New Jersey. About 15,000 Sephardic Iraqi Jews still live in the country today.

The Muslims were next. Many of them arrived as students and professionals in the 1970s to escape repression at the hands of the Baath Party, establishing a beachhead for the 40,000 Iraqis that would arrive in the USA from 1992 on.

The early arrivals included Azzam Alwash, the director of Eden Again/ Nature Iraq, who was born in Kut and spent his youth in Nasiriyah, where his father was a district irrigation engineer. He left in 1978 to attend college in the USA where he became a civil engineer. In 1998, he and his wife, geologist Suzanne Alwash, started Eden Again to bring attention to the environmental disaster caused by Saddam drying out the marshes of southern Iraq. After the fall of Saddam Hussein, Alwash quit his consultant practice to direct the Eden Again, which aims to restore the marshlands.

And there was Hind Rassam Culhane, who also came to the USA on a student scholarship and ended up working as a psychologist and a counsellor. She spent June 2003 to June 2004 in Iraq, where she worked as a senior education adviser to an Iraqi education reconstruction project involving secondary school teachers and administrators.

Each new crisis – the Iran–Iraq War, the Kuwait invasion, political repression and economic problems – brought more Iraqis. Only 1,516 emigrated in 1989 but their numbers jumped to 4,111 in 1992 after the first Gulf War. Immigration reached a high of 6,025 in 1994, dropped to 2,220 in 1998, then climbed to 4,985 in 2001, at which point immigration was basically frozen after the 11 September terrorist attacks.

According to the 2000 US census, 89,892 people of Iraqi descent live in the USA, less than 1% of the total foreign-born population of 31.1 million. Detroit has the largest population (30,569) of Iraqi-Americans, followed by Chicago with 9,513 and San Diego with 7,507. The states with the largest Iraqi populations are: Michigan, California, Illinois, Tennessee, Texas, New York, Arizona, Virginia, Missouri and Pennsylvania.

The last wave of immigrants in the 20th century were the Kurds, who left Iraq in 1996 after the USA learned that Saddam was planning to invade their territory. Not wishing another public relations fiasco similar to the worldwide publicity centred on starving Kurdish refugees marooned in Iran and Turkey during the first Gulf War, the USA secretly scooped up 6,600 Kurdish allies between September and December 1996. In a dramatic rescue known as Operation Pacific Haven that cost US$10 million, Kurds and their families were bussed into refugee camps in southeast Turkey. They were then flown from the US airbase at Incirlik to Guam, where they stayed for three months before being assigned their new homes in various US cities. Most have now become citizens and their de facto spokesman, Qubad Talabani, son of current Iraqi president Jalal Talabani, has set up shop in Washington. He constantly visits and lobbies government officials and media organisations on behalf of Kurds, as well as trying to interest businesses in investing in his country.

Kurds are concentrated in northern Virginia, Nashville, San Diego and Dallas. In Nashville, with the country's largest concentration at 8,000, some of the teenage boys have taken the lead of their fellow Hispanic immigrants by forming Kurdish street gangs, an unusual innovation for these normally model immigrants.

THE SAGA OF A KURDISH FAMILY IN THE STATES

We will call them the Afandis: a middle class family from Suleimaniyah that was swept up in Operation Pacific Haven, a huge effort by the US government in December 1996 to rescue more than 6,000 Kurds from Saddam's approaching forces. Anyone – and their families – who had anything to do with the CIA, an NGO or any foreign group was resettled in the United States.

For these Kurds, it was an opportunity of a lifetime: an all-expenses-paid trip to the USA with citizenship practically guaranteed. The Afandis had four daughters; the youngest in high school and the oldest in her mid-20s. Together they and thousands of others were bussed to refugee camps across the border in Turkey, near the southeastern city of Cizre. They could only take two suitcases each. This first step was pure misery; for years afterwards the family would talk about having to sit on wet ground in tents and be mocked by the Turks, until the Americans could transport them to the Incirlik air base, where private planes hired by the American military flew them via Bangkok to Guam.

Guam was a warm oasis where the Kurds were fed and treated well for about three months until arrangements could be made to find them homes. In March of 1997, the Afandis were shipped to Houston, a steamy and large southern Texas city which they despised. They headed for the northern Virginia suburbs of Washington, DC, where the climate was far more temperate and where there was already a growing Kurdish community.

By the time I met them that October, they were squeezed into a shabby two-bedroom apartment in Fairfax, Virginia. The father, who had been trained as an engineer, was placed in a tedious job making copies of documents for a large firm. The daughters landed jobs at fast-food restaurants or as bank tellers; their education in Iraqi universities was useless in the American education system.

'Nashville is cheap but the standard of living is high,' said Kirmanj Gundi, a Tennessee State University professor and a Kurd who came in the 1970s. 'We are so grateful to America for helping Kurds.'

Their fellow Iraqis are slowly working their way into the culture and in 2005, one immigrant even invaded Hollywood through the CBS reality show *Big Brother*. The contestant was Kaysar Ridha, a handsome Iraqi-American graphics designer from Irvine, California, who has a penchant for sweets, basketball and the actress Penelope Cruz.

Earlier, in 1996, John Kanno, an Assyrian Christian from Jelou, Iraq, who ended up as an electrical engineer in Stockton, California, started a weekly political show, *This Week in Politics*, on KBSV television that was broadcast via satellite to other Assyrians. And in what may have been a first for Iraqi immigrants in terms of politics, he unsuccessfully ran for U.S. Congress in California's 18th District.

Although Iraqi Americans are a sliver of the immigrant community in America, they were sought out as advisors in 2002 as the Bush administration was laying plans to invade. In 2002, the State Department assembled 32 Iraqi exiles to draft a report on the post-invasion future of Iraq. Unfortunately, most of their advice got ignored. During early 2003, the Pentagon drew together a team of 150 Iraqis living in the States and in Europe to return to their homeland

I was a volunteer who had offered to mentor them through the intricacies of American life. I soon learned that Kurds believed in an amicable system of arranged marriages. They had no sooner arrived in Virginia than a suitor from Britain showed up to court the eldest daughter. The two families knew each other from Suleimaniyah and within a few months, she had become a doctor's wife and the two had moved to London.

I helped them understand everything from the American credit card system to junk mail; the latter an amazing concept to people from a society that has no postal service. I helped them shop for new beds and badger customs officials for green cards. I took them to church and to a Jewish New Year celebration. When the youngest daughter began to flunk her courses at the local high school, I negotiated with the guidance counsellors on her behalf. In turn, they had me over on Sunday afternoons twice a month for huge Kurdish dinners, complete with the inevitable discussions about politics.

As the years passed, a second daughter married a young Kurdish surgeon, also from Britain, and moved there to join her sister. The youngest married a Syrian Kurd, moved to Qatar, then returned to the United States just in time to give birth to her daughter on American soil. The remaining daughter secured a diploma from an American university and continued on to dental school. The father found a better job with a local county planning department. The mother found part-time jobs as an Arabic translator.

They finally became US citizens in 2006. Getting to know them so whetted my appetite to find out more about this fascinating country that I visited Kurdistan in 2004, staying with many Afandi family members, who welcomed me with open arms.

Julia Duin

to help jumpstart democracy. A number of these exiles were recruited in meetings near Detroit, where the largest concentration of Iraqis live. Exiles, who ranged from oil company executives to nuclear physicists, were established in key posts in Iraq to advise the American administrators there. Others were later hired by the Coalition Provisional Authority for jobs such as rebuilding Baghdad's wastewater collection system and training female Iraqis on the art of running for office.

The rest of the American Iraqis – the vast majority of whom were in exile to avoid Saddam Hussein – were stunned when U.S. forces easily reached Baghdad. Democracy seemed just a step away.

'The vast majority of Iraqis supported the war, whereas the rest of the Arab Americans opposed it,' said Imad Hamad, regional director of the American Arab Anti-Discrimination Committee in Dearborn, Michigan:

The Shi'ite sector was especially vocal for the war. Later, they became frustrated with the administration as they saw major mistakes being committed. Many of them shifted to the Democratic Party in 2004 for that reason. They didn't want a continued occupation; they wanted an exit strategy for the US military forces. They are thankful to the United States for getting rid of the dictatorship of Saddam Hussein, but the present-day

14

killings and instability is not the scenario they envisioned. Now they are saying it was better there during Saddam's day – as bad as that was – than it is now.

'Assyrian Chaldean Americans, who were also in favour of the war, have also switched sides', said Joseph Kassab, executive director for the Chaldean Federation of America near Detroit:

> The majority seem to be against the war because it led to mass displacement of this ancient people. More than half of the 1.2 million Chaldeans before the war are either refugees or internally displaced people seeking shelter.

The most upbeat of the Iraqi immigrants remain the Kurds, for whom the war was a win-win situation.

'A vast majority of the Kurds welcomed the war, prayed for it and are grateful for the outcome,' said Kani Xulam, director of the American Kurdish Information Network in Washington, DC:

> They are sad at the way the cost of the war has been borne by the Americans, but if you ask the majority of Kurds, they are happy at the way things worked out.

Before the Americans pull out too many troops, he and many Kurdish leaders are hoping the USA will establish a permanent military base in their region.

'The Kurds have been murdered and gassed by their neighbours,' he said, 'so they prefer the Americans to them.'

15

Postscript

Geoff Hann
When reading some chapters of this book, and some of its bloodstained chronologies, Dante's 'Abandon hope all ye who enter here' springs to mind. Can people, any people, really be doing this to each other? Well yes of course they can, and they have been doing so for centuries. As this book went to press in March 2008 Iraq was on the verge of a menacing civil war. The Iraqi army began a battle with the Mehdi Army for control of Basra.

There are many contributing factors to the present situation in Iraq, not least the surprising ignorance and ineptitude displayed by the American and British governments in failing to implement sensible plans to rebuild the whole country after such a militarily successful war. Surely the decrepit state of Iraq's infrastructure and what would be needed to revive it, let alone the destruction caused by the war, should have been uppermost in the minds of those who took us to war. I have been a frequent visitor to Iraq for many years and even as a layman it was obvious to me how the structure of the country had deteriorated in so many ways. Obviously no-one who made the decisions wished to listen to their own experts.

The arrogance and, later, isolated ineptitude of Saddam Hussein – after all, who would dare to criticise or offer adverse advice to such a brutal dictator – in becoming involved in three wars almost one after the other ruined his people and eventually led to his downfall. These wars, in hindsight, were used to bolster his power position in the Middle East and to keep his own population under control with a 'guns and butter' policy. This traditional dictators' policy was notable in the early days of Nazi Germany and Mussolini's Italy and, at first, succeeded in Iraq. Saddam was a student of such history and in his early days, in pursuit of this policy, many social reforms and advancements were made.

Another major factor is the accompanying escalation in the confrontation between the West and Islam and its more extreme factions. Iraq has become its ideal playground. This confrontation is also fuelled by yet another factor, and not just in Iraq: the media. The increasingly sophisticated manipulation of various media forms by self-interested groups and governments does not encourage hope. The devastating effect of some major destructive device seen so instantly on our screens eventually produces a negative impression on us all. The positive but more mundane events are often not shown, which is something we should all complain about.

So, is there any hope, or indeed any reason, why a country such as Iraq should survive as an entity, and for the good of its people? Yes, I believe there is.

In approximately 90 years Iraq has progressed from being three neglected provinces (*vilayets*) of the worn-out Ottoman Empire, to being mandated, a kingdom, a self-governing country and a dictatorship – a mere bagatelle in historical terms. I am reminded of the Kassites, the longest ruling dynasty in Babylonian history – over 300 years, from circa 1600BC to 1300BC, admittedly a somewhat undue length of time. Their great ziggurat (now restored) can still be seen on the outskirts of Baghdad at Agargouf (see pages 303–4). History and time should not be measured over a mere four to five years, at the whim of politicians who make two or three visits, some of which are measured in hours.

I remember in 2002 when Saddam was ostensibly re-elected as president. The 'Nahm, Nahm, Saddam' slogan proliferated everywhere and supposedly 96% of voters had voted him in again. But no queues could be seen around any building. Post-Saddam, all over Iraq – and despite sectarian threats – the first free elections jammed polling stations.

Democracy Western-style, especially the American and British versions, may not be ideal for Iraq despite what we Westerners wish to believe. But progress towards rational government, reforms, elections, constitutions, and effective army and police forces, is being made. Opposition politics are also being honed. There have been many steps forward and plenty backward, but it's progress.

A regional federation, or even splitting Iraq into three separate states, is also being touted, but this seems to be the preference of those who do not have the will or stomach to see through their obligations to the Iraqi people. It should be noted that even the Kurds, who are in a better position than the rest of Iraq at the moment, do not wish to secede completely. The disadvantages of complete severance well outweigh the advantages. Yes, the Kurds have oil, but for how long would the West support an independent Kurdish state given the hostility of the surrounding countries?

Another reason for hope is something that was seen in Iraq in post-war 2003: the explosion of new **newspapers and magazines**, over 300 at the time. In Baghdad, Mosul and Basra in particular, everyone was eager to read and absorb news after years of oppression. Freedom of thought and determination to vote are something that established societies take for granted and often abuse by neglect. For Iraqis those freedoms are meaningful and offer a glimpse of hope for the future.

Oil, Oil, Oil – butter, butter, butter is probably the key not only to prosperity, but also to combat the sectarian violence that is being fostered by so many outside factions. **Oil** means money, and money means food, work, self-respect and infrastructure. Most people find it hard to support needless destruction of their own environment when their bellies are full. Vested interests in the Middle East and in the West do not wish for a settled, prosperous Iraq. But inevitably this will not last and oil will flow and transform it all. Then proper reconstruction in all sectors will happen. This is not to detract from the huge sums already spent by mostly Western and some Asian governments, who to their credit, although horrified by their now clear commitments, are still proclaiming involvement. One example has been the costly clearing of the Shatt al Arab waterways and harbours of sunken shipping, much of it dating back to the 1980s and 1990s.

The large population of Iraqis abroad is aching to return and rebuild the nation with their own wealth and experience.

Oil is not the only, or rather total, answer – there are so many other avenues to be explored. The sweet **dates** of the Basra region were once a principal export, justly famous for many centuries. Resuming proper commercial production will be a long business but very worthwhile.

Tourism in its many forms can be ready quickly if not immediately, once security is established. The clearing of the harbours around Basra is an invitation for cruise ships to stop and let their clients shop in the bazaars and make excursions to Ur, for example. Pilgrim traffic from the Gulf and Iran will grow immensely once shipping is made safer. Ancient Iraq, both north and south, offers endless opportunities for ancient and classical tours. Yes, there has been extensive looting, and yes much has been destroyed, some sadly for ever, but the major sites of Iraq are still extant. Much will need to be done of course, but all is not lost. The archaeological world is waiting for the opportunity to apply modern techniques to the established places and look for the lost sites of antiquity. The great Museum of Baghdad, once totally secure and aided by the world's art community, will become a focus for all lovers of ancient history. We have so much to look forward to. This is not only Iraq's heritage, but our heritage, and it will be preserved. The mountains of Kurdistan Iraq beckon the adventurous. Side by side with these developments is the opportunity to rebuild the hotels and restaurants, and small farmers will also develop their own accommodation markets. Tourism employs large numbers throughout the world, and for a few years a boom in building, allied industries and of course labour will take place.

I personally believe that we should all have courage, hold our collective nerves, look for the good news and continue to strive for progress. The future is bright for Iraq – the people are brave, courageous and willing to work hard if they can see a future that is more than mere survival. They have a wonderful heritage that we share also.

History is undecided. We should all set aside the psychology of failure, the mentality of defeat, the feeling of impotence and be confident that we can make a difference.

Appendix 1

TRAVELLING IN IRAQ

A curious business this travelling and tourism. More people, particularly Westerners in the guise of the army, security personnel, NGOs and business people, have visited Iraq since 2003 than ever before, yet there have been fewer religious pilgrims (mostly Iranian Shias), who once represented the bulk of the travellers to Iraq (over two million per year prior to 2003).

The country has been revealed in its nakedness, stripped to the bone and all aspects of its society exposed, but through this media attention we all know more about Iraq's geographical aspects and historical sites than we did before the war. The country has spectacular mountains and valleys in the north along the border with Turkey, and to the east borders Iran and the Zagros Mountains. The western border with Syria is mostly desert. The weather can be extreme; it is almost unbearably hot in the Baghdad region in summer (44°C plus), whilst Basra in the south has over 100% humidity. Conversely, Kurdistan Iraq in the north is extremely cold in the winter.

At first glance why would travellers want to visit Iraq? Well, because it is a very special place. Bisected by the Euphrates and Tigris rivers, which have always brought life to the country, it is rich in archaeology, history and religion, and is the cradle of mankind's birth, from nomadism to settlement. Now, in political terms, it is undergoing another test, that of the democratising practices of the West.

So what can the traveller do in Iraq? At the time of writing the security situation makes general travelling difficult, and in some places impossible, but this will not be the case forever and could change rapidly. One area, Kurdistan Iraq, has made itself secure by hiving itself off physically and politically from the rest of Iraq, and it is possible to travel within this area fairly easily. However, travelling outside of this area does require a full Iraqi visa and is not secure for foreigners; therefore it is recommended that you enter and exit through Turkey, and limit your travel to the Kurdish region at the present time. Flights are possible into Erbil and Suleimaniyah avoiding the overland routes but have their own problems and costs.

KURDISTAN IRAQ At the moment the KRG (Kurdistan Regional Government) pays lip service to the Baghdad central government and mostly governs itself, although it is ultimately dependent on its share of Iraq's wealth, or lack of it. Therefore direct tourism is now actively being encouraged and direct investment sought for the region's infrastructure. Erbil and Suleimaniyah boast airports operating to international standards,

Appendix 1 TRAVELLING IN IRAQ

A1

337

with increasing numbers of flights from Baghdad, Basra, Europe, Iran and the Gulf. Travellers arriving at Erbil and Suleimaniyah are granted Kurdistan Iraq visas on arrival. The visa is only good for ten days. After that you must register with the authorities in Erbil as a foreigner; this can take time and you are advised to take an interpreter with you.

Inexpensive flights can also be taken to the Turkish city of Diyarbakir (followed by road travel to Silopi and the border) or the Syrian city of Qamishli. However, the Syrian route direct to Kurdistan Iraq is currently not recommended for Western travellers.

Because of this, most visitors enter Kurdistan Iraq by road via Turkey, at the border crossing of Ibrahim Khalil, an hour from Silopi. This Turkish border point has much improved facilities and Kurdistan Iraq visas are also granted here on arrival. Once over the border, transfers by taxi or minibus are readily available to the town of Zakho, a mere 12km away. This town is on the edge of the huge transit parking lot for Turkish and Iraqi road travel, but it does have a magnificent Abbasid bridge, some hotels, and a terrible modern history full of refugees, invasions and massacres.

From Zakho, the main highway (Highway 2) goes to Mosul, connects with Highway 1 and then goes directly to Samarra and Baghdad. Kurdish Iraq lies mostly to the east of these highways and the KRG has built a network of roads bisecting this region without, for the most part, having to travel in Arab areas not under their control. All roads have checkpoints at intervals and all villages and towns have roadblocks at entry and exit points. This recent road-building is opening up many areas and places of scenic beauty, and a frenzy of speculative chalet and hotel building for tourism is taking place, notably at Shaqlawar, Rawanduz and Dokan.

Dohuk An hour down Highway 2 from **Zakho** brings you to the growing town of Dohuk. Pleasantly congenial, it is a headquarters for political parties and a hub for the many diverse villages of the area – Turcoman, Arab, Kurdish and Yezidi. The town has many restaurants, and food is plentiful and reasonably inexpensive, as it is almost all over Iraq. There are many hotels, the Sulav and the Shindokhu being particularly good, and moderately priced at around US$50 plus. The Jiyan is the premier hotel, but there are many simpler hotels in the town costing from US$20 per room.

Using Dohuk as your base there are many interesting places to visit within an hour or so of the town. The most important place for the Yezidi faith is the **Temple of Lalish**, a most interesting place to visit, as little is known by outsiders of this religion. Nearby is the Yezidi village of **Ain Safni**, which is home to the chief sheik of the religion and several important tombs. Also within reasonable distance is the **Bavian Gorge/Canal**, cut by the Assyrians in the 7th century BC to bring water to the fruit orchards and crops of the region, and lined by Assyrian reliefs in the gorge. These reliefs are the most outstanding and easily reached Assyrian remains in Kurdistan Iraq. Not far away is the village of **Agosh**, a mixed religious village of Muslims and Christian Arabs with a church, a mosque and special tombs.

A word of caution – please note that all visits to any of these villages should be checked for security reasons on the day that you travel.

Erbil It is possible to cut across country on roads that will take you to Rawanduz, to Dokan and to Suleimaniyah through mountains and valleys, but most travellers will want to visit the outstanding towns of the region first, so will travel first to Erbil (also known as Hewler or Howler), which is three hours away. Unfortunately, for security reasons it is advisable to avoid Mosul, only 35km away, and continue in the footsteps of Alexander the Great, past the Gaugamela battle site (where Darius III was defeated in 331BC) and crossing the Greater Zab River to reach the city of Erbil.

Erbil, seat of the Kurdistan Regional Government and dominated by its amazing ancient citadel, is growing at a pace that is almost frightening. Huge speculation and its accompanying monetary inflation make this a very busy place. There are many hotels, although not enough, and prices change constantly. The largest and most expensive upmarket hotel, at US$300 per room, is the Sheraton, which has a reasonable restaurant in its grounds, specialising in the traditional Iraqi fish dish *masgouf*, freshly caught and prepared. There are other hotels such as the Erbil Tower and the Chwarchra, from US$85 per room. In Shaqlawa, outside Erbil, a new **hotel** has opened, the Khanzad Hotel (e *khanzadhotel_shaqlawa@yahoo.com*), which has rooms ranging from US$150 to US$300. The British Consulate is located inside the hotel.

Places of interest to visit in Erbil include the **museum**, the **14th-century minaret** (now set in newly laid-out gardens), the **old bazaar** and the **citadel** itself. Ultimately the citadel will be one of the most exciting archaeological sites in the world. Already cleared of its inhabitants, little excavation has taken place so far, but with a known history going back to 4000BC, exciting discoveries are sure to be made once this gets underway in earnest. Make sure when there that you do not miss the Kurdish Carpet/Kilim Centre currently based in the citadel. Excursions from the city are possible, notably to the **4th-century Christian monasteries** of Der Mar Matti and Mar Benham (when possible).

Suleimaniyah The two–three hour journey from Erbil to the other major city of the region, Suleimaniyah, can be undertaken via two different routes. The first goes across country via Shaqlawa, the major holiday resort of Dokan Lake. This route goes through some amazing geological formations with tremendous views. Dokan Lake and its river, the Little Zab, is the premier resort for Suleimaniyah, and many chalets and hotels are currently under construction here.

The alternative route to Suleimaniyah is on Highway 2 via Kirkuk. We do not recommend the route at this time due to the instability of the ethnic divide, Arab/Kurdish, particularly around Kirkuk. Just before **Kirkuk** you pass the great ridge lined by Saddam's fortlets. An amazing sight, it was a defensive wall against Kurdish insurgents, not against other outside enemies. This oil-rich city is home to the tomb of the Prophet Daniel and some interesting mosques. However, its history since the discovery and expansion of its oil reserves in the 1920s has led to this town being one of the most dangerous in Iraq, with roadside bombs and ethnic violence commonplace. Originally a Turcoman city, the enforced population changes of the last 60 years involving Kurds, Turcomans and Arabs, and its history, ethnic pride and oil, make it a desirable prize for all. Its oil, if it comes under the complete jurisdiction of the KRG, could change the face of Iraq in terms of complete autonomy for the Kurds.

The highway from Kirkuk to Suleimaniyah is a good, fast road. Along the way, approximately 50km from Suleimaniyah, is the ancient site of **Jarmo**. One of the earliest villages known to man, it dates back to before 6000BC. However, little remains to be seen, even if you can locate it, but note that you may need an official escort once off the main road (see page 303).

Suleimaniyah is a modern city and most of what can be seen dates from the late 19th century. The heights above the city provide wonderful views. It is a pulsating place, full of young people enjoying the modern aspects of life. Mobile phones abound. At times the city just resembles one gigantic market. There are plentiful restaurants, many of which serve alcohol. Among the reasonably priced **hotels** are the Ashti Hotel and the Hotel Dilan, along Salim Street in the city centre. Prices start from US$75 per double room per night. Many new hotels are being constructed.

The heart of the city conceals the dreaded Red Security Building, better known to the Kurds as the Amma Suraka. Now being developed as a museum, it exemplifies the worst excesses perpetrated by Saddam's regime against the Kurds. Its underground cells are particularly grim. **Halabja**, the internationally known example of these excesses, can be found 90 minutes' drive to the south of Suleimaniyah, and is a must for travellers to the region (see page 182).

Iranian influence is prominent in Suleimaniyah, and there are several borders open to traffic between the two countries. In the north that of Haji Omra, or Piranshahar, is set in spectacular scenery. Unfortunately it is only open to local traffic, and can often be closed when epidemics such as cholera or bird flu strike.

Beyond Suleimaniyah The central border-crossing with Kurdistan Iraq and the closest to Suleimaniyah is Merwan. Again it is open only to local traffic. Just south of the Kurdistan region, and almost in the centre of Iraq at the end of the Baghdad/Baquba highway, is the main international border between Iraq and Iran, Khorasavi. This is the main crossing for Iranian pilgrims to the Iraqi holy places of Kerbala and Najaf, the premier shrines of the Shia branch of Islam. Westerners can cross here, but the approach to Baghdad is very insecure.

Due to the problems with crossing the various other border points, western Kurdistan road travellers will have to return to the north and Turkey to exit the Kurdish region. To see more of the country it is recommended that you travel from Suleimaniyah via Dokan Lake and travel along the side of the mountains to **Rawanduz**. This historical, tribal and ancient caravan town is perched on a spectacular gorge with tremendous views across the mountains. Now, it has a holiday village attached, with fine chalets and a restaurant. From Rawanduz there are a choice of routes – either the time-consuming but adventurous one further north on rough roads to Dohuk, or the more convenient, shorter one on good roads, cutting across to Erbil and Dohuk.

Practicalities in Kurdistan Iraq A few travel pointers: the Kurdish language is not an easy one. Arabic is understood but many youngsters will not use it, preferring to practise their English if possible. An **interpreter/guide** is advisable. Always check before an excursion or when travelling on for any problems that you may encounter that day regarding security. As everywhere in the Middle East, **shared taxis** are readily available, as are taxis for sole hire.

At the cab offices care is taken to ascertain your ethnic origin and intended destination with respect to your driver's ethnicity. Cost examples – from Dohuk to Baghdad a shared taxi costs 65,000 dinar per person and a complete car for sole use 250,000 dinar (in September 2007, US$1 was worth 1,236 Iraqi dinar, or ID). A shared taxi from Dohuk to Erbil costs 20,000 ID per person. **Security note:** there are probably 20-plus checkpoints on the road from Dohuk to Baghdad and it is most definitely not recommended for foreigners, other than those of Iraqi origin.

At the moment **mobile phones** do not always function as there are many blank spots. SIM cards are readily available for purchase. There are two major systems for SIM cards in Kurdistan Iraq: Sanatel in Erbil and Asia Cell in Suleimaniyah. You may need both systems depending on how far you travel; most Kurds carry two phones to accommodate both systems. There are internet cafés in the major cities, again not always functioning well, but mobile phones and internet services are improving almost daily. Erbil Airport has free high-speed **Wi-Fi**. For hotels and other centres, communication via email and mobile is erratic, as numbers are often changed. Finally, do not expect costs of anything to stay stable – this is an inflationary, speculative region. However, it is also an exciting, adventurous one, and there is much more to explore than we have briefly mentioned. See page 349 for more practicalities on travelling in Iraq as a whole.

THE REST OF IRAQ What follows is a very brief general guide to what a visitor to Iraq (Mesopotamia) should be able to cover in normal peaceful times, in order to achieve the most from their travels. We have briefly covered Kurdistan Iraq in the northeast and now suggest some itineraries for the rest of the country, as we did in the earlier book, *Iraq: the Bradt Travel Guide* (note: when reasonable normality resumes we shall produce a further edition of that guide). At the moment there are few hotels that can be used, and the rail network and sea approaches are little used. The borders are often closed and insurgency ebbs and flows over most of the main roads. Some cities are just not secure for travellers. There are many plans waiting to be implemented to recover this situation. Excitingly, throughout the country there will be a frenzy of building and rebuilding, hotels, restaurants and tourist centres notably in Baghdad, Basra, Mosul and the smaller provincial cities. The tourist hotels close to Hatra and Babylon are waiting for renovation, again plans have been made for the moment that these hotels are empty of the present occupiers and when security is in place. The Ministry of Archaeology and Culture has begun recruitment of the Protection Police for the sites throughout the country. The famous sites, such as Babylon, Ur, Uruk, Nimrud, Nineveh, Hatra and Assur, have plans drawn up for the establishment of tourist centres once the security situation improves. At the time of writing, Iraqi Airlines are looking to re-introduce direct flights from European capitals; this will bring in its wake a renovation of restaurants and services to facilitate connections to the airports and cities. The train system from Aleppo in Syria to Mosul, Baghdad and Basra, begun before World War I as a spur of the Orient Express, and famously used by Agatha Christie, is on hold, but many schemes are waiting in the wings to change this. Already the track surveys have been done.

Appendix 1 TRAVELLING IN IRAQ

A1

Mosul Still in the north of the country (Kurdistan Iraq is not all of the north), between the Syrian border and Kurdistan Iraq, lies the second city of Iraq, multi-ethnic and cultural Mosul. It houses a great provincial museum and many churches of all faiths of Eastern Christianity, often hidden down narrow alleys in the old part of the city. There are also some important mosques, notably Nebi Younis, the Mosque of the Prophet Jonah, once the Church of St John (sitting, incidentally, on the site of an Assyrian palace). Others are the Great Nurid Mosque (AD1172) and the Umayyad Mosque, built in AD637 by Utba bin Farqad al-Salami under Caliph Umar. Bordering the River Tigris, and being slowly swallowed by modern Mosul, is that most ancient city site, **Nineveh**, the last and largest capital of the Assyrian Empire (see pages 312–14). The city was destroyed in 612BC, but the massive stone bulls guarding its gates and the wonderful relief slabs can now be seen adorning the museums of London and Paris. Today at Nineveh careful restoration has taken place on some city gates, but sadly the famous excavated Palace of Sennacherib has been totally neglected. This huge site vividly conveys the might and power of the Assyrians at the peak of their empire.

Unfortunately, at the present time, the situation in Mosul resembles that of Baghdad, with an ethnic split between Kurds and Arabs, and with Turcomans caught in the middle. The city is not safe for foreigners to visit, but it will be again, and visitors will once more be able to walk along the Corniche; lined with modest hotels, from here you can visit all the sites of the town. The university area has some interesting restaurants where you were once guaranteed interesting conversations with students. But more importantly the city can be your base to visit the wonderful sites around it. For example, 25km north is the site of Khorsabad, an Assyrian capital for a brief 18 years, whose relief slabs form a great hall in the Baghdad National Museum.

Just 37km south of the city lies the magnificent site of **Nimrud**. Second capital of the Assyrians, this great city mound has been almost continually excavated since the time of Layard who first began here in 1840. The last and most astonishing discovery in 1989 of royal treasures from the time of Ashurnasirpal II (883–859BC) has happily survived the looting of Baghdad.

Some 112km south lies **Assur**, first capital and religious centre of the Assyrians. Washed by the Tigris, excavations have been continuous here until very recently. West of Assur and 100km southwest of Mosul lies the caravan city of **Hatra**, the most complete ancient site in Iraq. Dating from the 1st century AD, it is isolated out in the desert. Its magnificent city walls and *iwans* (vaulted arches, originating in Iran in the Sassanid era) decorated with reliefs are glorious in the light and blaze of sunset. It is also one of the very few sites in Iraq to have a guesthouse nearby.

For the traveller basing themselves in either Erbil or Mosul, a five-day itinerary would easily cover these and the ancient sites of the north. A few more days would include the Kurdish villages and mountains.

To the west of Mosul lies Eski Mosul, many ancient tells (mounds) and the town of **Sinjar**. Situated almost on the Syrian border and notably a Roman frontier city at one stage, it is an important centre of the Yezidi faith. At the present time it too is unsafe for Westerners, and indeed ethnic cleansing is going on there.

Travelling south – the Sunni Triangle Continuing directly south on Highway 1 from Mosul brings you to the Sunni Triangle, Samarra and Baghdad (see pages 217–26). You are entering strictly Arabic speaking regions with many roadblocks manned by different groups of men with diverse loyalties, to the US Army, Iraqi Army, Iraqi Police, militias and insurgents. All of the towns on these highways have had their share of violent notoriety. The railway junction Baiji is the next town on this road, closely followed by **Tikrit**. Saddam built an ornate palace here and many of his ministers had houses in the town. Saddam was born in this area, finally returning as a fugitive, and he was captured close by (see page 224). He and his sons are also buried nearby. It has other claims to fame, too: in the 7th century AD Tikrit was a Christian Bishopric with a famous cathedral, and in the 11th century AD Saladin, the medieval warrior and conqueror, was born here.

Continuing towards Baghdad through very flat desert terrain, the great spiral (helicoidal) **Minaret of Samarra** can be seen, heralding one of the most remarkable episodes of Islamic history, the moving of the caliphate under Mut'tasim from Baghdad, and the construction of a city in AD836, whose remains stretch for 20km. One of the gems of world architecture, the minaret stands next to a huge walled mosque and is also close to the palace built by the Abassid Caliph Mutawakkil. A much smaller copy of the minaret called **Abu Dulaf** is to be found some 22km to the north. In the modern city of Samarra is the golden dome of the Askari Mosque and the tomb of the Mahdi, much revered by the Shias (see pages 238–9). Tragically, in February 2006 this mosque and its two minarets were severely damaged and almost completely destroyed by insurgents. Already a budget has been proposed for their reconstruction.

Finally, it is a 112km flat run on an increasingly busy highway and through many roadblocks into the capital.

Baghdad At this juncture we should briefly describe the other major road routes into Iraq from Syria and Jordan in the west. There are two main border points with Syria, Abu Kamal, where the road runs parallel to the Euphrates via Haditha and Hit, and the Al Waleed border further south. The Jordanian Qadissiya border road connects with the southern Syrian border road before Rutba. Beginning your journey along one of these from Damascus or Amman offers a fine introduction to Mesopotamia through long stretches of desert. From Damascus it is 918km, and from Amman 844km, travelling on a superhighway via Rutba, Ramadi and Fallujah, names we have come to know only too well these last years! Indeed, these roads themselves have been infested with bandits (or 'Ali Babas', the Iraqi nickname for thieves) and insurgents. But again, this is slowly changing for the better.

Commercial flights are now operating in and out of Baghdad. Regular flights operate from Amman and Damascus with Royal Jordanian Airlines, Syrian Arab Airlines and Iraqi Airlines. There are also regular flights with Iraqi Airlines to Basra and Erbil etc. Due to the security measures in place at Baghdad Airport when you land, and the necessary road transfers into the city, it can be a fraught experience and is not for the faint-hearted.

The chaos, heartbreak and violence, mingled with a desperate determination to make everything work for the better, come across clearly in our pages on

Baghdad. So let us describe what the visitor should see in Baghdad in the better days to come. There will be the new sites, previously closed sites, the Saddam palaces and the Green Zone buildings, but those can be added in due course. Indeed, they will most probably deserve a day tour in themselves. For some time there will be the complications of a city divided along ethnic lines, but people have a habit of working around such obstacles.

City tour suggestions So, for the stopover tourist, business people and travellers, some one-day touring suggestions.

An early start to your city tour allows you to make time for the Kassite Ziggurat at **Argagouf**, a site 30km from the city centre (see pages 303–4). Dating from the 15th century BC it is probably the best ziggurat in Iraq. But if you are a really early bird then start your tour first at the **Mosque of Kadhimain**. Built in the 16th century on the site of the shrines of two of Prophet Mohammed's descendants, Musa Al-Kadhim and Muhammed Al Jawad, it is situated on the banks of the Tigris to the north of the city, and the shrine has a magnificent golden dome and impressive minarets. Opposite the mosque is a famous clothes market.

Returning towards the centre, next take the road past the railway station, with its marble symbol of British colonial architecture. If you have time visit the booking hall. Just before the station is the famous monument of **Zummarrud Khatun's Tomb**. Dating back to the late Abbasid period (1179–1225), it is remarkable for its octagonal shape. The **tomb of Sheik Omar Al-Sahrawadi** is on Sheik Omar Street. This famous mystic and theologian was born in Iran and died in Baghdad in 1225. The shrine has an extraordinary conical dome in the Seljuk style, and it is very tranquil and eminently photographable.

Close to the hub of the city is the modern-day **Martyrs' Monument**, which cost US$40 million to build. It commemorates the deaths in the Iran–Iraq War (1980–88). In a hall underneath the huge double-hearted, egg-shaped structure are war memorabilia and inscribed names of the dead.

The next stop could be the magnificent **Iraq National Museum**. It is the hope of the world that this museum can be brought to life again and display its wonderful artefacts once more. It has been announced that in 2008 two galleries will be open. Progress indeed!

As you come into the centre, lunch can be taken at the **Khan Mirjan**. Dating back to 1230 this old caravanserai has now been converted into a restaurant. Close by are the market streets, and the copper bazaar off Rashid Street. The **Armenian Orthodox Church** and the **Marjan Mosque**, famous for its brickwork, are also in **Rashid Street**. Note the British colonial architecture in this street.

Close by is also the **Suq Al-Ghazil Minaret**. Built in AD902 and restored in the 12th century, it has marvellous brickwork, probably the finest in Iraq.

On the riverbank and well worth a visit, the **Abbasid Palace** has a superb *iwan* or entrance arch, and was slowly being turned into a museum of Islamic art before the last war. The beautiful **Mustansiriya School** building, built under the Abbasids, a short walk away, has stunning Islamic architecture and brickwork. The **Sheik Abdul Kader Al-Gailani Mosque** in Kifah Street is a must for those interested in all aspects of Islam. The mosque was damaged in 2007.

These are just some of the sites of Baghdad and we have not mentioned **Tel Harmal**, the small 1850BC Sumerian site in the northern suburbs, or the

Great Arch of Crossed Swords, built by Saddam for his victory parades, now, post Saddam, one of the most-photographed monuments in Baghdad.

There are several one-day tours that can be taken from Baghdad outside of the city. As we have already mentioned there is Samarra, a two-hour road journey away to the north. A more leisurely excursion is to **Babylon**, an hour away. So redolent of history, this is the most reconstructed site in Iraq, but nothing can take away the pleasure of walking past the site of the Hanging Gardens of Babylon, or passing by the Processional Way to the foundations of the Ishtar Gate, with its fabulous mythical beasts inlaid in the brickwork. Not far away is the holy city of **Kerbala** and the golden domes of the **Shrine of Abbas and Hussein**, martyred grandsons of the Prophet and so beloved of the Shias. Mingling with the pilgrims is always an amazing experience. On your route back to Baghdad you can divert to visit the greatest single span brick-arch in the world, that of **Ctesiphon**. Of Parthian origin, dating from the 1st and 2nd centuries AD, it is remarkable that it has survived until today.

Another one-day tour for those mostly interested in Islamic culture and the holy cities is to visit **Kerbala**, for the shrines of Abbas and Hussein, and then on to **Najaf** for the tomb of Ali, the Prophet's son-in-law and 4th Imam of Islam. Then, 6km away is **Kufa**, the first Arab city founded in Iraq after the invasion in AD637, and where Ali was killed. The mosques in these cities are much venerated by the Shias. All the shrines and tombs in these holy places are magnificently clothed in gold, with wonderful tile work. More importantly, they are centres of religious thought and piety, expressed by the thousands of pilgrims who visit them each year. If, after this, you want to see more, then you can divert to **Ctesiphon** on your way back to Baghdad.

To these tours you can also add, although it would make for a long day, the desert palace fortress of **Ukhaidher**, now very much restored but still worth seeing. Some 127km from Baghdad and 45km from Kerbala, it is close to the shores of **Lake Razaza**. Also *en route*, and close by the lake, are the Neolithic **Al Tar caves**. Note: there is a border point with Saudi Arabia southwest of Ukhaidher. Known as the Haj road, it is only open for general traffic during the period of the Haj, the annual pilgrimage to Mecca.

To the south The journey from Baghdad to Basra, the other main city of Iraq, is possible in a long day, despite the heat in summer. There are three major roads south, Highways 6, 7 and 8, plus the latest Superhighway 9 (which avoids all the towns). Of course it is possible to fly, or maybe take the slow train, which was stopped at one time, but which is now operating again, departing Baghdad at 09.00 and arriving at Basra at 20.30 that evening.

To visit the south comfortably and to fit in all the major sites then you will need to break the journey by staying in provincial towns such as Hilla, Kerbala, Diwaniya, Samawa or Nasiriyah, depending of course on what sites are a must for you. With the exception of Kerbala, the hotels in these provincial towns, even in 2002, had seen the best of their years and were then in great need of renovation.

An ideal four/five-day tour from Baghdad

Day one Leaving Baghdad on the Hilla road, after about 30 minutes you can make a short visit to **Sippa**. This is a Sumerian site dating from the 4th millennium BC and its huge flood-protection bank/walls are still in place.

Appendix 1 TRAVELLING IN IRAQ

A1

Note: you will need a map to find the site. Travelling on to **Ukhaider**, the **Al Tar caves** site, **Najaf**, **Kerbala** and **Kufa** makes for an exhausting but uplifting day. But do not finish yet as there is another site, often neglected by travellers in the past, that of **El-Khifal**. This once Jewish village houses in an old synagogue building the 6th-century BC **Tomb of Ezekiel**, the Old Testament Prophet. This tomb has been a place of pilgrimage for many centuries. It has been converted to a Mosque and has many Muslim tombs also. The building was restored under the Mongols in the 14th century. Close by is a superb minaret built by a Mongol caliph. Leading up to these buildings is a gem of a small covered bazaar. Make an overnight stop in Kerbala or Hilla.

Day two Now the ancient world! **Babylon**: city of Nebuchadnezzar and the Hanging Gardens, the Processional Way and Ishtar Gate. There are also the restored Greek Theatre of Alexander and the site of the Tower of Babel to be seen on this vast site, all overlooked by one of Saddam's extravagant palaces. The city is a must for every visitor to Iraq, and you should take your time walking around the site. Some 15km south of Babylon is the ancient site of **Borsippa**. Dating back to the 3rd millennium BC it has interesting temples and a ziggurat, and is just waiting for modern archaeologists to start digging again. In the vicinity is the ancient Sumerian city of **Kish**, occupied from the Ubaid period in c 5000BC. The Akkadian King Sargon (2370–2316BC) is the most famous personality to have ruled here. There are two ziggurat mounds and numerous excavated streets and houses.

Day three Still exploring ancient Sumer, we travel further south on Highway 8 to turn off to **Nippur**. Occupied from the 6th millennium BC the city was a major religious centre and is famous for the Temple of Enlil. Its site is extensive and the approaches are covered with pottery sherds from the numerous excavations that have taken place here right up until 1990. An enormous collection of cuneiform tablets has come from the site. The ziggurat is a fine one, crowned with a medieval building from the 12th century AD. There are Kassite buildings and Achaemenid remains dating from 1000BC. But this day is crowned by a visit to **Uruk (Warka)**, one of the most important sites in Iraq. A turning off highway 8 some 30km after the town of Samawa, takes you past re-housed refugees from Saddam's destruction of the Marshes to this massive site, also known as Erech in the Bible. It was occupied from the 5th millennium BC until the 7th century AD. Only a fraction has been excavated and the ziggurat overlooks a site with palaces, temples and great city walls. The earliest writing system was devised here and developed into true cuneiform later; its history is that of Sumer, Akkad and Babylonia. The Greeks, Parthians and Sassanians also left their mark on this city, truly a wonderful archaeological site. **Nasiriyah** would be the best town to overnight in after what would have been a hot long day.

Day four Nasiriyah is an interesting town and was once the centre for visiting the adjacent **Marshes**. This area had a life of its own for many thousands of years, but reached its nadir when Saddam attempted to completely drain the region in the interests of his economy and security. On his demise the Marshes' decimated population immediately broke down some of the dams he had erected, and with international and much self-help, the Marshes have begun to recover somewhat to a semblance of the old way of life – small villages situated on banks of reeds only accessible by reed boats, with breeding water buffalo and fishing.

There is a road that travels from **Nasiriyah** through some of the Marshes to **Qurnah**, a place where the Euphrates and Tigris meet. But at this moment in time we have other fish to fry: the famous site of **Ur**, inhabited since Neolithic times and famously associated with Abraham. Not far from the town of Nasiriyah is the famous Ziggurat of Ur. Restored and imposing, it is eminently climbable for tourists, and overlooks this ancient city. The two harbours are plainly visible, as is the low outline of mud-brick walls. Unfortunately for archaeologists and tourists, the unexcavated part of the site is also part of a former Saddam airfield and is now in the hands of the US Air Force. However, the excavations by Woolley (see page 296) of the Royal Tombs in the 1920s, where the great treasures of Sumerian art and gold were found, can still be seen, as can the great pit where he excavated and dramatically announced to the world that the flood, as described in the Bible, was provable.

About 23km away lies the site of **Eridu**. This has been described as the oldest city site in Iraq. Eighteen continuous temples spanning at least 1,500 years have been excavated here. The site itself is isolated and can be difficult to access in wet conditions. Also, because of this isolation it has been targeted by looters and insurgents, making it dangerous to visit without an armed escort. Basra is approximately 168km further south.

Day five

Basra But the city warrants two days in any event. Founded in AD638 soon after the Arab conquest of Mesopotamia, the city of Basra vies with Mosul as the second city of Iraq. Certainly it is a big city, hot and humid for much of the year, and situated on the Shatt Al Arab, with many canals and waterways. Its date industry virtually collapsed during the three recent wars, but is still capable of supporting a large export business. Famous as a port for centuries, its modern aspects were a result of British development of its commercial position in the post World War I years. It has a big market for produce from the east, and was known for its easy attitude to all things that make ports lively places. A tour of the city of Basra should include a boat ride on the Shatt Al Arab. The creeks and little waterways off the Shatt are close to the Iranian border. There is a myriad of interesting bird life, and it is interesting to see the date palms, and also some of the old palaces, that line the waterway.

In the city itself the market is interesting and so are the old merchants' houses, dating from the turn of the 19th century. These houses were being restored, and hopefully that will continue in the future. Zubair is a suburb and the mosque here was founded on the site of the Battle of the Camel (AD656), the famous military encounter between A'ishah, the Prophet Mohammed's widow, and Ali, Mohammed's son in law and the fourth Caliph. There is also the famous Imam Ali Mosque, though only the minaret and courtyard remain of one of the earliest mosques in Iraq. Saddam ordered a new mosque on the site and this was completed in 2003.

Basra has had a range of moderate hotels and a major Sheraton Hotel, famously trashed on TV by looters while the military occupiers watched from a distance! Similarly, the striking statues pointing to Iran that Saddam placed on the riverbank by the Sheraton, along with his statue, disappeared to be melted down for scrap. There were many reasonable restaurants here, and it is hoped that hotels and restaurants will rise again in due course, once tourism can operate in the region.

The city has always had a turbulent history and today is no exception. It has been the headquarters of the British zone during this last war and now seems to be in control of factions allied to the majority, the Shia, who have introduced many Iranian-style religious, social and governmental policies. The port of Um Qasr is just a few kilometres away, and this has been cleared now of the damage of the last 30 years, and should make Basra a viable growing commercial port again. Pilgrim traffic from Iran (and in the future cruise liners) can dock in this region.

The Iranian border points are close to here. It is only 50km across the Shatt Al Arab and directly across a flat desert plain to the Iranian border point of **Sareh**, with Khorramshahr being the nearest Iranian city. South of Basra, **Safwan** is the border crossing point to Kuwait, and from there it is only 50km by road to Kuwait City.

Depending on your schedule you can return to Baghdad by air or by road, or continue on to Kuwait – but remember that you will need a visa for that country prior to entry. To create some variety, if you travel by road you may wish to opt for the northernmost highway (6) which will take you to **Qurnah**, the place where the Tigris and Euphrates rivers meet. At the resthouse there is Adam's Tree, and this is supposedly the site of the Garden of Eden (see page 271). On the highway north of Qurna is the small village of **Al Azair**, which houses the Tomb of Ezra, of Old Testament fame, and attached is a well-preserved synagogue. Further north is the large town of **Al Amarah**. Some 186km from Basra, this town has acquired fame for the ferocity of its insurgents in the last few years. It is a further 206km to the town of **Kut**. These last two towns are the bases for the powerful landowning tribal Sheiks. But Kut has its own special fame from World War I, when the Ottoman Turks besieged the British troops and achieved a great victory, which in turn redoubled the efforts of the British to ultimately defeat the Turks. Finally, it is another 176km to Baghdad.

Alternatively, retrace your steps to Nasiriyah and travel on Highway 7 to reach Kut that way. The road is not great, but you may fancy visiting **Wasit** – founded in AD703, its name means 'The Town in the Middle', it being equidistant from Kufa, Basra and Ahvas in Iran – and other places *en route*. There is no doubt that the superhighway is the quickest route, but it is undoubtedly the most boring.

Obviously, given the present climate (2008) the above itineraries are for the future, but they have worked well in the past. As already mentioned, there will be new itineraries to plan, for example those connected with Saddam Hussein. He built 40 palaces throughout Iraq, very few of which he personally used. Paranoid of an assassination attempt, he had staff in three palaces prepare dinner as he never revealed his itinerary. Many more religious sites and smaller archaeological sites have not been mentioned. With the treasures that Iraq has to offer, the future for tourism could be very bright indeed.

Given the uncertainty in Iraq at the time of writing, it is extraordinarily difficult to give hard practical facts for commercial visitors, let alone for tourists.

GETTING THERE

By land As we have already described in our travelling section (see page 338).

By sea This is limited at the moment, but will increase.

By air Flights are increasing, as is the confidence of all associated with them. As of March 2008 the following applies:

Kurdistan
Erbil

Frankfurt–Erbil e info@irak-reisen.com. Operated by Zozik Air.

Vienna–Erbil 00964 66 224 5470; www.austrian.com. Scheduled service operated by Austrian Airlines, 3 days a week, was suspended for some months but resumed 2 April 2008.

Dubai–Erbil (Dubai) 00971 4262 2250. Operated by Kurdistan Airlines.

Dubai–Erbil (Dubai) 00971 4223 3530. Operated

by Zagros Air.

Stockholm–Erbil e info@atroshair.com. Operated by Atrosh Air.

Istanbul–Erbil e crestafunda@hotmail.com. Operated by Fly Air.

Amman–Erbil www.rja.com.jo. Operated by Royal Jordanian Airlines.

Beirut–Erbil (Beirut) 00961 3682 255. Operated by Flying Carpet.

Suleimaniyah

Munich–Suleimaniyah www.zozik-air.com. Operated by Zozik Air.

Dubai–Suleimaniyah (Dubai) 00971 4266 8993. Operated by Azmar Air.

Tehran–Suleimaniyah (Tehran) 00982 1 8880 4467. Operated by Azmar Air.

Iraqi Airlines operates regular services to Erbil (3 times weekly) & Suleimaniyah, some direct, some via Baghdad from Amman, Damascus & Dubai; (Dubai) 00971 5080 44854; (Baghdad) 00964 1 537 2001/2002/2003; (London, IKB Travel Ltd) 0044 (0)20 7724 8455.

A new service (November 2007) has begun: Iraqi Airlines now flies from Mosul to Baghdad and back. Mosul Airport is now open for the first time in 14 years.

Iraq generally
International services to Baghdad

Amman–Baghdad (Amman) 00962 6566 6823. Operated by Royal Jordanian Airlines.

Amman–Baghdad (Baghdad) 00964 11 537 2001; (London IKB Travel Ltd) 0044 (0)20 7724 8455. Operated by Iraqi Airlines.

Note: connections to Basra can be made with both airlines. Damascus–Baghdad flights operated by Syrian Arab Airlines and Iraqi Airlines.

HOTEL ACCOMMODATION At the time of writing, the people entering Iraq fall into some main categories:

- **Iraqi nationals** visiting their families or exiles returning from abroad will stay with their families.

- **Islamic Pilgrims** (mostly from Iran), although diminished in numbers, always keep a low profile and stay at hostels or hotels by the Holy Shrines such as Kerbala and Najaf. Mostly they will enter overland by coach.
- **Foreign nationals** – mainly armed forces, government officials, security personnel and some business people. Most of these will have prior arrangements with specially secured hotels and premises for their use only. The Green Zone will host all of those with official business with the government etc.
- **Other persons** – potential tourists or independent business people. There are very few hotels that will now take foreign nationals.

Major Hotels

Baghdad The Al Rashid in the Green Zone; the Hotel Ishtar Sheraton and the Hotel Palestine, both in Fardous Square; Babylon Hotel in Karrada district; al Hamra hotel, off Jamiya Street in Jadriya district; and Mansour Melia hotel on Haifa Street. These are the 4/5-star hotels. There are many small hotels, which generally will not take foreigners. The risk is too great.

Mosul and Basra Hotels in Mosul and Basra have similar policies, and generally don't accept foreigners. In the provinces there is usually only one respectable hotel in any town and it may or may not take foreigners.

Kurdistan Iraq A different situation altogether: hotels in Kurdistan Iraq are delighted to accept foreigners, the only criterion being the depth of your pocket.

Dohuk The Jiyan Hotel (*4/5-star; www.jiyanhotel.com*); the Sulav Hotel (e *sulavhotel@yahoo.com*); the Shindokha Hotel (*4-star*; e *shindokha_hotel @yahoo. com*). There are others – the Harem Hotel, the Palace Hotel, the Al Rasheed Hotel – all of which are situated by the marketplace.

Erbil (Hewler) There are many hotels to choose from here. The best hotel at the moment is the Erbil International Hotel, loosely described as the Sheraton (*5-star*; e *info@erbilinthotel.com; US$277 dbl plus tax in Sep 2007*). Good moderate hotels are the Chwarchra Hotel (e *sandi4chra@yahoo.com; US$90*), the Erbil Tower Hotel (e *Erbil_tower@hotmail.com*) and the Hawler Plaza Hotel (e *hawler_plaza@yahoo.com*). No longer so good but inexpensive is the Shereen Palace Hotel in Sheik Mahmod Square (\ *00964 66 2226240; from US$30*).

Suleimaniyah There are many hotels scattered around the town and more are being built. Recommended are the Ashti Hotel (e *ashtihotel@hotmail.com; US$90 per dbl*) and the Hotel Dilan (\ *312627; US$75 per dbl*), both on Salim Street.

Out in the country In **Dokan**, a number of chalets exist along the main street and are usually around US$50–70 per chalet per night. **Rawanduz** The Pank Resort, with new chalets at US$50 per chalet. **Shaqlawa** There are many small hotels and chalets, many newly built. Prices range from US$50 to US$100-plus per night.

VISAS Visas are granted on arrival into Kurdistan Iraq for that region only.
Visas are required for Iraq by all passport holders except those holding Iraqi passports, invited persons and those on official business.
Fees: tourist visa US$30; entry visa US$40; multiple-entry visa US$100; residence visa US$150.
Note: foreign nationals are required to obtain an exit visa if they are travelling on any visa except a tourist visa, which has its set time period.
Visas should be obtained at Iraqi diplomatic missions abroad. See the website www.mofa.gov.iq for details.

TRAVEL AGENTS AND TOUR OPERATORS

Hinterland Travel 12 The Enterdent, Godstone, Surrey RH9 8EG, UK; ⌕/f 0044 (0)1883 743584; e hinterland@btconnect.com; www.hinterlandtravel.com. A UK-based tour operator for Iraq.

IKB (Travel & Tours) Ltd 230 Edgware Rd, London W2 1DW, UK; ⌕ 0044 (0)20 7724 8455; www.youshouldtravel.com. UK–Iraq flights & tours for Iraq, & general sales agents of Iraqi Airlines in the UK & Eire.

GIVING SOMETHING BACK

British Iraqi Friendship Society PO Box 633, 2 Old Brompton Rd, London SW7 3DQ, UK; e britsoc@aol.so.uk

The Enheduanna Society 199 Foundling Ct, The Brunswick Centre, Bloomsbury, London WC1N 1QF, UK; contact Fran Hazelton: ⌕ 0044 (0)20 7278 3624; e zipang03@btopenworld.com; www.zipang.org.uk. Brings together Iraqi & non-Iraqi storytellers, scholars & enthusiasts to develop their shared appreciation of Mesopotamian literature & spread this appreciation to as many people as possible.

Halabja Monument e halabjamonument@yahoo.com; www.halabjamonument.com. This project maintains, preserves & seeks funds for the protection & renovation of the monument & gardens to the dead of the Halabja gas attack.

Independent Film & Television College ⌕ 0044 (0)20 7272 9324/(0)20 8838 0692; e Iftvc_iraq@yahoo.co.uk. The college trains Iraqi filmmakers & supports their filmmaking by providing production facilities & information about funding & further training.

Kurdistan Save the Children, Northern Region 17 Moran St, Sunderland, Tyne & Wear SR6 8HZ, UK; e maureen@ksc-kcf.org. KSC has been working with children in various fields of child protection, sponsorship, health & education.

Medical Aid For Iraqi Children 26 Old Brompton Rd, London SW7 3DL, UK; ⌕ 0044 (0) 20 7581 2727: f 0044 (0) 20 7581 2767; www.maic.org.uk

The Organisation of Human Rights in Iraq e sahibalhakim@yahoo.com; www.alhakim.co.uk. This organisation defends the rights of all Iraqis, irrespective of their race, colour, creed, religion or origin. It collects documents of all violations of human rights in Iraq, plus photos, testimonies, illegal orders of executions, deportations, arrests, disappearances & other violations.

Stuff Your Rucksack www.stuffyourrucksack.com. A website set up by TV's Kate Humble, which enables travellers to give direct help to small charities, schools or other organisations in the country they are visiting. The website describes organisations that need your help & lists the items they most need.

World Wide Welfare c/o 124 Wandle Rd, Morden, Surrey SM4 6AE, UK; ⌕/f 0044 (0) 20 8640 3428; e bayan@worldwidewelfare.org.uk; www.worldwidewelfare.org.uk. Assists Iraqi refugees & internally displaced people & organises sponsorship for Iraqi orphans.

A1

Appendix 2

FURTHER INFORMATION

BOOKS AND WEBSITES
General introduction

Hunt, Courtney, *The History of Iraq*, Greenwood Press, London (2005).

Nakash, Yitzak, *Reaching For Power: The Shia In The Modern Arab World*, Princeton University Press, New Jersey (2006).

Polk, William, *Understanding Iraq*, I.B. Tauris, London (2006).

Stansfield, Gareth, *Iraq*, Polity Press, Cambridge (2007).

Thabit, Abdullan, *A Short History Of Iraq*, Harlow Pearson Education, Harlow (2003).

Tripp, Charles, *A History of Iraq*, Cambridge University Press, Cambridge (2002).

Vali, Nasr, *The Shia Revival*, W.W. Norton & Company, New York (2006).

The ancient kingdoms

Dalley, Stephanie (ed), *The Legacy of Mesopotamia*, Oxford University Press, Oxford (1988).

Leick, Gwendolyn, *The Invention of the City*, Penguin, London (2001).

McCall, Henrietta, *Mesopotamian Myths*, British Museum Press, London (1990).

Reade, Julian, *Mesopotamia*, British Museum Publications, London (2000).

Roux, Georges, *Ancient Iraq*, Penguin Books, Harmondsworth (1966).

Van der Mieropp, M, *A History of the Ancient Near East ca. 3000-323BC*, Blackwell, Oxford (2004).

The Abbasids, Ummayads and Ottomans

Hawting, G R, *The First Dynasty of Islam*, Croom Helm, London (1986).

Kennedy, Hugh, *The Prophet and the Age of the Caliphates*, Longman, London (1986).

Kennedy, Hugh, *The Court of the Caliphs: When Baghdad ruled the Muslim World*, Phoenix, London (2005).

Lyons, Malcolm, *Saladin: The Politics of the Holy War*, Cambridge University Press, Cambridge (1982).

20th-century Iraq

Aburish, Said, *Saddam Hussein: The Politics of Revenge*, Bloomsbury, London (2000).

Alsamari, Lewis, *Out of Iraq: The terrifying true story of one man's escape from the harshest regime of the modern era*, Bantam Press, London (2007).

Arnove, Anthony (ed), *Iraq under Siege*, Pluto, London (2000).

Childs, Nick, *The Gulf War*, Wayland, Hove (1988).

Goodman, Susan, *Gertrude Bell*, Berg Women's series, Leamington Spa (1985).

Graves, Robert, *Lawrence and The Arabs*, Jonathan Cape, London (1927).

Hassan, Hamdi, *The Iraqi Invasion of Kuwait: Religion, Identity and Otherness in the Analysis of War and Conflict*, Pluto Press, London (1991).

Jabbar, Faleh, *Why the Intifada Failed in Iraq since the Gulf War: Prospects for Democracy*, CARDRI (Committee Against Repression and for Democratic Rights in Iraq), Zed Books, London (1994).

Al-Khalil, Samir, *Cruelty and Silence*, Penguin books, London (1994).

Al-Khalil, Samir, *Republic of Fear*, Hutchinson Radius, London (1989).

Al-Khayyat, *Honour and Shame: Women in Modern Iraq*, Al Saqi Books, London (1990).

Simons, Geoff, *Iraq: From Sumer to Saddam*, Macmillan, London (1994).

Sluglett, Peter, *Britain in Iraq: Contriving King & Country*, I.B. Tauris, London (2007).

Sluglett, Marion and Peter, *Iraq since 1958: From Revolution to Dictatorship*, I B Tauris, revised paperback, London (2001).

The 2003 War and the Battle of Fallujah

Bellavia, David (with Bruning, John) *House to House: An Epic of Urban Warfare*, Simon & Schuster, London (2007).

Buzzell, Colby, *My War: Killing Time in Iraq*, G.P. Putman's Sons, USA (2007).

Cushman, Thomas, *A Matter of Principle: Humanitarian Arguments for War in Iraq*, University of California Press, California (2005).

Fawn, Rick and Hinnebusch, Raymond (eds) *The Iraq War: Causes & Consequences*, Lynne Rienner Publishers, Colorado (2006).

Hiro, Dilip, *Secrets & Lies: The True Story of the Iraq War*, Nation Books, New York (2004).

Pauly Jr, Robert, *Strategic Pre-emption: US Foreign Policy and the Second Iraq War*, Ashgate Publishing, Aldershot (2005).

Rai, Milan, *Regime Unchanged: Why the War on Iraq Changed Nothing*, Pluto Press, London (2003).

Ramesh, Randeep (ed), *The War We Could Not Stop: The Real Story for the Battle of Iraq*, Faber & Faber, London (2003).

Simpson, John, *The Wars Against Saddam: Taking the Hard Road to Baghdad*, MacMillan, London (2003).

Useful website
www.mnf-iraq.com

Post-Saddam Iraq

Ajami, Fouad, *The Foreigners' Gift: The Americans, the Arabs and the Iraqis in Iraq*, Free Press, New York (2005).

Alawi, Ali, *The Occupation of Iraq: Winning the War, Losing the Peace*, Yale University Press, Yale (2007).

Ali, Tariq, *Bush in Babylon: The Recolonisation of Iraq*, Verso, London (2003).

Baer, Robert, *See No Evil: The True Story of a Ground Soldier in the CIA's War on Terrorism*, Crown Publishers, New York (2002).

Bremer III, Paul (with McConnell, Malcolm), *My Year in Iraq: The Struggle to Build a Future of Hope*, Threshold Editions, New York (2006).

Byman, Daniel and Pollack, Kenneth, *Things Fall Apart: Containing the Spillover from an Iraqi Civil War*, Brookings Institution Press, Washington (2007).

Chehab, Zaki, *Iraq Ablaze: Inside the Insurgency*, I.B.Tauris, London (2006).

Cockburn, Patrick, *The Occupation: War and Resistance in Iraq*, Verso, London (2006).

Ferner, Mike, *Inside the Red Zone*, Prager Publishers, Westport (2006).

Foulk, Vincent, *The Battle for Fallujah: Occupation, Resistance and Stalemate in the War in Iraq*, McFarland & Company Inc, North Carolina (2007).

Galbraith, Peter, *The End of Iraq: How American Incompetence Created a War Without End*, Simon & Schuster, London (2006).

Hiro, Dilip, *Secrets and Lies: Operation 'Iraqi Freedom' and After*, Nation Books, New York (2004).

Jamail, Dahr, *Beyond the Green Zone: Dispatches from an Unembedded Journalist in Occupied Iraq*, Haymarket Books, Chicago (2007).

Kember, Norman, *Hostage in Iraq*, Darton, Longman and Todd, London (2007).

McCarthy, Rory, *Nobody Told Us We Are Defeated: Stories from the New Iraq*, Chatto & Windus, London (2006).

Packer, George, *The Assassins' Gate: America in Iraq*, Farrar, Straus and Giroux, New York (2005).

Parenti, Christian, *The Freedom: Shadows and Hallucinations in Occupied Iraq*, The New Press, New York (2004).

Phillips, David, *Losing Iraq: Inside the Post-war Reconstruction Fiasco*, Westview Press, New York (2005).

Al-Rehaief, Mohammed Odeh, *Because Each Life is Precious: Why an Iraqi Man Risked Everything for Private Jessica Lynch*, Harper Collins, New York (2003).

Ricks, Thomas, *Fiasco: The American Military Adventure in Iraq*, Penguin Press, New York (2006).

Riverbend, *Baghdad Burning: Girl Blog From Iraq Vols I and II*, Marion Boyars Publishers Ltd, London (2006).

White, Andrew, *Iraq: Searching for Hope*, Continuum, New York (2005).

Wilding, Jo, *Don't Shoot the Clowns: Taking a Circus to the Children of Iraq*, New Internationalist Publications, Oxford (2006).

Useful websites
www.iraqupdates.com
www.einews.com
www.uruknet.info Anti-occupation website
www.zaman.com
www.iraqrevenuewatch.org
www.idao.org Iraqi Democrats Against Occupation
www.iraqigovernment.org
www.anotherIraq.com Good news website about Iraq

Archaeological sites
Bogdanos, Matthew and Patrick William, *Thieves of Baghdad*, Bloomsbury, New York (2005).

Curtis, John and Reade, Julian E, *Art and Empire: Treasures from Assyria in the British Museum*, British Museum Press, London (2005).

Al-Radi, Nuha, *Baghdad Diaries*, Al Saqi Books, London (1998).

Polk, Milbry and Schuster, Angela (eds), *The Looting of the Iraq Museum, Baghdad: The Lost Legacy of Ancient Mesopotamia*, Harry N Abrams Inc, New York (2005).

Russell, John, *The Final Sack of Nineveh*, Yale University Press, New Haven (1998).

Useful websites

www.thebritishmuseum.ac.uk

http://oi.uchicago.edu/OI/IRAQ/iraq.html Lost Treasures from Iraq, at the Oriental Institute, University of Chicago

www.britac.ac.uk/institutes/iraq British School of Archaeology in Iraq

www.baghdadmuseum.org

Travels in Iraq

Arnold, Catherine, *Baghdad City Guide*, Bradt Travel Guides, Chalfont St Peter (2004). Out of print.

Blunt, Anne, *Bedouin Tribes of the Euphrates*, Cass, London (1968).

Dabrowska, Karen, *Iraq: the Bradt Travel Guide*, Bradt Travel Guides, Chalfont St Peter (2002).

Heude, Lieutenant William, *A Voyage up the Persian Gulf in 1817*, Longman, London (1819).

Niebuhr, Carsten, *Travels Through Arabia and Other Countries in the East*, R Morison and Son, Edinburgh (1792).

Thesiger, Wilfred, *Arabian Sands*, Collins, London (1959).

Useful website

www.hinterlandtravel.com

Art and culture

Baram, Amatzia, *Culture, History and Ideology in the Formation of Ba'thist Iraq*, MacMillan, London (1991).

Faraj, Maysaloun, *Strokes of Genius: Contemporary Iraqi Art*, Al Saqi Books, London (2001).

Al Hashimi, Miriam, *Traditional Arabic Cooking*, Garnet Publishing, Reading (1993).

Al-Janub, Tariq, *Studies in Medieval Iraqi Architecture*, Ministry of Culture, Baghdad (1982).

Al-Khalil, Samir, *The Monument*, Andre Deutsch, London (1991).

Stevens, E S, *Folk-tales of Iraq*, Oxford University Press, Oxford (1931).

Tatchell, Jo, *Nabeel's Song: The story of the Poet of Baghdad*, Sceptre, London (2006).

Baghdad

Chandrasekaran, Rajiv, *Imperial Life in the Emerald City: Inside Baghdad's Green Zone*, Bloomsbury, London (2007).

Coke, Richard, *Baghdad: The City of Peace*, Butterworth, London (1927).

Eames, Andrew, *The 8.55 to Baghdad*, Bantam, London (2004).

Gunning, Heyrick Bons, *Baghdad Business School*, London, Eye Books (2004).

Pax, Salam, *The Baghdad Blog*, Atlantic Books, London (2003).

Roberts, Paul William, *The Demonic Comedy: The Baghdad of Saddam Hussein*, Mainstream Publishing, Edinburgh (1999).

Wiet, Gaston, *Baghdad: Metropolis of the Abbasid Caliphate*, University of Oklahoma Press, Oklahoma (1971).

Useful website
http://riverbendblog.blogspot.com Weblog of an Iraqi woman

The north
Ahmed, Mohammed and Gunter, Michael, *The Kurdish Question and the 2003 Iraq War*, Mazda Publishers Inc, California (2005).

Astarjian, Henry, *The Struggle for Kirkuk: The rise of Hussein, Oil and the Death of Tolerance in Iraq*, Greenwood Publishing Group, Westport (2007).

Bird, Christiane, *A Thousand Sighs, A Thousand Revolts: Journeys in Kurdistan*, Random House (2004).

Bowen, Wayne, *Undoing Saddam: From Occupation to Sovereignty in Northern Iraq*, Potomac Books, Dulles (2007).

Bruinessen, Martin van, *Agha, Shaikh and State*, Utrecht University, Utrecht (1978).

Chaliand, Gerald, *The Kurdish Tragedy*, Zed Books, London (1994).

Cook, Helen, *The Safe Haven in Northern Iraq*, Human Rights Centre, University of Essex, Kurdistan Human Rights Project, Exeter (1995).

Hamilton, A M, *Road through Kurdistan*, Faber & Faber, London (1937).

Hiltermann, Joost, *A Poisonous Affair: America, Iraq and the Gassing of Halabja*, Cambridge University Press, Cambridge (2007).

Izady, Mehrdad, *The Kurds: A Concise Handbook*, Taylor and Francis Inc, Washington (1992).

McDowall, David, *A Modern History of the Kurds*, I B Tauris, London (1996).

Meiselas, Susan, *Kurdistan in the Shadow of History*, Random House, London (1997).

Middle East Watch, *Genocide in Iraq: the Anfal Campaign Against the Kurds*, Human Rights Watch, New York (1993).

O'Leary, Brendan, McGarry, John and Salih, Khaled (eds), *The Future of Kurdistan in Iraq*, University of Pennsylvania Press, Pennsylvania (2005).

Parry, Oswald, *Six Months in a Syrian Monastery*, London (1895).

Solecki, R, *Shanidar: The First Flower People*, Alfred Knopf, New York (1971).

Thornhill, Teresa, *Sweet Tea with Cardamom: A Journey Through Iraqi Kurdistan*, Pandora, London (1997).

Yildiz, Kerim, *The Kurds in Iraq: The Past, Present & Future*, Pluto Press, London (2007).

Useful websites
www.kurdmedia.com
www.kurdishart.net
www.kurdistanobserver.com
www.krg.org Kurdistan Regional Government
www.kdp.pp.se Kurdistan Democratic Party
www.puk.org Patriotic Union of Kurdistan

www.kurdistancorporation.com Kurdistan Development Corporation
www.theotheriraq.com

The south

Alderson, Andrew, *Bankrolling Basra: The Incredible Story of a Part-time Soldier, $1bn and the Collapse of Iraq*, Constable & Robinson, London (2007).

Chesney, General Francis Rawdon, *The Expedition for the Survey of the Rivers Euphrates and Tigris in 1835, 1836 and 1837*, Longman Green and Co, London (1850).

Maxwell, Gavin, *A Reed Shaken by the Wind*, Longman, London (1957).

Middle East Watch, *Endless Torment: The 1991 Uprising in Iraq and its Aftermath*, Human Rights Watch, New York (1992).

Nakash, Yitzhak, *The Shi'is of Iraq*, Princeton University Press, Princeton, New Jersey (1994).

Salim, S M, *Marsh Dwellers of the Euphrates Delta*, Athlone Press, London (1962).

Stewart, Rory, *Occupational Hazards: My Time Governing in Iraq*, Picador, London (2006).

Thesiger, Wilfred, *The Marsh Arabs*, Penguin, London (1964).

Wetlands Ecosystems Research Group, *An Environmental and Ecological Study of the Marshlands of Mesopotamia*, Amar Appeal Trust, London (1994).

Wiley, Joyce, *The Islamic Movement of Iraqi Shi'as*, Lynne Rienner, Boulder, Colorado (1992).

Useful websites
www.albasrah.net
www.sistani.org
www.iraqiparty.com Iraqi Islamic Party
www.islamicdawaparty.org

Minorities

Benjamin, Marina, *Last Days in Babylon: The story of the Jews of Baghdad*, Bloomsbury, London (2007).

Betts, R B, *Christians in the Arab East: A Political Study*, John Knox Press, Atlanta, Georgia (1978).

Al-Rashid, Madawi, *Iraqi Assyrian Christians in London*, Edwin Mellen Press, Lewiston, New York (1998).

Rejwan, Nissim, *The Last Jews of Baghdad: Remembering a Lost Homeland*, University of Texas Press, Texas (2004).

Shibblak, Abbas, *The Lure of Zion: the Case of Iraqi Jews*, Al Saqi Books, London (1986).

Tapper, Richard, *Some Minorities in the Middle East*, Centre of Near and Middle Eastern Studies, School of Oriental & African Studies, London University, London (1992).

Useful websites
http://members.tripod.lycos.nl/Kerkuk Kirkuk and Turcomans
www.themesopotamian.org
www.zowaa.org Assyrian Democratic Movement

Bibliography

Anthony, Lawrence, *Babylon's Ark: The Incredible Wartime Rescue of the Baghdad Zoo*, Thomas Dunne Books/St Martin's Press, New York (2007).

Bates, Daniel and Rassam, Amal, *Peoples and Cultures of the Middle East*, Prentice Hall, New Jersey (1963).

Bowen, Wayne, *Undoing Saddam: From Occupation to Sovereignty in Northern Iraq*, Potomac Books, Dulles (2007).

Dodge, Toby, *Inventing Iraq: The Failure of Nation Building and a History Denied*, C. Hurst & Co. London (2003).

Gibb, H A R, Kramers, J H, Levi-Provencal, E and Schacht, J (eds), *Encyclopedia of Islam*, Luzac and Co, London (1960).

Gunter, Michael and Ahmed, Mohammed, *The Kurdish Question and the 2003 Iraqi War*, Mazda Publishers, California (2004).

Haj, Samira, *The Making of Iraq, 1900–1963*, State University of New York Press, New York (1997).

Hayden, Tom, *Ending the War in Iraq*, Akashic Books, New York (2007).

Hitti, P K, *History of the Arabs*, Macmillan, London (1937).

Hunter, Erica, *The Dictionary of Religions*

Keegan, John, *The Daily Telegraph, War On Saddam: The Complete Story of the Iraq Campaign*, Daily Telegraph, London (2003).

Kenneth Kattan, *Mine was the last Generation in Babylon*

Al-Khalil, Samir, *The Monument*, Andre Deutsch, London (1991).

Kimball, Lorenzo, *The Changing pattern of Political Power in Iraq, 1958–1971*, Robert Speller and Sons, New York (1972).

Kjeilen, Tore, *Encyclopaedia of the Orient* (Online Encyclopaedia http://lexicorient.com/e.o/index.htm).

Kramer, Samuel Noah and The Editors of Life Books, *Cradle of Civilisation*, New York (1967).

Lloyd, Seton, *Twin Rivers*, Oxford University Press, Oxford (1943).

Longrigg, Stephen and Stoakes, Frank, *Iraq*, Ernest Benn Ltd, London (1958).

Longrigg, Stephen, *The Middle East, a Social Geography*, Duckworth, London (1963)

Lovejoy, Bahija, *The Land and People of Iraq*, J B Lippincott Company, New York (1964).

Metz, Helen, *Iraq: A Country Study*, Library of Congress, Washington (1988).

Penrose, Edith and Penrose, E F, *Iraq: International Relations and National Development*, E Benn, London (1978).

Polk, Milbry and Schuster, Angela (eds), *The Looting of the Iraq Museum, Baghdad: the Lost Legacy of Ancient Mesopotamia*, Harry N Abrams, Inc, New York (2005).

Sayyid, Fayyaz Mahmud, *A Short History of Islam*, Oxford University Press, Oxford (1960).

Schoenbaum, Thomas, *International Relations: the Path not Taken – using international law to promote world peace and security*, Cambridge University Press, Cambridge (2006).

Stark, Freya, *Baghdad Sketches*, Murray, London (1947).

Sweetman, Denise, *Kurdish Culture, a Cross-Cultural Guide*, Verlag fur Kultur und Wissenschaft, Bonn (1994).

Tatchell, Jo, *Nabeel's Song*, Doubleday Books, New York (2007).

Totton, Michael, *Where Kurdistan Meets The Red Zone*, Internet blog www.windsofchange.net

Tsimhoni, Daphine, *Nationalism, Minorities and Diasporas: identities and rights in the Middle East*, Tauris Academic Series, London (1996).

Warren, John and Fethi, Ihsan, *Traditional Houses in Baghdad*, Coach Publishing House, Horsham, UK (1982).

Whitehead, K J, *Iraq The Irremediable: a Time of Treachery, Intrigue and Murder*, K J Whitehead, London (1989)

Young, Gavin, *Iraq: Land of Two Rivers*, Collins, London (1980).

Young, Gavin, *Return to the Marshes*, Penguin, London (1989).

Index

Page numbers in bold indicate major entries; those in italic indicate maps.

Bradt Travel Guides

www.bradtguides.com

Africa

Africa Overland	£15.99
Algeria	£15.99
Benin	£14.99
Botswana: Okavango, Chobe, Northern Kalahari	£15.99
Burkina Faso	£14.99
Cape Verde Islands	£13.99
Canary Islands	£13.95
Cameroon	£13.95
Congo	£14.99
Eritrea	£15.99
Ethiopia	£15.99
Gabon, São Tomé, Príncipe	£13.95
Gambia, The	£13.99
Ghana	£15.99
Johannesburg	£6.99
Kenya	£14.95
Madagascar	£15.99
Malawi	£13.99
Mali	£13.95
Mauritius, Rodrigues & Réunion	£13.99
Mozambique	£13.99
Namibia	£15.99
Niger	£14.99
Nigeria	£15.99
Rwanda	£14.99
São Tomé & Principe	£14.99
Seychelles	£14.99
Sudan	£13.95
Tanzania, Northern	£13.99
Tanzania	£16.99
Uganda	£15.99
Zambia	£17.99
Zanzibar	£12.99

Britain and Europe

Albania	£13.99
Armenia, Nagorno Karabagh	£14.99
Azores	£12.99
Baltic Capitals: Tallinn, Riga, Vilnius, Kaliningrad	£12.99
Belarus	£14.99
Belgrade	£6.99
Bosnia & Herzegovina	£13.99
Bratislava	£6.99
Budapest	£8.99
Bulgaria	£13.99
Cork	£6.99
Croatia	£13.99

Cyprus see North Cyprus	
Czech Republic	£13.99
Dresden	£7.99
Dubrovnik	£6.99
Estonia	£13.99
Faroe Islands	£13.95
Georgia	£14.99
Helsinki	£7.99
Hungary	£14.99
Iceland	£14.99
Kiev	£7.95
Kosovo	£14.99
Krakow	£7.99
Lapland	£13.99
Latvia	£13.99
Lille	£6.99
Lithuania	£13.99
Ljubljana	£7.99
Macedonia	£14.99
Montenegro	£13.99
North Cyprus	£12.99
Paris, Lille & Brussels	£11.95
Riga	£6.99
River Thames, In the Footsteps of the Famous	£10.95
Serbia	£14.99
Slovakia	£14.99
Slovenia	£12.99
Spitsbergen	£14.99
Switzerland: Rail, Road, Lake	£13.99
Tallinn	£6.99
Ukraine	£14.99
Vilnius	£6.99
Zagreb	£6.99

Middle East, Asia and Australasia

China: Yunnan Province	£13.99
Great Wall of China	£13.99
Iran	£14.99
Iraq	£14.95
Iraq: Then & Now	£15.99
Kyrgyzstan	£15.99
Maldives	£13.99
Mongolia	£14.95
North Korea	£13.95
Oman	£13.99
Sri Lanka	£13.99
Syria	£14.99
Tibet	£13.99
Turkmenistan	£14.99
Yemen	£14.99

The Americas and the Caribbean

Amazon, The	£14.99
Argentina	£15.99
Bolivia	£14.99
Cayman Islands	£14.99
Colombia	£15.99
Costa Rica	£13.99
Chile	£16.95
Dominica	£14.99
Falkland Islands	£13.95
Guyana	£14.99
Panama	£13.95
Peru & Bolivia: The Bradt Trekking Guide	£12.95
St Helena	£14.99
USA by Rail	£13.99

Wildlife

100 Animals to See Before They Die	£16.99
Antarctica: Guide to the Wildlife	£14.95
Arctic: Guide to the Wildlife	£15.99
Central & Eastern European Wildlife	£15.99
Chinese Wildlife	£16.99
East African Wildlife	£19.99
Galápagos Wildlife	£15.99
Madagascar Wildlife	£15.99
North Atlantic Wildlife	£16.99
Peruvian Wildlife	£15.99
Southern African Wildlife	£18.95
Sri Lankan Wildlife	£15.99

Eccentric Guides

Eccentric America	£13.95
Eccentric Australia	£12.99
Eccentric Britain	£13.99
Eccentric California	£13.99
Eccentric Cambridge	£6.99
Eccentric Edinburgh	£5.95
Eccentric France	£12.95
Eccentric London	£13.99
Eccentric Oxford	£5.95

Others

Your Child Abroad: A Travel Health Guide	£10.95
Something Different for the Weekend	£9.99

WIN £100 CASH!
READER QUESTIONNAIRE

**Send in your completed questionnaire for the chance to win
£100 cash in our regular draw**

All respondents may order a Bradt guide at half the UK retail price – please
complete the order form overleaf.

(Entries may be posted or faxed to us, or scanned and emailed.)

We are interested in getting feedback from our readers to help us plan future Bradt
guides. Please answer ALL the questions below and return the form to us in order
to qualify for an entry in our regular draw.

Have you used any other Bradt guides? If so, which titles? . . . .
. . . .

What other publishers' travel guides do you use regularly? . . . .
. . . .

Where did you buy this guidebook? . . . .

What was the main reason you read our guide to Iraq?. . . . .
. . . .

What other destinations would you like to see covered by a Bradt guide?
. . . .

Would you like to receive our catalogue/newsletters?

YES / NO (If yes, please complete details on reverse)

If yes – by post or email? . . . .

Age (circle relevant category) 16–25   26–45   46–60   60+

Male/Female (delete as appropriate)

Home country . . . .

Please send us any comments about our guide to Iraq or other Bradt Travel Guides.
. . . .
. . . .
. . . .
. . . .

Bradt Travel Guides
23 High Street, Chalfont St Peter, Bucks SL9 9QE, UK
☎ +44 (0)1753 893444 **f** +44 (0)1753 892333
e info@bradtguides.com
www.bradtguides.com

CLAIM YOUR HALF-PRICE BRADT GUIDE!

Order Form

To order your half-price copy of a Bradt guide, and to enter our prize draw to win £100 (see overleaf), please fill in the order form below, complete the questionnaire overleaf, and send it to Bradt Travel Guides by post, fax or email.

Please send me one copy of the following guide at half the UK retail price

Title		*Retail price*	*Half price*
. . .	. . . .	. . . .	. . . .

Please send the following additional guides at full UK retail price

No	*Title*	*Retail price*	*Total*
. . .	. . . .	. . . .	. . . .
. . .	. . . .	. . . .	. . . .
. . .	. . . .	. . . .	. . . .

Sub total . . . .
Post & packing . . . .
(£2 per book UK; £4 per book Europe; £6 per book rest of world)
Total . . . .

Name . . . .

Address. . . . .

Tel . . . .   Email . . . .

☐ I enclose a cheque for £. . . . . made payable to Bradt Travel Guides Ltd

☐ I would like to pay by credit card. Number: . . . .

Expiry date: . . . / . . .   3-digit security code (on reverse of card) . . . . .

Issue no (debit cards only) . . . . .

☐ Please add my name to your catalogue mailing list.

☐ I would be happy for you to use my name and comments in Bradt marketing material.

Send your order on this form, with the completed questionnaire, to:

Bradt Travel Guides IRAQT&N
23 High Street, Chalfont St Peter, Bucks SL9 9QE
☎ +44 (0)1753 893444   f +44 (0)1753 892333
e info@bradtguides.com   www.bradtguides.com